The Wadsworth College Success Program

Your Guide to College Success

by *John W. Santrock & Jane S. Halonen*

We stand by you as a co-creator in the success of all your students

For over 20 years, Wadsworth College Success has provided materials and training to help institutions and their students achieve the goals set forth in first-year seminars. Our team of authors, advisors, and facilitators have developed textbooks and training workshops that show instructors and administrators how to bring out the best in their teaching, their institutions, and their students. Because no two institutions, nor two students, are exactly alike, we have found that there isn't one way that works for everyone. We strive to assist both instructor and student with flexible, customizable programs that can fit a wide variety of needs using any form of media (print, video, CD-ROM, Internet, etc.) that best accomplishes this endeavor.

To assist in your teaching and your students' learning, we offer outstanding teaching and learning tools to enhance John Santrock and Jane Halonen's **Your Guide to College Success: Strategies for Achieving Your Goals**, Second Edition, Media Edition:

The Wadsworth College Success Workshop Series offered regionally and on campuses nationwide
(See page 12)

Constance Staley's **Teaching College Success: The Complete Resource Guide** for training instructors right on your campus
(See page 12)

Instructor's Resource Suite: Manual and CD-ROM with all the help you may need to prepare your course
(See page 10)

ExamView™ Computerized Testing to enhance your range of assessment and tutorial activities
(See page 10)

Toll-Free Consultation Service available to all instructors 1-800-400-7609
(See page 11)

Three-Hole Punch Version of *Your Guide to College Success* for instant customization and flexibility
(See page 6)

Custom Publishing Options to meet your specific needs
(See page 6)

Student CD-ROM to add a new level of interactivity to the book
(See page 8)

InfoTrac® College Edition for instant access to a powerful online library
(See page 8)

WebTutor™, a Web-based teaching and learning
(See page 8)

CNN® Today: College Success Video Series with lecture-launching video clips
(See page 10)

Wadsworth Study Skills Videos to help students take charge of improving their grades
(See page 10)

A World of Diversity Videos that address communication and conflict resolution between cultures
(See page 10)

College Success Resource Center at http://success.wadsworth.com for interactive teaching and learning
(See page 9)

College Success Factors Index Assessment Web Site to help students discover their strengths and weaknesses in important areas
(See page 7)

Franklin-Covey Premiere Agenda Planners for success in time management
(See page 7)

Wadsworth Films for the Humanities and Sciences® Videos for timely tips
(See page 11)

Your College Success Videos to stimulate group discussions
(See page 11)

WADSWORTH
THOMSON LEARNING

An Enhanced Structure
Revised with Instructor Feedback!

In this major revision of their acclaimed text, John Santrock and Jane Halonen help students make the connections and develop the skills that are so vital to their success in college and in life. This enhanced Second Edition includes new integrated themes, a streamlined design, a strategy-oriented approach, and much more—all based on what instructors in the College Success course said they wanted in a book.

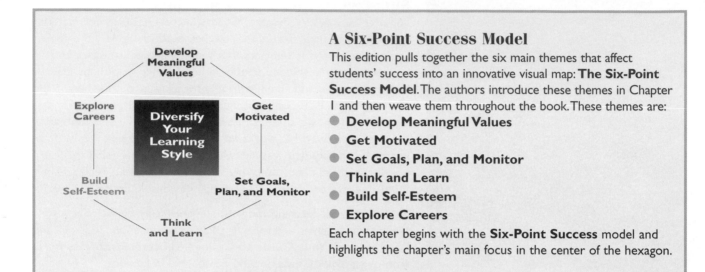

A Six-Point Success Model

This edition pulls together the six main themes that affect students' success into an innovative visual map: **The Six-Point Success Model.** The authors introduce these themes in Chapter 1 and then weave them throughout the book. These themes are:

- **Develop Meaningful Values**
- **Get Motivated**
- **Set Goals, Plan, and Monitor**
- **Think and Learn**
- **Build Self-Esteem**
- **Explore Careers**

Each chapter begins with the **Six-Point Success** model and highlights the chapter's main focus in the center of the hexagon.

Putting It All Together

A new, brief epilogue, *Putting It All Together*, helps students review the six main themes of the book and complete final, integrative self-evaluations. In this epilogue, the authors also encourage students to think about what the future holds for them and how the strategies they have learned in the course can help them manage their lives effectively.

Putting It All Together

How has the term or year gone so far? Are you mastering college? Have you put to good use many of the strategies we have described?

It's always good to take stock periodically where you are now, how things have gone, and where you're headed. This is a good time to reflect on the main themes of this book.

Stronger Emphasis on Active Strategies

The entire book is reconstructed with a very active, strategy-oriented approach. Virtually every heading has been changed as well as the emphasis of the discussion under the heading with an eye toward focusing more on strategies that will help students master the college experience. The authors spent considerable time choosing precise words that capture what students need to do to succeed in college.

Concentrate and Listen

Concentration is influenced by many things. For example, if you're an auditory learner or if you have a natural interest in the topic, extracting what you need from a lecture may not be hard. Other circumstances, though, will require you to take a more strategic approach to concentration.

You can do many things to minimize distractions:

1. **Sit near the front.** If you can't see or hear clearly, find a spot where you can.
2. **Reduce noise.** The instructor may not realize how noisy the room is for you, so do what you need to ensure your best hearing. Close doors and windows to reduce unwanted noise. Move away from chatty neighbors.
3. **Reduce Off-Task Pressures.** Get the sleep you need, and eat before class to quiet a growling stomach. If a specific worry keeps bothering you, write it down separately from your notes. Promise yourself that you'll worry about it later, so you can let it go for now.
4. **Stay Tuned In.** If something in the lecture distresses you—either content or delivery style—concentrate on identifying more precisely what bothers you and what you can challenge. Focus on hearing what you most likely will be tested on. Breathe deeply and use other stress-management techniques to stay in tune.
5. **Track Your Progress.** Keep records of how much time you spend paying attention. At the end of each class, estimate of what percentage of time you were on track, then write it on the upper right-hand corner of your notes. Try to make regular improvements in your rate.

Stay on Time to Reach Your Goals

Setting goals is a way of committing yourself to what you value and to what you seriously want to accomplish. As you attach actual dates and deadlines to those goals, your commitment gains focus.

Set Completion Dates for Your Goals

The first important principle in the art of managing time is to set completion dates for your goals and work out schedules to meet them. If you want to obtain a college degree, you might want to set a date of four to six years from now as your completion date depending on how much time each year you can devote to college. If your goal is to make one good friend, you might want to set a time of six weeks from now for achieving it. If your goal is to become the funniest person on campus, set a date for that as well.

Create Subgoals

Reaching goals is often easier if you break them down into intermediate steps or subgoals. In many cases, reaching a goal involves several activities. Say that one of your life goals is obtaining a college degree. You can break this down

Time Management

Time management, an essential topic for all students, is now covered exclusively in Chapter 3, while the discussion of money has been moved to Chapter 4 with campus resources.

Also Revised in this Edition:

- **The book has fewer chapters** (12) so students can better focus in on the essential material, whether they are taking a one-credit or three-credit course. The authors were able to reduce chapters by moving the discussion of values, which was a main theme of Chapter 14 in the first edition, to Chapter 1 and making it a major theme of the book—before students can set goals, they need to know what they value. Diversity coverage is integrated in a single chapter rather than two separate chapters, and is also integrated throughout other chapters as appropriate.

- **The topic of choosing careers is interwoven in many chapters**, helping students become better aware of themselves and how to prepare for a career—an essential reason for attending college.

- **Coverage of learning styles is completely rewritten** so that students can explore a broad spectrum of their abilities and natural tendencies, including the various learning modalities and personality preferences.

- **The new design in this edition reduces visual clutter.** Features are streamlined to reduce distractions and heighten focus. On any given spread of pages, students should be able to ask, "*So what?*" and immediately see what main idea is on the table.

Table of Contents

Changes to this Edition

An Inspiring Author Team that Teaches, Motivates, and Reinforces!

Bringing together the expertise of John Santrock, a prominent developmental psychologist, and Jane Halonen, a leader in critical thinking, this text/CD-ROM package emphasizes student self-awareness in pursuit of College Success goals. Innovative and pedagogically sound, **Your Guide to College Success** uses both the advantages of print and CD-ROM technology to address course topics from the standpoint of the individual student in the most effective way available today.

Powerful Pedagogy for Active Learning

Every chapter in **Your Guide to College Success** simultaneously motivates and reinforces learning with outstanding pedagogy:

_____ I choose appropriate places and times to study.
_____ I set reasonable goals for study sessions.
_____ I review regularly to learn course information better.
_____ I organize materials to make them easier to learn and remember.
_____ I use strategies to remember course information.
_____ I pursue deeper learning strategies when I can.
_____ I adapt my study strategies to suit different disciplines.
_____ I take my learning style into account when I study.
_____ I form study groups to expand my learning resources.

College Success Checklists at the beginning of each chapter outline the key success skills students will learn. This feature is converted to a self-scoring self-assessment on the CD-ROM and helps point students to the exercises they need most.

SELF-ASSESSMENT 1-1

Why Am I Here?

Different individuals want different things out of college. Think for a few moments about why you are here. The following items can help you to see how college might serve your needs. Place a check mark next to any of the items that apply to you.

I'm in college because
_____ It can help me learn and t
_____ It can help me get a good
_____ It can help me make a lot
_____ I'm avoiding having to find
_____ It's a good place to find a
_____ I want to have a good tim

Self-Assessments sprinkled throughout each chapter offer students the opportunity to examine a specific skill or characteristic. These Self-Assessments are included on the CD-ROM for easy scoring and interpretation.

ON-TARGET TIPS

Setting Daily Priorities

1. **Make up your daily to-do list before you go to bed at night.** Or do the list first thing in the morning. Set priorities. Estimate how much time it will take to complete each task.
2. **Identify the top-priority tasks and try to do these first.** Do them in the morning if possible.
3. **Raise your time consciousness.** Periodically look at or think about your list. Maybe you have a few items that take only a little time. Knock them off in 10 minutes here, 15 min-

On-Target Tips, praised by reviewers for their practical value, offer valuable strategies for improving College Success skills and are also included for easy reference on the CD-ROM.

Summary Strategies for Mastering College at the end of each chapter provide a final wrap-up of the key points discussed in the chapter.

Review Questions

1. What distinguishes good critical thinkers from bad ones?

_____

_____

_____

2. How can you improve your ability to ask good questions?

_____

Review Questions provide readers with an opportunity to further test their understanding of the chapter material.

Learning Resources for *Every* Student

Unlike exercises in other books, Santrock and Halonen's **Learning Portfolio** exercises take into account the heterogeneous nature of your student population and the fact that students learn in different ways. Students can choose from the different types of exercises within the **Learning Portfolio** section, or you can assign varied exercises to different students. The **Learning Portfolio**—found at the end of every chapter—offers five different kinds of exercises:

- **Reflect and Journal** to improve self-understanding
- **Learn by Doing** for hands-on experience
- **Think Critically** to develop problem-solving skills
- **Think Creatively** to develop a personal vision
- **Goal-Setting** for personal achievement

Other Motivating, High-Interest Features:

- **Images of College Success** begin each chapter with wonderfully motivating true College Success stories about people like Marian Wright Edelman, Oprah Winfrey, Amy Tan, and Albert Einstein. People of various backgrounds describe their college experiences, and while each experience is different, all have one thing in common—their personal success was derived from their college experiences.

- **"Feeling Features"** are sprinkled throughout every chapter to capture the student's attention in a more conversational style. **Staying Out of the Pits** boxes focus on information designed to motivate students to study. **Amazing But True Stories** describe attention-grabbing, true college experiences.

As smart as he was, Albert Einstein could not figure out how to handle those tricky bounces at third base.

- **Your Guide to College Success** is packed with over 30 cartoons and over 50 quotes chosen to get the reader laughing, relaxed, reflecting, and open to feelings of personal identification with the chapter material.

Learning Portfolio

Reflect and Journal

1. My Ideal Job
- Write down your ideal occupation choice.

_____
_____
_____

- Describe the degree you'll need for your ideal job, such as an AA, BA, MA, or PhD. How many years will this take?

_____
_____
_____

- On a scale of 1 to 10, estimate your chances of obtaining your ideal job.

1   2   3   4   5   6   7   8   9   10
Poor   Excellent

- Discuss these answers further in your journal.

_____
_____
_____
_____

Learn By Doing

1. Examine Your College Catalog
Look at your college's catalog. If you don't have one, your academic advisor can tell you where to get one. In most cases the admissions or registrar's office has copies.

- If you're not doing well in a particular class, you may want to consider dropping it. Look up the procedure for dropping a class and the latest date in the term you can do this.

_____
_____

- Look up the specialty or major you've chosen or that you're considering. What are the degree requirements for it? Is there a particular sequence of courses you should take?

_____
_____

2. Current Résumé and Future Résumé
Create a current résumé. List your education, work experience, high school or college campus organizations, and extracurricular activities. List any honors or awards you have achieved. Then write down what you would like your résumé to look like when you apply for your first job after college. By going to the Web site for this book, you can read about and see some examples of résumés.

_____
_____

3. Visit Your College's Career Center
Visit the career center at your college. Find out what materials and services are available. Get brochures about the careers that you're interested in. Consider making an appointment with a career counselor.

_____
_____

316 Chapter 12 • Explore Careers and Majors

Thorough, thought provoking, ...well organized, easy to read and understand, and sensitive to the needs of all kinds of students both inside and outside of the classroom.

Dorothy R. Clark,
Montgomery County
Community College

Covers skills, but adds the human touch.

Susann B. Deason
Aiken Technical College

Pedagogy Preview

Thomson Learning Custom Publishing
Creating the Perfect College Success Course

Thomson Learning Custom Publishing gives you the perfect opportunity to have your course exactly the way you want it. You can have Santrock and Halonen's text fully customized to your course and teaching style—a text built to provide the best learning outcome for your students.

Your Course, Your Way...

As the number one custom publisher for the College Success market, we have delivered over and over the personal touch that has helped match course materials to the course. We may have the solution you are looking for if you would like to:

- Supplement your current Wadsworth text with handouts, including campus-specific information like drop/add forms, important phone numbers, and dates. Also, if you want to add a map of the school or information on financial aid we can include that right into your book.

Your Guide to College Success at...
Northwestern State University

- Add a custom cover to your book, a cover that might include a picture of the school, your students, or the department.

- Add information to the unbound, three-hole punched version. We can put it all in a binder and add your materials—such as a syllabus.

- Combine materials from two or more Wadsworth books.

- Add the latest current events.

If you would like to learn more about adding a personal touch, ask your Thomson Learning sales representative or contact Thomson Learning Custom Publishing directly at 1-800-355-9983.

Holistic, high human interest...thoughtful.
Carol A. Copenhefer
Central Ohio Technical College

Engaging and participatory, between a workbook and a textbook.
Glenn Ricci
Lake Sumter Community College

To make it even easier...

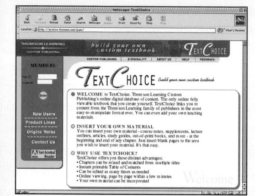

www.TextChoice.com

In just minutes, **TextChoice** allows you to:

- Mix and match chapters from different books
- View chapters online as you create your custom book
- Preview your finished book and make changes as necessary
- Add your own teaching material

For instant customization, punch it!

The easiest way to customize **Your Guide to College Success** with your own campus-specific materials is to choose our three-hole punch version of the text. Unbound, this version comes

with a front and back cover and with all of the pages conveniently three-hole punched so students can create their own course-specific binders. As with the bound text, this loose-leaf version comes packaged with *InfoTrac® College Edition* (see page 8).

Money-saving Opportunities for Your Students

Choose to bundle **Your Guide to College Success, Second Edition, Media Edition,** with any of these outstanding student resources and you'll help your students save money!

Franklin-Covey Premiere Agenda Planners
Wadsworth offers inexpensive planners designed specifically for college students by experts in time management—the Franklin-Covey Premiere Agenda team. Ask your Wadsworth representative for details on our latest calendar offerings.

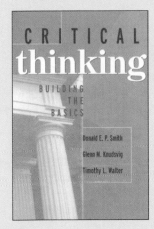

Critical Thinking: Building the Basics
by Donald E. P. Smith, Glenn M. Knudsvig, and Timothy L. Walter
One hundred pages of valuable guidance for improving learning through critical thinking. This guide helps students apply critical thinking strategies to master the material in their own textbooks.

Use bundle ISBN: 0-534-19284-X

How We Learn and Why We Don't
by Lois Breur Krause, Clemson University
Suitable for almost every course, *How We Learn and Why We Don't* is a relatively short, 60-page book designed to help students understand how they think, how they learn, and even perhaps why they don't think as clearly as they could or learn as much as they can. Beginning with a self-assessment, students are offered proven strategies to help them achieve better grades and to maximize and match learning profiles with their academic and career paths.

Today's Technology
for Today's Students

Your Guide to College Success integrates and is enhanced with course-leading technologies that meet the challenges and expectations of today's students and instructors.

Your Guide to College Success, Second Edition CD-ROM

Every student automatically receives an interactive CD-ROM FREE with every new copy of Santrock and Halonen's text. Designed to reinforce and extend the content of the text, the accompanying CD-ROM adds a new level of interactivity to the book's features. Every chapter on the CD-ROM includes self-assessments that direct students to the exercises, readings, and Internet resources that best meet their needs. In addition to the self-assessments, the CD-ROM includes exercises and tips from the text, quizzes, crossword puzzles, journal writing opportunities, Internet activities, and *InfoTrac® College Edition* exercises. The CD-ROM also includes the *Mission Statement Builder* exercise from Franklin-Covey Premiere Agenda Planners. The second edition of the CD-ROM is upgraded to include e-mail capabilities and a saving feature.

InfoTrac® College Edition

A FREE four-month subscription to this extensive online library is enclosed with every new copy of Santrock and Halonen's book, giving you and your students access to the latest news and research articles online—updated daily and spanning four years! This easy-to-use database of reliable, full-length articles (not abstracts) from hundreds of top academic journals and popular sources is ideal for launching lectures, igniting discussions, and opening whole new worlds of information and research for students. Exclusive to Wadsworth/Thomson Learning.

Available to North American college and university students only. Journals subject to change.

WebTutor™ on WebCT and Blackboard

WebTutor is a content-rich, Web-based teaching and learning tool that helps students succeed by taking the course beyond classroom boundaries to an anywhere, anytime environment. **WebTutor** gives students access to study tools that correspond chapter-by-chapter and topic-by-topic with the book, including flashcards (with audio), practice quizzes, and online tutorials. Professors can use **WebTutor** to provide virtual office hours, post syllabi, set up threaded discussions, and track student progress on the practice quizzes. **WebTutor** is easily customizable to specific course needs.

WebCT ISBN: 0-534-57209-X
Blackboard ISBN: 0-534-57210-3

Technology Resources

The Wadsworth College Success Resource Center

http://success.wadsworth.com

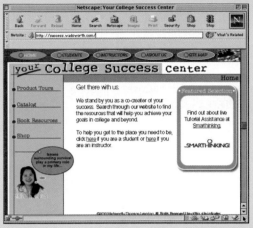

When you adopt Santrock and Halonen's text, you and your students have access to a rich array of teaching and learning resources that you won't find anywhere else. This outstanding site features everything from instructor resources to additional student study tips. It's the ideal way to make teaching and learning an interactive and exciting experience.

On the Instructor Page:

- **Complete listing of resources** for the College Success instructor
- **Workshop information** and registration
- **Teaching Tips** by instructors across the country—updated monthly
- **Sample syllabi** and ice-breaker activities
- **Tips for teaching** using *InfoTrac® College Edition* and the text-specific CD-ROM
- **Downloads** of Wadsworth's instructor materials for all Wadsworth/Thomson Learning textbooks
- **Links** to Wadsworth product tours and catalogs
- Information about reviewing and writing for Wadsworth/Thomson Learning

On the Workshops Page:

- Information about all of our different types of training events
- **Regional Workshops:** Listings, including dates and locations, topic information, and a printable copy of the registration form
- **On-Site Workshops:** Listings of all of our topics and information about all of our facilitators
- **Link to a tour** of *Teaching College Success* by Constance Staley—a binder filled with ideas and ready-to-produce materials for conducting a workshop on your campus

On the Student Page:

- **My College Experience,** where students tell their stories of how college affected their thinking and their lives
- **Study Skills Strategies** to help students make the most of their study time
- **Web links** that give students access to helpful tools and resources on the Internet
- **Quick Start Career Wizard** to help students build a career in today's competitive marketplace

Wadsworth Web Resources

Available exclusively on the Wadsworth College Success Web site—password protected!

College Success Factors Index

Developed by Edmond Hallberg, Kaylene Hallberg, and Loren Sauer

The perfect tool to help your students quickly assess their college success needs—and validate your college success program!

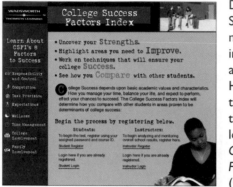

Does your College Success course make a difference in your students' academic success? Here's a survey that will give you the answers you're looking for! *The College Success Factors Index* survey (CSFI) is the perfect tool that allows you track the progress of students in the course—and at the same time show students what they need to work on to succeed.

Easy to take and affordable, in or outside of class!

CSFI is an 80-statement survey that students first take before they take the College Success course within the first year of college. While many assessments take up valuable class time, the CSFI tool is conveniently housed on the Wadsworth web site. Students can take the assessment on the Internet in a password protected area either in a lab, in their home, or at their workplace. All statements on the survey are based on eight important areas that have been proven to correlate with college success:

- Responsibility vs. Control
- Competition
- Task Precision
- Expectations
- Wellness
- Time Management
- College Involvement
- Family Involvement

How do they measure up?

When students finish the survey, they can immediately see their scores, based on how they compare with other students in college—the norm group. *The Norm group* is comprised of over 10,000 students nationwide in both four-year and two-year public and private institutions.

Getting the Advice They Need

This Wadsworth-CSFI Web site also presents intervention techniques related to the eight factors to help students improve their chances for success in college, as well as specific page references to Santrock and Halonen's text and other Wadsworth texts. There is also a special section for instructors with information and advice on how to administer, interpret, and report the data.

Now available online for the first time—only from Wadsworth!

Previously only available in paper form, the CSFI is now accessible to students and instructors via this exclusive arrangement with Wadsworth/Thomson Learning. A dedicated Web site makes it easy for students to take the survey and for schools to track the results. All administrators (and students) need is a password—available for a nominal price with the purchase of any Wadsworth textbook—to reach the protected Web site.

Instructor Resources

Instructor's Resource Suite: Manual and CD-ROM

prepared by Cynthia Jenkins, The University of Texas at Dallas, and Alice Lanning, University of Oklahoma

The manual includes additional ice-breakers and exercises, ideas on how to structure group and collaborative learning, alternative teaching strategies, specific suggestions for teaching each topic, chapter quizzes, and many other resources. The CD-ROM contains the entire instructor's manual, PowerPoint® slides, and CNN video clips in an easy-to-use search engine.

ISBN: 0-534-57212-X

ExamView® Computerized Testing

Enhance your range of assessment and tutorial activities—and save yourself time in the process. With **ExamView** you can easily create and customize tests! **ExamView**'s Quick Test Wizard guides you step-by-step through the process of creating and printing a test in minutes.

Cross-platform ISBN: 0-534-57207-3

Wadsworth College Success Transparency Package

Fifty color transparencies featuring helpful checklists, charts, and key points from College Success topics to help organize your classroom presentation.

ISBN: 0-534-56408-9

 **Toll-Free Consultation Service**

Available to all instructors: 1-800-400-7609

Video Presentation Tools

CNN® Today: College Success Video Series

Launch your lectures with riveting footage from CNN, the world's leading 24-hour global news television network. The **CNN Today: College Success Video Series** is an exclusive series jointly created by Wadsworth and CNN. Each video in the series consists of approximately 45 minutes of footage originally broadcast on CNN within in the last several years and selected specifically to illustrate the relevance of course topics to students' everyday lives.

CNN Today: College Success, 2000 Edition ISBN: 0-534-53754-5
CNN Today: College Success, 2001 Edition ISBN: 0-534-53799-5
CNN Today: College Success, 2002 Edition ISBN: 0-534-54140-2

Wadsworth Study Skills Videos

Volume I: Improving Your Grades features students talking to students and involves viewers in the issues that contribute to their success. *Volume II: Lectures for Notetaking Practice* features a series of college lectures that provide students with the opportunity to practice their note-taking skills.

Volume I ISBN: 0-534-54983-7
Volume II ISBN: 0-534-54984-5

A World of Diversity Videos

This powerful two-video set addresses communication and conflict resolution between cultures.

Volume I ISBN: 0-534-23229-9
Volume II ISBN: 0-534-23230-2

Wadsworth Films for the Humanities and Sciences® Videos

With timely and essential tips for getting the most from life inside and outside of the classroom, this series of films is sure to spark discussion and new ideas. Contact your Wadsworth/Thomson Learning representative for a complete list of titles.

Your College Success: Strategies for Success Video Series

This 12-part videocassette is designed to teach and stimulate lively group discussions. Based on the nationally acclaimed University 101 freshman seminar course directed by John Gardner and the University of South Carolina. Contact your Wadsworth/Thomson Learning representative for more information.

Instructor Resources

The Wadsworth College Success Workshop Series

We offer a variety of faculty development workshops regionally and on campuses nationwide throughout the year. Visit our Web site for dates and places: **http://success.wadsworth.com**. Topics at these workshops include active learning strategies to engage first-year students, motivating students, using technology, working with peer leaders, and ways to promote critical thinking.

Let us help you get the most out of Your Guide to College Success
When you adopt **Your Guide to College Success**, you may qualify to have one of our facilitators come to your campus to train your faculty on how to best use this learning-rich textbook for your College Success program. Please call one of our consultants at 1-800-400-7609 for more details.

Wadsworth Regional Workshop Series—join us at a location near you!
The College Success Regional Workshops appear in locations throughout the U.S., focusing on the unique features of College Success programs, active learning exercises you can use to enhance your lectures, and technology tools designed to improve introductory courses. Our regional workshops serve as wonderful gathering centers for instructors and administrators of College Success programs to meet and exchange ideas. See the Wadsworth College Success Web Site **http://success.wadsworth.com** to learn more about the seminars we offer throughout the year, throughout the country.

Or you can run a workshop on your own campus with a little help from Constance Staley . . .

Teaching College Success: The Complete Resource Guide
by Constance Staley

An all-inclusive package that contains everything you need to create your own tailored training program for College Success instructors! This resource includes a blend of content information (the nature of the College Success course, related theoretical approaches, and current national data) and experiential activities trainers can try with training groups and later with students. **Teaching College Success** contains an extensive array of print resources combined with dynamic PowerPoint® presentations.

ISBN: 0-534-53640-9

Dr. Staley knew the material. She explained things well and made me think how I can apply these ideas. The workshop was a wonderful investment in myself. Thanks!

Susann Deason
Aiken Technical College

I loved the variety of topics, current research on topics, and diversity of delivery methods!

Laynah Rogers
Evangel University

Motivating, inspirational, and fun.

Lenore Arlee
University of Oklahoma

Constance Staley was very knowledgeable and passionate about student success.

Denise Menchaca
GateWay Community College

Ideas for Instruction and Instructor Training	Videos & CD-ROMS	Media Resources for Instructors	Media Resources for Students
Instructor's Manual Exercises: • Strengths & Fears • Money Talks • Listen to the Coach • Why Do You Lack Motivation? • In-class Icebreaker Activity *Guest Speaker:* Invite a staff member from the college counseling center **Test Bank Questions** *Chapter 1:* 10 True/False, Multiple Choice, and Essay Questions *Available in a computerized test bank format:* **ExamView®** **Teaching College Success by Constance Staley** (Training manual & CD-ROM available for sale) *Module 1:* Training (and Freshman Course) Openers *Icebreakers:* • Group Résumé • Wheel in a Wheel • Hollywood Squares • Trading Places • If You Could be Me *Exercises:* • Spending Time • Get a Job • The Freshman Seminar • The Best of Times, The Worst of Times	**CNN Today: College Success 2000 Video** "Student Day" (3:06) "Campus Politics" (2:06) **CNN Today: College Success 2001 Video** "A Dorm Goes Drug Free" (2:39) **Your College Experience: Strategies for Success** Produced by the renowned First Year Experience Program at the University of South Carolina *Program 1: Keys to Success*	**Web Site** **http://success.wadsworth.com** *Resource Links:* • Cornell Trainer Network • The Beloit College's Class of 2004 Mindset *General Resources:* Download on… • How to have a successful first day of class—tips and activities • How to handle guest speakers in the classroom **Microsoft® PowerPoint® Slides** • Make the College Transition • Develop Meaningful Values • Get Motivated on Behalf of Your Values • Set Goals, Plan & Monitor, Think & Learn • Build Self-Esteem • Explore Careers **Transparency Acetates** • The Changing Life Goals of First-Year Students • Getting Motivated • Getting Help **WebTutor** Chapter 1 Course Management Tool for WebCT or Blackboard	**Web Site** **http://success.wadsworth.com** *Links to:* • An Online Student Survival Guide • How to Succeed as a Student • The National Clearinghouse for Academic Advising • Top Ten Tips for Surviving College • Color portraits of students with testimonials about college **Media Edition CD-ROM** *Self-Assessment* *Quiz* *Crossword Puzzle* *Journal* *InfoTrac College Edition* *Exercises from the Book:* • Why Am I Here? • What Are My Goals? • Evaluating My Self-Esteem • What Are My Values? • Manage Your Risk • College Graduation Day • The Magic Wand • Premiere Agenda's Mission Statement Builder *Bonus Exercises:* • Are You Reminiscing Too Much? • Saying "Thank You" • What Are the Odds? • Goal Tending • Was it Good For You? **College Success Factors Index Assessment Web Site** **http://success.wadsworth.com** • Responsibility/Control • Competition • Task Precision • Expectations • College Involvement **WebTutor** Text-specific study tools, including practice quizzes, online tutorials, and Web links, along with access to the Newbury House Online Dictionary **InfoTrac College Edition** *Keywords:* Marion Wright Edelman, values, motivation, goal setting, returning (adult) students, self-esteem, mastering college

Resource Integration Guide—Make the Connection!

Resource Integration Guide—Make the Connection!

Ideas for Instruction and Instructor Training	Videos & CD-ROMS	Media Resources for Instructors	Media Resources for Students
Instructor's Manual *Exercises:* • Examining the Learning Portfolio • Discussing Learning Styles • Using the Myers-Briggs Type Inventory • Former Students Come to Class • Do Groups Work? • Call Waiting • Tips for Teams • Faculty+Food *Guest Speaker:* Have a senior who has experienced academic difficulty come to class **Test Bank Questions** Chapter 2: 10 True/False, Multiple Choice, and Essay Questions *Available in a computerized test bank format:* **ExamView®** **Teaching College Success by Constance Staley** (Training manual & CD-ROM available for sale) *Module 2:* Teaching and Learning *Microsoft® PowerPoint® slides* 1-35: Learning Styles, Bloom's Taxonomy, Developing Integrity, Adult Learning Theory, and other slides about the process of learning *Handouts:* • Learning Style Inventory • Learning Styles and Strategies • Partial List of MBTI Resource Materials and Organizations	**Intelligence, Creativity, and Thinking Styles** (30 minutes) This video from *Films for the Humanities and Sciences®* explores how IQ relates to multiple intelligences & how teachers and parents can encourage creativity **Your College Experience: Strategies for Success** Produced by the renowned First Year Experience Program at the University of South Carolina *Program 3: Learning Styles*	**Web Site** **http://success.wadsworth.com** *General Resources:* Download on… • Active Learning • Critical Thinking • Interactive Learning **Microsoft® PowerPoint® Slides** • Know How You Learn • Regulate Your Effort • Launch Your Learning • Solve Problems with Instructors • Choose a "Stylish" Major **Transparency Acetates** • Myers-Briggs Styles • Myers-Briggs Scales • Teaching and Learning Styles **WebTutor** Chapter 2 Course Management Tool for WebCT or Blackboard	**Web Site** **http://success.wadsworth.com** *Links to:* • "Learning Style Inventory," where students can take a self-evaluation to see which learning style they prefer • "Multiple Intelligences and Technology," which discusses the importance of being aware of other people's learning styles • "Learning Services" which supports students at all levels of academia • Color portraits of students who have various learning styles **Media Edition CD-ROM** *Self-Assessment* *Quiz* *Crossword Puzzle* *Journal* *InfoTrac College Edition* *Exercises:* • The Cost of Cutting Class • Experiential Learning Preferences • Your Intelligence Profile: • Sensory Preference Inventory • Review a Syllabus • Connect with a Special Teacher • The "Stylish" Major • Career Cruising on the Web *Bonus Exercises:* • About Making the Connection • What is My Class Participation Style • Call Waiting: Dealing With Group Difficulties **College Success Factors Index Assessment Web Site** **http://success.wadsworth.com** • Task Precision **WebTutor** Text-specific study tools, including practice quizzes, online tutorials, and Web links, along with access to the Newbury House Online Dictionary **InfoTrac College Edition** *Keywords:* Robert Fulghum, multiple intelligences

Ideas for Instruction and Instructor Training	Videos & CD-ROMS	Media Resources for Instructors	Media Resources for Students
Instructor's Manual *Exercises:* • Creating a Term Timetable • Goal Tending • Goals Throughout Your Life • Not Now! • Does the Class Waste Time? • Me Spontaneous? *Guest Speaker:* Invite a panel of instructors from the University to talk about how they manage their time **Test Bank Questions** *Chapter 3:* 10 True/False, Multiple Choice, and Essay Questions *Available in a computerized test bank format:* **ExamView®**	**Time Management** (18 minutes) From the *Films for Humanities and Sciences®*, this video highlights three strategies students can use to manage time better **Wadsworth Study Skills Video, Vol. 1: Improving Your Grades** Time management is stressed as a way for students to make good grades **Your College Experience: Strategies for Success** Produced by the renowned First Year Experience Program at the University of South Carolina *Program 2: Time Management*	**Web Site** **http://success.wadsworth.com** *General Resources:* Download on... • Teaching Time Management—suggestions for teaching time management in a way that won't make students feel inferior **Microsoft® PowerPoint® Slides** • Control Your Life by Controlling Time • Stay on Time to Reach Your Goals • Plan for the Term, Week, Day • Never Procrastinate Again (Much) • Balance College, Work, Family, & Commuting **Transparency Acetates** • Controlling Your Time • Task and Time Plan • Timetable • Scheduling **WebTutor** Chapter 3 Course Management Tool for WebCT or Blackboard	**Web Site** **http://success.wadsworth.com** *Links to:* • Time Management Tips • Controlling Procrastination • Time Management Skills • Time Management Checklist **Media Edition CD-ROM** *Self-Assessment* *Quiz* *Crossword Puzzle* *Journal* *InfoTrac College Edition* *Exercises from the Book:* • Are You Studying Enough? • Weekly Plan • Link Goals with Time Spent in Activities • A New Kind of Cheese • Be More Precise • Make To-Do Lists • Time Wasters *Bonus Exercises:* • Creating a Term Paper • Are You a Procrastinator? • Creative Commuting **College Success Factors Index Assessment Web Site** **http://success.wadsworth.com** • Task Precision • Expectations • Time **WebTutor** Text-specific study tools, including practice quizzes, online tutorials, and Web links, along with access to the Newbury House Online Dictionary **InfoTrac College Edition** *Keywords:* Florence Griffith Joyner, time management, prioritizing, procrastination **Planners** *(can be bundled with text)* • *Deluxe Planner:* Attractive student planner can help students organize their busy days • *Basic Planner:* Less expensive than the Deluxe Planner, this compact organizer helps students manage their time

Resource Integration Guide—Make the Connection!

15

Resource Integration Guide—Make the Connection!

Ideas for Instruction and Instructor Training	Videos & CD-ROMS	Media Resources for Instructors	Media Resources for Students
Instructor's Manual *Exercises:* • Checking Out a Campus Newspaper • Show Me the Money • Big Night Out—For $20.00!! • Class Newsletter: Money-Saving Tips *Guest Speakers:* • Invite an experienced Residence Hall Advisor to class • Invite an upperclassman who became "over-involved" in school activities *Field Trips:* • Tour the campus by setting up a scavenger hunt • Invite the entire class to watch a play **Test Bank Questions** *Chapter 4:* 10 True/False, Multiple Choice, and Essay Questions *Available in a computerized test bank format:* **ExamView®** **Teaching College Success by Constance Staley** (Training manual & CD-ROM available for sale) *Module 9:* Technology Skills *Microsoft® PowerPoint® slides 1-24:* Designing Multimedia Class Projects, Creating Student Web Pages, and other slides relating to computers and technology *Handouts:* • PowerPoint Twelve-Point Exercise • Searching the Web • Refining Your Search • Evaluating Web Resources • Citing Internet Resources • Designing Effective Web Exercises	**CNN Today:**  **College Success 2000 Video** "College Tuition" (2:21) "College Costs" (1:49) "Student Jobs" (2:21) "Summer Jobs" (2:21) **CNN Today: College Success 2001 Video** "Financing College" (2:45) "College Students & Credit Cards "(2:07) "College Gambling" **Saving** (35 minutes) From the *Films for the Humanities and Sciences®*, this film shows how to postpone instant gratification and save for the future **Your College Experience: Strategies for Success** Produced by the renowned First Year Experience Program at the University of South Carolina *Program 7: Teacher and Student: Partners in Learning* *Program 8: An Information Age Introduction to the Library*	**Web Site** **http://success.wadsworth.com** *General Resources:* Download on... • Using Peer Leaders in the Classroom as a way for students to feel more connected to campus **Microsoft® PowerPoint® Slides** • Be a Great Money Manager • Connect with Your Campus • Connect with Computers **Transparency Acetates** • Budgeting • Money Managing Process • Financial Aid • Getting the Right Courses • Academic Advisors • Library: Touring Questions, 1 • Library: Touring Questions, 2 • Computers: Ten Questions • Computers: Overcoming Fears • Computers: Sources of Information **WebTutor** webTUTOR Chapter 4 Course Management Tool for WebCT or Blackboard	**Web Site** **http://success.wadsworth.com** *Links to:* *Financial Aid Info* • FASTWEB—Financial aid search through the Web • FinAid—Comprehensive list of financial aid resources • Nellie Mae • A College Student Budget *Computing* • What Is the World Wide Web? • How Do I Find Things on the Web? • How Do I Navigate the WWW? • What Will I Encounter on the Web? **Media Edition CD-ROM** *Self-Assessment* *Quiz* *Crossword Puzzle* *Journal* *InfoTrac College Edition* *Exercises from the Book:* • Campus Resources to Meet My Needs • Exploring Extra-Curricular Activities • Explore Campus Jobs • How Am I Doing with Computers? • $$$ • Uncover Web Treasures • Only the Best *Bonus Exercises:* • Visiting the Computer Center • My Annual Budget • My Monthly Budget **College Success Factors Index Assessment Web Site** **http://success.wadsworth.com** • Time • College Involvement • Family Involvement **WebTutor** webTUTOR Text-specific study tools, including practice quizzes, online tutorials, and Web links, along with access to the Newbury House Online Dictionary **InfoTrac College Edition** *Keywords:* Marc Andreessen, money management, credit card dangers, financial aid, academic advisors, college libraries, and the Internet

Ideas for Instruction and Instructor Training	Videos & CD-ROMS	Media Resources for Instructors	Media Resources for Students
Instructor's Manual *Exercises:* • Commit to Class • Concentrate & Listen • Capture Key Ideas • Connect Ideas • Note-Taking Strategies • Note-Taking Formats • Commit to Reading *Guest Speakers:* Invite a Reading Specialist to class to discuss reading strategies **Test Bank Questions** *Chapter 5:* 10 True/False, Multiple Choice, and Essay Questions *Available in a computerized test bank format:* **ExamView®**	**CNN Today: College Success 2001 Video** "College Students Buy Class Notes" (2:04) **Note-taking Video** (9 minutes) From the *Films for the Humanities and Sciences®*, this video features the Cornell note-taking system **Wadsworth Study Skills Video, Vol. 2: Lectures for Note-taking Practice** Have your students practice taking notes in a variety of lecture styles **Listening** (15 minutes) From the *Films for the Humanities and Sciences®* **Your College Experience: Strategies for Success** Produced by the renowned First Year Experience Program at the University of South Carolina *Program 4: Listening and Learning in the Classroom* *Program 5: A Sound Approach to Textbooks*	**Web Site** **http://success.wadsworth.com** *General Resources:* Download on… • Teaching Reading **Microsoft® PowerPoint® Slides** • Commit, Concentrate, Capture, Connect • Take Charge of Lectures • Take Great Lecture Notes • Take Charge of Your Reading • Mark or Take Notes from Reading **Transparency Acetates** • Serious About Learning • Participating • Distractions • Formats • Cornell Method Looseleaf • Cornell Sample Notes 1 • Cornell Sample Notes 2 **WebTutor** Chapter 5 Course Management Tool for WebCT or Blackboard	**Web Site** **http://success.wadsworth.com** *Links to:* • Six Reading Myths • How to Read Your Textbooks More Efficiently • Assess Your Reading Habits • SQ3R: A Reading Study Program • Reading Your Textbooks • How to Read Essays You Must Analyze • Mark Your Books • Suggestions for Improving Reading Speed **Media Edition CD-ROM** *Self-Assessment* *Quiz* *Crossword Puzzle* *Journal* *InfoTrac College Edition* *Exercises from the Book:* • Auditing Your Note-taking Style for Lectures • What's Your Reader Profile? • How Fast Do Your Read? • How Do You Read? • Analyze Your Sixth Sense *Bonus Exercises:* • Your Own System **College Success Factors Index Assessment Web Site** **http://success.wadsworth.com** • Task Precision **Web Tutor** Text-specific study tools, including practice quizzes, online tutorials, and Web links, along with access to the Newbury House Online Dictionary **InfoTrac College Edition** *Keywords:* College classes, listening, information processing

Resource Integration Guide—Make the Connection!

Ideas for Instruction and Instructor Training	Videos & CD-ROMS	Media Resources for Instructors	Media Resources for Students
Instructor's Manual *Exercises:* • Curiosity Doesn't Kill the Student • Study Nook • Your Teacher's Study Habits • High School Studying • Using American History (or Other) Notes • Memory Decay • Do You Have a Learning Disability? *Guest Speakers:* • Invite a professor from Women's Studies to talk about gender & learning • Invite a professor from Music to talk about the memorization tools needed for music **Test Bank Questions** *Chapter 6:* 10 True/False, Multiple Choice, and Essay Questions *Available in a computerized test bank format:* **ExamView®**	**CNN Today: College Success 2000 Video** "Drunken Memory" (1:42) **CNN Today: College Success 2001 Video** "Perfectionism" (3:20) **The Treatment of Attention Deficit Disorder in Adults** (29 minutes) From the *Films for the Humanities and Sciences®*, this Dartmouth Medical Center Production talks about how to treat ADD with drugs and by other means **Dyslexia: A Different Kind of Mind** (29 minutes) From the *Films for the Humanities and Sciences®*, this video explores the cognitive differences of people who have dyslexia **Strategic Learning** (10 minutes) From the *Films for the Humanities and Sciences®*, this video outlines a three-step approach to retaining information **Multimedia Study Skills** *Study Skills* From the *Films for the Humanities and Sciences®*, part one of this CD-ROM covers listening, remembering, and getting to the point of an assignment	**Web Site** **http://success.wadsworth.com** *General Resources:* Download on… • Active Learning **Microsoft® PowerPoint® Slides** • Plan Your Attack • Improve Your Memory • Pursue Deeper Leaning • Master Disciplines • Overcoming Learning Disabilities • Join a Study Group **Transparency Acetates** • Refining Skills • When to Study • How to Memorize 1 • How to Memorize 2 • Types of Teams **WebTutor** Chapter 6 Course Management Tool for WebCT or Blackboard	**Web Site** **http://success.wadsworth.com** *Links to:* • Study Skills Checklist: Find out your own habits and attitudes • Memory Theory & Techniques: This site will help students memorize the French language and historical dates • Study Distractions Analysis • Dartmouth Study Skills Center • University of Texas, Austin, Learning Skills Center Tips • Potter's Science Gems • "MathNerds" **Media Edition CD-ROM** *Self-Assessment* *Quiz* *Crossword Puzzle* *Journal* *InfoTrac College Edition* *Exercises from the Book:* • Early Bird or Night Owl? • Am I Ready to Learn and Remember? • Could I Have a Learning Disability? • Expanding Study Time • Call Waiting *Bonus Exercises:* • How Do I Make Groups Work? **College Success Factors Index Assessment Web Site** **http://success.wadsworth.com** • Task Precision **WebTutor** Text-specific study tools, including practice quizzes, online tutorials, and Web links, along with access to the Newbury House Online Dictionary **InfoTrac College Edition** *Keywords:* Jay Leno, mnemonics, study strategies, learning disabilities

Ideas for Instruction and Instructor Training	Videos & CD-ROMS	Media Resources for Instructors	Media Resources for Students
Instructor's Manual *Exercises:* • Assessing Study Groups • Test Files • Call Waiting (from Chapter 2 in student text) • Time Management & Tests • Healthy Test-prep • Special Help for Test-taking • Dropping Courses • Team Solution to Test Review • Test Taking Integrity • Is a Tutor Worth It? • Exam Kit—Help! *Guest Speakers:* • Invite a panel of upperclassmen to talk about test-taking strategies • Invite a rep from the Study Center to talk about test-taking techniques **Test Bank Questions** Chapter 7: 10 True/False, Multiple Choice, and Essay Questions *Available in a computerized test bank format:* **ExamView®**	**CNN Today:** CNN **College Success 2001 Video** "College Students Buy Class Notes" (2:04) **Your College Experience: Strategies for Success** Produced by the renowned First Year Experience Program at the University of South Carolina *Program 6: Making the Grade* **Your College Experience, Strategies for Success** Produced by the renowned First Year Experience Program at the University of South Carolina. Segments on study skills that can apply to test taking. **Multimedia Study Skills** *Test Preparation:* From the *Films for the Humanities and Sciences®*, part two of this CD-ROM gives advice about taking objective and subjective tests	**Web Site** **http://success.wadsworth.com** *General Resources:* Download on… • Student Assessment: Exams, Assignments, Grades: Describes strategies for making test-taking a positive experience for students. Tips for making tests that are both comprehensive & balanced **Microsoft® PowerPoint® Slides** • Get On With It • Get in Gear • Meet the Challenge • Make the Grade • Build Your Character **Transparency Acetates** • Long-term Strategies 1 • Long-term Strategies 2 • Short-term Strategies • General Strategies • Sample Essay Questions • Sample Essay Outline • Cheating (4 slides) • Identifying Behavior Problems **Web Tutor** webTUTOR™ Chapter 7 Course Management Tool for WebCT or Blackboard	**Web Site** **http://success.wadsworth.com** *Links to:* • Test Taking Skills (for taking essay tests) • Survival Strategies for Taking Tests • Checklist for Essay Tests **Media Edition CD-ROM** *Self-Assessment* *Quiz* *Crossword Puzzle* *Journal* *InfoTrac College Edition* *Exercises from the Book:* • Do I Have Test Anxiety? • How Well Do I Test? • Your Personal Honor Code • Decode Essay Instructions • Find Your Quiet Place *Bonus Exercises:* • Judging Exam Quality • Evaluate Your Exam Luck • Learn to Relax **College Success Factors Index Assessment Web Site** **http://success.wadsworth.com** • Responsibility/Control • Task Precision **WebTutor** webTUTOR™ Text-specific study tools, including practice quizzes, online tutorials, and Web links, along with access to the Newbury House Online Dictionary **InfoTrac College Edition** *Keywords:* Albert Einstein, studying for tests, essay tests, cheating, succeed on tests, multiple choice tests, memorization, study groups, test anxiety, relaxation techniques

Resource Integration Guide—Make the Connection!

Ideas for Instruction and Instructor Training	Videos & CD-ROMS	Media Resources for Instructors	Media Resources Resources for Students
Instructor's Manual *Exercises:* • Looking at a 1950's Science Textbook to Consider "Factual" Information • What Do You See?—Carefully Observing a Place on Campus • Cartoons—Humor & Creativity • Surprise!—for Creativity • Holistic Thinking *Guest Speakers:* • Invite a panel of professors to talk about critical thinking in their field • Invite employees from corporations to talk about critical thinking at work **Test Bank Questions** *Chapter 8:* 10 True/False, Multiple Choice, and Essay Questions *Available in a computerized test bank format:* **ExamView®** **Teaching College Success by Constance Staley** (Training manual & CD-ROM available for sale) *Module 8:* Communication Skills *Microsoft® PowerPoint® slides:* 20-23, Includes evaluating critical thinking and how focusing on critical thinking can change the way you teach	**CNN Today: College Success 2001 Video** "Mindful Living" (4:09) "Perfectionism" (3:20) **Intelligence, Creativity, & Thinking Styles (video icon)** (30 minutes) From the *Films for the Humanities and Sciences®,* this video explores how IQ relates to multiple intelligences & how teachers and parents can encourage creativity	**Web Site** **http://success.wadsworth.com** *General Resources:* Download on… • Critical Thinking **Microsoft® PowerPoint® Slides** • Think Critically • Reason • Solve Problems the "IDEAL" Way • Make Good Decisions • Think Creatively **Transparency Acetates** • Good Critical Thinkers 1 • Good Critical Thinkers 2 • Four Aspects of Critical Thinking • Four-Step Problem Solving • Brainstorming • Information Processing • Gardner's Seven Areas • Bloom's Thinking Skills • Lakota Medicine Wheel **WebTutor** Chapter 8 Course Management Tool for WebCT or Blackboard	**Web Site** **http://success.wadsworth.com** *Links to:* • How to Solve It: tips on how to critically solve problems • San Jose State's Interactive Critical Thinking Tutorial: exercises to help students prepare for critical thinking **Media Edition CD-ROM** *Self-Assessment* *Quiz* *Crossword Puzzle* *Journal* *InfoTrac College Edition* *Exercises from the Book:* • Claim Check • The Critical Difference • How Systematically Do I Solve Problems? • My Creative Profile • Claims Detector • A Question a Day • A Critical Rationale • The Great Debate • Creative Surfing **College Success Factors Index Assessment Web Site** **http://success.wadsworth.com** • Task Precision **WebTutor** Text-specific study tools, including practice quizzes, online tutorials, and Web links, along with access to the Newbury House Online Dictionary **InfoTrac College Edition** *Keywords:* Temple Grandin, creative thinking, mindfulness, "flow," finding flow

Ideas for Instruction and Instructor Training	Videos & CD-ROMS	Media Resources for Instructors	Media Resources Resources for Students
Instructor's Manual *Exercises:* • Writing from Within: Daily Journal • Writing a Self-Portrait Poem • Your Personal Writing "Slogan" • Practice Speaking in Public • Introducing Class Members *Guest Speakers:* • Invite an alum to talk about how writing is used at their work • Invite an alum to describe different public speaking situations required in business **Test Bank Questions** *Chapter 9:* 10 True/False, Multiple Choice, and Essay Questions *Available in a computerized test bank format:* **ExamView®** **Teaching College Success by Constance Staley** (Training manual & CD-ROM available for sale) *Module 8:* Communication Skills *Microsoft® PowerPoint® slides* 1-19 on teaching writing and speaking. *Handouts:* • Writing Exercises • Writing in the Freshman Seminar • Quotable Journals • Speaking Exercises	**On Writing** (25 minutes) From the *Films for the Humanities and Sciences®*, this video features interviews with some of the top writers in our time including Erica Jong and Gore Vidal **Speaking** (15 minutes) From the *Films for the Humanities and Sciences®*, this video gives methods for improving speaking	**Web Site** **http://success.wadsworth.com** *General Resources:* Download on… • Teaching Writing: Journal, Free-Writing, and Formal Writing: Gives advice on how to conquer these various types of writing with freshmen—when to encourage free thinking and when to have students buckle down and practice good form **Microsoft®** **PowerPoint® Slides** • Express Yourself! • Do Your Research • Write with Impact • Speak! **Transparency Acetates** • Habits of Effective Writers 1 • Habits of Effective Writers 2 • Three Steps • Writing Problems • Steps to Successful Speaking • Good Speaking 1 • Good Speaking 2 • GUIDE Checklist • PREP Formula • Feedback Form **WebTutor** Chapter 9 Course Management Tool for WebCT or Blackboard	**Web Site** **http://success.wadsworth.com** *Links to:* • How to Write and Revise a Rough Draft • Avoiding Plagiarism • MLA Guidelines for Citation from the Internet • The Elements of Style • Grammar and Style Notes **Media Edition CD-ROM** *Self-Assessment* *Quiz* *Crossword Puzzle* *Journal* *InfoTrac College Edition* *Exercises from the Book:* • What Are My Writing Strengths and Weaknesses? • What Are My Speaking Strengths & Weaknesses? • The Cost of Plagiarism • Creating a New Role • Debate Savvy *Bonus Exercises:* • Promoting Feedback **College Success Factors Index Assessment Web Site** **http://success.wadsworth.com** • Task Precision **WebTutor** Text-specific study tools, including practice quizzes, online tutorials, and Web links, along with access to the Newbury House Online Dictionary **InfoTrac College Edition** *Keywords:* Amy Tan, Internet resources, effective writing, writer's block, plagiarism, effective speaking

Resource Integration Guide—Make the Connection!

Ideas for Instruction and Instructor Training	Videos & CD-ROMS	Media Resources for Instructors	Media Resources Resources for Students
Instructor's Manual *Exercises:* • Listening & Critical Thinking • The Bill of Assertive Rights • Experienced Conflict Resolvers • Away from Home—Family Relations • Students with Partners • Mixed Messages • Take Part: Visit an Organization • Walk in Someone Else's Shoes *Guest Speakers:* • Invite a Rape Counselor or expert on rape to talk to the class • Invite a drama student to act out emotions nonverbally **Test Bank Questions** *Chapter 10:* 10 True/False, Multiple Choice, and Essay Questions *Available in a computerized test bank format:* **ExamView®**	**CNN Today: College Success 2001 Video** "Diversity Report Card" (2:40) "Controversy Over Affirmative Action" (2:23) "Students Experience Homelessness" (2:03) "Definition of Rape" (2:42) "Student Killed In Hate Crime" (2:25) **The videos listed below are from the** *Films for the Humanities and Sciences®*: **Listening** (15 minutes) Shows how listening can bring about greater awareness and understanding **Date Rape: Behind Closed Doors** (45 minutes) Explores the serious consequences of rape **Beyond Black and White: Affirmative Action in America** (58 minutes) **Expressing Yourself** (20 minutes) Gives tips on how to improve your communication **Sexual Harassment: Crossing the Line** (30 minutes) **Understanding Prejudice** (50 minutes) Discusses homophobia and multiculturalism **Hate & the Internet: Web sites & the Issue of Free Speech** (22 minutes) Narrated by Ted Koppel	**Web Site** **http://success.wadsworth.com** *General Resources:* Download on… • Diversity: Comprehensive look at how to teach a diverse classroom, how to promote unity, and how to make every student feel valuable • Personal Relationships: Tells how to deal with withdrawal-prone students; lists simple and effective ways to gain student trust **Microsoft® PowerPoint® Slides** • Communicate Effectively • Develop Good Relationships • Appreciate Diversity **Transparency Acetates** • Eight Keys • Formula for Assertiveness • Keeping Relationships Positive • Nonverbal Cues • Barriers to Verbal Communication • Ten Reasons to Join • Attitude Scale • Examples of Sexism • Improving Relations, 1 & 2 **WebTutor** Chapter 10 Course Management Tool for WebCT or Blackboard	**Web Site** **http://success.wadsworth.com** *Links to:* • Virtual Community Multicultural Resources • Family Relations • LatinoLink • PlanetOut • American Visions Society (site features African-American artists and writers) • Ipopcorn.com (site for Asian-American students) • Everywoman's Center **Media Edition CD-ROM** *Self-Assessment* *Quiz* *Crossword Puzzle* *Journal* *InfoTrac College Edition* *Exercises from the Book:* • Do You Blow Up, Get Down & Dirty, or Speak Up? • The Boyfriend & the Dumpster • What Does Touch Communicate? • Evaluate Your Attitudes toward Diverse Others *Bonus Exercises:* • Are You Androgynous? **College Success Factors Index Assessment Web Site** **http://success.wadsworth.com** • Task Precision • Competition • Expectations **WebTutor** Text-specific study tools, including practice quizzes, online tutorials, and Web links, along with access to the Newbury House Online Dictionary **InfoTrac College Edition** *Keywords:* Oprah Winfrey, effective communication, nonverbal communication, being assertive, conflict resolution, relationships, loneliness, diversity, prejudice, stereotyping, men's issues

Ideas for Instruction and Instructor Training	Videos & CD-ROMS	Media Resources for Instructors	Media Resources for Students
Instructor's Manual *Exercises:* • Your Personal Health Style • Create an Exercise Plan • About Sleep—Zzzzz • What Do You Eat? • About Smoking • Discussing Drugs and Alcohol • Music to Your Ears: Using Music to Help Combat Stress • Boosting Confidence—For You and Your Friends • Thinking About Depression **Test Bank Questions** *Chapter 11:* 10 True/False, Multiple Choice, and Essay Questions *Available in a computerized test bank format:* **ExamView®**	**CNN Today:** **CNN** **College Success 2001 Video** "Binge Drinking" (2:06) "A Dorm Goes Drug Free" (2:39) "College Butts Out" (1:54) "AIDS 101" (1:56) "Mindful Living" (4:09) **The videos listed below are from the *Films for the Humanities and Sciences®*:** **Binge Drinking: The Right to Party?** (22 minutes) Visits colleges where alcohol has become a hot topic **The Truth About Alcohol** (30 minutes) Describes why alcohol is so popular and the deadly consequences of misuse **Handling Stress: Today and Tomorrow** (30 minutes) Coping strategies for stress **Sleeping Well** (28 minutes) Ways to improve your sleep habits **What's Eating You? A Guide to Sensible Dieting** (30 minutes) Shows a balanced way to lose weight **The Relaxation Response** (30 minutes) Guides students through relaxation exercises	**Web Site** **http://success.wadsworth.com** *General Resources:* Download on... • Teaching About Drugs, Alcohol & Sexuality **Microsoft®** **PowerPoint® Slides** • Link Values, Motivation, Goals, and Self-Esteem • Pursue and Maintain Physical Health • Be Mentally Healthy **Transparency Acetates** • Lifestyle and Poor Health • Sleep Better 1 & 2 • Methods for Managing Stress • Risk Reduction for Sexual Assault • Secondary Effects of Binge Drinking • Beliefs (Alcohol & Drugs) • Annual Consequences • Drinks & GPA **WebTutor** **WebTUTOR** Chapter 11 Course Management Tool for WebCT or Blackboard	**Web Site** **http://success.wadsworth.com** *Links to:* • What to Eat and When to Eat It • Fronske Health Center, Northern Arizona University • Duke University "Healthy Devil" Online Guide to Health Concerns • The Alternative Medicine Page • Prevention Primer • Wisconsin Clearinghouse for Prevention Resources • Yahoo Nutrition Sites **Media Edition CD-ROM** *Self-Assessment* *Quiz* *Crossword Puzzle* *Journal* *InfoTrac College Edition* *Exercises from the Book:* • What Is My Health Style? • Do I Abuse Drugs? • Am I Depressed? • Keeping an Eating Journal *Bonus Exercises:* • How Emotionally Intelligent Are You? **College Success Factors Index Assessment Web Site** **http://success.wadsworth.com** • Competition • Expectations **WebTutor** **WebTUTOR** Text-specific study tools, including practice quizzes, online tutorials, and Web links, along with access to the Newbury House Online Dictionary **InfoTrac College Edition** *Keywords:* Arnold Schwarzenegger, healthy lifestyle, exercise, eating disorders, smoking, drinking, AIDS, stress, depression

Resource Integration Guide—Make the Connection!

Chapter 12: EXPLORE CAREERS AND MAJORS

Ideas for Instruction and Instructor Training	Videos & CD-ROMS	Media Resources for Instructors	Media Resources for Students
Instructor's Manual *Exercises:* • Defining Goals • Your Route: Finding out What Courses to Take • Using the College Catalog • Considering a Two-Year College • Finding a Mentor • Interviews: Role Playing • An Informal Way to Consider a Major *Guest Speaker:* Invite a staff member from the career center to speak to the class **Test Bank Questions** *Chapter 12:* 10 True/False, Multiple Choice, and Essay Questions *Available in a computerized test bank format:* **ExamView®**	**CNN Today:**  **College Success 2000 Video** "Student Jobs" (2:21) "Summer Jobs" (2:21) "Americorps" (2:13) **Your College Experience:**  **Strategies for Success** Produced by the renowned First Year Experience Program at the University of South Carolina *Program 10: Major, Career, and Transfer Planning* **The videos below are from the** *Films for the Humanities and Sciences®:* **How to Find and Keep a Job** (30 minutes) Expert advice on landing a job **Interview Tips** (30 minutes) Guides viewers through the interview process **Web Résumés** (30 minutes) Examines Web résumés and resume alternatives **The Exceptional Employee: A Guide to Success on the Job** (30 minutes) What it takes to be a valuable employee **Jobs: Not What they Used to Be—The New Face of Work in America** (57 minutes) Highlights companies that stress teamwork & technology skills	**Web Site** **http://success.wadsworth.com** *General Resources:* Download on… • Teaching Values— How to strengthen the "value muscle" in students so they are prepared for their careers and future **Microsoft®** **PowerPoint® Slides** • Get Motivated to Explore Careers • Map Out an Academic Path • Examine Career and Job Skills **Transparency Acetates** • Getting the Right Courses • Academic Advisors • Admissions Advisors • Current Résumé • Ideal Résumé **WebTutor** Chapter 12 Course Management Tool for WebCT or Blackboard	**Web Site** **http://success.wadsworth.com** *Links to:* • The Catapult on JobWeb • Bureau of Labor Statistics 2000-01 Occupational Outlook Handbook • Career Resource Center • JobWeb • Summer Jobs • Net-Temps • Job Search Links **Media Edition CD-ROM** *Self-Assessment* *Quiz* *Crossword Puzzle* *Journal* *InfoTrac College Edition* *Exercises from the Book:* • Coursework for an Associate Degree or Certificate • A Four-or Five-Year Academic Plan • Current Résumé and Future Résumé • How Good Are Your Communication Skills? • My Values and My Career Pursuits • My Self-Management Skills • Why Do People Choose Particular Careers? *Bonus Exercises* • Matching Your Career Interests with the Fastest-Growing Jobs **College Success Factors Index Assessment Web Site** **http://success.wadsworth.com** • Expectations • Wellness **WebTutor** Text-specific study tools, including practice quizzes, online tutorials, and Web links, along with access to the Newbury House Online Dictionary **InfoTrac College Edition** *Keywords:* Bernard Shaw, exploring careers, majors, academic plans, ideal job candidate, college work experience

Media Edition

Your Guide to
COLLEGE
SUCCESS

Strategies for Achieving Your Goals

SECOND EDITION

John W. Santrock
University of Texas, Dallas

Jane S. Halonen
James Madison University

WADSWORTH

TM

THOMSON LEARNING

Australia • Canada • Mexico • Singapore • Spain
United Kingdom • United States

WADSWORTH

THOMSON LEARNING

Executive Manager, College Success: Elana Dolberg
Assistant Editor: MJ Wright
Project Manager, Editorial Production: Trudy Brown
Print/Media Buyer: Mary Noel
Permissions Editor: Joohee Lee
Production Service: Greg Hubit Bookworks
Text Designer: Diane Beasley

Photo Researcher: Terri Wright
Copy Editor: Molly Roth
Cover Designer: Bill Stanton
Cover Image: Werner Bokelberg, The Image Bank
Compositor: New England Typographic Service
Text and Cover Printer: Transcontinental

Wadsworth/Thomson Learning
10 Davis Drive
Belmont, CA 94002-3098
USA

For more information about our products, contact us:
Thomson Learning Academic Resource Center
1-800-423-0563
http://www.wadsworth.com

International Headquarters
Thomson Learning
International Division
290 Harbor Drive, 2nd Floor
Stamford, CT 06902-7477
USA

UK/Europe/Middle East/South Africa
Thomson Learning
Berkshire House
168-173 High Holborn
London WC1V 7AA
United Kingdom

Asia
Thomson Learning
60 Albert Street, #15-01
Albert Complex
Singapore 189969

Canada
Nelson Thomson Learning
1120 Birchmount Road
Toronto, Ontario M1K 5G4
Canada

Library of Congress Cataloging-in-Publication Data
Santrock, John W.
    Your guide to college success : strategies for achieving
your goals / John W. Santrock, Jane S. Halonen—2nd ed.
        p. cm.
    Includes bibliographical references and index.
    ISBN 0-534-57205-7
    1. College student orientation—United States—
Handbooks, manuals, etc. I. Title: College success.
II. Halonen, Jane S. III. Title.
LB2343.32.S26 2002
378.1'98—dc21
                                    2001017981

Contents

CHAPTER 3

Be a Great Time Manager 53

CHAPTER 4

Connect with Money, Campus, and Computers 77

CHAPTER 5

Take It In: Notes and Reading 101

CHAPTER 6

Enhance Your Study Skills 133

CHAPTER 7

Succeed on Tests 161

CHAPTER 8

Expand Your Thinking Skills 189

CHAPTER 9

Refine Your Expression 217

CHAPTER 10

Communicate and Build Relationships 243

CHAPTER 11

Be Physically and Mentally Healthy 269

CHAPTER 12

Explore Careers and Majors 297

Putting It All Together 319

Preface

A Major Revision

The first edition of *Your Guide to College Success* was very well received. Both instructors and students praised the book for its active learning strategies designed for all styles of learners, the student self-assessments, the high-interest writing style, and the colorful contemporary design.

We continued to listen to instructors and students and have substantially improved the book in its second edition. With new, integrated themes based on what instructors of college success courses told us they wanted in a book, a reorganization within chapters to place a much stronger emphasis on active strategies, fewer chapters, an entire chapter devoted to managing time effectively, expanded and improved coverage of learning styles, the inclusion of many new topics and the deletion of others, new and improved learning and study aids, a dynamic new design and layout, and line-by-line revision of existing material, *we are confident that the closer you look, the more you will be surprised and pleased by these changes.*

New, Integrated Themes

The second edition of *Your Guide to College Success* has six main themes that make up most of Chapter 1, "Manage Your College Success": develop meaningful values; get motivated; set goals, plan, and monitor; think and learn; build self-esteem; and explore careers. These themes are explored throughout the book.

We believe these are the keys to college success—the main things that students need to do to master their college experience. After the six themes have been discussed in Chapter 1, they will appear again in every chapter of the book, both in the content of the chapter and in visual images.

At the beginning of each chapter, students will see a hexagon, *The Six-Point Success Model,* with the six themes linked together and the chapter's main focus in the center of the hexagon. For example, the Chapter 1 graphic looks like this:

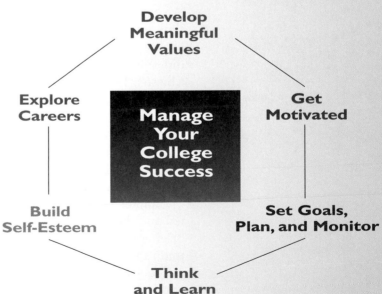

Within each chapter, students also will see horizontal linkages that include one or more of the six main themes. These horizontal linkages visually show important connections between the six main themes and the content of a particular chapter. For example, in Chapter 3, "Be a Great Time Manager," one set of horizontal linkages is:

This set of linkages appears just after students have read about the importance of setting completion dates for their goals.

Stronger Emphasis on Active Strategies

Virtually every heading in the book and each discussion that follows has been changed with an eye toward focusing more on strategies that will help students master the college experience. For example, in Chapter 1, one main heading is "Get Motivated on Behalf of Your Values," followed by subheadings "Show Confidence and Enthusiasm," "Realize That You Are in Command," "Persist," "Be Internally Motivated," and "What If You Are Bored?" followed in turn by an examination of these strategies for reducing boredom: "Explore Some New Avenues," "Tune in to Moments of Inspiration," and "Make Sure It Is Your Motivation."

We have reconstructed the entire book to reflect this active, strategy-oriented approach. We spent considerable time on choosing precise words that capture what students need to do to succeed in college.

Fewer Chapters: 14 to 12

We extensively surveyed instructors who teach the college success course, and they told us that they often did not get through the entire book of fourteen chapters. They recommended that we reduce the book to twelve chapters. We did this by moving the discussion of values, which was a main theme of Chapter 14 in the first edition, to Chapter 1 and making it a major theme of the book. Indeed, the more we talked with students and instructors, the more we realized that before students get motivated and set goals, they need to know what is important to them. So early in Chapter 1, we ask students to examine their values, to really dig into what is important to them. Further, discussions of values appear throughout the book; the material has been presented in the context of various topics rather than in a stand-alone chapter.

Chapter 14 of the first edition also had students integrate what they had studied and thought about in previous chapters. This task is now covered in a new, brief epilogue, "Putting It All Together." In the epilogue, students review the six main themes of the book and complete final, integrative self-evaluations. The epilogue also encourages students to think about what the future holds for them and how the strategies they have learned in this course can help them manage their lives effectively through the remainder of college and thereafter.

Instructors requested that the discussion of diversity and relationships be integrated into a single chapter rather than two. We have done this in Chapter 10, "Communicate and Build Relationships." Diversity remains an important topic throughout the book, appearing in many places, including chapter-opening stories, photographs, critical-thinking exercises, and so forth.

An Entire Chapter Now Devoted to Time Management

In the first edition of the book, managing time and money were discussed in the same chapter. Instructors told us that managing time is so important that it should be the focus of an entire chapter. So, Chapter 3, "Be a Great Time Manager," is now devoted exclusively to managing time effectively. The discussion of managing money effectively is now part of Chapter 4, "Connect with Money, Campus, and Technology."

Expanded and Improved Coverage of Learning Styles

Because instructors told us that they wanted more material on learning styles, we have made this topic the main focus of Chapter 2. Specifically, we have expanded exploration of multiple intelligence, included a new assessment of sensory preferences, and provided new practical suggestions to improve study strategies as they relate to learning styles.

New Topics and Features

Many new topics and features are presented in the second edition of *Your Guide to College Success.* They include the following:

Chapter 1: Manage Your College Success

- Evaluating why you are here (includes a new self-assessment)
- Developing meaningful values (includes a new self-assessment)
- Getting motivated on behalf of your values
- What to do if you are bored
- Setting goals, planning, and monitoring your progress (includes a new self-assessment)
- New linkages: Establish values, get motivated, and set goals, plan, and monitor
- Focusing on what is important in thinking and learning
- The importance of joining the information age
- How to build self-esteem including a new self-assessment
- Exploring careers

Chapter 2: Diversify Your Learning Style

- Expanded exploration of multiple intelligence
- New assessment of sensory preferences in learning style
- New practical suggestions to improve your study strategies as they relate to learning style
- Exploration of the role of reflection and impulse control in learning
- Guiding questions to improve self-regulation

- Linkage of learning styles to potential careers
- New cartoons

Chapter 3: Be a Great Time Manager

- Control your life by controlling time
- New self-assessment on time wasters
- New linkages: set goals, plan steps to meet them, set dates for steps, and monitor your progress
- New section on creating subgoals
- New section on choosing the right planning tools
- New self-assessment: "Are You Studying Enough?"
- New example of a to-do list
- Expanded coverage of balancing college, work, family, and community with several new strategies
- New linkages: identify needs to balance, set reasonable goals for each, plan for each goal, and integrate your planning across goals

Chapter 4: Connect with Money, Campus, and Computers

- Entire discussion of managing money effectively (new to this chapter)
- New self-assessment on managing money effectively
- New linkages: skills with technology, better learning, college goals, and the career you want/technology skills in your career
- New self-assessment: "How Am I Doing with Computers?"
- New on-target tips that focuses on critically evaluating Web information

Chapter 5: Take It In: Notes and Reading

- An inspiring new chapter opener about Brooke Ellison
- Improved examples of note taking, especially the Cornell system
- More systematic application of a simple framework for maximizing gains from study time

Chapter 6: Enhance Your Study Skills

- New study strategies that compensate for learning disabilities
- More comprehensive suggestions regarding how to master reading in different disciplines

Chapter 7: Succeed on Tests

- More systematic discussion of preparing for different kinds of tests
- A roster of positive strategies for better test performance
- Improved strategies for writing better essay-test responses
- Help in decoding college vocabulary in test instructions
- New suggestions for coping with failure
- Stronger linkage between personal values and avoiding cheating

Chapter 8: Expand Your Thinking Skills

- Expanded discussion of critical thinking in college
- New suggestions for strategies to develop criticism
- A new exploration of reasoning
- Practical examples to improve reasoning skills
- New strategies for avoiding bad decision making
- Examples of creative thinking from young inventors
- Testing creative potential with a new self-assessment

Chapter 9: Refine Your Expression

- Expanded suggestions for completing research projects
- Improved discussion about navigating the library
- Clarification of the kinds of writing projects college will require
- Improved solutions for coping with delivery problems in speeches

Chapter 10: Communicate and Build Relationships

- New linkages: communication skills, better learning and grades, higher self-esteem, and reaching long-term and short-term goals
- All-new diversity topics
- New discussions of culture, ethnicity, gender, and sexual orientation

Chapter 11: Be Physically and Mentally Healthy

- New section at the beginning of the chapter: "Link Values, Motivation, Goals, and Self-Esteem"
- New linkages: value physical and mental health; get motivated to practice physical and mental health; set physical and mental health goals, plan, and monitor progress; and build self-esteem
- New linkages: exercise, brain cells, think and learn, and reach academic goals

Chapter 12: Explore Careers and Majors

- Discussion of achievement motivation and other material moved to Chapter 1 as "Get Motivated."
- Expanded focus on careers and majors
- New section, "Where Am I in Exploring Careers?"
- New section, "Choose Career Options That Match Your Values."
- New self-assessment: "My Values and My Career Pursuits."
- New information about occupations with fast growth and high pay that are expected to show the largest numerical growth in jobs from 1998 to 2008
- New linkages on values, career goals, and major or specialization
- New section on self-management skills and a new self-assessment, "My Self-Management Skills"

Epilogue: Putting It All Together

- New feature that encourages students to reflect on the six major themes of college success that have been emphasized, how they are doing in regard to these themes, and what lies ahead in their future
- Includes several self-evaluative exercises

More Cartoons and Humor

Learning proceeds better when students are in a good mood and enjoy what they are doing. Instructors and students told us that they loved the cartoons in the first edition and encouraged us to include more of these. We did. Instructors and students also asked us to insert more humor into the content of the chapters. We did this in four ways:

1. In some of the headings—for example, "Never Procrastinate Again (Much)" in Chapter 3, "Be a Great Time Manager"

2. In the writing—for example, a story about a student with huge credit-card debt who lost his car, drum set, and credit rating to the Repo Man in Chapter 4, "Connecting with Money, Campus, and Technology"
3. In inserts on Staying Out of the Pits and Amazing College Stories—for example, "It's Noon Thursday. Here Comes the Beer Truck" and "The Boyfriend and the Trash Dumpster" in Chapter 10, "Communicate and Build Relationships"
4. In some of the quotations in the margins—for example, YOGI SIGHTING: "If you don't know where you are going, you might wind up someplace else."—Yogi Berra, *20th-Century American Baseball Player*

New and Improved Learning and Study Aids

Instructors heartily endorsed many of the learning and study aids that we included in the first edition of the book, especially the on-target tips, self-assessments, and learning portfolio. Here are the new and improved learning and study aids in the second edition:

Beginning of Chapter The first edition opened with a chapter outline, checklist, and a preview. The second edition now opens with an upbeat heading (For example, Chapter 1: "Where Are You Now?"), brief coverage of chapter themes, and a checklist that students fill out regarding what their current skills and knowledge are regarding the chapter themes.

Instructors told us they loved the chapter opening stories, so we kept them but replaced several of them. Also, a hexagon appears at the beginning of each chapter; in each hexagon, the six major themes of the book are linked together around the main focus of the chapter. At the top of this page we have also included a brief description of the main ideas of each chapter.

Horizontal Linkages One or more times within each chapter, horizontal linkages appear that include some aspect of the main themes of the book integrated with the topic that is being discussed at that point in the chapter. The horizontal linkages further help students integrate the main themes of the book with the ideas being explored in a particular chapter.

Self-Assessments Self-assessments were extremely popular in the first edition, and instructors told us they wanted more. We added several new ones and made the others easier to score and interpret.

On-Target Tips This popular feature in the first edition was retained. Several times in each chapter, students read these inserts that focus on precise strategies for mastering the college experience. In many cases, we have added numbers or bullets to these tips to make them easier to understand.

 CD-ROM Icon A CD-ROM icon appears next to many features in each chapter. This icon indicates that the feature also appears on the book's accompanying CD-ROM, adding a new level of interactivity to this second edition.

End of Chapter The end-of-chapter material includes several changes. *"Summary Strategies for Mastering the College Experience"* has now been numbered and bulleted for more precise coverage of the chapter's main ideas. Also the six major themes of the book and the main topic of the chapter appear at the top of the summary page to encourage students to think about the chapter in relation to these integrative themes.

The *learning portfolio,* another popular feature of the first edition, has been retained. The learning portfolio consists of the following sections, each with one or more exercises for students to carry out: Reflect and Journal, Learn by Doing, Think Critically, Think Creatively, and Work Toward Goals. We fine-tuned the items in the learning portfolio, and when a majority of instructors said to replace an item, we did.

The end-of-chapter material also includes a series of *review questions,* which help students to summarize some of the main ideas in the chapter.

Dynamic New Design and Layout

The design and layout have been extensively changed in this new edition. Headings are larger, more frequent, and more meaningful. The layout is less cluttered and easier to study. For example, in the first edition there were four boxed inserts on different themes. These have been reduced to two in the second edition: Staying Out of the Pits and Amazing College Stories. The colors used are brighter and more dynamic, replacing the pastels of the first edition.

Ancillaries

Teaching Aids for the Instructor

Instructor's Resource Suite: Manual and CD-ROM (0-534-57212-X)
by Cynthia Jenkins, The University of Texas at Dallas
Alice Lanning, University of Oklahoma
The manual includes additional ice-breakers and exercises, how to structure group and collaborative learning, alternative teaching strategies, specific suggestions for teaching each topic, chapter quizzes, and many other resources. The CD-ROM contains the entire instructor's manual, PowerPoint slides, and CNN video clips in an easy-to-use search engine. With this CD-ROM, programs can customize the instructor's material to fit their course syllabus in an easy step-by-step process.

Thomson Learning WebTutor™ on WebCT and Blackboard
WebTutor on WebCT: (0-534-57209-X)
WebTutor on Blackboard: (0-534-57210-3)
This Web-based learning tool gives students access to study tools that correspond chapter by chapter and topic by topic with the book. Professors can use WebTutor to provide virtual office hours, post syllabi, set up threaded discussions, and track student progress on the practice quizzes.

Toll-free telephone consultation services 1-800-400-7609 for helpful advice and information about our products and services.

Custom Publishing Options. Faculty can select chapters from this and other Wadsworth College Success titles to bind with their own materials (campus maps, syllabi, etc.) into a fully customized book. For more information, visit our Web site at **www.wadsworth.success.com**.

Wadsworth College Success Workshop Series. We offer a variety of faculty development workshops regionally and on campuses nationwide throughout the year. Visit our Web site for dates and places: **www.wadsworth.success.com**.

Teaching College Success: The Complete Resource Guide (0-534-53640-9). By Constance Staley
An all-inclusive package that contains everything instructors need to create their own tailored training program for college success! This resource includes a blend of content information and experiential activities for trainers to try with training groups and later with students.

ExamView from Wadsworth/Thomson Learning . . . including online testing!
Cross-Platform Windows and Macintosh (0-534-57207-3). Create, deliver, and customize tests and study guides (both print and online) in minutes with this easy-to-use assessment and tutorial system.

Wadsworth College Success Transparency Package (0-534-57417-3). Fifty color transparencies featuring helpful checklists, charts, and key points from college success topics to help organize classroom presentations.

CNN Today: College Success Video Series
ISBN: 0-534-53754-5 CNN VIDEO-COLLEGE SUCCESS, 2000 Edition
ISBN: 0-534-53799-5 CNN VIDEO-COLLEGE SUCCESS, 2001 Edition
ISBN: 0-534-54140-2 CNN VIDEO-COLLEGE SUCCESS, 2002 Edition
Organized by topics covered in college success courses, these videos are divided into small clips that are excellent for launching class discussion.

Wadsworth Study Skills Video, Volume 1: Improving Your Grades (0-534-54983-7). This video features students talking to students and involves viewers in the issues that contribute to their success.

Wadsworth Study Skills Video, Volume 2: Lectures for Notetaking Practice (0-534-54984-5). This video features a series of college lectures that provide students with an opportunity to practice their note-taking skills and instructors with an opportunity to assess student skills.

World of Diversity Video, Volume 1 (0-534-23229-9) & Volume 2 (0-534-23230-2). This powerful two-video set addresses communication and conflict resolution between cultures.

Learning Aids for the Student

Three-Hole Punch Version of the Text (0-534-57206-5). This is the easiest way to customize *Your Guide to College Success* with your own campus-specific materials.

Your Guide to College Success, Second Edition CD-ROM. Every student will automatically receive an interactive CD-ROM FREE with every new copy of Santrock and Halonen's text. Designed to reinforce and extend the content of the text, the accompanying CD-ROM adds a new level of interactivity to the book's features. Every chapter on the CD includes self-assessments that direct students to the exercises, readings, and Internet resources that best meet their needs. In addition to the self-assessments, the CD-ROM includes exercises and tips from the text, quizzes, crossword puzzles, journal-writing opportunities, Internet activities, and InfoTrac College Edition exercises. The CD-ROM also includes the Mission Statement Builder exercise from Franklin/Covey Premiere

Agendas. The second edition of the CD-ROM is upgraded to include e-mail capabilities and a saving feature.

College Success Factors Index Assessment Web Site. Developed by Edmond Hallberg, Kaylene Hallberg, and Loren Sauer, this self-assessment tool using 80 self-scoring statements is designed to help students discover their strengths and weaknesses in eight important areas that can affect their success in college. Students can access this assessment in a password protected site on the Wadsworth Web site. Student passwords are available for purchase with this text.

InfoTrac College Edition. Updated daily! An online library featuring access to the full text of articles from hundreds of publications. A four-month subscription is packaged with every copy of this text.

The Wadsworth College Success Resource Center Web Site: www. wadsworth.success.com. When they adopt Santrock and Halonen's text, instructors and their students have access to a rich array of teaching and learning resources that they won't find anywhere else. It's the ideal way to make teaching and learning an interactive and exciting experience.

Franklin-Covey/Premiere Agenda Planners. Wadsworth offers inexpensive planners designed specifically for college students by experts in time management—the Franklin-Covey/Premiere Agenda team. Ask your Wadsworth representative for details on our latest calendar offerings.

Critical Thinking: Building the Basics (0-534-19284-X). By Donald E. P. Smith, Glenn M. Knudsvig, and Timothy L. Walter. One hundred pages of valuable guidance for improving learning through critical thinking. Helps students apply critical-thinking strategies to their own textbooks.

Acknowledgments

We owe special thanks to Elana Dolberg for guiding this revision. Her insights and enthusiasm helped to create a much better book. Thanks again to Alan Venable, our developmental editor and friend, whose heart and mind fill this manuscript. We also continue to appreciate the leadership and support of Wadsworth CEO, Susan Badger. We also thank our spouses—Mary Jo Santrock and Brian Halonen—for their enthusiastic support of our work, patient tolerance of our work habits, and good-humored companionship.

We would also like to extend our appreciation to the reviewers who offered their time, opinions, and suggestions to improve our book. Thank you.

Reviewers

Alicia Andrade-Owen, California State University, Fresno; Diane D. Ashe, Valencia Community College; Carol A. Copenhefer, Central Ohio Technical College; Dorothy R. Clark, Montgomery County Community College; Susann B. Deason, Aiken Technical College; M. Katherine Grimes, Ferrum College; Cynthia Jenkins, University of Texas, Dallas; Alice Lanning, University of Oklahoma; Alison Murray, Indiana University/Purdue University Columbus; Christina Norman, University of Oklahoma; Glenn Ricci, Lake Sumter Community College; Regina C. Schmidt, Texas Woman's University; Mary Walz-Chojnacki, University of Wisconsin-Milwaukee; Kimberly Vitchkoski, University of Massachusetts, Lowell; and David M. Parry, Penn State Altoona.

Manage Your College Success

Where Are You Now?

By entering college you've embarked on an important journey. What is life like as you make this transition?

To evaluate where you stand right now, place a check next to the items that apply to you. Leave blank the items that do not apply to you.

_____ I know what I value.

_____ I know what I want from college and am motivated to get it.

_____ I am good at setting goals, planning, and monitoring my progress.

_____ I know my long-term and short-term goals.

_____ I link my motivation, goal setting, planning, and monitoring to my values.

_____ I have good thinking and learning skills as well as good computer skills.

_____ I feel good about myself.

_____ I've given some serious thought to careers I might pursue.

As you read about Marian Wright Edelman on the next page, think about what her values are, how motivated she is, and how she is in control of her life.

David Young-Wolff/Stone

IMAGES OF COLLEGE SUCCESS

Marian Wright Edelman

Marian Wright Edelman founded the Children's Defense Fund in 1973. For more than two decades she has worked to advance the health and well-being of children in the United States. When she was fourteen, her father died. The last thing he told her was to let nothing get in the way of her education. Four years later she entered Spelman College in Atlanta. Challenged by college, Edelman responded by working hard. Beginning in her junior year, she won scholarships to study in Paris and Moscow. Edelman later commented that the experiences abroad showed her that she could navigate the world and do just about anything.

The Gamma Liaison Network/Theo Westenberger

Marian Wright Edelman (left) mastered the college experience and went on to become a powerful advocate for improving the lives of children.

In her book *The Measure of Our Success*, Edelman (1992) highlighted several lessons for life for college-aged students. Among these worthwhile lessons are the following:

- **Create opportunities.** Don't think that you are entitled to anything you don't sweat and struggle for. Take the initiative to create opportunities. Don't wait around for favors. Don't assume a door is closed. Push on it until you get it open.

- **Challenge yourself to do things right.** Everyone makes mistakes. Don't be afraid of taking risks or being criticized. It's the way you learn to do things right. It doesn't matter how many times you fall down. What matters is how many times you get up.

- **Don't ever stop learning and improving your mind.** College is a great investment. But you can't just park your mind there as if everything you need to know will be poured into it. Be an active learner. Be curious and ask questions. Explore every new horizon you can.

Learn more about Marian Wright Edelman.

Develop Meaningful Values

Explore Careers

Manage Your College Success

Get Motivated

Build Self-Esteem

Set Goals, Plan, and Monitor

Think and Learn

S*uccess in college? The key is knowing what things you value and setting goals to reach them. If you know your goals, you will have no trouble deciding what you need to learn and motivating yourself to learn it. If you let your values steer you through college, you'll feel good about yourself. You'll also prepare yourself to do great things beyond college. In this and every chapter, you'll be able to assess where you are now, what you need to change, and how to change.*

Make the College Transition

Life is change and college is change. Whether you have entered college right out of high school or as a returning student, you'll need to adapt to this new place. What unexpected things are going on around you? What's different? What changes are you going through as you make this transition?

The High School–College Transition

One first-year student said that a difference between high school and college is that in high school you can't go off campus for lunch because you aren't allowed but that in college you can't do this because you can't afford it. Another student said the difference between high school and college is that in college it's much more difficult to figure out the course schedule of the man or woman you have a crush on in order to figure out where he or she will be on campus at a certain time so you can "accidentally" say hello.

You can probably come up with many other differences between high school and college. For instance, *college classes are much larger, more complex, and more impersonal.* You most likely knew the principal of your high school, who may have greeted you in the hall. Your teachers in high school probably knew your name and maybe your family. In college, however, your instructors may not know your name or recognize your face outside class.

In college, attendance may be up to you. Although some of your instructors will require attendance, many won't. If you miss class it's your responsibility to find out what you missed. Most instructors do not allow makeup work without a reasonable, well-documented explanation.

College instructors give fewer tests. They may hold you responsible for more than what they say in class. Some won't let you make up tests.

In college, nobody treats you like a kid anymore. You have more independence, choice, and responsibility. You are more on your own about how you use your time than you were in high school.

*L*ife is change.
Growth is optional.
Choose wisely.

Karen Kaiser Clark
20th-century American author

ON-TARGET TIPS

Returning-Student Strategies

- *Evaluate your support system.* A strong and varied support system can help you adapt to college. If you have a partner or family, their encouragement and understanding can help a lot. Your friends can also lend support.

- *Make new friends.* As you seek out friends of different ages, focus on meeting other older students. You'll find that many other older students also juggle responsibilities and are anxious about their classes.

- *Get involved in campus life.* The campus is not just for younger students. Check out the organizations and groups at your college. Join one or more that interest you.

- *Don't be afraid to ask for help.* Learn about the services your college offers. Health and counseling services can help you with the special concerns of older students. These include parenting and child care, divorce, and time management. If you have any doubts about your academic skills, get some help from the study skill professionals on your campus.

You have to do much more reading in college. More of your work will need to be done outside class. You may be expected to make your own decisions about what information from your reading is most important for you to remember.

Good grades are harder to get in college. In many colleges, there is more competition for grades than in high school, and instructors set the bar higher for an A or B.

Your college classmates may be more diverse in age and backgrounds. Look around. You'll probably see more older individuals and more people from different cultures than you did in your high school.

Strengths of Returning Students

An increasing number of students start or finish college at an older age than before (Sax & others, 2000). More than one out of five full-time students today is a returning student. About two-thirds of part-time students are also returning students. Some are working full time, are married, have children or grandchildren, some are divorced, retired, or changing careers. Some have attended college before.

If you have entered or returned to college at an older age you may experience college differently than recent high school graduates do. You may have to balance your class work with commitments to a partner, children, a job, and community responsibilities. This means you may have less flexibility about when you can attend classes. You may need child care or have special transportation needs. As an older student you may lack confidence in your skill and abilities or undervalue your knowledge and experience.

Despite such challenges, as a returning student you bring specific strengths to campus. These include a wide range of life experiences that you can apply to issues and problems in class. Your multiple commitments may stimulate you to be more skilled than younger students in managing your time. You may have greater maturity in work habits and more experience participating in discussions. You may also face setbacks more easily. Failing a pop quiz, for instance, is not likely to feel devastating for those who have experienced greater disappointments in life. See the tips listed in "Returning-Student Strategies."

Why Are You in College?

As you make the transition to college, you need to be aware of why you're here. What are your reasons for being in college? Before you continue reading, complete Self-Assessment 1-1 to evaluate your motivation to be here.

Are you here for the "right" reasons? That is, do your reasons for being in college connect with what you think is important in life? What *are* your values?

Barbara Stitzer/PhotoEdit

If you're a first-year student just out of high school, what kind of transitions do you have to make? If you're a returning student, what transitions do you need to deal with?

Why Am I Here?

Different individuals want different things out of college. Think for a few moments about why you are here. The following items can help you to see how college might serve your needs. Place a check mark next to any of the items that apply to you.

I'm in college because
____ It can help me learn and think more effectively.
____ It can help me get a good job.
____ It can help me make a lot of money.
____ I'm avoiding having to find a job.
____ It's a good place to find a mate.
____ I want to have a good time.
____ It's a way to prove my self-worth.
____ It's a way to get away from home.
____ My parents made me go.
____ My friends are here.
____ There are things that I can learn here better than anywhere else.
____ I want to learn more about what I can do with my life.
____ I couldn't think of anything else to do at this point.

Reflect on which of these reasons, as well as others not listed, are motivating you to be in college. Are these the best reasons to be in college? To succeed in the academic aspects of college, do you need to rethink your motivation? Evaluate your reasons in a journal. Is college where you really want to be now?

Develop Meaningful Values

Just what are "values"? Values are our beliefs and attitudes about the way we think things *should* be. They involve what is important to us. We attach values to all sorts of things: politics, religion, money, sex, education, helping others, family, friends, self-discipline, career, cheating, taking risks, self-respect, and so on. As the contemporary U.S. columnist Ellen Goodman commented, "Values are not trendy items that can be traded in."

Your character is what you really are.
John Wooden
former UCLA basketball coach

One of the most important benefits of college is that it gives you the opportunity to explore and develop your values. Why is this so critical? Our values represent what matters most to us, so they should guide our decisions; knowing our values helps us to clarify what we want to do. Without seriously reflecting on what your values are, you may spend too much time in your life on things that really aren't that important to you. Clarifying your values will help you determine where to direct your motivation and which goals you really want to go after.

Sometimes we're not aware of our values until we find ourselves in situations that expose them. For example, you might be surprised to find yourself reacting strongly when you discuss religion or politics with other students.

ON-TARGET TIPS

Clarify Your Values

Stephen Covey and his colleagues (Covey, Merrill, & Merrill, 1994) recommend the following to help you clarify your values (use your watch to go through the timed exercises):

1. Take one minute and answer this question: *If I had unlimited time and resources, what would I do?* It's okay to dream. Write down everything that comes into your mind.

2. Go to Self-Assessment 1-2 and review the list of five values that are the most important to you.

3. Take several minutes to compare this list with your dreams. You may be living with unconscious dreams that don't mesh with your values. If you don't get your dreams out in the open, you may spend years living with illusions and the feeling that you somehow are settling for second best. Work on the two lists until you feel that your dreams match up with your values.

4. Take one minute to see how your values relate to four fundamental areas of human fulfillment: physical needs, social needs, mental needs, and spiritual needs. Do your values reflect these four needs? Work on your list until they do.

Spend some time thinking about and clarifying your values. This will help you determine what things in life are most important to you. As one step toward clarifying your values, complete Self-Assessment 1-2.

There are other ways to clarify values. Steven Covey (1989) has helped many individuals do this. He stresses that each of us needs to identify the underlying principles that are important in our lives and then evaluate whether we are living up to those standards.

Covey asks you to imagine that you are attending your own funeral and are looking down at yourself in the casket. You then take a seat, and four speakers (a family member, a friend, someone from your work, and someone from your church or community organization) are about to give their impression of you. What would you want them to say about your life? This reflective thinking exercise helps you to look into the social mirror and visualize how other people see you. See "Clarify Your Values" for some other helpful tips from Covey.

Although you're unlikely to register for a course titled "Character 101," your experiences in college (both in and out of the classroom) will contribute to your character and integrity. Most instructors expect you to behave in a way that promotes trust in the classroom. For example, they expect you to complete and submit your own work on projects, not cheat on tests, not plagiarize the work of others, and show respect for others' opinions.

Abiding by these behaviors most likely will help you respect and feel good about yourself. Not practicing integrity can bring forth negative feelings such as distress, misery, shame, anxiety, and humiliation. It can also cause such problems as failing courses, losing friends, or being expelled from school.

By clarifying your values, you gain a better idea of where to direct your energy and motivation. The following sections are intended to help you build a strong connection between values, motivation, and personal goals.

"I've got the bowl, the bone, the big yard. I know I _should_ be happy."

What Are My Values?

This list presents a wide variety of values. Place a check mark in the spaces next to the ten values that are the most important to you. Then go back over these ten values and rank order the top five.

_____ Having good friendships and getting along well with people
_____ Having a positive relationship with a spouse or a romantic partner
_____ Self-respect
_____ Being well-off financially
_____ Having a good spiritual life
_____ Being competent at my work
_____ Having the respect of others
_____ Making an important contribution to humankind
_____ Being a moral person
_____ Feeling secure
_____ Being a great athlete
_____ Being physically attractive
_____ Being creative
_____ Having freedom and independence
_____ Being well educated

_____ Contributing to the welfare of others
_____ Having peace of mind
_____ Getting recognition or becoming famous
_____ Being happy
_____ Enjoying leisure time
_____ Being a good citizen and showing loyalty to my country
_____ Living a healthy lifestyle
_____ Being intelligent

Other Values
List any values important to you

_____

_____

_____

My five most important personal values are

1. _____

2. _____

3. _____

4. _____

5. _____

As you review your selections, think about how you got these values. Did you learn them from your parents, teachers, or friends? Or did you gain them from personal experiences? How deeply have you thought about each of these values and what they mean to you? Think about whether your actions support your values. Are you truly living up to them? Do they truly reflect who you are?

Get Motivated on Behalf of Your Values

Consider the values and motivation that Terry Fox, a young Canadian, must have. Fox ran 3,339 miles across Canada, averaging a marathon run each day for five months. He performed this tremendous feat as an amputee and a survivor of cancer, to raise money for cancer research. Before his run, Terry had set a goal and was intensely motivated to reach it. He wanted his life to have a purpose and to make a difference in this world. He surpassed his goal.

Whether or not we can ever match Terry Fox's motivation, the lesson is clear. When we want something badly enough, we expend the energy and effort to get it. This book describes many strategies that will help you to succeed in college, but all the strategies in the world won't help you unless you become motivated to learn them and use them.

How can you become motivated to succeed in college?

UPI/Corbis-Bettmann

Terry Fox exemplifies the importance of getting motivated, planning, and setting goals in life. He spent considerable time planning his run. Although he faced some unforeseen obstacles, such as ice storms, he reached his goal.

Show Confidence and Enthusiasm

When you face something difficult, it's easy to think that you can't do it. Believe in yourself. You'll never reach your dreams or attain your goals if you don't think you can. Try to view problems and hurdles as challenges to be overcome, not stresses that overwhelm you. Think about how good you'll feel about yourself when you face challenges rather than avoid them, when you achieve rather than fail.

Realize That You Are in Command

Shaq Goes Back

We put in a lot of effort and believed in ourselves.

Shaquille O'Neal, *after winning the 2000 NBA Championship.*
Note: Shaq left LSU before graduating to play in the NBA but recently returned to college and obtained his undergraduate degree in 2001.

Don't be trapped by the difficulty of your college experiences. Students who feel trapped say things like "I'm not very good at this." This kind of thinking actually increases anxiety and may cause students to do worse. Instead, it's best to say positive things to yourself. Believe in yourself and your ability. Tell yourself, "I'm going to make it. I can do it. This is a challenge I'm going to face and overcome. I'm going to control it and not let it control me. I'm in command of what happens, and it's going to be good."

Persist

Getting through college is a marathon, not a 100-yard dash. Studying a little here and a little there won't work. To be successful you have to study a lot almost every day for weeks and months at a time. You'll often need to make small sacrifices to gain long-term rewards. College is not all work and no play, but if you mainly play you will pay for it by the end of the term. Remember, from the beginning of the chapter, Marian Wright Edelman's advice not to feel entitled to anything you don't sweat and struggle for.

Be Internally Motivated

Being internally motivated means seeing yourself as responsible for your achievement and believing that your own effort is what gets you to your goals. If you don't do well, don't blame it on bad luck or another person. Face the music and think about what you can do better to accomplish what you want. Moping around won't help. You have the power to develop a plan.

Being internally motivated does not mean doing everything in isolation. Surround yourself with other motivated people. Ask individuals who are successful how they motivate themselves. Find a mentor, such as an experienced student, an instructor, or a teaching assistant you respect, and ask his or her advice on motivation.

What If You Are Bored?

You may be fired up about college, enjoying all your courses—you couldn't be happier. Or you may not be enjoying it at this stage. You may already feel bored with it and other aspects of your life. If you fall into the latter camp, what can you do about it?

Explore New Avenues For starters, think more deeply about the values you listed in Self-Assessment 1-2. What interests do these values suggest? To explore these interests, you can get to know some new people, seek out new situations, ask new questions, read new books, and examine your school's catalog again for new ideas and possibilities that turn on your mind.

Tune in to Inspiration Keep track of the moments in the day or week when you feel the most energetic and inspired because of what you are doing or what you see and hear around you. What do these moments tell you about how to become less bored?

Make Sure It Is Your Motivation Some first-year college students lack motivation because they have not teased apart their parents' "shoulds" from their own, sometimes opposite, interests and motivations. Examine your motivations and interests. Are they yours, or are you currently acting as a "clone" to fulfill your parents' or someone else's motivations and interests? Your motivation will catch fire when you are doing what YOU want to do.

University of South Carolina football coach Lou Holtz said that if you're bored with life—you don't get up every morning with a burning desire to do things—you don't have enough goals. Let's explore the importance of goals in mastering college.

> *The true harvest of my daily life is a little star dust caught, a piece of a rainbow I have clutched.*
> Henry David Thoreau
> 19th-century American author

Set Goals, Plan, and Monitor

How important are goals? Former NBA star Julius Erving, who went on to be very successful in business, summed up the importance of goals this way: "Goals determine what you are going to be."

As we've seen, you begin by determining your personal values. Then you find your motivation to act on them. The next step is using your self-knowledge and energy to set specific goals, plan how to reach them, and monitor your progress:

For example, say that one of the values you chose in Self-Assessment 1-2 was being well educated. If so, then it's important for you to become motivated to incorporate this value into your everyday activities. And it's important for you to set educational goals, plan how to reach these goals, and monitor your progress toward the goals.

Value	Motivation	Set Goals, Plan, and Monitor
Become well educated	Get motivated to incorporate educational activities into my daily life.	Set educational goals, plan how to reach these goals, and monitor my progress toward these goals.

Or suppose that one of the values you clarified in Self-Assessment 1-2 was "contributing to the welfare of others." If so, then it's important to motivate yourself to engage in activities that contribute to the welfare of others and to set goals pertaining to this area of your life. One such goal might be to participate in at least one service learning activity per month, such as volunteering at a nursing home for the elderly.

Linking your values, motivation, goal setting, planning, and monitoring will help make your college life run more smoothly. If you engage in this process regularly, not only will college make more sense to you but you also will greatly enhance your chances of mastering it.

Students vary a lot in how much they set goals, plan, and monitor their progress. The students who never do these things usually don't excel in college. Those who do excel realize that the time they take to set goals, plan, and monitor their progress will pay off in helping them get done what they need to get done on time. When students don't set goals, don't plan, and don't monitor their progress, time tends to slip away until it's too late for them to accomplish what they want.

Now let's explore eight ways that you can effectively incorporate setting goals, planning, and monitoring into your college life.

Set Goals That Are Challenging, Reasonable, and Specific

For every goal that you set, ask yourself, "Is it challenging? Is it reasonable? Is it specific?" When you set challenging goals, you commit to improving yourself. Be realistic, but stretch yourself to achieve something meaningful. Also, when you set goals, be concrete and precise. A diffuse goal is, "I want to be successful." A precise, concrete goal is, "I want to achieve a 3.5 average this term."

Set Long-Term and Short-Term Goals

Have both long-term and short-term goals. Some long-term goals take years to reach, such as becoming a successful teacher or getting into medical school. Other goals are more short-term, such as doubling study time next week or perhaps simply not drinking this weekend.

Plan to Reach Your Goals

A goal is nothing without a means of achieving it. Good planning means getting organized mentally, which often requires writing things down. It means getting your life in order. It means controlling your time and your life, instead of letting your world and time control you.

Manage Your Time

Learning takes a lot of time. Your life as a college student will benefit enormously if you become a great time manager. If you waste too much time, you'll find yourself poorly prepared the night before an important exam, for instance. If you manage time well, you'll have time to relax before exams and other deadlines. Time management will help you be more productive and less stressed, with a better balance between work and play.

Chapter 3 is all about managing time. Among other things, it will explain the importance of linking time management to your goals, how to set priorities, strategies for eliminating procrastination, and the value of monitoring your time.

A goal is a dream with a deadline.
Napolean Hill
Contemporary American author

Live One Day at a Time

In *Even Eagles Need a Push*, David McNally (1990) suggests that as you set goals and plan, you should also live your life one day at a time. Make your commitments in daily bite-sized chunks. The artist paints one stroke at a time. Don't let long periods of time slip by when you aren't working on something that will help you reach your goals.

The U.S. Olympic speed-skating champion Bonnie Blair described how she thinks about and acts on goals every day: "No matter what the competition is, I try to find a goal that day and better that goal."

Overcome Obstacles

Sometimes, on the way to our goals, unforeseen obstacles get in the way. Although Terry Fox had planned his trans-Canada run flawlessly, he did not anticipate some of the circumstances that arose: severe headwinds, heavy rain, snow, and icy roads. In his first month of running, Fox averaged only 8 miles a day, far below his plan. But he kept going and picked up the pace in the second month to get back on track to reach his goal. So it may be for you. As you go through the weeks and months ahead, check your progress toward your goals. If obstacles arise, motivate yourself to overcome them and push forward.

It's Noon Thursday. Here Comes the Beer Truck.

One first-year student showed up at college motivated to do well. He never partied much in high school and really did not have plans to party and drink much in college. But things changed quickly. By the luck of the draw, his first roommate's father owned a major national brewery. The roommate conned one of the drivers who worked for his dad's company to deliver several kegs to him each week. Every Thursday around noon the beer truck pulled up and unloaded the kegs. And the party was on.

The student from the beer company family was a fun-loving, persuasive fellow. It didn't take long for him to convince his more naive, serious roommate that he was missing out on a lot of fun. How did it all end? Their parties went on several months before they got thrown out of the dorm. With all Fs at the end of the term, both were kicked out of school.

For several months, as they played and partied, their immediate gratification felt great. By the end of the term, they began to wonder where all the fun had gone.

Commit

Commit yourself today to setting goals and reaching them. A true commitment is a heartfelt promise to yourself that you will not back down. Some people have dreams and good intentions but lack the commitment to make dreams come true. If reaching big goals sounds like hard work, consider the alternative: living an uncommitted life. A person who is uncommitted sees no compelling reason to get up in the morning. One day follows another, the only goal being to make it through the day.

Monitor Your Progress

Monitoring your progress toward your goals will help you discover new courses of action for improving your academic performance. Without this monitoring, you'll likely fall behind in a class. With the monitoring, you'll improve your ability to keep up with assignments and to learn how much time it takes to do well in the class.

Get Started Now

Get started today on your goals for the term, for next week, and for tomorrow. Map out your plans. Put your plan into action and monitor your progress toward your goals. Self-Assessment 1-3 will help you begin to express some goals.

Setting goals, planning, and monitoring your progress are so important to college success that you will be asked to complete exercises using these skills at the end of each chapter of the book. You will also be asked to review the results of the self-assessments and the checklist you fill out in each chapter. Based on your review, you'll complete a one-page goal-setting exercise that contains a simple, orderly process for achieving any goal:

1. Select the goal that you want to work on.
2. Determine strategies or steps to achieve the goal.
3. Consider any obstacles you'll need to remove.
4. Line up additional resources.
5. Commit to a date by which you should reach the goal.
6. State how you'll know that you have reached the goal.

Practicing these goal-setting, planning, and monitoring exercises now will help you to develop them into lifelong skills.

Yogi Sighting

If you don't know where you are going, you might wind up someplace else.

Yogi Berra
20th-century American baseball player

What Are My Goals?

By completing the following statements, you should get a better idea of what your goals are. Earlier you examined your values. You might want to look at your responses to Self-Assessment 1-2. Your values can help you formulate your goals. Remember that goals can be academic (such as getting straight As this term) or personal (such as forming at least two good friendships this term). A good strategy is to set goals that are challenging but achievable. Be sure to make your goals as concrete and specific as possible.

My main goals in life are

1. _____

2. _____

3. _____

4. _____

My main goals for the term are

1. _____

2. _____

3. _____

4. _____

My main goals for tomorrow are

1. _____

2. _____

3. _____

4. _____

Return to this self-assessment tomorrow evening. How did you do in reaching your four goals for tomorrow? Are your goals for these three time frames—life, term, and tomorrow—in sync?

Think and Learn

Have your values, motivation, and goals steered you into college? Is this where you belong?

Above all, college is a place to think and learn. More specifically, it is a place to practice thinking reflectively, critically, and productively. Keep an open mind about different ideas and decide for yourself what you believe. Evaluate, analyze, create, solve problems, and poke holes in arguments. Be prepared to show "why" and back up your assertions with solid evidence. Don't just stay on the surface of problems. Stretch your mind. Become deeply immersed in meaningful thinking.

You learn when you adapt and change because of experience. Make it a high priority to learn from both your successes and failures. Make a commitment not to make the same mistake twice.

Here now are some strategies for becoming an outstanding learner.

Focus Your Talents and Skills

Some courses may put you to sleep because they don't tie in well with your needs and current interests. Others may spark new interests, even make you passionate about a subject. Where you "catch fire" and become highly motivated to learn will point you to a successful future.

Remember that not all learning takes place in the classroom. If a topic in class seems interesting to you, explore it more deeply. Scan books and journals on the topic and pick out several to read more closely.

Explore Your Learning Styles

Some people learn mainly by doing things themselves. Others learn best by watching or listening to someone lecture. Still others learn best by reading, while others get the most from field projects or laboratory experiments.

Your college work will help you to sort through the ways you prefer to learn. In Chapter 2 you'll explore learning styles extensively and determine the styles at which you excel. You'll also learn some strategies that can improve your flexibility in using learning styles. This exploration of learning styles will then continue throughout the book.

Master Effective Work Skills

College and success in life require self-discipline and good work habits. These habits will help you become not only a better student in college but also a valuable employee, a skilled professional, or a resourceful entrepreneur afterward. This book shows the best ways to stay on task, on time, and under budget. The strategies presented will give you more hours not only for study but also for play and sleep.

To succeed in college you need many work skills such as knowing how to take good notes, participate in class, collaborate with other students, and interact with instructors. You also need good study and test-taking strategies and good reading, writing, and speaking skills. Chapters 2–9 will provide you with a solid foundation and extensive strategies for improving these skills.

DILBERT reprinted by permission of United Feature Syndicate, Inc.

Join the Information Age

To get the most out of your college education, you need to be familiar with computers. We encourage you to take every opportunity to use the computer and learn how to use emerging standard computer applications such as word processing, e-mail, and the World Wide Web effectively.

If you don't already have good computer skills, developing them will make your college life much easier and improve your chances of landing a good job later. To be blunt, if you don't develop computer skills, you are likely to get left behind.

Can you think of a career in which computers aren't used? From the humanities to the sciences, we now are squarely in the middle of the information age and technological revolution.

Throughout the book, you'll find strategies using technology to your advantage in both college and your career. For example, Chapter 3 presents the benefits of electronic planners. Chapter 4 explores other strategies for using computers. On the Web site for this book you can connect with many other Web sites that have information that can help you master college. The CD-ROM that accompanies this book also provides these Web sites.

Develop a Learning Portfolio

To help you experience many different types of learning, we have included a Learning Portfolio section at the end of each chapter. This section has five types of exercises:

Reflect and Journal These exercises will help you improve your self-understanding by having you complete journal entries. Completing them will enhance your writing skills and give you the other benefits of keeping a journal. For example, James Pennebaker (1990), a professor at the University of Texas at Austin, found that first-year students who write in a journal cope more effectively with stress and are healthier than those who don't.

Learn by Doing These exercises involve action projects such as conducting interviews, participating in discussions, taking field trips, and putting together presentations. Most of the projects help you to solve problems and practice report writing. Some include collaborating with others.

© 1973 News America Syndicate, Mell Lazarus

Think Critically These exercises help you to practice thinking more deeply, productively, and logically. In some, you will evaluate evidence. In others, you may criticize an idea. Your critical insights may be expressed in critiques, memos, reports on group discussions, and so forth.

Think Creatively These exercises will help you pursue new insights alone and with other students. You may be asked to write creatively or try your hand at drawing images, inventing quotations, or crafting posters. Some exercises will encourage you to brainstorm with other students.

Work toward Goals We described these exercises earlier in the chapter under the importance of setting goals, planning, and monitoring. Completing these exercises will help you develop concrete objectives and plans for mastering college.

Your instructor will help you choose which assignments to complete for your learning portfolio. In addition to the exercises at the end of the chapter, you may want to include other chapter exercises, such as the checklist and self-assessments in your portfolio. You also may want to include some or all of the on-target tips and the summary strategies for mastering college that appear in each chapter. Throughout the term, your learning portfolio will grow. In fact, you may want to keep adding to it as you continue through college.

Build Self-Esteem

Building self-esteem will improve your chances of college success. What is self-esteem? Sometimes called self-worth or self-image, it is your general evaluation of yourself—how you feel about you, the image you have of yourself.

Many things in your life contribute to your self-esteem: how much you have succeeded or failed, how much the people around you (parents, friends, peers, teachers) positively evaluate you or criticize you, whether you tend to be optimistic or pessimistic, and so forth.

What is your current level of self-esteem? To evaluate your self-esteem, complete Self-Assessment 1-4. You also can visit a campus counselor for a more personalized assessment.

Evaluating My Self-Esteem

Reflect on each of the following statements. Place a check mark under "Agree" if the statement describes you, under "Disagree" if it does not on the whole.

	Agree	Disagree
1. On the whole, I am satisfied with myself.		
2. At times I think I am no good at all.		
3. I feel that I have several good qualities.		
4. I am able to do things as well as most other people.		
5. I feel I do not have much to be proud of.		
6. I feel useless at times.		
7. I feel that I'm a person of worth, on at least an equal plane with others.		
8. I wish I could have more respect for myself.		
9. All in all, I am inclined to feel that I am a failure.		
10. I take a positive attitude toward myself.		

Scoring: For items 1, 3, 4, 7, and 10, for each time you checked "Agree," give yourself 1 point. For items 2, 5, 6, 8, and 9 each time you answered "Disagree," give yourself 1 point. Your highest possible score is 10, your lowest possible score is 0. The higher your score, the higher your self-esteem; the lower your score, the lower your self-esteem. Students with high self-esteem are likely to score in the 8–10 range, and those with low self-esteem, 3 or below.

In interpreting your score, remember that this self-assessment is a rough estimate and that your score may fluctuate depending on the mood that you were in when you filled it out. Do you think that your score reflects your level of self-esteem? If your score is low, why do you think it's low? Apply some strategies for improving self-esteem.

Building self-esteem will give you the confidence to tackle difficult tasks and create a positive vision of the future. It will help you reach your goals and give you the confidence to act on your values.

If you have low self-esteem, commit to raising it. Here are some good strategies for increasing self-esteem (Bandura, 2000; Bednar, Wells, & Peterson, 1995):

*T*he greatest discovery of any generation is that human beings can change their lives by changing their attitudes.

Albert Schweitzer
20th-century French missionary

Believe in Yourself

Above all else, believe in yourself. Have confidence in your ability to succeed and do well in your life. Believing that you can make changes in your life is a key aspect of improving your self-esteem. Individuals who don't think they can change their lives often never even take the first step to improve themselves.

Monitor what you do and say to yourself. Putting yourself down will only lower your self-esteem. Take responsibility for yourself and believe in your abilities.

Remember, though, that if you have legitimate weaknesses in skill areas, such as math or English, just thinking positive thoughts won't be enough. You'll also need to work hard to improve your skills. This may involve obtaining support through tutoring, study skills workshops, and the like.

Identify Causes of Low Self-Esteem

Identifying the sources of low self-esteem is critical to increasing self-esteem. Is your low self-esteem the result of bad grades? Is it due to living with people who constantly criticize you and put you down? Explore ways to change these sources.

Define Important Areas of Competence

Students have the highest self-esteem when they perform competently in the areas of their lives that matter to them. If doing well in school is important to you, then doing well academically will increase your self-esteem. If you value being well connected in society, having a great social life will increase your self-esteem. Consider actor Arnold Schwarzenegger. He did not stop at his physical achievements. He also took college courses in business to give him added competence and self-esteem to launch a film career and other enterprises.

Achieve

Achievement boosts self-esteem. Learning new skills can increase achievement and self-esteem. For example, learning better study skills can improve your GPA. This, in turn, might do wonders for how you feel about yourself this term and will also pay off in the long run.

Get Emotional Support and Social Approval

Emotional support and social approval can increase your self-esteem. When people say nice things to us, are warm and friendly to us, and approve of what we say and do, our self-esteem improves. Sources of emotional support and social approval include friends, family, classmates, and counselors. Seek out supportive people. Find ways to give support back to them.

Cope

Self-esteem also increases when we tackle a problem instead of fleeing. Coping makes us feel good about ourselves. When we avoid coping with problems, they mount up and lower our self-esteem.

"It took a long time before I could look myself in the mirror and say, 'I'm Frosty the Snowman, and I like me.'"

Explore Careers

By working on ideas about careers you will be able to link your short-term and college goals with some of your long-term life goals and be motivated by your long-term prospects.

What do you plan to make your life's work? Is there a specific career or several careers that you want to pursue? If you have a career in mind, how certain are you that it is the best one for you?

An important aspect of college is training for a career. Each of us wants to find a rewarding career and enjoy the work we do. If you're a typical first-year student, you may not have any idea yet of which particular career you would like to pursue. That's okay for right now, especially if you're currently taking a lot of general education courses. But as you move further along in college it becomes ever more important to develop your ideas about a career.

As long as you keep searching, the answers will come.

Joan Baez
Contemporary American folksinger

The Rewarding Connection between College and Careers

Choosing a career based on a college education will likely bring you a higher income and a longer, happier life. College graduates can enter careers that will earn them considerably more money in their lifetimes than those who do not go to college (Occupational Outlook Handbook, 2000–2001). In the United States, individuals with a bachelor's

"Your son has made a career choice, Mildred. He's going to win the lottery and travel a lot."

First-year students at a college career center. Your college's career center is an excellent place to find out information about potential careers.

Michael Newman–PhotoEdit/Picture Quest

degree make over $1,000 a month more on average than those with only a high school diploma. Individuals with two years of college and an associate degree make over $500 a month more than those who only graduated from high school. Over a lifetime, a college graduate will make approximately $600,000 more on average than a high school graduate will! College graduates also report being happier with their work and have more continuous work records than do those who don't attend or don't finish college.

How would you like to give yourself several more years of life? One of the least-known ways to do this is to graduate from college. If you do, you will likely live longer than your less-educated counterparts. How much longer? At least one year longer. And if you go to college for five years or more, you are expected to live three years longer than you would if you had only finished high school.

Master Content and Develop Work and People Skills

A successful career often involves three things:

1. Gaining specialized knowledge of the content of a particular field (like electrical engineering or English)
2. Having good work skills, especially those involved in communication and computers
3. Having good personal skills, including being able to get along with people, high self-esteem, and working from one's own values, motivations, and goals

Your college experiences will give you plenty of opportunities to develop your talents in these three areas.

Chapter 12 explores careers and majors. Throughout the book other connections to the long-term question of careers will be made.

Learn with *InfoTrac College Edition*

InfoTrac College Edition

Look up these articles and search for more on topics that sparked your interest while reading this chapter.

Marian Wright Edelman A voice for the poor in D.C. Arthur Jones. *National Catholic Reporter.* March 24, 2000. v36, i21, p4.

Transition to College The freshman experience: The case of Alice, Dorothy, Peter, and Wendy. Harris C. Faigel. *College Teaching.* Summer 1998. v46, n3, p115.

Values On developing human values. Gerald A. Larue. *The Humanist.* Nov 1998. p38.

Mastering College Speech for a high school graduate: A parent gives his son several words of indispensable advice. Roger Rosenblatt. *Time.* June 9, 1997. v149, N23, p90.

Summary Strategies for Mastering College

Know what things you value and set goals to reach them.

1 Make the College Transition

- If you're making the transition from high school to college, think about the ways that college differs from high school. Remind yourself that change can be challenging and requires you to adapt. Let go of some old ties and securities. Get some new friends.
- If you're a returning student, evaluate your support system, make new friends, get involved in campus life, and don't be afraid to ask for help. Evaluate how you may need to balance your class work with commitments to partners, children, jobs, and the community. Realize that you bring certain strengths to campus.
- Understand your motivation for being in college.

2 Develop Meaningful Values

- Become aware of your values.
- Identify the underlying principles in your life.
- Examine your academic values.

3 Get Motivated on Behalf of Your Values

- Be confident and enthusiastic.
- Be in command.
- Be persistent.
- Be internally motivated.
- Reduce boredom by exploring new avenues, tuning in to moments of inspiration, and making sure that your motivation is truly your own.

4 Set Goals, Plan, and Monitor

- Link goal setting to motivation and values.
- Set goals that are challenging, reasonable, and specific.
- Set long-term and short-term goals.
- Plan.
- Manage your time.
- Live your life one day at a time.
- Overcome obstacles.
- Commit.
- Monitor your progress.

5 Think and Learn

- Focus your talents and skills.
- Explore your learning styles.
- Develop effective work styles.
- Join the information age.
- Develop a learning portfolio.

6 Build Self-Esteem

- Believe in yourself.
- Identify the causes of low self-esteem.
- Define important areas of competence.
- Achieve.
- Get emotional support and social approval.
- Cope.

7 Explore Careers

- Begin to research, think, and talk with others about possible careers.
- Be aware of the advantages of a college education.
- Master content and develop work and people skills.

Review Questions

1. What challenges do you and other students face in making the transition to college?

_____

_____

_____

_____

_____

2. How will your own values, motivation, and goal setting help determine your success in college?

_____

_____

_____

_____

_____

_____

_____

3. According to this chapter, can you increase your motivation to do well in college? If so, how? If not, why not?

_____

_____

_____

_____

_____

_____

_____

4. Imagine giving a talk to high school students on the importance of setting goals, planning, and monitoring progress toward goals. What would you tell them? What would you tell an audience of older and returning students?

_____

_____

_____

_____

_____

_____

5. What can be done to improve self-esteem?

_____

_____

_____

_____

_____

_____

Learning Portfolio

⊙ Reflect and Journal

1. Your New Life

Think about the changes that have taken place in your life since you started college.

- What is different?

  _____
  _____
  _____

- What excites you the most about your life and opportunities in college?

  _____
  _____
  _____
  _____

2. What Interests You the Most in Life?

- How can college feed that interest?

  _____
  _____
  _____

3. Conscious Coping

- Describe the most stressful experience you have had so far in college.

  _____
  _____

- What made it so stressful?

  _____
  _____

- How did you cope with it?

  _____
  _____

- Were you successful?

  _____
  _____

- If the problem still bothers you, how do you plan to cope with it?

  _____
  _____
  _____

⊙ Learn by Doing

1. Why College?

Self-Assessment 1-1 asked you to explore your motivation to be in college. Get together with several other first-year students and compare your reasons. In your journal, compare your motivation to be here with that of other students.

_____
_____
_____
_____
_____
_____
_____
_____
_____
_____
_____
_____
_____

2. Toward Your Future

Think about a career that you might want to pursue. Search the Internet to find out as much as you can about it. Try to find out entry requirements, recommended majors, and salary ranges. Use e-mail, the phone, or personal contact to talk with someone in that field about how he or she likes it and whether it might be right for you.

_____
_____
_____
_____
_____
_____
_____
_____
_____
_____
_____

Think Critically

1. Manage Your Risk

Many college students don't get past their first year. Think about your own risks related to dropping out of college. Make a list of the factors that could undermine your ability to succeed in college. Describe how you plan to overcome these potential obstacles.

_____
_____
_____
_____
_____
_____

2. College Graduation Day

Imagine the day you will graduate from college. Describe what you hope your family, friends, classmates, and teachers will say about you as a college student.

_____
_____
_____
_____
_____
_____
_____

3. Explore This Book

Study the table of contents of this book. Leaf through the chapters. What topics are going to be particularly helpful to you? Quickly scan those topics for ideas that you may want to start using now.

_____
_____
_____
_____
_____
_____
_____
_____
_____
_____
_____
_____
_____
_____
_____
_____
_____

Think Creatively

1. The Magic Wand

Suppose your teachers granted you a magic wand to make three changes to improve your academic life. What three changes would you make and why?

_____
_____
_____
_____
_____
_____
_____
_____
_____
_____
_____

2. Your Hero

As you read about the inspiring example of Terry Fox, you probably recognized how heroic his fund-raising efforts were, given his physical disability. Fox demonstrated that motivated individuals can overcome even severe limitations. Find a photograph of someone else you consider inspiring. Decide why you selected this hero and how you may be similar to him or her. Post it on your wall.

_____
_____
_____
_____
_____
_____
_____

Work Toward Goals

Review the results of the self-assessments you completed in this chapter. Also review the opening checklist. Based on your review, select a relatively short-term goal that you want to work on now.

1. What is that goal? (*Hint:* Is it challenging, reasonable, and specific?)

_____

_____

_____

_____

_____

2. What strategies will you use to achieve your goal? (*Hint:* Can you organize your strategy into a series of smaller goals?)

_____

_____

_____

_____

_____

3. What obstacles may be in your way as you attempt to make these positive changes?

_____

_____

_____

_____

_____

4. What additional resources might help you achieve your goal? (Use the CD-ROM that comes with this book for access to some useful leads.)

_____

_____

_____

_____

_____

5. By what date do you want to accomplish your goal?

_____

_____

_____

_____

_____

6. How will you know you have succeeded?

_____

_____

_____

_____

Diversify Your Learning Style

2

Different Strokes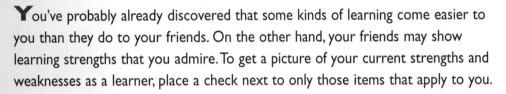

You've probably already discovered that some kinds of learning come easier to you than they do to your friends. On the other hand, your friends may show learning strengths that you admire. To get a picture of your current strengths and weaknesses as a learner, place a check next to only those items that apply to you.

_____ I know my greatest strengths and weaknesses as a learner.

_____ I know whether I favor visual, auditory, or tactile sensory modes

_____ of learning.

_____ I can describe types of learning experiences that are easiest for me.

_____ I like to study one thing in depth rather than several things more
superficially.

_____ I have started out my classes on the right foot.

_____ I deal well with different teaching styles.

_____ I get along well with my instructors and I know how to solve problems
I may have with them.

_____ I can describe career options that fit with my learning style.

On the next page consider what the writer Robert Fulghum has to say about using all of your talents and preferences to get the most from college.

Jeff Greenberg/PhotoEdit

IMAGES OF COLLEGE SUCCESS

Robert Fulghum

Robert Fulghum's amazing writing career started with a column for a newsletter at the church where he was pastor. One of his columns talked about the lifelong value of the ideas contained in simple sayings directed toward children. For example, "Share everything," "Play fair," and "Clean up your own mess" were lessons that Fulghum believed to be as important in helping adults get along as they were for children.

A kindergarten teacher in the congregation was so impressed by one essay that she sent it home with the children in her class. One child's parent was a literary agent who thought that Fulghum's writing would have broad appeal in such complex times. She was right. *All I Really Need to Know I Learned in Kindergarten* topped the *New York Times* bestseller lists for 209 weeks.

Is it true that Fulghum really learned everything he needed to know in kindergarten? No. But his earliest school experiences laid a foundation for the wisdom that would evolve through the rest of his education and his life. Fulghum began at the University of Colorado. When his father became ill, Fulghum transferred to Baylor University to be closer to home. In these and later experiences, he developed a rare capacity to analyze his own experiences and mine them for simple truths. College also helped him to learn to write and to build the self-discipline to pursue a challenging career as a writer.

Robert Fulghum, author of the best-selling book *All I Really Need to Know I Learned in Kindergarten.* Did Fulghum really learn everything he needed to know in kindergarten?

Barbra Witt

Fulghum observes, "The older I get, the more I realize the importance of exercising the various dimensions of my body, soul, mind, and heart. Taken together, these aspects give me a sense of wholeness. I want to be a whole human being" (Fulghum, 1997). Fulghum insists that the path to wholeness is learning to use all aspects of yourself.

Learn more about Robert Fulghum.

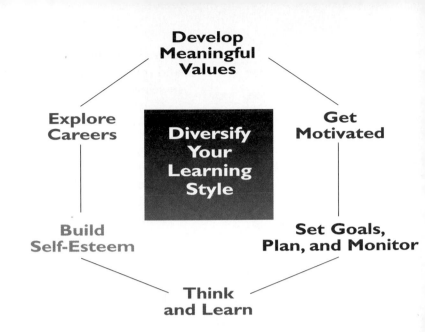

Develop
Meaningful
Values

Explore
Careers

**Diversify
Your
Learning
Style**

Get
Motivated

Build
Self-Esteem

Set Goals,
Plan, and Monitor

Think
and Learn

A ll of us learn a little differently, according to individual abilities and preferences. To reach your goals, it's important to understand how you learn and to look for ways to become more versatile.

Know How You Learn

How you learn is sometimes called your learning style. People differ in how easily they learn, but describing the differences isn't easy. When you learn, many things at once can influence how well you acquire new information and skills.

Know Your Learning Style ⟷ **Set Learning Goals and Monitor Progress** ⟷ **Think and Learn** ⟷ **Reach College and Career Goals**

This chapter will help you explore several different dimensions of your learning profile to maximize your success in college and beyond. For example, your basic intellectual skill in specific areas will influence your success and even your career direction. How teachers present information will also determine how easy it is for you to learn. You also have preferences about how you use that information to promote long-term learning. In combination, these dimensions can influence how well you succeed in academic and other areas of college life. Let's start with the basic intelligence that you bring to college.

Your Intelligence Profile

Perhaps at some point in your past, someone measured your intelligence. On the basis of your intelligence quotient (IQ) score you may have been able to skip a grade or qualify for special help in school. Recently psychologists have begun to question the notion that we can capture individual intelligence with a single number.

The psychologist Howard Gardner (1989) proposed that we would be wiser to consider several types of abilities rather than a single measure of intelligence. He formulated his theory of "multiple intelligence" based on observing patterns in different sets of skills. For example, brain-damaged individuals

*T*here's only one corner of the universe you can be certain of improving and that's your own self.

Aldous Huxley
20th-century British author

sometimes show significant disabilities in certain skill sets. Child prodigies and other individuals with exceptional talents demonstrate superior abilities in selected skill sets.

Gardner suggested that these sorts of abilities cluster in eight different areas, or *domains:*

- **Verbal-Linguistic Skills:** sensitivity to and appreciation of word meanings and the function of language
- **Logical-Mathematical Skills:** orderly use of reasoning, logic, and mathematics to understand and explain abstract ideas
- **Musical Abilities:** appreciating, performing, or creating music or the elements of music, such as rhythm or pitch
- **Bodily-Kinesthetic Awareness:** coordinated and skilled use of objects in the environment, involving both gross and fine motor skills
- **Spatial Skills:** accurate perception and reproduction of spatial images, including strong navigation and artistic skills
- **Interpersonal Abilities:** meaningful discrimination and interpretation of the behavior and moods of others
- **Intrapersonal Abilities:** accurate self-perception, including a refined capacity to identify and represent complex personal emotions and motives
- **Naturalist Abilities:** understanding, relating to, classifying, and explaining aspects of the natural world

Gardner argued that these domains are independent of one another. Human beings can be highly developed in one area but not in others. According to Gardner, most college courses tend to emphasize verbal-linguistic and logical-mathematic intelligences at the expense of other important skill areas.

You may suspect that you're naturally more gifted in some areas than in others. Learning in those areas is simply easier for you than in others. You may even resist taking required courses that don't fall within those easy areas. However, most college programs are committed to developing a broad base of skills. So, for example, even if you don't have strengths in logical-mathematical skills, you'll probably have to take some basic courses that require those skills.

Take a moment to complete Self-Assessment 2-1. This inventory should help you identify your intellectual strengths. It can also help you predict which courses will be relatively easy or difficult for you. For example, if your strengths lie in spatial skills, then a required art history course may be a surprisingly happy learning experience. If the area of interpersonal abilities is your main strength, then you'll likely do well in courses that focus on group work.

As smart as he was, Albert Einstein could not figure out how to handle those tricky bounces at third base.

© 2000 by Sidney Harris.

Half of being smart is knowing what you are dumb about.
David Gerrold
Contemporary science fiction writer

On the other hand, if algebra is "Greek" to you, you'll have to work much harder to grasp the concepts than will the mathematically gifted person seated next to you. You may want to get help right away before you get too far behind in a course that doesn't match your talents. Find a study partner who demonstrates the intelligence that you need to develop. Or work with your study skills center on campus to help you take advantage of your learning strengths and style.

Your Intelligence Profile

Indicate your strengths by identifying all the characteristics that apply to you. Mark the space using the following codes:

2 = very much like me
1 = somewhat like me
0 = not like me

Verbal-Linguistic
_____ I like to read.
_____ I enjoy finding out the meanings of new words.
_____ I appreciate humor involving wordplay.
_____ I enjoy telling or writing poems or stories.
_____ I recall written or verbal material well.

Logical-Mathematical
_____ I like working with symbols.
_____ Math comes fairly easy to me.
_____ I like to analyze and solve problems.
_____ I like to discover logical weaknesses in an argument.
_____ I enjoy listening to a good debate.

Musical
_____ I enjoy singing or making rhythmic sounds.
_____ I like to listen to favorite tapes and records.
_____ I sometimes make up my own tunes.
_____ I would enjoy learning to play a new musical instrument.
_____ I enjoy music deeply even when it has no lyrics.

Bodily-Kinesthetic
_____ I enjoy working with my hands.
_____ It's hard for me to sit still for long periods.
_____ I am good in at least one sport.
_____ I enjoy a well-executed physical movement.
_____ I'm physically comfortable with my body.

Spatial
_____ I can easily visualize objects.
_____ I tend to find beauty in things that others don't.
_____ I can usually get around without going the
_____ wrong way.
_____ I enjoy working on arts, crafts, or drawing.
_____ People often comment on my "good taste."

Interpersonal
_____ I like to be around people, and I make friends easily.
_____ I have a knack for remembering names and faces.
_____ I have demonstrated natural leadership tendencies.
_____ I notice subtle differences among people.
_____ I understand people better than many other people do.

Intrapersonal
_____ I prefer solitary activities to group work.
_____ I enjoy quiet time.
_____ I am very sensitive to emotional experiences.
_____ I know myself very well.
_____ I prefer to have a few deep friendships rather than lots of friends.

Naturalist
_____ I have a strong curiosity about how nature works.
_____ I enjoy looking for patterns in things.
_____ I can learn more easily outdoors than indoors.
_____ Science classes tend to be easy for me.
_____ I have at least one collection that I keep in careful order.

Add up your scores in each category. This inventory can reveal which multiple intelligence area is a relative strength and which is a relative weakness. In which dimensions did you score the highest? In which did you score the lowest?

The Match Game

How can you adapt your skills when your instructor isn't a good match for your sensory learning style?

- If you are an **Auditory** Learner, your best match will be instructors who LECTURE.

  When your instructor doesn't lecture:
  1. Concentrate on the spoken words.
  2. Rehearse key ideas in your head.
  3. Identify key concepts in your notes.
  4. Summarize the key themes of the class out loud to a study partner.
  5. Pay less attention to visual supports that may distract you.

- If you are a **Visual** Learner, your best match will be instructors who LECTURE WITH IMAGES.

  When your instructor doesn't use visual supports:
  1. Draw your own related pictures and graphs in your notes.
  2. Use arrows in your notes to highlight connections.
  3. Seek out related media that support or review key concepts.
  4. Try to visualize imagery that will help you remember.
  5. Create two or three images that capture the essence of the class.

- If you are a **Tactile** Learner, your best match will be instructors who use ACTIVE LEARNING.

  When your instructor doesn't use active learning:
  1. Make notes that highlight how the content is connected to you.
  2. Form a study group to give you a chance to discuss key ideas.
  3. Imagine how the information will have practical value for you.
  4. Record class information on index cards.
  5. Select the two or three cards that represent the key ideas for each session.

This knowledge can also help you choose a major. Later in this chapter, you'll be asked to consider what kinds of majors might be consistent with your intelligence profile.

Sensory Preferences

A second dimension that contributes to your learning style is your sensory preference for receiving information. Do you prefer to get input about the world through your ears, eyes, or sense of touch? Which sensory mode you prefer will influence how easily you can learn in different academic situations. (In Chapter 5, we give you some tips on how to make the most of lectures regardless of the sensory channel that you prefer).

Auditory Learning The majority of your course experiences will likely be lectures. Typically, the professor talks . . . and talks . . . and talks . . . while you try to take notes on the most important ideas. This traditional approach assumes that you have skills in auditory learning.

Some lucky people are good *auditory learners*. They can absorb a lecture without much effort. They may not even need to take careful notes to learn from listening. Auditory learners may avoid making eye contact with anyone in the class so they can concentrate on catching the stream of spoken language in the lecture.

Visual Learning Many of us have an easier time learning from lectures with visual components such as pictures, diagrams, cartoons, or demonstrations. *Visual learners* employ their strengths by picturing words and concepts they hear as images. Then they capture these images on paper for a quick review. Visual learners also benefit from the use of charts, maps, notes, and flash cards when they study.

Visual learners may easily become distracted when professors provide no visual anchors in their lectures. They may become overwhelmed when professors use slides with dense terminology and lecture at the same time. In this situation, visual learners may need to tune out the auditory information and focus on what they can see, for the most efficient processing.

Tactile or Kinesthetic Learning Some people may also be *tactile* or *kinesthetic learners*. They prefer touch as their primary mode for taking in information. Unfortunately, very few classes provide an opportunity for tactile learners to use their preferred sensory mode. Art, recreation, and technical classes related to careers involving manual procedures are among the most prominent examples.

Sensory Preference Inventory

Place a check mark in the appropriate space after each statement. Use the scoring procedures at the end to evaluate your sensory profile.

	OFTEN	SOMETIMES	SELDOM
1. I can remember best about a subject by listening to a lecture that includes information, explanations, and discussion.			
2. I prefer to see information written on a chalkboard and supplemented by visual aids and assigned readings.			
3. I like to write things down or take notes for visual review.			
4. I prefer to use posters, models, or actual practice and [do] other activities in class.			
5. I require explanations of diagrams, graphs, or visual directions.			
6. I enjoy working with my hands or making things.			
7. I am skillful with and enjoy developing and making graphs and charts.			
8. I can tell if sounds match when presented with pairs of sounds.			
9. I remember best by writing things down several times.			
10. I can easily understand and follow directions on maps.			
11. I do best in academic subjects by listening to lectures and tapes.			
12. I play with coins or keys in my pockets.			
13. I learn to spell better by repeating words out loud than by writing the words on paper.			
14. I can understand a news article better by reading about it in the newspaper than by listening to a report about it on the radio.			
15. I chew gum, smoke, or snack while studying.			
16. I think the best way to remember something is to picture it in your head.			
17. I learn the spelling of words by "finger spelling" them.			
18. I would rather listen to a good lecture or speech than read about the same material in a textbook.			
19. I am good at working and solving jigsaw puzzles and mazes.			
20. I grip objects in my hands during learning periods.			
21. I prefer listening to the news on the radio rather than reading about it in the newspaper.			
22. I prefer obtaining information about an interesting subject by reading about it.			
23. I feel very comfortable touching others, hugging, handshaking, etc.			
24. I follow oral directions better than written ones.			

Scoring: Place the point value on the line next to the corresponding item number below. Add the points in each column to obtain your Preference Score for each (VPS, APS, TPS). Your highest score indicates your sensory learning preference.

OFTEN = 5 points [ ] [ ] [ ]   SOMETIMES = 3 points [ ] [ ] [ ]   SELDOM = 1 point [ ] [ ] [ ]

VISUAL		AUDITORY		TACTILE	
NO.	PTS.	NO.	PTS.	NO.	PTS.
2	_____	1	_____	4	_____
3	_____	5	_____	6	_____
7	_____	8	_____	9	_____
10	_____	11	_____	12	_____
14	_____	13	_____	15	_____
16	_____	18	_____	17	_____
19	_____	21	_____	20	_____
22	_____	24	_____	23	_____
VPS =	_____	APS =	_____	TPS =	_____

Use what you learn from this inventory to develop learning strategies that will support your learning style.

Source: Barsch, R. (1990). *The Barsch Learning Style Inventory.* Novato, CA: Academic Therapy Publications. All rights reserved.

Tactile learners faced with auditory learning situations should write out important facts and perhaps trace the words that they have written. They can make up study sheets that connect to vivid examples. In some cases, role-playing can help tactile learners learn and remember important ideas.

Self-Assessment 2-2 gives you an opportunity to identify the sensory mode on which you rely most. Then, in the on-target tip, you can review the strategies that can help you learn more effectively, particularly if you find yourself in situations that aren't a good fit for your learning style. See also "The Match Game."

Experiential Learning Preferences

Besides differing in intelligence domains and sensory preferences, people also differ in how they like to learn about and work with ideas. Here are four distinctive ways based on David Kolb's (1984) work on experiential learning. We also explore how experiential preferences relate to strengths in multiple intelligence and sensory preferences.

Learn by Doing Although some people can learn passively simply by listening, watching, or reading, those with active learning preferences fare better when they learn by doing through problems or games and simulations, for example. They like to apply principles through fieldwork, lab activities, projects, or discussions.

Many kinds of classes are ideal for learning by doing. These include science and math classes as well as career-oriented classes, such as business and nursing. Learners who prefer visual and tactile sensory modes of learning benefit from active learning strategies. Active learning strategies also tend to appeal to people with refined intelligence in spatial skills and bodily awareness.

Unfortunately, many professors don't take this active learning preferences into account. By simply lecturing away, they reinforce the tendency of many students to regard learning as a spectator sport.

Learn by Reflecting Reflecting here means having an opportunity to compare incoming information to personal experience. Reflective learners prefer classes such as the humanities in which they can learn by observing rather actively participating. They enjoy learning that is rich in emotional content. Reflective learners often show preferences for learning through auditory sensory channels because these situations provide the least interference for thoughtful, quiet reflection.

Reflective learners tend to demonstrate strengths in intrapersonal intelligence as well. Because they like to look carefully at a situation and think about its meaning, they often set reasonable goals and achieve them. Reflective students enjoy taking time to respond to and reflect on the quality and accuracy of their answers (Kagan, 1965). Because they're good at problem solving and decision making, they like to set their own goals for learning (Jonassen & Grabowski, 1993). Whether or not

"Personally I'm a doer."

you are primarily a reflective learner, you can probably improve your learning by noticing connections with your own experience and by staying aware of your learning goals.

Reflective students also enjoy journal writing, project logs, film critiques, and essay questions, all of which let them show their reflective skills. They prefer intimate discussions of content over group discussions.

Learners who reflect carefully about ideas may not be the quickest to answer questions in class, because a question may provoke a great deal of thinking and remembering before the learner can arrive at a conclusion. Regrettably, professors seldom allow much time for careful reflection in class.

Learn by Critical Thinking Critical thinkers relish learning situations that encourage them to grapple with ideas in ways that push beyond memorizing facts. They enjoy manipulating symbols, figuring out unknowns, and making predictions. They like to analyze relationships, create and defend arguments, and make judgments. Critical thinkers are often good with abstract ideas, even in the absence of concrete examples or applications. Classes that are theoretical in nature or emphasize logical reasoning, model building, and well-organized ideas are especially appealing to critical thinkers.

Good critical thinkers perform especially well in courses that appeal to verbal-linguistic, logical-mathematical, and naturalist intelligences. They tend to be comfortable in lecture-based classes that primarily rely on auditory sensory channels, although they can also exercise critical-thinking strategies in other learning situations to make course ideas more engaging. Debates and other opportunities to exchange ideas appeal especially to critical thinkers.

Learn by Creative Thinking In contrast, creative thinkers thrive in learning situations that offer opportunities for unique personal expression. Although humanities and arts classes particularly develop creative thinking, opportunities can be found in other courses, too. Creative thinkers prefer to write stories, brainstorm, solve problems in original ways, design research, and so forth. They think more holistically, meaning that they try to consider a broad range of information in their problem solving. They may even enjoy violating the rules if it helps them come up with a unique solution or viewpoint.

Creative thinking is the hallmark of artists who demonstrate musical and spatial intelligence, respectively relying on auditory and visual sensory processing. Creativity also underlies the development of new theories, research strategies, novels, and computer games. That is, creative thinking can be expressed in all domains of multiple intelligence.

What learning processes do you prefer? Complete Self-Assessment 2-3 to identify your preferences among these experiential learning processes.

Experiential Learning Preferences

Each choice here captures an aspect of how people prefer to learn. Think about each choice in relation to yourself.

Choose all items that apply. Circle the number in front of the item.

When I have to learn how to operate a new piece of equipment, I
1 Watch someone who knows how to operate the equipment.
2 Carefully study the owner's manual.
3 Fiddle with the dials until I produce a desired effect.
4 Ignore the instructions and make the equipment suit my purposes.

What I like best about lectures is (are)
1 The chance to record the ideas of an expert.
2 A well-constructed argument about a controversial issue.
3 Illustrations using real-life examples.
4 Inspiration to come up with my own vision.

My class notes usually look like
1 Faithful recordings of what the instructor said.
2 Notes embellished with my own questions and evaluations.
3 Outlines that capture key ideas.
4 Notes with drawings, doodles, and other loosely related ideas or images.

I prefer assignments that involve
1 Emotional expression.
2 Analysis and evaluation.
3 Solving practical problems.
4 Creative expression.

In class discussion
1 I'm a watcher rather than a direct participant.
2 I'm an active, sometimes argumentative participant.
3 I get involved especially when we discuss real-life issues.
4 I like to contribute ideas that no one else thinks about.

I would rather work with
1 Stories about individual lives.
2 Abstract ideas.
3 Practical problems.
4 Creative ideas.

My learning motto is
1 "Tell me."
2 "Let me think this out for myself."
3 "Let me experiment."
4 "How can I do this uniquely?"

Interpretation: Look over your responses. Use the following code for each question to determine your preferred experiential learning process:

1 = Learning by reflecting

2 = Learning by critical thinking

3 = Learning by doing

4 = Learning by creative thinking

The alternative with the most checks is your preferred learning process. You may discover that you strongly favor a particular approach. Or you may find that your preferences are spread across several categories. Your experiences in college will help you develop your skills in all areas so you will become more flexible and more resourceful.

Think Strategically about Your Learning

Understanding your learning style (multiple intelligence strengths + sensory preferences + experiential learning preferences) can help you succeed in any classroom. Think of your learning style as providing the basic tools that can help you solve common classroom problems.

Find out about Instructors' Styles The next time you register for class, invest some time in identifying which instructors have a teaching style that suits your learning style. Interview seasoned students. Go beyond questions about whether the instructor is "good." You can guess by now that "good instructor" means different things to people with different learning styles. Ask *how* they teach. For example, does the instructor

- Lecture the entire period?
- Involve the class in discussion?
- Use active learning strategies?
- Offer any note-taking supports such as outlines?
- Show enthusiasm for students?

Build Strengths across the Styles As you meet each challenge that college offers, your learning resources will expand. You may discover abilities you never thought you had. Working harder in skills that don't come easily can improve how easily you learn.

Help from the Learning Portfolio. As noted in Chapter 1, the Learning Portfolio sections at the end of each chapter build on the four processes of learning that you just read about. Choose exercises at the end of each chapter that will help you stretch and grow in new ways. Don't choose only activities or assignments that let you stay in your comfort zone. Your investment will make you more versatile as you face new learning challenges in the future.

Help through Improved Planning. Recall that the Learning Portfolio sections end with "Work toward Goals." This feature provides systematic practice in goal setting and achievement. Regardless of other elements of learning style, setting realistic goals and planning effective strategies for achieving them can improve your chances of college success. Impulses can be a good thing. They can urge us into action and help us take wise risks. However, you'll benefit even more from careful planning. Some people develop very disciplined approaches to setting goals and monitoring progress. In Chapter 3, you'll get some help in improving your time-management skills by practicing goal-related skills.

Regulate Your Effort

Success in college is not determined just by your natural talents and preferences. You must make some important decisions and choices about how and when to apply yourself. We hope these questions sound familiar and that they are already on your mind.

Accomplishment results from staying in touch with your values and motivation.

How hard do I want to work?

Some college courses will be so intriguing that you'll naturally be drawn in deeply. It will be easy to learn, because the content and instructor's approach match your interests, learning style, and abilities. However, you may find yourself wanting to devote just enough time and energy to get by. This will happen in courses that have little bearing on your ultimate goals or when you're short on time. These contrasting examples illustrate *surface* versus *deep* learning styles.

Surface learning means studying the minimum amount you need to learn. Surface learners rely primarily on rote memory, often exercised at the last minute. These learners tend to be motivated by grades or feedback from the teacher.

Surface learning can be risky. On the whole, surface learners are much less likely than deep learners to do well in college. Ultimately, surface learners may have serious problems in their chosen major if they need to remember what they learned only shallowly in prior courses. Still, you may choose to be a surface learner in some courses so that you can devote more time to deep learning in other courses.

Deep learners set a goal of truly understanding the course ideas. Such learners tend to construct their learning experiences actively. They enjoy the process of learning for its own sake and use a lot of thinking skills. Deep learners remember what they learn longer. If your interests parallel those of the course, deep learning may not be much effort. It might even be fun.

Every time you're confronted with a learning opportunity, you must decide how deeply you with to learn in order to succeed in college overall. Do you need to work hard in this particular course, or do you need merely to break the surface? Keep your level of effort and motivation in line with your broader goals and values.

I have trouble jumping in to class discussions, because they seem to take off before I'm ready! Is there such a thing as being too reflective?

Students process information at various speeds. This can create some interesting class conditions. Some people respond quickly and are accurate and insightful in their contributions. Sometimes rapid responding is impulsive, producing ill-formed and off-target ideas. In general, impulsive students tend to make more mistakes than do students who carefully reflect on their experience (Jonassen & Grabowski, 1993). However, some reflective individuals may think forever about a problem and not ever speak.

If the course rewards careful reflection as well as discussion, participating in class may not be required for success. However, here is an area where you can expand your skills. Make a note of the kinds of questions the instructor presents for discussion. Prepare answers based on what you think your instructor will ask. By carefully reflecting ahead of time, you should be able to cut your processing time in class.

Amateurs hope.
Professionals work.

Garson Kanin
20th-century playwright

I feel stifled by detailed assignments. Can I get away with being creative?

It depends. If you stray in a way that enhances the point of the assignment, the instructor may be pleased with your initiative. If you exceed the minimum criteria, most instructors will think of you as hardworking and creative. However, if you drift from the intended purpose, the instructor will see your work as deficient and possibly defiant. It's best to check with your instructor ahead of time to make sure that your creative approach will work.

Is it always best to work by myself or should I try to work with others?

In almost every career domain, working with people is becoming more and more common and important. This is a skill that is worth developing. However, you also must learn the skills involved in independent work, because the majority of evaluation and testing in college and beyond will put you alone in the spotlight. Think of your peers as additional resources who can help you learn. However, be sure to ask your instructor whether group effort may be inappropriate or unethical. To help you improve your group work skills, each Learning Portfolio section includes group exercises.

I can already tell I won't have enough time to do well in all my classes. How should I choose where to work hardest?

In general it's a bad idea to do poorly in many classes when you can improve your standing by dropping a class or two. If you find that you're giving short shrift to several classes, consult with your advisor about dropping the course that will have the least negative impact on your schedule. To help build your confidence, it may be wise to stay in courses that overlap your natural talents.

How do I decide when to stay safe and when to take a risk? What happens if I fail?

Students just starting out in college often feel like imposters. They worry that giving the wrong answer in class will forever brand them as stupid and alienate them from the other students. But going to college isn't just about acquiring knowledge. It's about personal change. Many people believe that the impact of a single failure can be a more powerful lesson than a string of successes. College should be a safe place in which to take thoughtful risks as you learn and change from both success and failure.

Launch Your Learning

Your earlier experiences in school, from kindergarten to high school, have taught you a great deal about what your teachers expect. This section explores how to get the most of your *college* classroom experiences—regardless of your learning style.

Create a Good First Impression

College instructors expect you to have academic common sense. Knowing how to develop relationships with your instructors is an important part of that common sense. Some guidelines, which sound suspiciously like Robert Fulghum's rules, can help you get off on the right foot.

Common sense is perhaps the most equally divided, but surely the most underemployed, talent in the world.
Christiane Collange
Contemporary French writer

- **Buy the right stuff.** You won't look like a serious student if you don't have the required books.
- **Be prepared.** If you read assignments *before* class, you'll ask better questions and impress your instructors with your motivation to learn. You'll also get more out of the lecture or discussion.
- **Do the work on time.** Coping with deadlines in serious business in college. Many students are surprised when they learn that college deadlines are not as flexible as they were in high school.

  If you miss a deadline, you may not be able to negotiate an extension. Most instructors do not extend deadlines to individuals without justification. Many believe that doing so isn't fair to students who do their work on time.
- **Use the syllabus.** A course syllabus comprehensively describes how the instructor expects the course to proceed. The syllabus can include the course objectives, reading list, grading policies, and other information that applies throughout the term.

  The syllabus also can give hints about the instructor's teaching style. It may contain helpful hints on how to study for tests. Some instructors hold students responsible for reading all materials listed in the syllabus. This can be a surprise at test time if you thought that your class notes would be enough.
- **Play straight.** The syllabus may or may not discuss cheating or other moral issues. However, your college's student handbook will outline the code for academic integrity on your campus. If caught violating this code, you face a range of unpleasant consequences, from severe (expulsion from school) to more lenient (zero on the work submitted).

FIGURE 2-1
How to Get on the Wrong Side of an Instructor

Some behaviors that disturb and distract instructors and students alike (Appleby, 1990).

BEHAVIORS THAT SHOW QUESTIONABLE MATURITY
Talking during lectures
Chewing gum, eating, or drinking noisily
Being late and leaving early
Creating disturbances
Wearing hats
Putting feet on desks or tables
Being insincere or "brownnosing"
Complaining about work load
Acting like a know-it-all
Wearing headphones

BEHAVIORS THAT SHOW INATTENTION
Sleeping during class
Cutting class
Acting bored or apathetic
Not paying attention
Being unprepared

Packing up books and materials before class is over
Asking already answered questions
Sitting in the back rows when there are empty seats in front
Yawning obviously
Slouching in seat
Asking "Did we do anything important?" after missing class
Not asking questions
Doing work for other classes in class
Reading the newspaper in class

MISCELLANEOUS IRRITATING BEHAVIORS
Cheating
Asking "Will this be on the test?"
Being more interested in grades than in learning
Pretending to understand
Blaming teachers for poor grades
Giving unbelievable excuses
Wearing tasteless T-shirts

- **Stay cool.** The best classes run on respectful and civil behavior. Respect does *not* mean that you can't challenge or ask questions. In fact, many instructors (but not all) regard student questions as an essential part of classroom learning. However, all instructors expect participation to be civil (calm, polite, and efficient rather than prolonged, pointless, or profane). Figure 2-1 describes other behaviors that can get in the way. See also "Ask It This Way."

- **Be There.** As mentioned in Chapter 1, college involves a higher level of personal responsibility than most students experienced in high school. This freedom can be alluring and intoxicating. Especially when instructors do not require attendance, you may be tempted to skip classes. What's wrong with skipping class?

    1. It's expensive. See Figure 2-2 to calculate how much a skipped class will cost.
    2. It harms your learning.
    3. It harms your grades.
    4. It annoys those who end up lending you their notes to copy. (If you must miss a class, be sure to borrow notes from someone who is doing well in the course!)

Size up Your Instructors

Before your college years are over, you'll experience all kinds of instructors. Teaching styles are every bit as diverse as learning styles. Teachers will vary not only in their disciplines but also in their enthusiasm, competence, warmth, eccentricities, and humor. What about your teachers will matter the most to you? How do these variations among your instructors relate to your learning style?

The Student-Centered Teacher Some instructors focus on developing students' intellectual growth in their assigned courses. They tend to run their classes with a variety of activities chosen to motivate student interest and heighten learning. They may use small group discussions, film clips, and student performance as part of their teaching. The activities they provide appeal to a broad range of learning styles. Finally, such instructors depart from their original plans because they believe that a new direction serves the students' learning better; in these cases, class tends to become spontaneous.

If you learn best when you have the opportunity to apply course concepts to practical examples, then student-centered approaches probably will appeal to

"Is the homework fresh?"

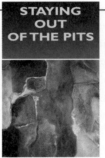

STAYING OUT OF THE PITS

Ask It This Way

When you can't attend a class, don't ask your instructor, "*Did I miss anything important?*" Although it may be innocent, your question implies that your instructor regularly spends time on unimportant information. Instead, ask "*Can I make up any of the work I missed?*" Or you can talk with a classmate to help you get caught up.

FIGURE 2-2
The Cost of Cutting Class

How much tuition did you pay for this term?

How many credits must you take on your campus to be considered full-time?

Divide the full-time hours into your tuition dollars (cost per credit hour):

How many credit hours does the course you're most tempted to avoid have?

Multiply the course credit hours by the cost per credit hour (cost of the course):

How many classes meet in this course over the term?

Divide the cost of the course by the number of classes:

The final calculation represents the financial loss that happens every time you cut this class.

you. Your obligation to learn in such classes tends to be simple: Work at as deep a level as you can manage. Because the instructor is likely to include activities that appeal to your learning preferences, chances are good that you will succeed in the course.

However, you might prefer the structure and efficiency of a well-designed lecture, particularly if you're a good auditory learner and like to memorize. If so, what can you do to survive the student-centered class?

- Outline your reading.
- Try to anticipate what the course will cover.
- Talk with the instructor about the course and how it's working for you.
- Form a study group to work more systematically on the key ideas.

The Content-Centered Teacher Content-centered teachers typically use lectures as their primary teaching method. The learning climate in lecture-based courses tends to be highly structured, paced by the lecturer's strategy for covering material in a meaningful way. Instructors expect students to take careful notes to prepare for tests. Most college classes are lectures. Thankfully, there are good lecturers who tell stories and use humor to get their information across in an interesting way.

Some learning preferences fit well with lecturing. Auditory learners tend to fare best in lectures. In fact, students who thrive in these environments might well consider college teaching as a potential career.

Visual and tactile learners or learners who prefer active learning experiences simply have to work harder to adapt their learning style to the demands of content-centered courses. If you face this challenge, learn to make systematic and perhaps creative notes during the course, or at least work with the notes creatively when you study. Generate practical examples that help you form concrete connections with the course material. Form a study group that can help you talk about and play with course concepts.

If a content-centered instructor offers you the option of writing a paper, grab it! The challenge gives you an opportunity to hone your writing skills. Because you get to choose your topic, the paper will likely be the most interesting thing you do in the course.

If you cannot take things by the head, take them by the tail.
Arab proverb

Connect with Instructors

Instructors respond the most positively to students who show interest and enthusiasm for their course. Later in the term, instructors have an easier time cutting some slack for students who have been responsive and responsible in the earlier weeks. When test scores fall between two grades, those students who seem to care about their work are the ones who get bumped up instead of down.

Is it possible to get acquainted with your instructors in large classes? The answer is yes, although doing so may be challenging. By asking intelligent questions during class or visiting during office hours, you can stand out even in very large classes. Interviewing an instructor for this course can help you practice getting to know your instructors on an informal basis.

Research indicates that seeking contact with faculty outside the classroom is associated with staying in college and graduating with honors (Astin, 1993). How can you get your instructors to take a special interest in you? "Become a Distinctive Student" gives some tips.

Solve Problems with Instructors

If you're lucky, you may not have to solve relationship problems with your instructors. However, four problems may prompt you to take action:

- There is a serious mismatch between your abilities and the level of the course.
- Appropriate personal boundaries with instructors are challenging to manage.
- You and your instructor disagree about the completion status of your work.
- You need to make a complaint about an instructor's actions.

Resolve a Mismatch

Courses are unsatisfying if the instructor does not teach at a level the students can handle. In some of these courses students feel overwhelmed by an instructor who is talking over their heads. In other cases, instructors offer too little challenge and students feel cheated.

To resolve either problem, first talk with your classmates to verify that others are struggling too. Then, preferably with one or two other concerned students, request an appointment with the instructor and present your concerns directly. Many instructors will be pleased with your initiative and grateful for the feedback. Others will be less enthusiastic but can give you suggestions about how to cope with their demands. If you can't resolve the mismatch through talking with the instructor, consider withdrawing from the course and taking it again later with a different instructor.

Manage Boundaries

Most instructors give clear signals about how and when they can be contacted. Instructors usually have office hours. They can and should respond to student questions or concerns during those periods as part of their professional responsibilities.

Instructors differ in their enthusiasm about being contacted outside class or office hours. Some provide home phone numbers and encourage you to call whenever you have questions. Others request not to be disturbed at home, because they want to separate their professional and personal lives. It is easy to see how students get confused about how and when to contact their instructors. If your instructors have not specified that they can be reached at home, use memos, voice mail, office-hour visits, or the time just after class to ask questions or maintain contact.

Friendships between instructors and students pose an especially complex boundary problem. Many instructors believe that friendship with students is

ON-TARGET TIPS — Become a Distinctive Student

- **Sit in the front.** The most motivated and interested students often sit close to the instructor to minimize distractions and create the opportunity for informal discussion before or after class.
- **Bring articles or clippings to class related to the course.** Instructors like to see you make independent connections between what you're learning and your life outside the classroom. They may incorporate your ideas into the class and remember you for making the contribution.
- **Take advantage of existing opportunities to get to know your instructors informally.** On some campuses, faculty sponsor informal gatherings to help you network with others. You also can join student clubs with faculty sponsors. These are great opportunities to get to know the faculty as people.
- **Visit during your instructor's office hours.** Most instructors identify their office hours when the course begins. Check in with your instructor about something you found interesting or were confused about from class discussion. Ask the instructor to review your notes to see whether your note-taking skills are on target.
- **Use e-mail to connect, if that is an option.** Many instructors like to communicate with their students via e-mail. This is a great option if you're shy or the instructor seems hard to approach.
- **Actively seek a mentor.** After you engage an instructor's interest in you, find out about the instructor's availability to serve as your mentor, someone who can give you guidance beyond the classroom and help you find other opportunities to develop. This can be the most meaningful connection you make in college in person.

> *The university is not engaged in making ideas safe for students. It is engaged in making students safe for ideas.*
>
> Clark Kerr
> *Former president of Stanford University*

a bad idea. They don't want to do anything that could compromise their objectivity. Other instructors believe that they can be objective in grading the work of a student-friend.

Keep Copies of Your Work

When an instructor and student dispute whether work has been completed, the burden of proof falls on the student. Get in the habit of making copies of your papers. Then, if a paper gets lost or misplaced, you can easily replace it. Keep returned projects in a safe place so you can retrieve them if the instructor has failed to record and grade them. When the term is over and your instructor has filed your grades, retain your best work for your academic portfolio. This will help you track your progress over time and will give you samples that may help in future job applications.

Complain If Necessary

You have several options when an instructor's conduct upsets you. First, recognize that the instructor is the authority in the class. Weigh carefully how upset you are against the possible consequences of confronting an instructor who holds greater power and probably more credibility than you do.

If you have a complaint about a class, start by talking directly with your instructor. By describing the problem and offering your interpretation, you may be able to solve the problem quickly and fairly.

If you decide to complain, explain your concerns directly to the instructor. Ask for an appointment. Present your concerns and offer evidence to support it. If this is unsuccessful, appeal in writing to the instructor's immediate supervisor. In most cases, this supervisor is the department head or coordinator, who will hear you out and determine what steps to take. If the supervisor fails to take action and you still need further resolution, ask for an appointment with that person's supervisor, most likely the academic dean. At each stage of the chain of command, the person will review what attempts you have made already to resolve the problem before he or she does anything about it.

As one cautionary note, you're unlikely to have much luck appealing a final grade unless you can identify discriminatory treatment or a specific error in the instructor's judgment. Most colleges regard instructors as the final authority in grading and rarely overturn their grades.

◉ Choose a "Stylish" Major

Once you're off to a successful start in your classes, you can turn some attention to what the future holds.

A college degree can be a passport to a professional career, but a well-chosen major can produce a greater number of opportunities that are linked to your interests and skills. Your learning style should influence which career you pursue and the major you choose to help you get there.

Diversify Your Learning Style ↔ Match Your Major to Your Style ↔ Explore Career Options

Target an Intelligent Career

One way to start planning your future is to link your natural intellectual talents to possible career options. Gardner's theory of multiple intelligences has been used to explore the relationship between intellectual ability and career choice. See Figure 2-3 for some typical and creative career choices based on the multiple intelligence model.

FIGURE 2-3
Intelligent Career Choices

The theory of multiple intelligences suggests that intellectual strengths predict career choices. Review some traditional and less-conventional careers linked to different domains of intelligence.

Intelligence Domain	Traditional Careers	Less Conventional Careers
Verbal-Linguistic	author reporter teacher librarian attorney advertising specialist politician	talk-show host poet children's book writer crossword puzzle maker campaign manager
Logical-Mathematical	engineer scientist mathematician statistician insurance specialist computer expert claims adjuster	physicist astronomer astronaut
Intrapersonal	novelist psychologist philosopher	advice columnist feature writer
Interpersonal	politician social worker sales manager psychologist public relations specialist nurse, doctor, or other health care giver	religious leader

FIGURE 2-3 (continued)
Intelligent Career Choices

Intelligence Domain	Traditional Careers	Less Conventional Careers
Musical	performer singer music teacher	composer conductor sound effects specialist
Spatial	engineer architect surgeon painter sailor Web designer fashion designer	mapmaker sculptor billboard designer
Bodily-Kinesthetic	artisan actor athlete dancer coach	professional juggler professional skater health writer
Naturalist	conservationist agricultural specialist floral designer museum curator librarian botanist	safari director antique specialist baseball card expert game-show winner

Find the Right Mix

Every college major tends to emphasize certain learning styles more than others. Consider these examples:

- Marcia has always shown a particular talent for music. She prefers the kind of hands-on learning that she experiences in her music classes over courses where she passively takes notes on concepts. Her auditory skills are especially well developed. Because she is also effective working with others, her major of music education represents a natural outgrowth of her skills (*musical and interpersonal intelligences + auditory sensory preference + active-learning preference*).
- Darnell enjoys classes where he can sit, listen, and think carefully about the issues. He especially enjoys writing assignments that allow him to reflect on the significance of the ideas, particularly if he has to take apart an issue and form some judgments. He enjoys learning new and complex words. He is thinking about opting for a journalism major (*verbal-linguistic and intrapersonal skills + auditory sensory preference + reflecting and critical-thinking preferences*).

- Carra enjoys taking risks. She likes to combine her strengths in mathematics and her growing ability to deal effectively with others in action-oriented projects. She finds that she learns best when she can apply principles in hands-on situations. Carra believes a business major will complement her entrepreneurial style (*logical-mathematical and interpersonal intelligences + tactile sensory preference + active-learning preference*).
- Bruce has never been a big fan of reading or writing, but he keenly appreciates courses that allow him to be physically active. He likes the hands-on activities that his kinesiology classes offer and is considering a career in recreation management (*bodily awareness intelligence + tactile sensory preference + active-learning preference*).
- Portia has a vivid visual imagination. She prefers classes where she can express her creative impulses. She is thinking about a career in graphic design (*spatial intelligence + visual sensory preference + creative-thinking preference*).

Review the results of your self-assessments in this chapter. What career directions and majors does your learning style suggest? If no obvious directions appear, consider consulting with a career-counseling specialist on campus who can help you make more concrete links between your learning style and possible majors and careers.

Keep a Flexible Outlook

You may be fortunate to have natural talents in many areas. You may discover many new abilities through your college experiences. Don't close off your options by locking yourself into a career path too soon.

Sandra's story offers a good example of this. Both of her parents and her old brothers were lawyers. Like them, she was especially skilled in verbal-linguistic intelligence and enjoyed a good debate. But she was surprised to discover how much she enjoyed the community service work that she was required to do in her sociology class. By her junior year, she abandoned her pre-law major in favor of social work. Eventually she found great career satisfaction in managing a residential home for delinquent teenagers.

After you commit to a specific major, stay flexible about what the future may bring. As you'll see in Chapter 12, the career you ultimately pursue may not even have emerged yet as an option. Versatility as a learner will give you more choices about where you want to go in your major and your career.

Learn with *InfoTrac College Edition*

InfoTrac College Edition

Look up these articles and search for more on topics that sparked your interest while reading this chapter.

Robert Fulghum True love: Stories told to and by Robert Fulghum. *Publisher's Weekly.* Jan. 27, 1997. v244, i4, p91.

Multiple Intelligences All kinds of smarts. Stefanie Weiss. *NEA Today.* March 1999. v17, i6, p42.

Integrating learning styles and multiple intelligences. Harvey Silver, Richard Strong, Matthew Perini. *Educational Leadership.* Sept. 1997. v55, i1, p22.

Summary Strategies for Mastering College

Diversify Your Learning Style to Get the Most From College

1 Know How You Learn

- Identify your intellectual strengths and weaknesses.
- Understand how your sensory preferences shape your learning.
- Recognize what learning processes help you learn best.
- Develop adaptive strategies based on your learning style.

2 Regulate Your Effort

- Commit to deep learning when time and resources permit.
- Focus on classes where you are likely to do well, even if it means dropping a course to give you extra time.
- Pursue group work to refine your people skills.
- Don't be afraid to make mistakes. It may be a powerful source of learning.

3 Launch Your Learning

- Create a good first impression through proper preparation.
- Determine whether your instructor is student centered or content centered.
- Get acquainted with instructors.

4 Solve Problems with Instructors

- Talk personally with your instructor outside of class to see if you can resolve your concerns.
- Respect the boundaries established by your instructors to avoid grading complications.
- When you have a serious complaint, consider talking with the instructor's supervisor, usually the head of the department, to get help in resolving the problem.

5 Choose a "Stylish" Major

- Consider majors with courses that match your learning style.
- Stretch your ability to use different learning styles in order to have more career options later.

Review Questions

1. What are the eight types of intelligence that Gardner identified? On which ones are you strong or weak?

_____

_____

_____

_____

_____

_____

2. Describe your learning style in terms of its sensory and experiential preferences. What are the strengths and weaknesses in your style?

_____

_____

_____

_____

_____

_____

3. Is it possible to develop a more versatile learning style? If so, how can it be done?

_____

_____

_____

_____

_____

4. What are some important things to do to get off on the right foot in class?

_____

_____

_____

_____

5. How does learning style relate to choice of major and career planning?

_____

_____

_____

_____

Learning Portfolio

Reflect and Journal

What Did You Learn in Kindergarten?

You have already invested many years in your education. Think about the kinds of classroom experiences you had before college.

- How are college classes similar to your earlier educational experiences?

  _____

  _____

- How are they different?

  _____

  _____

- Are teachers different in college than at earlier levels?

  _____

  _____

- Will any lessons from kindergarten, grade school, or high school serve you well in college?

  _____

  _____

- In which ones are you likely to be a deep learner?

  _____

  _____

- Which ones are more likely to produce shallow learning—where you will probably do just enough to get by?

  _____

  _____

- How would you plan to study in each case?

  _____

  _____

The Deep End of the Pool

You probably recognized when you read about deep and surface learning that how comfortable you are as a learner may depend on the context. For example, you may easily comprehend complex ideas in a subject that you find intrinsically interesting. When subjects don't intrigue you, your efforts may feel shallow.

Think about the courses you are registered for this semester:

_____

_____

_____

_____

Learn By Doing

1. Connect with a Special Teacher

Make an appointment with the instructor who seems most approachable to you. Interview that instructor. Find out how your instructor's interest in the discipline began. As the main theme of your interview, ask for advice on what you can do to get the most from college and how to avoid pitfalls. Try asking a few questions about the instructor's own experience as a first-year college student. Compare those answers with your own experience.

_____

_____

_____

_____

_____

_____

_____

_____

2. Review a Syllabus

Consult the syllabus from the course you expect to be the most difficult for you. Examine it carefully, then try to predict how the class will proceed. Ask yourself questions like these:

- How labor intensive will the course be?

  _____

- Where will the peak periods of effort occur?

  _____

- How should I pace my reading?

  _____

- Will there be an opportunity to develop my group work skills?

  _____

- How can I connect with the instructor if I run into a problem?

  _____

Think Critically

1. The Stylish Major

You have probably given some thought to the kind of major for which you would be best suited. Think about whether the major you've declared or to which you're most inclined is best suited to your learning style.

- What major are you considering?

  _____

  _____

- What intelligences fit best with this major?

  _____

  _____

- What sensory preferences might work best in this major?

  _____

  _____

- What learning process might be most emphasized in this major: reflection, active learning, critical thinking, or creative thinking?

  _____

  _____

- What is your conclusion about how well you might be suited to this major based on your learning style?

  _____

  _____

2. Career Cruising on the Web

Write a one-sentence description of your learning style based on the results of your self-assessments in this chapter. What are your dominant intelligence domains? Sensory preferences? Experiential learning preferences? Then conduct a Web search to identify five career options that would fit with your learning style. Be sure to include some unconventional career choices.

_____

_____

_____

_____

_____

_____

_____

_____

_____

_____

_____

_____

Think Creatively

1. Everything I Need to Know I Plan to Learn in College

Look through Robert Fulghum's book, *Everything I Need to Know I Learned in Kindergarten.* Write down 10 simple truths that might serve as the draft for a college-level version of his book.

_____

_____

_____

_____

_____

_____

_____

_____

_____

2. Your Learning Metaphors

Think about what it feels like for you to learn in the college classroom. Do you feel like a sponge, soaking up every detail you can? Do you feel like a juggler? A prisoner? A butterfly? Are there other metaphors that describe your student experience? Describe or draw your metaphor and explain its significance.

_____

_____

_____

_____

_____

_____

_____

_____

Work toward Goals

Review the results of the self-assessments you completed in this chapter. Also review the opening checklist. Based on your review, select a relatively short-term goal that you want to work on now.

1. What is that goal? (*Hint:* Is it challenging, reasonable, and specific?)

_____

_____

_____

_____

2. What strategies will you use to achieve your goal? (*Hint:* Can you organize your strategy into a series of smaller goals?

_____

_____

_____

_____

3. What obstacles may be in your way as you attempt to make these positive changes?

_____

_____

_____

_____

4. What additional resources might help you achieve your goal? (Use the CD-ROM that comes with this book for access to some useful leads.)

_____

_____

_____

_____

5. By what date do you want to accomplish your goal?

_____

_____

_____

_____

6. How will you know you have succeeded?

_____

_____

_____

_____

Be a Great Time Manager

3

Beat the Clock

What you do with your time is critical to your success in college and beyond. Highly successful scientists, business people, and other professionals say that managing their time on a daily basis is crucial to reaching their goals.

How strong is your current ability to manage time effectively? To begin, evaluate how good you are at managing time. Place a check mark next to only those items that apply to you.

_____ I use time well to reach my goals.

_____ I use a paper or electronic planner to manage my time effectively.

_____ I have created a term calendar and monitor it regularly.

_____ I make weekly plans and monitor how I use my time each week. I also set priorities and do daily to-do lists.

_____ I treat my academic commitment as a serious job.

_____ The time I spend on academics equals or exceeds the time I spend on leisure, play, recreation, sports, and watching TV.

_____ I don't procrastinate much.

_____ I'm good at balancing my academic life with the other demands in my life.

As you read about Florence Griffith-Joyner on the next page, think about what a great time manager she was and how this contributed to her success in life, competition, and career.

Flo-Jo

Time especially is important in the lives of athletes who race against a clock. Florence Griffith-Joyner, or "Flo-Jo," beat the clock not only in track but also in her life.

As an Olympic athlete, Flo-Jo smashed Olympic and world records in the 100-meter and 200-meter dashes. In college, she had to juggle many aspects of her life to be successful. In addition to being a full-time college student and athlete, she worked and commuted to school. She managed her time well enough to run impressively in college and also to achieve high grades. Because she was so focused on doing well academically and because she needed to work to help pay for her college, however, she almost did not compete in track in her first year of college at California State-Northridge.

Despite doing well academically as a first-year student, Flo-Jo could not afford to return for her sophomore year, so she worked as a bank teller until the Northridge track coach helped her apply for financial aid. When her track coach took a job at UCLA, she transferred there and became the NCAA champion in the 200-meter event.

Flo-Jo's development of time-management skills in college served her well later. A typical day for her after college involved working for four hours on a public relations project for one of her sponsors, a long track workout, $1\frac{1}{2}$ hours in the weight room, a sprint home to cook dinner, a workout in the evening, and writing after dinner.

Flo-Jo grew up in poverty in the Watts area of Los Angeles and was intensely motivated to find a career—in sports and afterward—that would give her a more prosperous life. However, she never forgot her past and frequently gave back to the community. She often returned to speak to children and urged them to place academics ahead of athletics in their lives. Setting priorities for her time was something that she always did well.

Unfortunately, Florence Griffith-Joyner died unexpectedly at age 38. In her book, which was published after her death (Griffith-Joyner & Hanc, 1999), she talked about the importance of commitment and determining the best times of the day to do whatever is most important.

David Boe/Corbiss Bettmann

"When you have been second best for so long, you can either accept it or try to become the best. I made the decision to try to be the best."
—Florence Griffith-Joyner

Learn more about Florence Griffith-Joyner.

To reach your goals and still be able to live a balanced life, you need to do two things:

1. Plan and monitor your time with your goals in mind
2. Take steps to minimize procrastination and distractions

Control Your Life by Controlling Time

Many college students feel overwhelmed with all they have to do. Yet some of the busiest and most successful students get good grades *and* find enough leisure time. How do they do it? They control their life by controlling their time.

How often have you said or heard people say, "I just don't have enough time"? Tough luck! Each of us has the same amount of time—24 hours, or 1,440 minutes, a day—yet individuals vary enormously in how effectively they plan and use their hours and minutes.

You can't really change the nature of time or buy more of it than you're given. What you can change is how you manage *yourself* in relation to time. You alone control how *you* use it. Once you've wasted time, it's gone and can't be replaced.

There are many ways to waste time, such as surfing the Web, daydreaming, socializing, worrying, or procrastinating. To evaluate some ways and reasons that you might waste time, complete Self-Assessment 3-1.

You can reap many benefits by controlling your time:

- **Be more productive.** More effectively using your time will make you productive in college. You'll have the hours you need to write that long term paper. Effectively managing your time will help you get better grades.
- **Reduce your stress.** Poorly managing your time will increase your stress. Imagine that you haven't really been studying much and all of a sudden the day before an important exam arrives. Panic! Tension builds and stress escalates. Effectively managing your time will help you reduce the stress in your life.
- **Improve your self-esteem.** Learning to manage time effectively will increase your self-esteem. Wasting a lot of time will make you feel crummy about yourself.

While we are postponing, life speeds by.

Seneca
1st-century Roman philosopher

"Hey, I'll get to the meeting on time. It's those creative types you ought to be checking on."

Time Wasters

To spot some ways and reasons that you might waste time, place a check mark next to the items that apply to you.

_____ Talking on the phone
_____ Listening to music
_____ Watching TV
_____ Playing computer games
_____ Surfing the Web
_____ Daydreaming
_____ Socializing
_____ Not being able to say "no"
_____ Worrying
_____ Having weak reading or study skills

_____ Not being able to concentrate
_____ Not planning adequately
_____ Not spending enough time on what's important
_____ Too much time spent with friends who drop by
_____ Not being organized
_____ Not being able to make decisions
_____ Procrastinating
_____ Not being self-disciplined
_____ Other

From this list select the three ways and reasons you waste the most time:

1. _____

2. _____

3. _____

What can you do to reduce the number of hours you lose in these three time wasters?

_____

_____

_____

_____

_____

_____

_____

_____

_____

_____

- **Achieve balance in your life.** Developing good time-management skills and actively using them will let you achieve a more balanced life. You'll miraculously have enough time for school, work, home, family, and leisure.
- **Conquer multitasking.** As you go through college, there will be times when you think you need to be several places at once. Of course, you can't be two places at the same time without doing serious bodily damage to yourself. You can't be at a club meeting when you need to be at the library studying for a test.

    In college and in your career, you'll need to juggle many different tasks. "Multitasking" is a way of life in today's busy, complex world. Individuals who are good at this are the most likely to succeed in college and beyond. Being a great time manager will let you conquer multitasking, as it did for Florence Griffith-Joyner.
- **Establish an important career skill.** College provides you with an opportunity to work on developing many skills that you can carry forward into a career. Being a great time manager is one of these. In most careers, to be successful you'll not only need to complete many different tasks, but also need to complete them quickly and by a deadline.
- **Reach your goals.** The act of setting goals and planning how to reach them will help you live the life you want to live. You need time to reach your goals, so the better you can manage time, the bigger you can dream.

Stay on Time to Reach Your Goals

Setting goals is a way of committing yourself to what you value and to what you seriously want to accomplish. As you attach actual dates and deadlines to those goals, your commitment gains focus.

Set Goals ⟷ Plan Steps to Meet Them ⟷ Set Dates for Steps ⟷ Monitor Your Progress

Set Completion Dates for Your Goals

The first important principle in the art of managing time is to set completion dates for your goals and work out schedules to meet them. If you want to obtain a college degree, you might want to set a date of four to six years from now as your completion date depending on how much time each year you can devote to college. If your goal is to make one good friend, you might want to set a time of six weeks from now for achieving it. If your goal is to become the funniest person on campus, set a date for that as well.

Create Subgoals

Reaching goals is often easier if you break them down into intermediate steps or subgoals. In many cases, reaching a goal involves several activities. Say that one of your life goals is obtaining a college degree. You can break this down

"Doctor, have you any advice to offer a young man who would love to be a physician but whose crowded schedule simply doesn't permit time for medical school?"

into either four subgoals (if you're in a four-year degree program) or two subgoals (if you're in a community college). Each subgoal can be the successful completion of a year in your degree program. These subgoals can be broken down into exams, quizzes, term papers, amount of time you plan to study each week, and so on. Figure 3-1 illustrates this strategy.

The more you can order steps or subgoals into a series, the more easily you can accomplish each. Writing a good term paper involves many tasks that you can break down into fairly orderly stages. Table 3-1 provides an example of how this might work. In your planning, work backward from the final due date, reserving enough time for each step. You can apply this same approach to many college goals.

Be sure to assign a completion date to each intermediate step. Without doing this, time often sprouts wings and flies away. Before you know it, you won't have time to do all of the tasks necessary to do well on a project. For example, in writing an important paper, you might end up doing only a crude first draft because you didn't have enough time to revise or to accept an instructor's offer to give you feedback.

Revisit Your Goals Regularly

Periodically examine how well you're working toward your goals. After writing down your goals, place the list where you can easily see it from time to

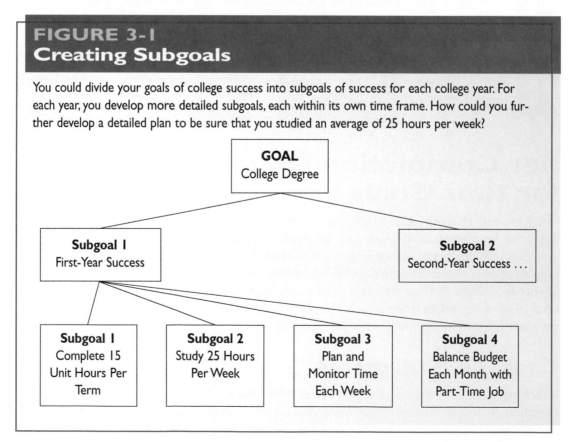

FIGURE 3-1
Creating Subgoals

You could divide your goals of college success into subgoals of success for each college year. For each year, you develop more detailed subgoals, each within its own time frame. How could you further develop a detailed plan to be sure that you studied an average of 25 hours per week?

GOAL
College Degree

Subgoal 1
First-Year Success

Subgoal 2
Second-Year Success ...

Subgoal 1
Complete 15 Unit Hours Per Term

Subgoal 2
Study 25 Hours Per Week

Subgoal 3
Plan and Monitor Time Each Week

Subgoal 4
Balance Budget Each Month with Part-Time Job

time, such as on a calendar or taped to the inside of your personal address book. If after a week or month you're falling behind, evaluate what you can do to get back on track.

TABLE 3-1
Steps for Completing a Term Paper

GOAL: Psychology Term Paper	
Subgoals/Intermediate Steps	Deadline
1. Meet with instructor to explore topic for paper	10/1
2. Conduct library research on topic	10/15
3. Write several draft outlines of paper	10/22
4. Meet with instructor to go over topic and proposal	10/29
5. Write first draft of paper	11/15
6. Edit first draft	11/22
7. Write second draft of paper	11/29
8. Meet with instructor for further feedback on paper	12/6
9. Make final adjustments, write final draft, and proofread	12/13
10. Turn in paper	12/20

Plan for the Term, Week, and Day

Break down your time by term, week, and day. As you create plans for coordinating your time within these three time frames, always keep in mind the importance of breaking your goals down into subgoals and intermediate steps. Also think about the tools you'll need to do this planning.

Time moves slowly, but passes quickly.
Alice Walker
Contemporary U.S. author

Choose the Right Planning Tools

The two basic types of planning tools are paper-and-pencil planners and electronic planners.

Paper-and-Pencil Planners The traditional mode of planning involves using a paper-and-pencil planner. Among the most effective and popular of these are the Franklin and Franklin Covey planners. Originally offering only the Franklin planner, Franklin joined with time-management expert Steven Covey, author of *The Seven Habits of Effective People* (1989), to create a second type of planner, the Franklin Covey. The Franklin Covey planner especially encourages you to think about your goals and values as you set up your time-management program. For example, it asks you to set a long-range goal, write down the value of that goal or what its role is in your life, and then list the intermediate steps and their deadlines for reaching the goal. The Franklin Covey planner comes in a college version called the Franklin Covey Collegiate Planner.

Paper-and-Pencil Planner

Palm Pilot

Electronic Planners Several electronic time-management systems are also available. The Franklin Covey time-management program comes in an electronic form, as do others. On the Web site for this book you can find links for exploring electronic planners.

The computer versions of the planners often are most effective for long-range planning. For short-term tasks, like to-do lists, paper planners often work best. However, some smaller electronic devices (such as a Palm Pilot) can be used effectively for many time-management tasks.

Create a Week-by-Week Calendar

You'll benefit enormously by mapping out a week-by-week plan for the entire term. Get a calendar that covers the current month and the next three to four months. Some colleges provide a term calendar that identifies breaks and holidays. Your college catalog also may provide this information.

If you don't already have a calendar for the term, pages 61–63 provide a grid of the days and weeks to create one. Write in the weeks and number the days. Write in vacations and holidays. Then get out your course syllabi and write down dates and deadlines for exams, major homework assignments, and papers.

Consider coding different courses by color. History might be in red, English in blue, biology in green, and so on. Using colored pencils allows you to revise schedules easily. Highlight exam dates with a marker or write them in large letters.

After you've written down your exam and other task dates on the calendar, look at the dates. Think about how many days or weeks you'll need to study for major exams and write major papers. Mark the days or weeks in which these tasks will be your main priorities.

Keep a spare copy of your term calendar in case you lose the original. You might want to carry one calendar with you when you go to classes. Post the other one on your bulletin board or keep it in your desk.

Your term calendar is not etched in stone. Check it regularly and decide whether you need to modify it. Your circumstances may change. An instructor might add another assignment or two or change a test date. You might find out that you need more study time than you originally predicted for a particular course.

Create and Monitor a Weekly Plan

Former Chrysler Corporation CEO and President Lee Iacocca credited his weekly plan as the key to his success. Even if your life goal is not to run a mammoth corporation, weekly planning skills will serve you well long after college.

On pages 62 and 63, you'll find a grid on which to map out your weekly plans. You might want to make a number of photocopies of it so that you will have enough for the entire term. Or you can use the weekly planning grids in a commercial paper-and-pencil or electronic planner.

Before you start filling in the grid, before you make out your weekly plan, examine your term plan to identify your week's main priority. Then ask yourself these questions about the next week (see pages 62–63):

Week-by-Week Calendar

Week of	MONDAY	TUESDAY	WEDNESDAY	THURSDAY	FRIDAY	SATURDAY	SUNDAY
_____							
_____							
_____							
_____							
_____							
_____							
_____							
_____							
_____							
_____							
_____							
_____							
_____							
_____							
_____							
_____							
_____							
_____							

⊙ Weekly Plan

		MONDAY		TUESDAY		WEDNESDAY	
		Plan	Actual	Plan	Actual	Plan	Actual
AM	6:00						
	7:00						
	8:00						
	9:00						
	10:00						
	11:00						
	12:00						
PM	1:00						
	2:00						
	3:00						
	4:00						
	5:00						
	6:00						
	7:00						
	8:00						
	9:00						
	10:00						
	11:00						
	12:00						
AM	1:00						
	2:00						
	3:00						
	4:00						
	5:00						

- What do I expect to accomplish?
- What will I have to do to reach these goals?
- What tasks are more important than others?
- How much time will each activity take?

THURSDAY		FRIDAY		SATURDAY		SUNDAY	
Plan	Actual	Plan	Actual	Plan	Actual	Plan	Actual

- When will I do each activity?
- How flexible do I have to be to allow for unexpected things?

In the *Plan* column on the grid, fill in your class hours, regular work commitments, and other routine tasks. Then fill in the remainder of the things you plan to do next week.

*P*lease. No crises next week.
My schedule already is full.
Henry Kissinger
20th-century Secretary of State

A good strategy is to fill in the *Plan* column at the end of the preceding week. Put it together on Friday afternoon or Sunday evening at the latest. The plan takes no more than a half hour for most students, yet it can save you at least an hour a day that week!

During the week, monitor your schedule closely all week to see whether you carried out your plans. A good strategy is to sit down at the end of each day and write in the *Actual* column what you actually did that day. Compare what you planned to do with what you actually did. Analyze the comparison for problems and plan some changes to solve the problems.

Use the weekly planner in concert with your term planner each week of the term. Every Friday, pull out your term planner and see what your most important priorities are for the following week. Make any changes that are needed on the term planner. Then get out your Xeroxed copy of the weekly plan and write down what you plan to do next week.

Allocate Time for Studying and Other Activities As you construct your weekly plan, be sure to put enough time aside for doing assignments outside of class. In a national survey, the more hours students spent studying or doing homework, the more they liked and stayed in college, improved their thinking skills, graduated with honors, and got into graduate school. Students who have higher grades and graduate with honors are less likely than students who have lower grades and don't graduate with honors to watch TV or spend time partying (Astin, 1993).

Evaluate how much time you have allocated in your weekly time plan for activities such as studying, watching TV, and partying. To find out how much time you actually study each week and whether it's enough, see Self-Assessment 3-2.

Swiss Cheese and Set Time Two strategies for getting the most out of your weekly plan are called *Swiss cheese* and *set time*. The time-management expert Alan Lakein (1973) describes the Swiss cheese approach as poking holes in a bigger task by working on it in small bursts of time or at odd times. For example, if you have 10–15 minutes several times a day, you can work on a math problem or jot down some thoughts for an English paper. You'll be surprised at how much you can accomplish in a few minutes.

If you're not a cheese lover, the set time approach may suit you better. In this approach, you set aside a fixed amount of time to work on a task. In mapping out your weekly plans, you may decide that you need to spend six hours a week reading your biology text and doing biology homework. You could then set aside 4–6 P.M. Monday, Wednesday, and Saturday for this work.

Plan for Tomorrow

You live your life one day at a time, and you reach your goals the same way. How do you think that your term and weekly planning work for you on a daily level?

Set Priorities and Use To-Do Lists Great time managers figure out what the most important things are for each day and allocate enough time to get them done. Figuring out the most important things to do involves setting priorities. An effective way to set priorities is to create a manageable to-do list. Your goal is to complete at least all of your priority items on the list. A no-miss day is one after which you can cross off every item. If that turns out

Are You Studying Enough?

How much time should you spend studying or doing homework each week? 5 hours? 10? 20? 40? Estimate how many hours you think you need to study outside class in college if you want to get good grades:

_____ Hours

How many hours each week do you currently study outside of class?

_____ Hours

Many students underestimate the number of hours they need to study. One guideline suggests that for every hour you spend in class you need to study two to three hours outside class each week, if you want to get great grades. Thus, if you're taking 12 hours of classes, you need to study 24–36 hours a week outside class.

Multiply the number of credit hours you're taking by 2 or 3 to determine the range of hours you need to study each week outside class to get high grades:

_____ × 2 or 3 = _____ or _____
Number of Credit Hours

How are you doing? Are you spending enough time studying to get the grades you want? What changes will you need to make in your weekly and daily schedules? Do you want to redo your weekly or term plans?

_____

_____

_____

_____

_____

_____

_____

_____

_____

_____

_____

_____

_____

_____

_____

_____

_____

_____

Setting Daily Priorities

1. **Make up your daily to-do list before you go to bed at night.** Or do the list first thing in the morning. Set priorities. Estimate how much time it will take to complete each task.

2. **Identify the top-priority tasks and try to do these first.** Do them in the morning if possible.

3. **Raise your time consciousness.** Periodically look at or think about your list. Maybe you have a few items that take only a little time. Knock them off in 10 minutes here, 15 minutes there. Keep your priorities in focus. Make sure you get your number-one priority done before it is too late in the day.

4. **Toward the end of the day, examine your to-do list.** Evaluate what you have accomplished. Challenge yourself to finish the few remaining tasks.

to be impossible, make sure that you finish the most important tasks. For some good strategies, see "Setting Daily Priorities."

The time-management expert Stephanie Winston (1995) recommends blocking out time each day for the one task you think will benefit you the most. For example, you might have a major paper in English due in three weeks that counts as one-third of your grade. Each day, assign yourself one task related to the paper. For example:

- *First Day:* Go to library and survey topics.
- *Second Day:* Narrow topics.
- *Third Day:* Select topic.
- *Fourth Day:* Construct outline.
- *Fifth Day:* Write first two pages.
- *And so on.*

Figure 3-2 shows one student's to-do list. Notice that this student has decided which tasks are the most important and put some time frames on when to do the tasks.

You might want to create a blank to-do list form similar to the one shown in Table 3-1. Then you could photocopy it to use each day. Commercial planning tools, especially electronic planners such as the Palm Pilot are often good for doing to-do lists. Or you might just take a notepad and create a to-do list on it each day.

FIGURE 3-2
Sample To-Do List

To Do

The Most Important:
1. **Study for Biology Test**

Next Two:
2. **Go to English and History Classes**

3. **Make Appointment to See Advisor**

Task	Time	Done
Study for biology test	Early morn., night	
Call home	Morning	
Go to English class	Morning	
Buy test book	Morning	
Call Ann about test	Morning	
Make advisor appt.	Afternoon	
Go to history class	Afternoon	
Do exercise workout	Afternoon	

Do successful people really use to-do lists in their everyday lives? For the most part, yes. Lists help them keep track of the tasks they want to complete.

But making a list is not enough. You also need to defend your priorities from unnecessary interruptions, such as telephone calls and drop-in visitors. To avoid such unwanted intrusions,

- Unplug the phone.
- Get an answering machine.
- Hang a DO NOT DISTURB sign on the door.
- Tell visitors that you're too busy to talk with them. Promise to get back to them when you've finished what you're doing.

Tune in to Your Biological Rhythms It has been said that people will accept an idea better if they're told that Benjamin Franklin said it first. Indeed, Benjamin Franklin did say, "Early to bed, early to rise, makes a man healthy, wealthy, and wise." Some of us are "morning people." However, others of us are "night people." That is, some students work more effectively in the morning, while others are at their best in the afternoon or evening. Evaluate yourself. What time of day are you the most alert and focused? For example, do you have trouble getting up in the morning for early classes? Do you love getting up early but feel drowsy in the afternoon or evening?

If you're a night person, take afternoon classes. Conduct your study sessions at night. If you're a morning person, choose morning classes. Get most of your studying done by early evening.

What can you do if you hate getting up early but are stuck with early morning classes? Start your day off properly. Many students begin their day with too little sleep and a junk-food breakfast or less. Does this description fit you? If so, try getting a good night's sleep and eating a good breakfast before you tackle your morning classes. You may even discover that you're not a "night person" after all. Exercise also is a great way to get some energy and be more alert when you need to be—and is often more effective than caffeine.

Never Procrastinate Again (Much)

Procrastination often hurts many students' efforts to become good time managers. Do you tend to put off until tomorrow what you need to do today? Procrastination can take many forms (University of Illinois Counseling Center, 1984):

- **Ignoring the task, hoping it will go away.** A midterm test in math is not going to evaporate, no matter how much you ignore it.
- **Underestimating the work involved in the task or overestimating your abilities and resources.** Do you tell yourself that you're such a great writer that you can grind out a twenty-page paper overnight?
- **Spending endless hours on computer games and surfing the Internet.** You might have fun while you're doing this, but will you have to pay a price for it?
- **Deceiving yourself that a mediocre or bad performance is acceptable.** For example, you may tell yourself that a 2.8 grade point average (GPA) will get you into graduate school or a great job after graduation. This mindset may deter you from working hard enough to get the GPA you need to succeed after college.

Better three hours too early than a minute too late.

William Shakespeare
16th–17th-century English playwright and poet

Let Me Count the Ways (Instead of Working)

Here is one student's ten best excuses for procrastinating:

1. I work best under time pressure so I'm going to wait and study later.
2. I'm too tired.
3. It's morning and I'm a night person—my body clock is out of sync.
4. My horoscope says it's a bad day for me.
5. It's too nice outside to be in here studying.
6. Study tonight? No way, my favorite TV shows are on.
7. This is going to give me a headache. I'm going to do something else.
8. Even if I do it, it probably won't be good enough, so why do it?
9. Ten years from now, will it really matter if I don't do this right now?
10. I think I'll wait until later when I become more motivated.

- **Substituting a worthy but lower-priority nonacademic activity.** For example, you might clean your room instead of studying for a test. Some people say, "Cleanliness is next to godliness," but if it becomes important only when you need to study for a test, you are procrastinating.
- **Believing that repeated "minor" delays won't hurt you.** For example, you might put off writing a paper so you can watch *Allie McBeal* or the World Wrestling Federation. Once the one-eyed monster has grabbed your attention, you may not be able to escape its clutches.
- **Dramatizing a commitment to a task rather than doing it.** For example, you take your books along on a weekend trip but never open them.
- **Persevering on only one part of a task.** For example, you write and rewrite the first paragraph of a paper, but you never get to the body of it.
- **Becoming paralyzed when having to choose between two alternatives.** For example, you agonize over whether to do your math homework or your English homework first. You get neither done.

Here are some good strategies for overcoming procrastination:

- **Put a deadline on your calendar.** This creates a sense of urgency. You might put deadline Post-its on the mirror and in other places you can see them at strategic times during the day. Think about other ways that you might create urgent reminders for yourself.
- **Get organized.** Some procrastinators don't organize things effectively. Develop an organized strategy for tackling the work you need to do.
- **Divide the task into smaller jobs.** Sometimes we procrastinate because the task seems so complex and overwhelming. Divide a larger task into smaller parts. Set subgoals of finishing one part at a time. This strategy can often make what seemed to be a completely unmanageable task an achievable one. For example, imagine that it's Thursday and you have fifteen math problems due on Monday. Set subgoals of doing five by Friday evening, five more by Saturday evening, and the final five by Sunday evening.
- **Take a stand.** Commit yourself to doing the task. One of the best ways to do this is to write yourself a "contract" and sign it. Or, tell a friend or partner about your plans.
- **Use positive self-statements.** Pump yourself up. Tell yourself things that will get you going, such as the following (Keller & Heyman, 1987):

  "There is no time like the present."

  "The soon I get done, the sooner I can play."

  "It's less painful if I do it right now. If I wait, it will only get worse."
- **Build in a reward for yourself.** This gives you an incentive to complete all or part of the task. For example, if you get all of your math problems done, treat yourself tonight to a movie you've been wanting to see. What other types of rewards can you give yourself for completing an important task?

Balance College, Work, Family, and Commuting

Time management is particularly challenging for college students who also hold a job, have a partner or children, or commute. If you face these challenges, for the next term you can schedule your classes at the earliest possible time during registration. This will get you the classes you want at the times you want. You can also talk with other students who share similar challenges.

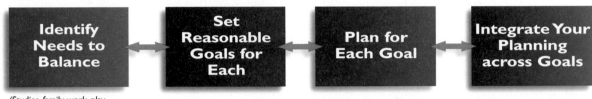

Identify Needs to Balance ← → **Set Reasonable Goals for Each** ← → **Plan for Each Goal** ← → **Integrate Your Planning across Goals**

(Studies, family, work, play, commuting, other)

Here are some additional time-management strategies for students with these special needs.

Balance College and Work

Managing time can be hard if you work to pay for college. For both part-time and full-time students, those who work full-time are less likely than students who work part-time or not at all to complete college, have high grade point averages, graduate with honors, or go on to graduate school (Astin, 1993). If you need to work, here are some suggestions.

Limit Work If Possible It's best not to work more than 10–20 hours. Full-time students who work more than 20 hours a week get lower grades than students who work fewer hours do. They are also much more likely to drop out of college.

Work on Campus If Possible Whether part-time work is positive or negative for college students depends on where they work. In general, a part-time job off campus is an academic minus (Astin, 1993). However, a part-time job on campus is an academic plus. Why does it matter whether you work part-time off campus or on campus? The answer has to do with involvement. Students who work part-time on campus will likely be connected with other students and faculty. This more than compensates for the time students devote to the part-time job.

Investigate Work-Study Options Some jobs can help you develop your skills for future careers. Others are good just for the money. Some companies pay for the courses of their student employees. Look for jobs and programs that suit your needs and goals.

Evaluate Your Course Load Carefully consider how many classes you are taking and how much work each one requires. You might want to take a reduced class load to give you more time for studying and work.

Balance College and Time with Partners and Children

Time is especially precious if you have a spouse, partner, or children. Communicating and planning are important assets in balancing your family time and academic time.

Talk with Your Partner Communicate with your partner about his or her importance in your life. Set time aside for your partner. Plan ahead for tasks that require extra study time. Inform your partner about test dates and other deadlines. After you've created your weekly and term calendars, let your partner see how you plan to use your time. If your partner is also a student, you may be able to coordinate your schedules so you can spend free time together. If one person works and another is in school, perhaps work-related activities can be coordinated with school/study time, and vice versa.

Build in Study Time at School If you have a partner or child, try to do some studying while you're still at school. Use time between classes, for example. Possibly arrive at school 30 minutes before your first class and stay 30 minutes after your last class to squeeze in uninterrupted study time.

Be Creative in How You Manage Time with Children If your child has homework, do yours at the same time. Take a break for ten minutes or so for each hour you study at home, and play or talk with your child. Then go back to your studying. If your children are old enough to understand, tell them what your study routine is and ask for their cooperation. Consider having your children play with other children in the neighborhood during your study hours. If your children are young, this might be arranged under another parent's supervision. Or try to swap child care with other student parents. Also check into child care and community agencies that may provide services and activities for your children in the before-school and after-school hours.

Use Commuting Time Effectively

If you commute to class, you already know how much time disappears on the road. Commuting students tend also to have family and work commitments that cut into study time. Courses may be available only at inconvenient times. Conflicts in schedules can make it difficult for commuters to take part in study sessions and other learning opportunities. Solving such scheduling problems requires good time management. See "Commute Boosters" for some good commuting strategies.

ON-TARGET TIPS

Commute Boosters

- Save time by consistently using to-do lists and weekly plans.
- Audiotape your instructors' lectures if they let you. Play them back on the way home or on the way to school.
- Rehearse what you learned in class today on your way to work, school, or home.
- If you carpool with classmates, use the commuting time to discuss class material with them.
- Use a backpack or briefcase to carry books and papers that you use each day. Organize the materials you plan to use the next day at school the night before. Then put them in your satchel.
- Exchange phone numbers with other students in your classes early in the semester. Call them if you need to discuss class issues or if you need their notes for a class you missed.
- Create a personal commuter telephone directory. Important phone numbers might include those of your instructors and their secretaries or teaching assistants, the library, student services, study partners, and other campus resources.

Managing the time demands of college may mean reorganizing how you spend time with significant others in your life. Commuting also presents special time demands.

Learn with *InfoTrac College Edition*

InfoTrac College Edition

Look up these articles and search for more on topics that sparked your interest while reading this chapter.

Florence Griffith-Joyner Flo-Jo, Diva of the Dash. Joy Duckett Cain. *Essence*. Dec. 1998. v29, i8, p174.

Time Management A get-real guide to time management. Donna J. Abernathy. *Training and Development.* June 1999. v53, i6, p22.

Prioritizing First things first: Prioritizing and time management—keeping up grades, working at internships, and holding down a job. James A. Perry. *The Black Collegian*. Oct. 1997. v28, n1, p54.

Procrastination What are the effects of procrastination? *Brown University Child and Adolescent Behavior Letter.* Jan. 1998. v14, i1, p3.

Balancing College and Family

Summary Strategies for Mastering College

Manage time effectively in order to reach your goals.

1 Control Your Life by Controlling Your Time

With great time management you can do the following:
* Be more productive and reduce your stress.
* Improve your self-esteem.
* Achieve balance in your life and conquer multitasking.
* Find career success and reach your goals.

2 Stay on Time to Reach Your Goals

* Set completion dates for your goals.
* Create subgoals and intermediate steps to goals.
* Revisit your goals regularly.

3 Plan for the Term, Week, and Day

* Choose the right planning tools.
* Create a week-by-week calendar.
* Create and monitor a weekly plan. Allocate time enough time for studying and other activities. Remember how many hours a week you need to study outside class to make good grades. Monitor this closely.
* Plan for tomorrow by setting priorities and managing to-do lists every day. Make sure you get your most important priority done. In deciding when to carry out tasks, examine your daily biological rhythms.

4 Reduce Procrastination

* Beware of procrastination's many faces.
* Tackle procrastination by setting deadlines on your calendar and becoming better organized.
* Divide the task into smaller jobs and make a commitment to each.
* Use positive self-statements and reward yourself.

5 Balance College, Work, Family, and Commuting

* Balance college and work by limiting work and working on campus if possible. Evaluate your course load. Manage your time.
* Balance college and time with partners and children by practicing good communication, planning study time at school, and being creative in how you manage time with children.
* Use commuting time effectively.

Review Questions

1. How can becoming a great time manager help you control your life? What benefits does someone who effectively manages time enjoy?

_____

_____

_____

_____

_____

_____

2. What are some good strategies for staying on time to reach your goals?

_____

_____

_____

_____

_____

_____

_____

_____

3. What advice would you give someone who wants to create a week-by-week term calendar? A weekly planner? A to-do list?

_____

_____

_____

_____

_____

_____

_____

_____

4. What are some good strategies for tackling procrastination?

_____

_____

_____

_____

_____

_____

_____

5. Describe ways to balance your academic life with all of the other demands in your life.

_____

_____

_____

_____

_____

_____

Learning Portfolio

Reflect and Journal

1. Who's in Charge?

We discussed many different ideas about managing time, such as developing a term plan, creating a weekly plan, setting priorities and consistently creating to-do lists, and tackling procrastination.

- What are your current strengths and weaknesses with regard to managing time?

_____

_____

_____

_____

_____

- What do you plan to do to address your weaknesses?

_____

_____

_____

_____

_____

_____

2. Are You Studying Enough?

Respond in writing to the question at the end of Self-Assessment 3-2 about whether you're studying enough.

_____

_____

_____

_____

_____

_____

_____

_____

_____

_____

_____

_____

_____

_____

_____

_____

_____

Learn by Doing

1. Make To-Do Lists

For the next several days, make a to-do list for each day. Create the list before you go to bed each night. Prioritize the items and jot down how much time each activity is likely to take. Then periodically review the list the next day and check off the activities you completed. Remember to complete your number-one priority before it gets too late in the day. At the end of the week, evaluate how much the lists made your days more manageable and organized.

_____

_____

_____

_____

_____

_____

_____

_____

_____

2. Put Swiss Cheese into Action

The Swiss cheese approach involves poking holes in bigger tasks by working on them in small bursts of time or at odd times. List your biggest task for next week. You should have some set time to work on it. However, also try to work on it in small bursts when you have a little time here, a little time there. At the end of next week, come back to this activity and write down how much more time you were able to sneak in on the big task by taking the Swiss cheese approach.

_____

_____

_____

_____

_____

_____

_____

_____

_____

Think Critically

1. Be More Precise

Following are some vague plans. Make them more specific.

Vague: I'm going to start getting to school on time.
Precise: _____
_____
_____
_____
_____

Vague: I plan to watch TV less and study more.
Precise: _____
_____
_____
_____
_____

Vague: I'm going to quit wasting my time.
Precise: _____
_____
_____
_____
_____
_____

2. Link Goals with Time Spent in Activities

- In what waking activities do you spend more than three hours a week?
_____
_____
_____
_____

- How does each of these activities relate to your goals?
_____
_____
_____
_____

- Examine your reasons for participating in activities that are unrelated to your goals.
_____
_____
_____
_____
_____

Think Creatively

1. Jump Starts

In this chapter we described some strategies for reducing procrastination. Get together with some other students and brainstorm about strategies for reducing procrastination.
_____
_____
_____
_____
_____
_____
_____
_____
_____
_____
_____
_____
_____
_____
_____

2. A New Kind of Cheese

We described the Swiss cheese and set time approaches to using your time more productively. Come up with a catchy title for a time-management approach that works for you. Write down its title and briefly describe it.

Title of approach:
_____

Description of approach:
_____
_____
_____
_____
_____
_____
_____

Work toward Goals

Review the results of the self-assessments you completed in this chapter. Also review the opening checklist. Based on your review, select a relatively short-term goal that you want to work on now.

1. What is that goal? (*Hint:* Is it challenging, reasonable, and specific?)

_____

_____

_____

_____

_____

2. What strategies will you use to achieve your goal? (*Hint:* Can you organize your strategy into a series of smaller goals?)

_____

_____

_____

_____

_____

3. What obstacles may be in your way as you attempt to make these positive changes?

_____

_____

_____

_____

_____

4. What additional resources might help you achieve your goal? (Use the CD-ROM that comes with this book for access to some useful leads.)

_____

_____

_____

_____

_____

5. By what date do you want to accomplish your goal?

_____

_____

_____

_____

_____

6. How will you know you have succeeded?

_____

_____

_____

_____

_____

Connect with Money, Campus, and Computers

Resources and More Resources

You want to be independent, but even the most successful college students don't do it all alone. They get connected—find the resources that will help them master college. They manage their money effectively and find out what financial resources are available to them. They know the best resources on campus for what they need. They get to know the people on campus who can help them if they run into problems. They use computer resources to their advantage.

To evaluate your current connections to important resources, place a check mark next to only those items that apply to you.

_____ I've made a yearly and monthly budget.

_____ I'm not getting into trouble with my credit cards.

_____ I've explored financial aid options for college.

_____ I know what campus resources are available to meet my needs.

_____ I know how to use library services.

_____ I plan to participate in one or more extracurricular activities.

_____ I use the Internet for e-mail and to search for information.

_____ I use a word processing program for most of what I write.

As you read about Marc Andreessen on the next page, think about how he used campus financial resources to support his college success and how he used technology resources to embark on a remarkable career.

IMAGES OF COLLEGE SUCCESS

Marc Andreessen

During his senior year at the University of Illinois, Marc Andreessen supported himself as a lab technician on campus, making $6.85 per hour. Within two years, he was worth more than $50 million. This change in finances resulted from the public offering of stock in Netscape Communications, the company he cofounded in 1994. Obviously not all on-campus employment leads to making a fortune. But Andreessen's story is a great example of making the best of campus resources.

The Internet is an international network of computer systems connected by telephone lines. It's been around for a long time, but in the past it was a trouble-

Marc Andreessen's **taming of the Internet demonstrated powerful problem-solving skills.**

some array of disorganized information that was difficult for most users to navigate. In his senior year, Andreessen worked with six other students to create Mosaic software, the first browser that facilitated access to the Web. A subsequent partnership with Jim Clark produced *Netscape,* a browser that could search the Web ten times faster than *Mosaic.* When the company offered *Netscape* shares to the public, the stock price zoomed from $28 to $75 per share. In 18 short months *Netscape* grew to 1,100 employees. By 1996, eighty million users were visiting the *Netscape* Web site daily.

Some computer experts suggested that Andreessen's *Netscape* was like a David going up against the Goliath of Bill Gates' Microsoft. When *Netscape* was bought out by AOL in the late 1990s, Andreessen stayed with AOL for a few months then quit. Now in the twenty-first century he has ventured out on his own again seeking new challenges in the world of technology.

Learn more about Marc Andreessen.

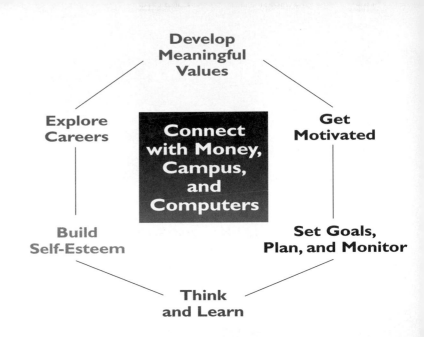

To master college and reach your goals, you need good resources. Three important resources are money, the campus, and computer technology. If you connect effectively with these, your college life will be easier, less stressful, and more productive.

Be a Great Money Manager

Money is a concern for many college students, as it was for Marc Andreessen. In a recent national survey of first-year college students, more than half were concerned about financing college and one in five students had major concerns (Sax & others, 2000). Nothing will disconnect you from college faster than running out of money. How do people get into debt? They simply spend more money than they have. To get a handle on your current money-management skills, complete Self-Assessment 4-1.

I finally know what distinguishes man from the beasts: Money worries.

Jules Renard
19th-century French novelist

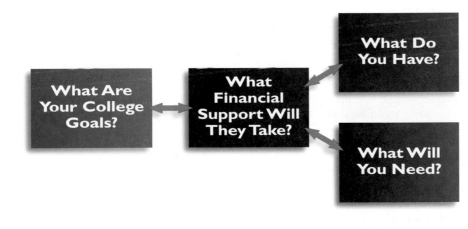

Just Say No to Plastic

Credit cards are a quick route to spending more money than you have. A credit card essentially provides you with a loan. In most cases, individuals pay back this loan with a minimum monthly payment that includes interest added to the bill. As months go by, more items are charged to the credit card but only a minimum payment is made. The charges and interest pile up. Before you know it, you're in over your head.

Too Good to Be True If the credit card offers you get in the mail seem too good to be true, they probably are. Promises of 2 percent interest for the first three months are great--for three months! Credit card offers like

_____ I know how much my basic expenditures are going to be this year.

_____ I know how much my expenditures will be this month.

_____ I don't use credit cards much.

_____ I know the interest rate on my credit card(s).

_____ I'm good at pinching pennies.

_____ I am not a compulsive buyer; I have good control over my spending habits.

_____ I know what financial aid I might be eligible for at my college or university.

_____ I have a good idea of how much debt I will have at the end of my first year of college.

_____ I know how much money I will owe when I graduate from college.

_____ I have several good strategies for reducing my expenses.

_____ I have already set financial goals for this year and planned how to attain them.

Look back over this list. The more check marks you see, the better your financial health. The more blanks you see, the more attention you need to give to your college finances.

Are you a good money manager? Or do you have a lot of work to do on monitoring your finances and improving your money-management skills? Can you think of ways you could improve your money management?

these can easily lure you into living beyond your means and quickly lead you to pay interest rates as high as 19 percent. If you're not sure what that means, sign up for business math.

Used in moderation, credit cards usually do not cause a problem. However, always keep in mind what credit really is: paying for the privilege of using someone else's money. Abusing credit cards will place you in serious financial danger.

Here Comes the Repo Man Consider Erik Papczun, a student at Kent State University. He lost it all—including his credit rating—to the Repo Man. How did he get into such a serious financial mess? Eric had no trouble getting twenty credit cards. He started accumulating them in his first year of college. By his junior year he owed more than $30,000! Among his purchases were a $6,000 car and $2,000 drum set. Bill collectors started showing up and repossessed the car, drums, and other purchases, embarrassing him in front of his friends. Eric graduated from college when he was 22 but it took him until he was 27 to pay off all of his college credit card debts. His credit history was not cleared until he was 31.

After college Eric took a job with a consumer credit union and became one of the founders of the Kent State Student Credit Union. To try to help college students avoid his mistakes, Eric gives talks to first-year students on the importance of managing money effectively. In these talks he concludes with two main points:

- Don't assume that only "losers" get into financial trouble. Eric was successful academically and socially in college but still found financial ruin. Ironically, he not only majored in finance but also was the treasurer of the student body.
- Don't bury your head in the sand. Be aware of any developing financial problems and do something about them.

Alternatives to Credit Cards As you can see, using credit cards to compensate for poor financial planning can lead to disaster. What are some alternatives to credit cards? They include debit cards, prepaid long-distance calling cards, and checking accounts in which funds are deposited each month. You can also send e-mail instead of making long-distance calls on credit cards.

If you choose to use a credit card, try to pay your bill in full each month. At least pay more than the monthly minimums. Also avoid late payments, for which you may be charged.

The best alternative to credit cards is to be a great money manager. What does that take? In one word: *budget*.

Credit cards are easy for college students to get. No job, no credit history—you can still get them. However, running up big debts on credit cards has become a major problem for many college students. What are some alternatives to credit cards?

Budget Wisely

A *budget* is a plan that lets you see whether your input of money (total income) meets your output of money (total expenditures). It also helps you match the timing of income and expenditures. A good budget anticipates cash-flow problems. These arise when you don't have enough money to pay your bills when they're due. A good budget also alerts you to necessary adjustments such as postponing expenditures, getting more income sooner, and using credit to better advantage.

Assess Your Income and Expenses for the Academic Year Examine the sources of your income. They likely consist of one or more of the following: parents, spouse, grandparents, savings, financial aid, and work.

Also evaluate your expenses. A good strategy is to list fixed expenses and variable expenses separately. Fixed expenses are unavoidable costs. For college students these include tuition and fees, books, supplies, and housing.

Variable expenses are flexible costs that you can change if needed. These include food, transportation, phone and utilities, clothing, laundry/dry cleaning, entertainment, and hair care/beauty treatments.

To compute your income and expenses for the academic year, go to the CD-ROM for this book. After you have summarized your total income and expenses, does your estimated annual budget show a negative balance? If so, you need to find ways to increase your income or decrease your variable expenses. If you want to decrease your variable expenses, a good way to start is to put together a budget for a shorter time frame.

Create a Monthly Budget By creating a monthly budget each month for several months, you can get a better sense of whether your annual budget is working. Your sources of income and your expenses will be similar to those described in the discussion of annual budgets.

The Case of the Pizza Addiction

Robert, a first-year student, loved pizza. He ordered pizza every night, had it delivered to his room, and paid for it with a check.

The first month or so this didn't pose any problem. But Robert wasn't very good at balancing his checkbook. And the pizza chain wasn't very forgiving about the string of bad checks Robert eventually and unknowingly wrote.

A policeman showed up at Robert's dorm one night with a warrant for his arrest. Robert was escorted to the police station and locked up. It cost his parents $200 to bail him out.

If you have a checking account, keep track of how much money is in your account. Write down the amount of each check you write. Keep track of the totals.

To compute your monthly budget, again go to the Web site for this book. There you can create and print out your specific plan for income and spending.

When you add up your income and expenses for next month, is your balance negative? If so, explore ways you can reduce your variable expenses. "Pinch Pennies" lists several money-saving tips.

Be Prepared for Unexpected Expenses

No matter how hard you try, you can't anticipate every little thing that crops up. Life has a way of presenting us with unexpected expenses or diminished income. Your car might break down. Your utility rates might go up. Someone might break into your room and steal something. Your part-time job might end. Friends may ask you to go on a road trip this weekend.

In many cases, you can't predict or prevent such circumstances. What you can do is consistently maintain a positive budget month to month. Then, you'll have more money coming in than going out when a financial emergency arises. Also, try to anticipate any financial roadblocks that might crop up so that you're at least emotionally prepared to handle them.

"Good day, Madam. I'm working my son's way through college."

Balance Your Checkbook

Many college students have checking accounts. If you have one, you know that your checkbook lets you keep a running summary of your transactions.

An important strategy is to keep track of how much money is in your account. Be sure to write down the amount of each check you write and keep track of each total. Consider using overdraft protection in case you mess up and write a check without adequate funds in your account.

Know Your Financial Resources

Be aware of your financial resources, both current and potential ones (in case you run into financial trouble). The sources of money that first-year students use to pay for college expenses are shown in Table 4-1 on page 84. Notice that parents or family are the main source for most college students. Also notice that work, loans, grants, and scholarships are common sources.

More than seven million undergraduates—slightly less than half—receive some form of financial aid. The federal government provides approximately $25 billion of financial aid for undergraduates each year.

Pinch Pennies

Here are twenty-two ways to save money (McDonald, 1994):

- Make your own lunch.
- Shop around. Fight the urge to buy the first item you see.
- Don't allow yourself to be pressured. Resist high-powered sales tactics.
- Learn when to say no. Ask yourself whether you can really afford what you're thinking about buying. Will it fit into your budget?
- Try bartering instead of spending. For example, agree to watch a friend's children for a few hours in exchange for a good meal.
- Reduce the number of shopping trips you make; every time you walk into a store, you may be tempted to spend money.
- Clip coupons, keep them organized, and use them when needed.
- Borrow clothes or accept hand-me-downs from friends and relatives.
- Buy clothes only on sale, never at full retail price. Buy secondhand clothes.
- Visit a cosmetology or barber school to have students cut your hair.
- If you have to pay extra for utilities, use fans instead of air conditioning in warmer months.
- If you have a car, plan your excursions to use gas efficiently.
- Check newspapers for special prices on lunches or dinners.
- Take advantage of college discounts on movies, sporting events, musicals, plays, and so on. These discounts are often substantial.
- Attend campus entertainment events, which are usually cheaper than commercial entertainment.
- Take advantage of your college's library services. Read their books, magazines, and newspapers instead of buying them, for example.
- Use your college's exercise facilities rather than joining a health club.
- Regularly leaf through the campus newspaper to find discounts on food, movies, and so on. Just because it's listed as a discount, though, doesn't mean it's a good deal. Be sure to compare prices.
- Ask other students about the least expensive supermarkets, drug stores, restaurants, and so on.
- Ask yourself whether what you're buying is practical. Peer pressure, fads, and trends can become very expensive.
- Be prepared to change your attitude when necessary. For example, some people think that the most expensive item is the best item, but you don't always get what you pay for.

In addition to federal loans and grants, many scholarships are available. A good initial strategy is to contact the financial aid office at your college. Find out what scholarships are available. Many national organizations, businesses, churches, and other agencies have scholarships for students. Check the Wadsworth Web site for places to find out about scholarships.

Connect with Your Campus

It costs you nothing to connect with your campus, yet nothing will help you more than knowing and using your campus resources. You probably have visited some of them already—the book store for textbooks and study supplies, the student center or commons to check out bulletin boards or pick up a newspaper.

TABLE 4-1
First-Year Students' Sources of Money

Source	Received Any Aid From	Received $1,500 or More From
Parents or family	76%	52%
Spouse	1	1
Savings (summer work)	50	8
Savings (other)	30	7
Part-time job (on campus)	22	2
Part-time job (off campus)	23	2
Full-time job while in college	3	1
Pell Grant	23	5
Supplemental Educational Opportunity Grant	6	1
State scholarship or grant	16	4
College work-study grant	13	1
Other college grant	26	15
Vocational rehabilitation funds	1	1
Other private grant	10	3
Other government aid (ROTC, BIA, etc.)	3	2
Stafford/Guaranteed Student Loan	30	14
Perkins Loan	9	2
Other college loan	10	6
Other loan	7	4
Other	4	2

© 1982 Universal Press Syndicate

Tom Wilson

An important goal in college is learning how to solve your personal problems and get your needs met. Many campus resources can help you attain these goals. You can learn a lot about the best campus resources on your own if you set a goal of obtaining information about them and aren't afraid to ask questions. Use Self-Assessment 4-2 to get started.

Stay Healthy

Many campuses have fully equipped medical centers for students. Health care services may offer blood testing, health screenings, pregnancy tests, flu shots, and educational programs, as well as regular physicians' care. Smaller campuses may offer access to a nurse or health specialists trained in emergency care. Find out the phone numbers for these services. Carry them with you. When health emergencies arise, contact an employee of the campus or call the campus switchboard to explain the situation and request urgent help.

Campus Resources to Meet My Needs

First, cross off any items that you know you won't need. Add any other locations that you think you will need. Then answer yes or no after the items not crossed off. Next, write down the location of the campus resource and any notes you want to make about the resource, such as its hours and phone number.

Does My Campus Have	Yes or No	Location/Notes
Career services center?	_____	_____
Student testing center?	_____	_____
Math laboratory?	_____	_____
Performing arts center?	_____	_____
Campus security?	_____	_____
Financial aid office?	_____	_____
ROTC service?	_____	_____
TV or radio station?	_____	_____
Work-study program?	_____	_____
Writing lab?	_____	_____
Health center?	_____	_____
Travel agency?	_____	_____
Mental health services?	_____	_____
Language lab?	_____	_____
Intramural sports office?	_____	_____
Student government office?	_____	_____
Post office?	_____	_____
Lost and found?	_____	_____
Printing service?	_____	_____
Banking center?	_____	_____
Computer labs?	_____	_____
Multimedia and graphics lab?	_____	_____
International students' center?	_____	_____
College newspaper office?	_____	_____
Religious services?	_____	_____
Campus cinema?	_____	_____
Lost and found?	_____	_____
Other _____	_____	_____
Other _____	_____	_____
Other _____	_____	_____

Compare your information with that of others in the class. How are you doing in discovering resources on your campus? Put the information about resources in the planner that you carry with you on campus. Note: This list is also on the Web site for this book, where you can easily tailor the list to meet your own needs and print out a copy of it.

Keep Safe

Personal safety is an important concern on all campuses. Security personnel monitor the campus for outsiders and sometimes provide escorts after dark. If you feel unsafe or spot activities that you think may threaten the well-being or property of others, call the campus switchboard or security and report your suspicions or concerns.

Most campuses teem with activity. Unfortunately, they do attract people who find busy places ideal for stealing. No matter what the size of your campus, possessions that can be converted to cash can disappear. Keep your personal belongings locked up when you are not around. Consider insuring valuable property.

Exercise good judgment about the risks you take. You'll be meeting many people. Most of them will enrich your life, but some may try to take advantage of you. Be careful about lending money or equipment, especially to people you've just met. Exercise your street smarts on campus to avoid potential exploitation.

You may sometimes feel pressured by friends to take safety risks, such as drinking inappropriately, taking drugs, or hanging out in places that don't feel safe. Don't succumb to friendly pressures to do things that place you at risk. True friends have your best interests at heart. If you feel pressure to take risks, it's time to reevaluate your friendships.

Get Help from Advisors, Academic Support Services, Counselors

Most people on campus will be eager to help you in your quest to master college. Whether you want information or training, here are some things you can do to get the help you need (Canfield & Hansen, 1995):

- **Ask as though you expect to get help.** Your tuition dollars pay for assistance in the classroom, the library, or even the cafeteria line. Ask with authority. You may be able to enter that restricted part of the library merely by acting like you know what you're doing. High self-esteem gives you the confidence to do these kinds of things.
- **Ask someone who is in a position to help you.** You may have to do some homework to find out who can help you best. If someone you approach can't deliver, ask whether that person knows of someone else who might be able to help you.
- **Ask clear and specific questions.** Even those who enjoy helping students don't like to have their time wasted. Think ahead about what you need and what level of detail will satisfy you. Take notes so you won't have to ask to go over the same ground twice.
- **Ask with passion, civility, humor, and creativity.** Enthusiasm goes a long way toward engaging others to want to help you. A polite request is easier to accommodate than a loud, demanding one. Sometimes problems yield more readily to a playful request. A clever request is just plain hard to turn down. Although this approach can entail more risk, the results can be very satisfying. But size up whether your instructors will appreciate a humorous approach. If not, your good intentions and creativity may backfire.

Connect with Your Academic Advisor

Perhaps the most important helper on campus will be your academic advisor. Navigating academic life by yourself is not a good idea. Your academic advisor has important information about your course requirements that can help you realize your plans. Advisors can explain why certain courses are required and can alert you to instructors suited to your preferred learning style.

Plan to confer with your advisor regularly. When it's time to register for next term's courses, schedule a meeting with your advisor early in the registration period. Bring a tentative plan of the courses that you think will satisfy your requirements. Be open if the advisor offers you compelling reasons for taking other courses. For example, your advisor may suggest that by taking some harder courses than you had planned, you can prepare yourself better for the career you have chosen. Your advisor will help you reach your career objective as efficiently as possible, but not by compromising solid preparation.

Some advisors may not have regular office hours. To maximize your effectiveness and efficiency, call your academic advisor for an appointment before dropping by. If you put your concerns in writing before the appointment, your advisor will have some time to work on your specific issues before you come to your appointment. See "A Memo to Your Advisor" to help you get started.

If the "chemistry" between you and your academic advisor isn't good, confront that problem with your advisor. Say what behaviors make you feel uncomfortable. Recognize that your own actions may have something to do with the problem. You need an advisor you can trust. If you can't work out a compromise, request a change to find an advisor who is right for you.

ON-TARGET TIPS

A Memo to Your Advisor

When you need to contact instructors or academic staff members to help you solve a problem, notify them in advance about your needs. A standard memo format will help you set the context for the meeting. Be sure to include your telephone number and good times to reach you in case a change in scheduling is necessary. For example:

Memo
To: Dr. Charles
From: Tyrell Wilkins
Re: Changing majors
Date: 9/27

I would like to meet with you during your 11 A.M. office hour on Monday, 10/5. I am thinking about changing majors but I want to find out whether this could delay my graduation. Please e-mail me or call me any weekday evening after 7 P.M. if the proposed time doesn't work for you. Thank you!

Phone: 555-3300
E-mail: tykins@omninet.edu

Learn about Academic Support Services

Most campuses provide access to specialists who can assist you with academic problems. If you're struggling, you might want to look into the sorts of specialized services offered on your campus. For example, many study skills specialists are qualified to do diagnostic testing to determine the nature of your learning difficulties, or they can refer you to specialists who provide this service. They can suggest compensating strategies for your assignments and may be able to give you some directions about taking courses with instructors who are more sympathetic with your struggle to learn. They can also set up and monitor additional study supports, including tutoring and study groups, to get you accustomed to the demands of college-level work.

Seek Counseling for Personal Concerns

College life is often challenging on a personal level. Talking to a counselor or therapist may provide the relief you need. Large campuses have mental health departments or psychology clinics. They may have therapists and counselors on site who will give you the support you need on a one-to-one or a group basis. The fee for such services either will be on a sliding scale (meaning that the cost is proportional to your income), covered by your health insurance policy, or covered by your tuition.

Either I will find a way or I will make one.

Sir Philip Sidney
16th-century English poet and soldier

Some student services offer topic-specific support groups, such as a group for single mothers returning to college or one for students struggling with English as a second language. In support groups you can meet others who have problems similar to yours. Their advice and experience may be helpful. Ask the counseling center or dean's office about support groups on campus.

If you do not find a group that addresses your concern, consider creating one. Most support groups start from the concerns of one or two students. The student services office will usually assist you with the advertising and the room arrangements to help your group get off the ground.

Tap the Library

Libraries may not seem a likely site for adventure. But think about it. Each visit to the library can be a treasure hunt. The treasure might be a bit of information, an opportunity to go online, or a chance to check out a new book from your favorite author. The sooner you get a feel for how the library works, the more useful it will be to you.

One of your classes may arrange a tour. If not, ask a librarian for help in getting oriented. Librarians can give you a schedule of library tours or provide you with maps or pamphlets to help you search independently. Although librarians may look busy when you approach them, step up and ask for help. Most of them enjoy teaching others how to use the library. If you find an especially friendly librarian, cultivate the relationship. A librarian friend can be a lifesaver.

What do you need to know in order to use the library effectively? The following questions may help you organize your first tour of the library:

- How can I check out materials? What are penalties for late returns?
- Do instructors place materials on reserve? How does this work?
- What interesting or helpful journals does the library have?
- Is the library catalog online or on cards? Are some things online and others not?
- Can I arrange interlibrary loans to get materials not available in my college library?
- What kinds of reference materials are available? Are the abstracts of published research on microfilm or in books?
- Where are "the stacks" and when can I use them?
- What technological resources does the library have that will help me succeed in college?

Pursue Extracurricular Activities

Participating in extracurricular activities improves your changes of meeting people who share your interests.

Many choices for activities are usually listed in the campus handbook or advertised in the student newspaper. Many majors sponsor clubs that allow you to explore careers through field trips or special speakers. If you're interested in journalism, you can work on the college newspaper or yearbook. Prospective drama students can audition for plays. Students interested in business can join an entrepreneur's group to examine how business people manage their lives and work. Intramural and campus sports are available. Some clubs promote service to others.

It may seem like your study life is too full to accommodate fun. However, leisure activities are important for balance in your life. The campus may hold dances, concerts, campuswide celebrations, or other events to help you meet people, relax, and have fun. Extracurricular activities of any kind can also help you develop leadership skills and manage multiple commitments.

As valuable as extracurricular activities are, your involvement can also create problems. Some activities are expensive. If your income is limited, look for ones that don't wipe out your cash. Sometimes you get too involved. Before you know it, you may have more commitments than you can manage and too little time to study. Have fun, but keep your larger goals in mind.

Enrich Your Cultural Life

Your campus and community may offer unique opportunities for cultural enrichment. Because most campuses are training grounds for artists and performers, they often operate an art gallery for student work or the work of invited artists. They also host live performances in music, dance, and theater to showcase student and faculty talent, as well as outside professional performers. In the community, museums, galleries, theaters, the symphony, and political gatherings can all enrich your learning.

Most college students have spiritual concerns. Campus ministries usually coordinate religious activities for various denominations. These may be formal religious services or social groups where you can simply get together with others of a similar faith. You can not only practice your faith but also expand your network of friends with common values. Of course, religious services are also available off campus.

In summary, connecting to the campus and community through extracurricular and cultural activities offers you great opportunities to sample new pursuits as you search for a meaningful major or career.

Overcome Limitations

In the last decade, the number of college students with a disability has increased dramatically. Today more than 10 percent of college students have some form of physical or mental impairment that substantially limits their major life activities.

Colleges are required to make reasonable accommodations to allow students with a disability to perform up to their capacity. Accommodations can be made for motor and mobility impairments, visual and hearing deficits, physical and mental health problems, and learning disabilities.

If you have a disability, determine what support you need to succeed in college. The level of service a college provides can be classified as follows:

- **Minimal support.** Students generally adapt to the college and advocate for their own services and accommodations.

Jon Riley/Tony Stone Images

Many individuals overcome physical disabilities and other limitations to become successful college students. What are some services that colleges provide for individuals with physical limitations?

- **Moderate support.** The campus offers a service office or special staff to help students with advocacy and accommodations.
- **Intense support.** The campus provides specific programs and instructional services for students with disabilities.

Among the academic services that may be available on your campus are

- **Referrals for testing, diagnosis, and rehabilitation.** Specialists who can help in this area may be on or off campus.
- **Registration assistance.** This involves consideration regarding the location of classrooms, scheduling, and in some cases waivers of course requirements.
- **Accommodations for taking tests.** Instructors may allow you to have expanded or unlimited time to complete tests. You may be able to use a word processor or other support resources during the test.
- **Classroom assistance.** Someone may be assigned to take notes for you to translate lectures into sign language. Or instructors may allow their lectures to be taped for students with impaired vision or other disabilities.
- **Special computing services and library skills.** Support services on campus are finding inventive new ways to interpret written texts to overcome reading and visual limitations.

This section has discussed social connections on campus. But computer resources are also important. Let's turn to them now.

Connect with Computers

Computers can make your college life easier. They can support your efforts to think and learn, help you reach many of your college goals, and provide a foundation for building important career skills.

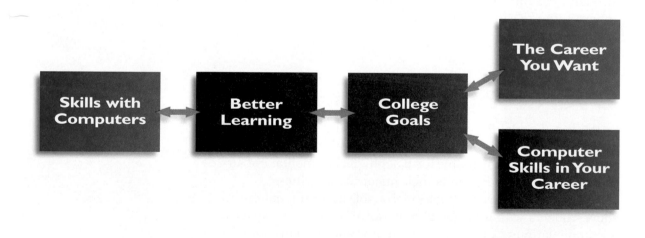

Get up to Speed

If you've had little chance to become familiar with computers, several strategies will help you get up to speed. You should be able to become computer literate by making good use of the free computer labs on campus. Many campus computer labs are open early and close late to promote student access. Some

How Am I Doing with Computers?

1. How advanced are your computer skills? Do you use them productively on a regular basis? Or have you avoided using them? Place a check mark next to each item you use regularly:

___ E-mail
___ The Internet
___ Word-processing program(s)
___ Research databases
___ Graphics and presentation software
___ Spreadsheet programs

If you did not place a check mark next to some items, use your knowledge of goal-setting, planning, and monitoring to learn the particular skills.

2. Are any of the following aspects of computers a problem for you? Place a check mark next to any item that's a problem or is becoming a problem for you.

___ I spend too much time on computer games.
___ I spend too much time surfing the Web.
___ My time on the computer is cutting into my sleep.
___ Using computers so much has kept me from having a good social life.
___ I've begun to develop problems in my hands, wrists, or arms because of excessive
___ computer use.
___ I've tried to cut back on my overuse of the computer but I haven't been able to control this.

If you checked off any of the items, computer time may be consuming too much of your life. Use your motivational and goal-setting skills to help overcome your problem.

campuses have computer labs in the residence halls. Take a beginning computer class to start learning the skills you'll need in a computer-dependent world. Or find part-time work that involves computers so you can earn a paycheck while you learn these valuable skills.

See Self-Assessment 4-3 to see where you stand regarding computer use.

Explore the Internet

The Internet is a major force in the academic world and elsewhere (Poole, 1998). You've probably noticed the widespread use of World Wide Web addresses in advertising. If you are an experienced "Web surfer," you know how your own work patterns have changed since you begin using this tool. If you have not personally experienced the astounding capabilities of the Web, find ways to gain access and get good at using it.

The future world of today's college students will depend on computers, which have already transformed the education landscape of colleges.

E-Mail E-mail allows ongoing Internet conversations with people who share your interests. For example, some of your instructors may require discussions online using a class listserve. Such discussions allow you to practice the language of the course and can improve your understanding of course concepts. Some instructors welcome questions via e-mail because it's often more convenient than office hours for both parties. Technologically oriented instructors are often remarkably open to developing online relationships with their students. Some may be even more open to online chats than face-to-face discussions.

Your campus may provide you with a free e-mail account. Most campuses that have not yet provided this service are hard at work raising funds to do so. If your campus does not offer such accounts, you can join a full-range commercial service for about $20 per month. If you have an e-mail address, consider getting some cards printed with your name and e-mail address to facilitate building your own electronic community. Once you have your own e-mail address, it will be easy to send private mail to others, participate in listserves, visit Web sites, and download a variety of resources available on the Internet.

World Wide Web (WWW) The World Wide Web is both the most exciting and the most frustrating development on the Internet (Kurose & Ross, 2001). The excitement comes from the impressive variety of information presented in pictures, sounds, and dazzling graphics available to anyone with a browser. The Web lets you move easily from one piece of information to other related information by clicking "buttons" on a Web site. In this way you can search through a "web" of connected sites. When you find a site that you especially like and wish to revisit, you can create bookmarks that let you return there directly.

The frustration comes from the sheer quantity of information available on the Web. Entering a key word on the search engine of a browser may result in the browser listing thousands of possible resources, or "hits." You may have no easy way to separate the valuable ones from the "noise." Visiting every site takes too long. This explains why some students report that they spent hours

Not all computer time has to be spent in physical isolation. If you're spending too much time alone on a computer, start collaborating with others at least some of the time when using the computer.

on the Web but still couldn't find answers to the questions that prompted their search.

Many organizations and businesses offer information on the Web that pertains to college subjects. For example, a class studying AIDS may find a lot on the Web about AIDS, including current research on medication, legal concerns, and support groups. Because many Web pages are updated frequently, this information may be among the most current professional research available. Unfortunately, some Web sites don't get updates, so their information may be out of date. The Web also contains a lot of junk. It does not currently have the same quality control procedures that you would find in the academic journals in your college library. Get in the habit of examining the information about the maintenance of the Web site. It will help you judge the currency and value of the information posted. The tips in "Critically Evaluate Web Information" should help you judge what you read on the Web.

Surfing the Web can be wonderful experience—sometimes maybe too wonderful. Most users report that hours can slip away while they're using the Web. Be prepared to invest some time if you choose to use this helpful tool.

Reprinted by permission. www.cartoonstock.com.

Use a Word-Processing Program

Word-processing programs on a computer make the process of writing and rewriting papers easier because you can make changes without having to retype most of your work (Tiene & Ingram, 2001). You can also select different print types, called *fonts*, and use other features to highlight or underline key sections of your work. With most word-processing programs, you can incorporate headers (standard headings at the top of each page), page numbers, and footnotes easily. Many programs will also develop your reference list, placing it in the conventional format for the discipline in which you're writing. Perhaps most helpful of all are the features that allow you to check spelling, grammar, and word count when your paper is completed. Of all of the tips for success in this book, one of the most important is *Learn to use a word processor and write all your papers on it*.

Word processing also involves some hazards. If you don't make a habit of saving your work often, you can end up with nothing to print. Spell-checkers do not substitute for good proofreading, because spell-checking will identify words that are misspelled but not words that are misused. For example, most won't catch the difference between *there* and *their* or *to, too,* and *two*. The worst problem associated with word processing is that it might encourage you to procrastinate and therefore lose revision time, because your first draft can look very professional. Better papers are better because the writer allowed some time to think again and revise.

Critically Evaluate Web Information

ON-TARGET TIPS

1. **How Accurate Is the Information?**
   Do you have any way of checking the accuracy of the content?

2. **How Authoritative Is the Information?**
   What authority or expertise do the creators of the Web site have? How knowledgeable are they about the subject matter? For example, there is a big difference between the information about space launches provided by an armchair amateur and that given by NASA.

3. **How Objective Is the Information?**
   Is the information presented with a minimum of bias? To what extent is the site trying to push a particular idea and sway opinions versus presenting facts?

4. **How Current Is the Information?**
   Is the content of the site up to date? When was the Web site last updated?

5. **How Thorough Is the Coverage?**
   Are topics covered in sufficient depth? What is the overall value of the content?

TABLE 4-2
Helpful Library Research Databases

Research Coverage	Title
Behavioral sciences	PsychInfo/PsychLit
	Sociological Abstracts
Business	PROMT
	ABI/INFORM
Education	ERIC
Humanities	Economic Literature Index
	Historical Abstracts
	Humanities Abstracts
	Philosopher's Index
Natural science	BIOSIS
	MEDLINE
News reports	Associated Press
	NEXUS
	Reuters
Reference	Books in Print
	Dissertation Abstracts
	Academic Index
	Britannica Online

Use Computers in Other Ways to Reach Your Goals

Using e-mail, the World Wide Web, and word-processing programs regularly will help you succeed in college and thereafter. In many careers, successful individuals rely on these computer tools on a daily basis. You may also want to consider three other tools—research databases, graphics and presentation software, and spreadsheet programs—that can help you enormously if the task at hand is appropriate for their use.

Research Databases Your campus library houses electronic databases that you can use for research assignments. Each database uses key words, years, or authors to direct you to specific articles in the professional literature. Table 4-2 lists some of the most frequently used academic databases. You may find other uses for databases as well. For example, business classes may explore how to keep track of inventory or potential customers. If you get a part-time job at the college, you may be working with databases of alumni addresses or bookstore inventories.

Graphics and Presentation Software

Graphics packages let you express yourself visually. They allow you to copy and design images, create animations, develop charts and graphs, and make impressive computer-driven presentations. Some of your courses may have graphic requirements. In other classes, graphics can improve the content and aesthetic appeal of your work.

PowerPoint is an especially powerful presentation software tool. If you have to do a class presentation, Power-Point can help you organize it and create a dynamic, visually attractive format for it. Many successful individuals in a wide range of careers use PowerPoint, saying that it has made the art of presenting a lot easier and more professional, and makes presentations much more interesting for the audience.

Spreadsheet Programs Spreadsheet programs perform calculations on numerical data. For example, you can enter data from a chemistry experiment into the columns of a spreadsheet and set up the spreadsheet program to calculate and summarize the results. Students who major in business are likely to use spreadsheets in marketing analyses, business plans, and financial projections. Your instructors will probably tell you which spreadsheet programs will best suit your needs.

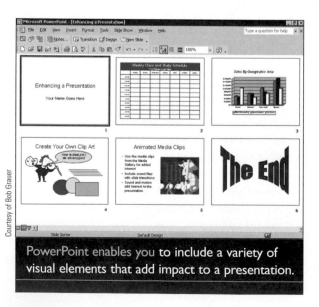

Courtesy of Bob Grauer

PowerPoint enables you to include a variety of visual elements that add impact to a presentation.

Avoid Computer Addiction

It's hard to pry some people away from their computers. Some computer technology fans are so dedicated to their computers that they neglect their work or studies. How can a computer be so addictive?

- **The compelling opportunity to explore the world.** Casual surfing of the Internet can take you in many directions. Anyone with a healthy curiosity can find it hard to stay away from the vast and varied sources of information that computers can reach.
- **The obsessive attraction of computer games.** The thrill of good performance is rewarding. It's easy to keep playing "just one more time" to see whether you can better your score. Hours slip by as you gradually refine your game skill and lose your real social connections.
- **The seduction of electronic relationships.** An electronic relationship between two people can feel profound, because the absence of physical cues may allow you to connect to another person in a novel way. Without the other elements of real life intruding, such exchanges can lead to deeper emotional involvement and reward than a user may currently experience in face-to-face relationships. However, this sense of intimacy can be based on half-truths or even lies, because you have no real way of knowing who the other person is. In any case, such relationships can be compelling and time-consuming. If you find yourself favoring "e-friends" over "real-friends," think twice!

Reprinted with permission of Carole Cable.

Learn with *InfoTrac College Edition*

InfoTrac College Edition

Look up these articles and search for more topics that sparked your interest while reading this chapter.

Marc Andreessen What's it really like to be Marc Andreessen? Rick Tetzeli. *Fortune.* Dec. 9, 1996. v134, i11, p136.

Money Management Five money mistakes to sidestep. Lena Sherrod. *Essence.* Aug. 2000. v31, i4, p90.

Credit Card Dangers

Financial Aid for College Help with college costs. *Financial Executive.* July 2000. v16, i4, p14.

Academic Advisors

College Libraries

Campus Involvement

The Internet The Internet: More than we can imagine. John Patrick. *Financial Executive.* May–June 1999. v19, i3, p14.

Computer Addiction

Summary Strategies for Mastering College

To master college and reach your goals, you need good resources.

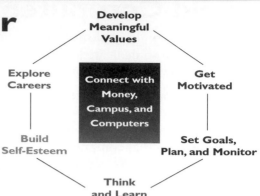

1 Be a Great Money Manager

- Say no to credit cards or at best use them sparingly and intelligently.
- Balance your checkbook.
- Budget wisely.
- Assess your income and expenses for the academic year.
- Create a monthly budget.
- Be prepared for unexpected expenses.
- Know your financial resources.

2 Connect with Your Campus

- Know which campus resources you need now or might need in the future. Find out their locations, hours, and phone numbers. Keep this information in a planner you carry with you.
- Stay healthy and use your campus health services when needed.
- Keep safe and know how to contact the campus security personnel when you need them.
- Connect with your academic advisor, who can be one of your most important campus resources.
- Learn about academic support services, such as help for writing and math. Find out if tutoring and study groups are available.
- Seek counseling if you have or develop personal concerns.
- Tap library resources.
- Participate in one or more extracurricular activities but don't spend so much time in these that they interfere with your academic work.
- Become culturally enriched by learning about and going to some cultural activities at your college and in the community.
- If you're a student with a physical limitation, learn about and use the campus resources that are available to you.

3 Connect with Computers

- Get up to speed and become computer literate. If you don't own a computer, use campus labs. Consider taking a computer class.
- Use e-mail.
- Learn to use the World Wide Web to support your success in college. Be sure to evaluate the accuracy and quality of information on the Web.
- Use a word-processing program for most or all of your writing. If you can't yet, learn how as soon as possible.
- Learn to use research databases, graphics and presentation software, and spreadsheet programs. Learn to use PowerPoint to make great presentations.
- Avoid computer addiction.

Review Questions

1. Discuss some of the problems that can develop with credit cards. If you use credit cards, how can you use them wisely?

_____

_____

_____

_____

_____

2. Apart from credit card issues, what are some other principles of good money management?

_____

_____

_____

_____

_____

_____

3. What kinds of campus connections matter? Name at least five.

_____

_____

_____

_____

_____

_____

4. What are some important computer skills that will help you succeed in college?

_____

_____

_____

_____

_____

5. What are some signs of computer addiction?

_____

_____

_____

_____

_____

Learning Portfolio

 Reflect and Journal

1. Improve Your Budget

List the three most important things you can do to improve your ability to balance your budget this term.

a. _____
_____
_____
_____

b. _____
_____
_____
_____

c. _____
_____
_____
_____

2. Dealing with Computers

Go back to Self-Assessment 4-3, "How Am I Doing with Computers?" What computer skills do you have? Do you have any fears or problems regarding computers? What are they? How can you address them?

_____
_____
_____
_____
_____
_____
_____
_____
_____
_____
_____
_____

Learn By Doing

1. Explore Campus Jobs

Perhaps the fastest way to do this is to go to the financial aid office on campus. Ask for a list of available part-time jobs. Do any of these jobs appeal to you? Will any help you develop skills toward a future career? Describe the jobs that best link up with future careers.

_____
_____
_____
_____
_____
_____
_____
_____
_____
_____
_____

2. Explore Extracurricular Activities

Locate or create a list of available extracurricular events or meetings. Identify those that appeal to you most, then attend one or two. Decide whether you want to make these activities a regular part of your college life.

_____
_____
_____
_____
_____
_____
_____
_____
_____
_____
_____

Think Critically

1. Analyze Your Own Credit Rating

Contact a local credit bureau or a reference librarian to help you identify the main factors that affect a person's credit rating. If you have a credit history, ask the credit bureau for a report of your credit rating and evaluate how you've done so far.

_____

_____

_____

_____

_____

_____

_____

_____

_____

_____

_____

_____

_____

_____

_____

_____

_____

2. Uncover Web Treasures

Select a topic that you're learning about in one of your courses. Enter it as a key word on an Internet browser such as Yahoo, Netscape, or Google. Visit the Web sites that look like they would give you the best information.

You also might want to ask your instructors for the best Web sites in their subject areas. Go to these sites, then write about your experience. Did you uncover some helpful information? Why or why not?

_____

_____

_____

_____

_____

_____

_____

_____

_____

_____

_____

_____

_____

Think Creatively

1. Only the Best

Ask students you trust and who have been on campus longer than you about where to locate at least five of the following:

- Best cheap, hot breakfast
- All-night food store
- Local businesses that give student discounts
- Best software
- Live music
- Best pizza
- Best coffee
- Free or cheap movies
- Best place for quiet conversation
- Best place to exercise
- Best bulletin board
- Best place to dance
- Discount bookstores
- Cheap photocopies
- Best place to view the stars

2. Your Cognitive College Map

You may have received a campus map as part of your orientation materials. Draw your own map as well. On it, emphasize the aspects of campus that are most important to you by drawing them larger and more stylized. You might also try constructing the map using computer graphics.

_____

_____

_____

_____

_____

_____

_____

_____

_____

_____

_____

_____

_____

_____

_____

Work toward Goals

Review the results of the self-assessments you completed in this chapter. Also review the opening checklist. Based on your review, select a relatively short-term goal that you want to work on now.

1. What is that goal? (*Hint:* Is it challenging, reasonable, and specific?)

_____

_____

_____

_____

_____

2. What strategies will you use to achieve your goal? (*Hint:* Can you organize your strategy into a series of smaller goals?)

_____

_____

_____

_____

_____

3. What obstacles may be in your way as you attempt to make these positive changes?

_____

_____

_____

_____

_____

4. What additional resources might help you achieve your goal? (Use the CD-ROM that comes with this book for access to some useful leads.)

_____

_____

_____

_____

5. By what date do you want to accomplish your goal?

_____

_____

_____

_____

6. How will you know you have succeeded?

_____

_____

_____

_____

Take It In: Notes and Reading

5

Be Selective

To succeed in college, you need to take charge of new ideas and make good judgments about their importance to your learning. In other words, you need to learn strategies for being *selective* about the information you take in. To see where you are right now, place a check mark next to only those items that apply to you.

_____ I'm very organized about the way I take information from lectures, group work, and textbooks.

_____ I use many strategies to figure out what's most important to learn.

_____ I know how to keep myself focused during difficult lectures.

_____ I'm familiar with different note-taking methods.

_____ I can explain why certain places are better suited for reading than others.

_____ I know the difference between primary and secondary research sources and the value of each.

_____ I use various strategies to read more effectively and efficiently.

_____ I use my notes to improve my learning as well as my test performance.

As you read the heroic story of Brooke Ellison, consider how you could benefit from the successful strategies she used to decide what to learn.

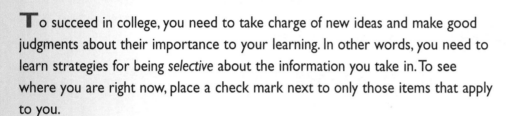

Frank Siteman/Stock, Boston

IMAGES OF COLLEGE SUCCESS

Brooke Ellison

Brooke Ellison's life took an unexpected turn as she passed the fire station walking to school on her first day in the seventh grade. A car struck her, paralyzing her from the neck down and rendering her unable to breathe. She credits the prompt response of emergency workers and police for saving her life. However, the accident left Ellison a quadriplegic.

A tragedy of this magnitude would prompt many people to throw in the towel, but Ellison claims that the accident inspired a deeper faith: "My situation has given me a different perspective on life. I see things with different eyes. I see the value in things that are sometimes overlooked by other people—having family and friends, being able to appreciate a beautiful, sunny day. These are things I came so close to losing" (Gewertz, 2000).

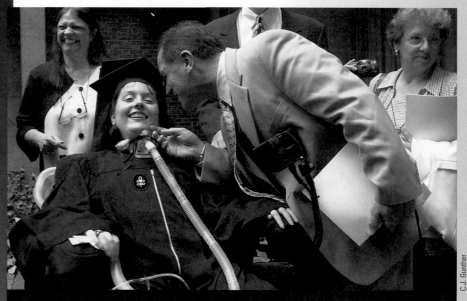

Congratulated here by her father, Brooke Ellison graduates from Harvard with a degree in cognitive neuroscience. Her mother (left) helped her overcome tremendous physical obstacles in reaching her academic goals.

When Ellison gained entry into Harvard, the challenges of college life for a student with such substantial physical limitations were daunting. Ellison's mother moved into her dorm at Harvard to help her with everything from her health care needs to turning pages.

Ellison graduated from Harvard with a degree in cognitive neuroscience. She is drawn to research on regenerating spinal tissue, because she is optimistic about her prospects for recovery. Her own studies on resilience suggest that people can learn how to be hopeful in the face of extraordinary obstacles to success.

Learn more about Brooke Ellison.

M otivate yourself by adopting helpful strategies to select, think about, and learn new ideas that college has to offer.

Commit, Concentrate, Capture, Connect

By now you must recognize that college requires you to sift through and master an extraordinary amount of information. Extracting what you need from lectures and textbooks is no small feat, especially given the differences in learning styles that make some tasks more challenging than others.

This chapter describes a simple, easy-to-remember approach for sorting through information and making good decisions about what you want to learn—the "four C's":

- *Commit* yourself to do your best work.
- *Concentrate* to eliminate distractions and focus on the material.
- *Capture* critical information.
- *Connect* new ideas to what you already know.

This approach can help you choose the most helpful information from your classes and your reading.

T he only place you find success before work is in the dictionary.

May V. Smith
American government specialist

Take Charge of Lectures

First let's apply the four C's to getting the most from classes. Begin by knowing your motivation, and the rest will flow.

Commit to Class

Some classes will be exciting from start to finish. You'll look forward to these lectures and linger after each. It's easy to follow through on your commitment to learning when courses match your learning style or personal interest.

When the content of the class or the style of the lecturer is not a good match, making a strong commitment to attend class is even more important. This commitment involves more than just showing up, however. You commit to the work involved as well.

Before each class, get ready to learn. If you can, arrive a few minutes early and review the notes from the last class or glance over your reading assignment. Identify any areas that are difficult to understand and think about questions that could clarify them. These strategies will help you anticipate how the class will flow and what ideas will be most important.

Be on time. Well-organized instructors often use the first few minutes of class to review the previous class. This review allows you to rehearse what you've been learning. Like reviewing your notes, it also sets the stage for how the upcoming class will unfold, which will help you get organized so you can figure out what's important and what isn't.

Concentrate and Listen

Concentration is influenced by many things. For example, if you're an auditory learner or if you have a natural interest in the topic, extracting what you need from a lecture may not be hard. Other circumstances, though, will require you to take a more strategic approach to concentration.

You can do many things to minimize distractions:

1. **Sit near the front.** If you can't see or hear clearly, find a spot where you can.
2. **Reduce noise.** The instructor may not realize how noisy the room is for you, so do what you need to ensure your best hearing. Close doors and windows to reduce unwanted noise. Move away from chatty neighbors.
3. **Reduce off-task pressures.** Get the sleep you need, and eat before class to quiet a growling stomach. If a specific worry keeps bothering you, write it down separately from your notes. Promise yourself that you'll worry about it later, so you can let it go for now.
4. **Stay tuned in.** If something in the lecture distresses you—either content or delivery style—concentrate on identifying more precisely what bothers you and what you can challenge. Focus on hearing what you most likely will be tested on. Breathe deeply and use other stress-management techniques to stay in tune.
5. **Track your progress.** Keep records of how much time you spend paying attention. At the end of each class, estimate what percentage of time you were on track, then write it on the upper right-hand corner of your notes. Try to make regular improvements in your rate.

Instructors differ in their ability to lecture. Some make learning easy; others make it tough. Sometimes students react differently to the same lecturer. For example, some are enchanted by a lecturer who shares personal anecdotes; others find these examples annoying and time wasting. Develop your skills at listening so that you can compensate for any skills in speaking that the instructor may lack. See "Tame That Tough Lecture" for some pointers.

Tame That Tough Lecture

The Fast-Talking Lecturer

Enthusiastic instructors may talk too fast for you to catch what they're saying. When you're confronted with a fast talker,

- **Say "Slow down."** Most fast-talking instructors know that they talk too fast. Many appreciate getting feedback so they can adjust their pace.
- **Encourage the instructor to write down the key terms.** Seeing them written down will help you understand them. Also, while the instructor writes on the board, you may be able to catch up.
- **Focus on the major thrust, not the detail.** Fast talkers are hardest for students who attempt to take notes word for word. Concentrate on the major ideas instead.

The Bewildering Lecturer

Some instructors simply use more sophisticated language than you may be used to hearing. When your instructor is hard to understand,

- **Prepare for class carefully.** If you do the assigned readings before class, you'll already be familiar with many key terms.
- **Ask for restatements.** If you persist in asking for interpretations when instructors' language is too complex, many will simplify it to avoid losing the time it takes to reexplain.
- **Change your attitude.** Think about this kind of instructor as eloquent rather than obtuse. He or she gives you extra education for your tuition dollar. You may emerge from the class with an enriched vocabulary.

The Disorganized Lecturer

Some lecturers organize poorly. They go off on tangents or don't teach from an organized plan. If you have a chaotic instructor,

- **Look at the big picture.** Concentrate on the larger themes so you won't feel overwhelmed by disconnected details.
- **Form a study group.** Pool your resources to make sense of the teaching.
- **Impose connections.** Use note-taking strategies that will help you see the connections between the ideas. Try to organize the lecture materials to give them some structure, such as creating an outline.

The Tedious Lecturer

Instructors give boring lectures because they have lost interest in their work or don't understand classroom dynamics well. Some instructors even suffer from stage fright. If you have a boring instructor,

- **Make connections.** Breathe more life into the lecture by applying what you hear to what you already know.
- **Ask questions that encourage examples.** Stories have a natural appeal. They can arouse and sustain attention. By requesting an illustration of a key point, you may help the instructor add life to the lecture. Although this may be easiest to accomplish in small classes, you can also ask for examples in visits during office hours.
- **Show active interest in the lecture.** Maintain good eye contact, nod your head, and smile occasionally to motivate teachers to give you more.

To succeed, you need to concentrate. One way to do this is to listen actively. On average, speakers talk at about 150 words per minute, and listeners can usually process words at about 500 words per minute (Nichols, 1961). This means that even when instructors talk very fast, you should have plenty of time to understand them. Put that extra time to best use through *active listening*.

Active listeners sort through the information they hear and figure out what's most important. They connect what they hear with things that they already know. Although it's

Reprinted by permission of Vivian Scott Hixson.

hard work, active listening is an efficient way to get the most from a lecture. The next sections provide some specific strategies to build your active learning skills.

In contrast, passive listeners merely write down the instructor's words without necessarily understanding the ideas or making judgments about their importance. This approach shifts actual learning to a later time, when the ideas have already faded. Don't delay the job of understanding. Putting it off not only makes ideas harder to learn, it also takes time from preparations for the next assignment.

Capture Key Ideas

Some instructors will help you spot their main ideas by starting with a preview, outline, or map of the material that a lecture will cover. Others won't but will still expect you to grasp their organization (even when it's obscure) and recognize key ideas. What are some strategies you can use to recognize key points?

Identify Key Words and Themes Often these are ideas that the instructor repeats, highlights, illustrates with examples, or displays on a blackboard or screen. Most courses are organized around a central set of terms. Any unfamiliar term or phrase is a new idea you need to learn. Such terms often represent the specialized language of the discipline you're studying.

Recognizing broader themes may be more challenging. Sometimes your instructor will give you an overarching theme to help you organize what you're about to hear. If the instructor does not, make a point to think about what theme the details of the lecture suggest and how they relate to any themes from previous lectures. Try to keep the big picture in mind so you don't feel overwhelmed by the details.

Relate Details to the Main Point Instructors use stories, examples, or analogies to reinforce your learning of the main points. Their stories are usually intended to do more than entertain. Check to make sure you understand why the instructor chose a particular story or example.

Work on your "Sixth Sense" It seems that some students just know when an instructor is covering key ideas, especially material that's likely to be on the test. They sit, pencils poised, and wait for the instructor to get to the good stuff. Actively categorize what your instructor is saying by asking questions such as

- Is this statement central to my understanding of today's topic?
- Does this example help clarify the main ideas?
- Is this a tangent (an aside) that may not help me learn the central ideas?

Listen for Clues Pay special attention to words that signal a change of direction or special emphasis. For example, note when a concept or topic comes up more than once. Such a topic is likely to show up on an exam. Transition speech, such as "in contrast to" or "let's move on to" or even "this will be on the next exam," signals changing topics or new key points. Lists usually signify important material that is also easy to test. Instructors are most likely to test for ideas that they consider exciting, so listen for any special enthusiasm.

Save Your Energy Don't write down what you already know. Besides covering new material, lectures usually overlap some of the material in required textbooks. If you have read your assignment, you should be able to recognize when the lecture overlaps the text. Open your text and follow along, making notes in the margins where the instructor stays close to the text. Pay closer attention when what you hear sounds unfamiliar.

Connect Ideas The best listeners don't just check in with the speaker from time to time. They work at listening by using strategies to create more enduring impressions of the lecture and to escape daydreaming.

Paraphrase What You Hear If you can't translate the ideas from a lecture into your own words, you may need to do more reading or ask more questions until you are able to do so.

Relate Key Ideas to What You Already Know When you can see how the course ideas connect to other aspects of your life, including your experiences in other courses or contemporary events, the ideas will be easier to remember. For example, if you're studying in sociology how societies organize into different economic classes, think about how those ideas apply to the neighborhood where you grew up.

Look up Unknown Words Use a dictionary in class to look up words you don't know. If the instructor is moving quickly, write the word at the top of your notes and look it up right after class.

Anticipate When you guess the direction that the class will take, you can come up with examples that make ideas more compelling. You can also ask questions. No matter what form your anticipation takes, it will help you stay actively involved with the ideas in the lecture.

Take Great Lecture Notes

Successful students take good notes. The quality of their work is based on the quality of their drive. By connecting your work in lectures with your future prospects, you can find the energy to excel.

A successful note-taking style reflects not just the complexity of the course content and lecturer's style but your own learning preferences as well. If you're a visual learner, use images, arrows, or other graphic organizers to help you remember the important material more easily. Color-code parts of your notes or draw sketches. Use any strategy that will help the key ideas stand out. If you're an auditory learner, you may thrive in lectures; however, you may be tempted to take down every word. See "It's Not Dictation" for some good advice.

Good Lecture Notes ← → Strong Learning ← → Success in Courses ← → Greater Career Possibilities

FIGURE 5-1
The Cornell Method

The Cornell method separates running notes taken during class from summary phrases and an overall summary or comments added after class. To review, cover the material on the right and practice recalling it from the cues on the left.

Dr. Kong -- Psychology 21   Tues. 9-14-02

Topic: Optimism & Pessimism -- Seligman's theory

Success:

2 keys or 3?

Talent and desire, 2 keys to success. Is there a 3rd key -- "optimism"? (= expecting to succeed)? The real test = how you react when something bad happens. Give up or fight on?

Lab studies on learning/unlearning helplessness

Psych lab experiments can teach dogs to be helpless. If dog is trained to think it has no control over when it will get shocked, it starts acting helpless even when it could jump away & not get shocked. Same type thing happens to people in childhood. If they don't think they can change things, they act helpless: pessimistic. But you can also train a dog out of being helpless. All depends on expecting to be or not be in control.

How optimists vs. pessimists explain bad events.

Pessimist:

"P P P"

1. Personal -- "Bad things are my fault."
2. Permanent -- "Can't get better."
3. Pervasive -- "Affects everything I do."

Optimist:

1. Impersonal -- "Bad things not my fault."
2. Momentary -- "Can change tomorrow."
3. Particular -- "Doesn't affect the rest of me."

Pessimism → depression

Everyone can get depressed, but pessimists stay depressed longer. Why? Because of how they explain things.

Therapy = Change explanations

Cognitive therapy: Change the way pessimist explains things to cure their depression. How? First get them to hear what they tell themselves when things go bad. Then get them to change what they say.

Seligman found that desire and talent don't always win. Optimism also important. Pessimists can become "helpless" in hard times. Optimists recover faster. Training pessimists to think more optimistically might reduce depression.

Q: But how does it work? Find out Thursday!

Five Good Formats for Taking Notes

Once you get beyond the idea of taking notes verbatim, you have numerous good options. Choose one that suits your learning needs. Here are several popular note-taking methods.

The Cornell System Draw a vertical line down your looseleaf or notebook page about 2½ inches from the left edge of the page (Figure 5-1). Draw a horizontal line across the page about 2 inches from the bottom. Use the largest area on the right side of the page to take your notes during class. After class is over, use the blank left side of the page to write short headings or questions for each part of your notes. Use the bottom of the page for a summary or other comments and questions.

The Cornell system creates a great tool for reviewing. Cover up the right-hand portion of the page and use the phrases or questions on the left side as prompts. As you read each prompt, practice recalling the details on the right.

Outlining An outline summarizes key points and subpoints (see Figure 5-2). The summary of headings at the outset of each chapter of this book is also an outline. When you use an outline form, the results are neat and well-organized. Naturally, outlines are easiest to create when the lecture itself is well-organized. Some outliners don't use numbers and letters because the task is too distracting. They simply use indentations to signify subpoints.

STAYING OUT OF THE PITS

It's Not Dictation

The worst strategy students can adopt when taking lecture notes is trying to get down every word the instructor says. They become *transcribers*, trying to reproduce the lecture word for word. This approach to note taking pays off for secretaries but not for students.

Recall the time advantage that the listener has in processing information. You can usually think and listen more than three times faster than a speaker can talk. Transcribers do well if they can get down 80 to 90 words a minute using shorthand. On the other hand, students who transcribe instructor's words without using shorthand may write at less than 20 words per minute (Kierwa, 1987). By concentrating on capturing individual words, they get only a portion of the message and certainly miss the big picture.

FIGURE 5-2
Take It In

This format provides a logical treatment that makes good use of readings.

Chapter 5
Target Information

I. Commit, Concentrate, Capture, Connect
    A. Identifying what you need is hard work
        1. from lecture
        2. from text
    B. 4-part approach can help make good decisions

II. Take Charge of Lectures
    A. Commit to the course
        1. Not hard to commit when interest is high
        2. When not a good match . . .
            a. Be present
            b. Be ready
            c. Be punctual

    B. Concentrate
        1. Overcome distractions
            a. Sit near front
            b. Reduce noise
            c. Reduce off-task pressures
            d. Stay tuned in
            e. Track your progress
        2. Adapt to Teaching Styles
            a. To cope with fast talkers
                (1) Tell them "Slow down"
                (2) Ask them to write down key words
                (3) Focus on key ideas
            b. To cope with bewildering lecturers . . .

Summary Method In this approach, you monitor the lecture for critical ideas and pause at intervals to summarize what you think is most important. Writing summaries may be somewhat time-consuming, but it helps you take responsibility for judging what is crucial and relating that to other aspects of the course. It's also an effective way to handle a disorganized lecturer.

Concept Maps A concept map provides visual cues about how ideas are related (see Figure 5-3). You can try mapping for both organized or disorganized lectures. It may work or it may get too messy. Some students construct concept maps after class from lecture notes as a way to review the material.

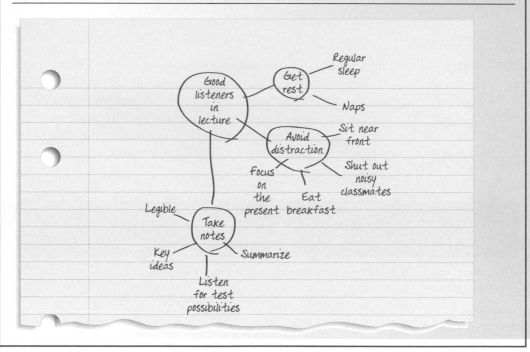

FIGURE 5-3
The Concept Map

A concept map is a helpful tool for visual learners. It displays the key ideas in a lecture or resource and shows how the ideas relate to each other.

Fishbone Diagram Some students use a conceptual map called a fishbone diagram (see Figure 5-4). This method is used by business managers to explore how problems have developed (Ishikawa, 1986). First, the problem or outcome is identified and printed in the head of the fish. Then primary factors are identified and connected like ribs to the backbone of the "fish." Finally, each rib is elaborated with spurs showing more detail. The method is often used by groups because individual contributions are easy to insert into the diagram. It can also be used for individual note-taking or reviewing.

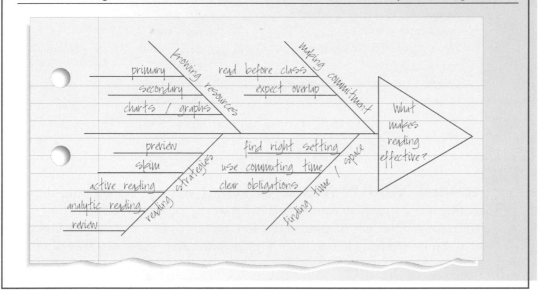

FIGURE 5-4
The Fishbone Diagram

A fishbone diagram is a helpful note-taking format to address cause-effect relationships or to use when working in a group. Write the problem or topic in the fish's head and identify the main factors as the large bones in the fish skeleton. Elaborate each factor to complete the diagram.

Finer Points on Taking Notes

You'll learn a great deal by taking careful notes. Whichever format you choose, combine it with the following strategies:

Identify the Session Clearly Be sure to include the topic or title of the lecture, if any, along with its date. This makes it easier for you to track down specific information when it's time to review.

Take Notes from All Relevant Input Some students believe that only the instructor's input is worth recording. However, the instructor may treat any class material as fair game for testing, even when it's introduced by other students. Remember to summarize the relevant details from videos or films that are shown in class.

Don't Erase Mistakes Erasing takes more time than drawing a line through an error. Drawing a line also lets you restore the information later if you need it.

Use Abbreviations You can use standard abbreviations to record information quickly. Figure 5-5 shows some common abbreviations. You can also develop your own abbreviations for words that you need to write often. For example, you can abbreviate academic disciplines, such as *PSY, BIO, EN,* and *LIT*. When terms are used regularly throughout the course, develop abbreviations for them as well. For example, *EV* might stand for *evolution* or *A/R* for *accounts receivable*. When you use personalized abbreviations, write their meanings inside the cover of your notebook as a handy reference.

FIGURE 5-5
Common Abbreviations for Notes

Using your own abbreviations or the standard abbreviations in this list will save you time when you take notes.

i.e.	= that is (to clarify by restating a point)	→	= leads to
e.g.	= for example (to clarify by adding a typical case)	<	= less than
		>	= more than
vs.	= versus (to identify a contrasting point)	k	= $1,000 (as in 10 k for 10 thousand; k = kilo)
∴	= therefore (to come to a conclusion)	~	= approximately
∵	= because	??	= I'm confused
w/	= with	*	= important, testable
w/o	= without	@	= at

Review Your Notes Often Have you ever waited until the night before a test to review your notes? Did it work? Perhaps you found that it pays to make regular use of your notes. Review your notes right after class if you can. Some students like to rewrite their notes after class as a way of consolidating information. If you don't rewrite, at least reread your notes to add whatever might be missing. You may also want to highlight certain phrases, identify the key points, or revise notes that are unclear.

Review your notes between classes to consolidate your learning. Some students review notes from the previous class just before the next meeting of the course as a way to get back into the subject.

Tape Lectures Selectively Some students like to tape lectures as a backup for the notes, but it isn't always a good idea. Tape the lecture only if you

- Need the complete text of a lecture, as when the content is extremely difficult or tricky
- Have a learning disability that hinders listening carefully or accurately
- Have a plan for how to listen regularly to the tapes
- Take advantage of commuting time to listen
- Must be absent but can get a classmate to tape for you

Without a plan or special need to justify taping, you will end up with a pile of cassettes that you never listen to. You may also not listen as carefully as you might the first time but still not use the tape.

Organize Your Materials for Easy Retrieval A separate notebook or compartment in a binder for each subject can improve your efficiency. Three-ring binders allow you to rearrange and add pages. Write on only one side of the page to make your notes easy to arrange and review later. Some students, especially tactile learners, use index cards because they're easy to carry, organize, and review.

Request Feedback about Your Notes Especially in classes where you struggle with note taking, see your instructor during office hours and ask for help. Ask whether you are capturing the main ideas in your notes; if not, discuss ways to improve your note taking.

Auditing Your Note-Taking Style for Lectures

	Always	Sometimes	Never
I approach listening as an active learner.	_____	_____	_____
I select note-taking formats to suit the various courses I take.	_____	_____	_____
I organize my notes in one place.	_____	_____	_____
I label the lecture with title and date.	_____	_____	_____
I take notes from all participants in class.	_____	_____	_____
I concentrate during class.	_____	_____	_____
I work to build my vocabulary.	_____	_____	_____
I strike errors instead of erasing them.	_____	_____	_____
I try not to write dense notes. I leave space for adding more notes later.	_____	_____	_____
I listen for directional cues or emphases.	_____	_____	_____
I avoid shutting down when I have a negative reaction to what I hear.	_____	_____	_____
I highlight key ideas or themes.	_____	_____	_____
I use abbreviations to save time.	_____	_____	_____
I personalize my notes.	_____	_____	_____
I review my notes after class.	_____	_____	_____
I pay attention to the quality of my note-taking process as I go.	_____	_____	_____
I would consider asking the instructor for help in constructing better notes.	_____	_____	_____

Results: *Look at the pattern of the responses that you made on this assessment. Your best note-taking strategies are reflected in checks in the* Always *column on the left. If the majority of your checks fall in the* Always *column, you are establishing a good foundation for study with your note-taking practices. Now look at the items marked* Never. *What would it take for you to add each of these items to your note-taking toolbox?*

Evaluate Your Note-Taking Strategy When a test is returned, examine the structure of your notes to see what accounted for your success. Continue to practice the strategies that served you well. Modify practices that may have made it hard for you to learn or test well. You can also audit your own style of listening by completing Self-Assessment 5-1. The results will show where you can improve.

Take Charge of Your Reading

The four C's—Commit, Concentrate, Capture, and Connect—work as well for reading as for note taking. A systematic approach to reading will allow you to achieve your reading goals and make your learning efficient.

Commit to Reading Goals

Some students assume that reading assignments aren't all that important because they think the instructor will cover the material in class. This is not a wise assumption. Many instructors assign reading as a related but independent resource; they do not review the readings. Successful students complete assigned readings *before* class to prepare to understand the lecture. Connections and overlaps between the lecture and reading reinforce their learning. Another reason to complete reading assignments is that you may be called on to report your impressions of the reading. It's embarrassing when you haven't got a clue what to say.

Plan Time and Space to Concentrate

College reading takes concentration. Schedule blocks of time for reading in a place where you won't be interrupted. On your main schedule, set aside times for study. Clear other concerns from your mind so you can concentrate.

Students differ about where they prefer to read. Many like the library. Others find it *too* quiet or too full of distracting people. You may want to try out a few settings to find out which work best for you.

If you can spend only a little time on campus, you may face particular challenges in securing quiet space and uninterrupted time. Some commuters on public transportation can read and review while they travel. If you're stuck with reading an assignment in a noisy environment, you may want to wear headphones with familiar instrumental music just loud enough to block distractions. If you have a long drive to school, you can listen to taped classes.

If you have to combine reading with child care,

- Plan to read during nap times, after the children have gone to bed, or before they get up.

Francis Hogan/Electronic Publishing Services Inc. NYC

If you have to read in distracting environments, minimize the distraction. For example, on a crowded bus you might want to read while listening to music played at a low level on headphones.

- Set a timer for 15 minutes and provide activities that your children can do at the table with you. Let them know that at the end of 15 minutes—when the timer goes off—everyone will take a play break.
- Find other students with similar child-care needs. Pool your resources to hire a regular baby-sitter or trade baby-sitting services to free up more time for reading.

Capture and Connect

How you read will depend on your interest level, the complexity of the material, the time you have to do the reading, and your reading skill. If you're very interested in a topic and already know something about it, you may not need disciplined strategies to comprehend the reading. Just dive in and take notes.

But what if the reading is unfamiliar and difficult? Read both selectively and systematically. Your system will probably include some of the following types of reading: preview, skimming, active reading, analytic reading, and review (see Figure 5-6). "Reading Strategies for Different Situations" recommends some combinations for different reading tasks.

ON-TARGET TIPS

Reading Strategies for Different Situations

- When you want to develop understanding of the ideas:
  Preview → Active reading → Review
- When you want to practice critical thinking about your reading: Preview → Analytic reading → Review
- When you have trouble retaining what you read:
  Preview → Skim → Active reading → Review → Review
- When you don't have time to read for mastery: Skim → Review (pay close attention to summaries and boldface terms)

FIGURE 5-6
Elements of Your Reading Plan

Approaching your reading assignments strategically means adopting different reading strategies. The type of reading you choose depends on your available time, the complexity of the material, and your motivation to master the ideas. As you go from top to bottom of the pyramid, the intensity of your effort increases: You become more involved with the material, and the reading task becomes more demanding. The consequences of your review may return you to the reading to skim, read actively, or read analytically.

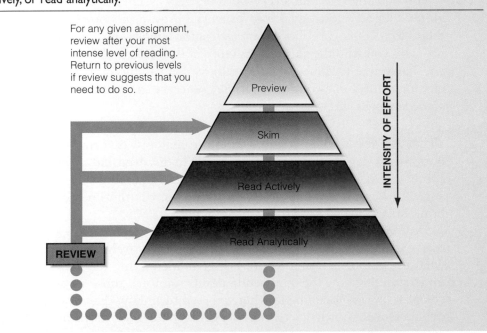

For any given assignment, review after your most intense level of reading. Return to previous levels if review suggests that you need to do so.

INTENSITY OF EFFORT

Preview

Skim

Read Actively

Read Analytically

REVIEW

Preview Dave, an education major, always previews his reading assignment no matter what the subject. Previewing helps him estimate how intense his effort will need to be and how much time it will take to complete the assignment. During the preview, Dave looks at

- **The context for the assignment.** To see how the assignment fits into the course, Dave thinks about the class activities that have led up to the assignment.
- **The length of the reading.** By applying his reading speed to the number of pages in the assignment, Dave can estimate how long he will need to devote to the job.
- **The structure and features of the reading.** A good time to take a reading break is at the end of a section. Knowing a text's structure can help Dave plan well. Textbook features such as summaries can help him rehearse his learning.
- **The difficulty of the reading.** Higher-level material may require more than one reading.

Skimming Whereas previewing helps you size up the reading, skimming covers the content at a general level. When you skim, you read at about twice your average rate. Focus on introductory statements, topic sentences (usually the first sentence in the paragraph), and boldface terms. Slow down to examine summaries carefully.

Karen, a management major, likes to skim a text before she settles down to read more intensely. Skimming gives her a sense of the kind of information her assignment contains. She recognizes that the concepts in many of her courses overlap. By skimming the material, she can see where the assignment contains new ideas that she'll have to read more carefully.

Markie, a full-time communications major with a half-time job, doesn't always have the time to read her assignments as thoroughly as she should. Rather than abandoning her reading, she skims some assignments. She usually reserves the strategy for easier courses so she can concentrate more intensely on her tougher courses.

You don't need to read every word of every assignment (Frank, 1996). Your ability to read selectively improves as you grow accustomed to how readings relate to a course and how your instructor chooses test material. Skimming provides you with the surface structure of the ideas in the text when that is all you have time for. Successful skimmers can usually participate in class discussions with some confidence if they rehearse the main ideas and have read some key passages.

Active Reading Takima, a music major, was distressed to reach the bottom of a page of her science book only to discover that no information had come across. You've probably experienced something similar. It's easy to engage in empty reading. Your eyes track across the lines of text but your brain fails to register anything meaningful.

One way to prevent the wasted time of empty reading or to avoid having to read the same material again is to read texts *actively*. Immerse yourself in what the author is trying to say. Focus on identifying the main ideas and on understanding how the supporting points reinforce those ideas. Also work at constructing the meaning in what you read by linking the information to your own personal knowledge or experience. Use these questions as guidelines for active reading:

Some books are to be tasted, others to be swallowed, and some few to be chewed and digested.

Francis Bacon
*16th-century English statesman
and philosopher*

- Have I ever experienced anything similar to what is described in the reading?
- How does this relate to things I already know?
- How might this be useful for me to know?
- Do I like or agree with these ideas?
- How does the reading relate to current events?

Active readers form as many links as possible between their personal experience and knowledge and what they're reading.

Analytic Reading Joshua, majoring in pre-med, likes to read his assignments intensely. Like other analytic readers, he likes to break ideas open or dig underneath their surface. He tries to spot flaws in the writer's logic and identifies which elements are clear and which are confusing. He compares the quality of the work to that of other works he has read. He examines whether the materials are persuasive enough to change his own viewpoint. Good analytic readers question both the author and themselves as they dig their way through a reading. The following questions may help you become an analytic reader:

- What are the author's background and values? Do these influence the writing? How?
- Does the author's bias taint the truthfulness of what I'm reading?
- What implicit (unstated) assumptions does the author make?
- Do I believe the evidence?
- Is the author's position valid?
- Are the arguments logically developed?
- What predictions follow from the argument?
- What are the strengths and weaknesses of the argument?
- Is anything missing from the position?
- What questions would I want to ask the author?
- Is there a different way to look at the facts or ideas?
- Would these ideas apply to all people in all cultures or in all situations?

Review An anthropology major, Sanjay likes to review his reading assignments to help consolidate his learning. He reviews his notes immediately after class and before he begins his next reading assignment. Reviewing the assignment makes the main points stand out and makes them easier to remember.

Think of reviewing as an opportunity to test yourself on your own comprehension. Question yourself on details or write out summaries of what you've read.

The quality of your notes can make all the difference when it's time to study for a test. With well-constructed notes that you have reviewed systematically after your classes, your final review should be a breeze.

Primary and Secondary Sources

There are two general types of readings for courses: primary sources and secondary sources. A *primary source* is material written in some original form. Autobiographies, speeches, research reports, scholarly articles, government documents, and historical journal articles all might be viewed as primary source readings. For example, you may read the U.S. Constitution as a primary source in your political science class.

> **R**eading a book is like re-writing it for yourself. You bring to a novel, anything you read, all your experience of the world. You bring your history and you read it in your own terms.
>
> Angela Carter
> *20th-century British writer and educator*

Flip Chalfont/The Image Bank

Effective note-taking involves material not only from lectures but also from your readings.

Secondary sources summarize or interpret primary sources. A magazine article that discussed politicians' interpretations of the Constitution would generally be considered a secondary source. Textbooks are secondary sources that try to give a comprehensive view of information from numerous primary works.

You have many more opportunities to read primary sources in college than you did in high school. Most people find reading original works exhilarating. For example, reading a speech by Frederick Douglass about the abolition of slavery will likely stimulate you more than reading interpretations of his speeches. However, primary sources are usually more difficult to read than secondary sources. Original works must be chewed and digested.

Interpreting original ideas yourself is also more challenging than accepting others' interpretations. When reading primary sources, learn as much as you can about the intentions of the authors and the historical context in which they were writing. Understanding a historical period will help you interpret texts written at that time.

Master Reading in Different Disciplines

As you've already discovered, some readings are harder than others for you. Obviously, you'll learn material more easily than not if it matches an area in which you have special interests and intellectual strengths. However, liberal arts programs almost always require reading about topics that don't come naturally. In some readings, technical terms may slow you down. Other readings may require more imagination.

Let's explore some tips that will help you read in areas that are challenging for you.

Literature In literature courses you study poetry, novels, plays, and short stories. Appreciation of these forms comes most easily to people who enjoy reflective learning and who like to think critically. For them, many great works provide delight. But what strategies can help you when reading literature is challenging?

- **Use your imagination.** Try to visualize the action. Participate at the level the author intended: Use as many senses as the author used—taste, smell, sound—as you recreate the author's world in your imagination.
- **Look for connections.** Are any of the experiences like your own? Do the characters remind you of anyone you know?
- **Make the author real.** Search the Internet for a good biography or personal details about the author that might help you understand the author's motivation to create the work.
- **Make a chart.** If the reading is complex, make a list of key figures as they are introduced so you can easily review as the story progresses.

- **Predict what will happen.** Once you understand the direction the work is taking, see if you can anticipate what happens next.
- **Read aloud.** Some great works are savored best when read aloud. Find a study partner and share the task.

History

Some students love history because they believe that we are all the walking expression of history. History texts provide a great opportunity to use your imagination and will come alive if you let it. Good readers in history put conscientious effort into seeing how events, places, and people are interconnected.

- **Put yourself in the picture.** As you read about events, think about how you might have reacted to them at the time.
- **Change history.** Try to predict an alternative course of history by changing a critical event or two. How might the ripple effects have changed some element of your life?
- **Imagine or draw the timeline.** Try to articulate a casual link from one event to the next over time.
- **Make it into a movie.** Imagine a cast of stars taking the roles of the historical figures you're reading about. It may help you visualize the action better.

Natural and Social Science

The sciences can be especially challenging because of the level of abstraction in some scientific writing. The terminology presented in the sciences represents a kind of shorthand that allows scientists to communicate with each other. Learning these terms can be a challenge without some helpful strategies.

- **Keep a running glossary of terms.** Treat the sciences like a foreign language. Each new term stands for a concept. Study the meaning of each.
- **Accept the role of numbers.** If you aren't comfortable with numbers, you may be turned off by the practice of measurement and statistics that pervade most sciences. When numbers accompany text, spend extra time understanding their significance.
- **Think practically.** See if you can come up with a practical application of the scientific relationships you're reading about.
- **Look for links in the news.** The sciences regularly issue progress reports that may enhance your understanding or clarify concepts.
- **Cruise the Internet.** Chances are good that the Internet will provide ideas that will help you with the terms. You may also find information about the scientists themselves that will help make the enterprise feel more real to you.
- **Look for overlaps.** Where does your life intersect with the scientific ideas you're trying to learn?

"All very well and good—but now we come to chart B."

© Gahan Wilson.

What's Your Reader Profile?

Check the alternative that best describes you as a reader.

1. When I have an assignment to read,
   _____ a. I'm usually enthusiastic about what I'll learn.
   _____ b. I like to wait to see whether what I have read will be valuable.
   _____ c. I'm generally apprehensive about reading assignments because I'm afraid I won't understand them.

2. What is my attitude toward the authors of my college books?
   _____ a. I think of them as human beings with an interesting story to tell.
   _____ b. I haven't really given the writers much thought.
   _____ c. I think of them as people who will probably talk over my head.

3. When I plan my reading,
   _____ a. I think about how the assignment fits in with the objectives of the course.
   _____ b. I review the prior assignment to set the stage for current work.
   _____ c. I plunge in so I can get it done.

4. I take breaks
   _____ a. To consolidate the information I read.
   _____ b. To help me study longer and more productively.
   _____ c. Whenever I lose interest in my reading.

5. When I don't know a word,
   _____ a. I look it up, write it down, and practice it.
   _____ b. I try to figure it out from the context of the sentence.
   _____ c. I usually skip over it and hope it won't make too much difference in the meaning.

6. When I can't understand a sentence,
   _____ a. I reread the sentence more carefully.
   _____ b. I try to figure out the sentence from the context of the paragraph.
   _____ c. I skip the sentence, hoping it will make sense later.

7. When the whole assignment confuses me,
   _____ a. I try to find more materials that will shed some light on my confusion.
   _____ b. I ask the instructor or someone else for ideas about how to cope with the assignment.
   _____ c. I tend to give up on it.

8. When I read,
   _____ a. I try to read as fast as I can while still understanding the meaning.
   _____ b. I try to sweep as many words as I can at a glance.
   _____ c. I take it one word at a time—speed doesn't matter to me.

Results: Alternatives "a" and "b" of each question indicate successful reading habits. Revisit any "c" alternatives that you marked. Think about possible causes of these less-successful patterns. You may benefit from a visit with a reading specialist on campus who can help you figure out how to make As and Bs by practicing more "a"s and "b"s.

Finer Points on Reading

Use Self-Assessment 5-2 to see your current reading profile. Then consider these additional strategies for improving your reading skills.

- **Stay positive.** Keep a positive attitude. Others have succeeded before you. If they could manage, so can you. If you approach your reading with a feeling of defeat, you may give up instead of pulling through.
- **Make the author your companion.** Most authors envision themselves talking to their readers as they write. As you read, imagine talking to the author as a way of making your reading more lively. When you approach the reading as one end of a conversation, it may be easier to make comments, to see relationships, and to be critical.

- **Pace yourself according to difficulty level.** When you're naturally drawn to a reading or it fits in well with your abilities or interests, you may not have to struggle to get the key ideas. However, you may need to read some difficult writing three or four times before it begins to make sense. We all struggle with hard material—that's normal.

- **Take breaks.** Plan to take breaks at regular intervals throughout a reading session. How long you can read between breaks depends on how hard you have to work to grasp the ideas. Examine the material to see whether there are natural breaks, such as the ends of sections, that correspond to your attention span.

    Reward yourself when you've completed each reading goal. Go for a walk, visit briefly with someone, or do some pleasure reading. When you have two or more kinds of reading to complete, do the harder or duller one first, while your concentration is stronger.

- **Shift gears when you do not make progress.** A fresh start may be required if you find yourself reading and rereading the same passage. Try writing a note on the reading. Take a break. Get something to drink. Call a classmate to confer about your struggle. Return to the passage with an intention to read more slowly until the clouds part.

- **Read other sources if the reading is confusing.** Sometimes an author's style is hard to comprehend. For nonfiction, find a clearer book on the same topic at the library or bookstore. Make sure that it covers things similar to your assigned text. Browsing the Internet may be helpful as well.

    Some bookstores sell guides to certain disciplines that may help to clarify basic ideas. Keep your introductory textbooks as references for when you are challenged in later, tougher courses. Get help from an instructor or tutor in finding other sources.

- **Build your vocabulary.** College is a great place to expand your vocabulary. In the process of learning the specialized languages in a discipline, you'll also expand your general vocabulary. Get a dictionary and use it often for words you don't know. Once you look up a word, practice using the word to help you remember it. On an index card, keep a list of new words and their meanings. Use it as a bookmark.

    If you don't have a dictionary nearby when you need it, you may be able to use "word attack" skills to understand a word. That is, you can often divide a word into parts that give you hints about the meaning. Knowing common prefixes and suffixes can help (see Figure 5-7). You also may be able to figure out the meaning of the word from the rest of the sentence.

- **Work on reading faster.** Fast readers tend to be more effective learners than slow readers are, not only because they remember more of what they read but also because they save valuable time (Armstrong & Lampe, 1990). Learn your reading speed by completing Self-Assessment 5-3.

    You can improve your reading speed by concentrating on processing more words with each sweep of your eye across a line of text. For example, if you normally scan three words at a time, practice taking in four words with each scan or scan to read whole phrases instead of individual words. You can also ask to have your reading abilities tested formally by reading specialists at the college. They can help you identify specific problems and solutions.

How Fast Do You Read?

Select a text from one of your courses. Set a timer for five minutes and start reading. When the timer goes off, stop reading. Count the number of lines you read in the five-minute period. Pick several lines at random in the text and count the number of words in the lines. Multiply the number of lines you read by the average number of words per line. This will give you an approximation of the total of words you read in the five-minute period. Finally, divide by five to produce your reading speed in words per minute.

Content area: _____

Date of assessment: _____

Number of lines read: _____

$\times$ Number of words per line: _____

$=$ Approximate total words   _____

Divided by 5 (minutes)   _____

Approximate words per minute   _____

How does your reading speed compare with these average speeds for different kinds of reading (Skinner, 1997)?

Skimming	800 words per minute
Active reading	100–200 words per minute
Analytic reading	Under 100 words per minute

Results: *use this estimate as a baseline for your reading speed. If the material was well suited to your interest areas, you were probably able to read within the range for effective active reading. If the material was very familiar, your rate was probably higher, approaching the rates found in skimming. If your reading rate was below 100 words per minute, this may be a cause for concern. Although that reading rate is acceptable for complex materials, a slower reading rate on routine materials predicts that you may have difficulty keeping up with your reading assignments. Consider going for a more thorough evaluation of your reading strengths and weaknesses at the campus study skill center. Professional assistance can pinpoint the problem and make your future reading strategies much more successful.*

FIGURE 5-7
Word Attack Skills

Prefixes (word beginnings) and suffixes (word endings) provide clues about word meanings. Here are some common examples from Latin and Greek.

Prefixes	Meaning	Example
a, ab	without or not	*a*theist: nonbeliever in God
ad	to	*ad*vocate: to speak for
ambi	both	*ambi*valent: uncommitted
con	together	*con*vention: formal gathering
de	from or down	*de*spicable: abhorrent
dis	not	*dis*interest: boredom
ex	over	*ex*aggerate: to magnify
hyper	above	*hyper*active: overactive
hypo	under	*hypo*dermic: under skin
mono	single	*mono*lingual: speaking one language
non	not	*non*responsive: not reacting
pro	forward	*pro*duction: process of making
re	back, again	*re*vert: return to former state
sub, sup	under	*sub*ordinate: in a lower position
trans	across	*trans*pose: to change places

Suffixes	Meaning	Example
-able, -ible (adjective)	capable of	respons*ible*: in charge
-ac, -al, -il (adjective)	pertaining to	natur*al*: related to nature
-ance, -ence (noun)	state or status	dalli*ance*: playful activity
-ant, -ent (noun)	one who does	serv*ant*: person who waits on others
-er, -or (noun)	one who does	contract*or*: one who builds
-ive (adjective)	state or status	fest*ive*: partylike
-ish (adjective)	quality of	fool*ish*: like a fool
-less (adjective)	without	heart*less*: harsh, unfeeling
-ly (adjective/adverb)	like	miser*ly*: like a miser
-ness (noun)	state of	peaceful*ness*: state of peace

One bad habit that many students fall into is *subvocalizing,* or concentrating on sounding out words as they read. Some students actually mouth words as they read, which is quite inefficient. However, others subvocalize with their mouths closed. The problem with subvocalizing is that it dramatically slows down your reading because it limits your reading speed to how fast you talk. Concentrating on reading phrases or passages is much more efficient. Your reward for "keeping your mouth closed" is faster reading with more time to spare.

■ **Set goals.** Plan how much to read. Make commitments that will help you feel more responsible for what you've read. Join a study group or promise to tutor another student who needs help. Some students negotiate with their instructors about how they can contribute to class on a given day. This strategy is especially helpful for shy students.

Mark or Take Notes from Readings

Just as there are several ways to take notes from lecture, there are several ways to boil down readings. In general, of course, your goal should be to capture the main ideas and show how secondary information connects and supports them.

Choose a Good Method

There are three general strategies for taking reading notes. The first two are for books you own. The third involves creating an external set of notes.

Highlight Text Using a highlighter helps many students concentrate as they read and makes it easier for them to review for tests. Ideally, you should highlight topic sentences, key words, and conclusions, which usually make up much less than one-quarter of a text.

Although this strategy may keep you engaged with the reading, it presents several hazards. You may highlight too much material so that you are faced with rereading nearly the entire text when you review. Also, simply highlighting does not show why you highlighted a passage. And when it's time to review, you still need to carry the complete text with you. Finally, if you sell your text after the course is over, the highlighting may reduce its value.

Personalize Text Some students find that they can absorb a text more easily by drawing symbols and writing summary notes in the margins. To make your learning more vivid, you can draw arrows or thumbs-down signs when you disagree, and circle key terms. Of course, this also may reduce the book's resale value.

Finer Points on Notes

- **Write your notes in your own words.** Translating an author's words into your own increases the personal connections you make to the material and makes it easier to remember. It also helps you avoid plagiarism when you use the notes to write a paper. When you literally lift the words of an author from a text and later present these words as your own, you are stealing the thoughts and expressions of another. Instructors may view this as laziness or deceit and may penalize you. See Figures 5-8 and 5-9 for an example of good note-taking.
- **Avoid writing things down that you don't understand.** You simply won't understand some ideas on first reading. You may feel tempted to write down unclear ideas with the intention of returning to them later. Don't. Instead, mark the passage with a question and do what you can to clarify it before you record it and move on.
- **Think and record in pictures.** Try to turn information from the text into some other form, such as a list, table, graph, or picture, to make it easier for you to recall. Diagrams and tables can also be tools for summarizing.

FIGURE 5-8
Highlighted Notes

Minorities and Stardom
Stark, R. (1994). Sociology. 5th Edition

NBA = African-American?

The majority of players on every team in the National Basketball Association are African-American. White boxing champions are rare. A far greater proportion of professional football players are African-American than would be expected based on the size of the African-American population. Furthermore, African-Americans began to excel in sports long before the Civil Rights Movement broke down barriers excluding them from many other occupations. This has led many people, both African-American and white, to conclude that African-Americans are born with a natural talent for athletics. How else could they have come to dominate the ranks of superstars?

main question →

The trouble with this biological explanation of African-Americans in sports is that it ignores an obvious historical fact: It is typical for minorities in North America to make their first substantial progress in sports (and, for similar reasons, in entertainment). Who today would suggest that Jews have a biological advantage in athletics? Yet at the turn of the century, the number of Jews who excelled in sports far exceeded their proportion in the population. And late in the nineteenth century, the Irish dominated sports to almost the same extent as African-Americans have done in recent decades.

example: Jews showed same pattern 19th cent.

By examining an encyclopedia of boxing, for example, we can draw accurate conclusions about patterns of immigration and periods at which ethnic groups were on the bottom of the stratification system. The (Irish) domination of boxing in the latter half of the nineteenth century is obvious from the names of heavyweight champions, beginning with bareknuckle champ Ned O'Baldwin in 1867 and including Mike McCoole in 1869, Paddy Ryan in 1880,

John L. Sullivan in 1889, and Jim Corbett in 1892. The list of champions in lower-weight divisions during the same era is dominated by fighters named Ryan, Murphy, Delaney, Lynch, O'Brien, and McCoy.

Early in the twentieth century, Irish names became much less common among boxing champions, even though many fighters who were not Irish took Irish ring names. Suddenly, champions had names like Battling Levinsky, Maxie Rosenbloom, Benny Leonard, Abe Goldstein, Kid Kaplan, and Izzy Schwartz. This was the Jewish era in boxing.

Then (Jewish) names dropped out of the lists, and (Italian) and eastern European names came to the fore: Canzoneri, Battalino, LaMotta, Graziano, and Basilio; Yarosz, Lesnevich, Zale, Risko, Hostak, and Servo. By the 1940s fighters were disproportionately African-American. Today, (African-American) domination of boxing has already peaked, and Hispanic names have begun to prevail.

history of boxing:
Irish ↓ Jews ↓ Italians ↓ Af. Am.

The current overrepresentation of African-Americans in sports reflects two things: first, a *lack of other avenues to wealth and fame*, and second, the fact that minority groups can overcome discrimination most easily in occupations where the *quality of individual performance is most easily and accurately assessed* (Blalock, 1967). These same factors led to the overrepresentation of other ethnic groups in sports earlier in history.

1.
2. } *key ideas*

It is often difficult to know which applicants to a law school or a pilot training school are the most capable. But we can see who can box or hit a baseball. The demonstration of talent, especially in sports and entertainment, tends to break down barriers of discrimination. As these fall, opportunities in these areas for wealth and fame open up, while other opportunities remain closed. Thus, minority groups will aspire to those areas in which the opportunities are open and will tend to overachieve in these areas.

this is why

FIGURE 5-9
Cornell Notes on Reading

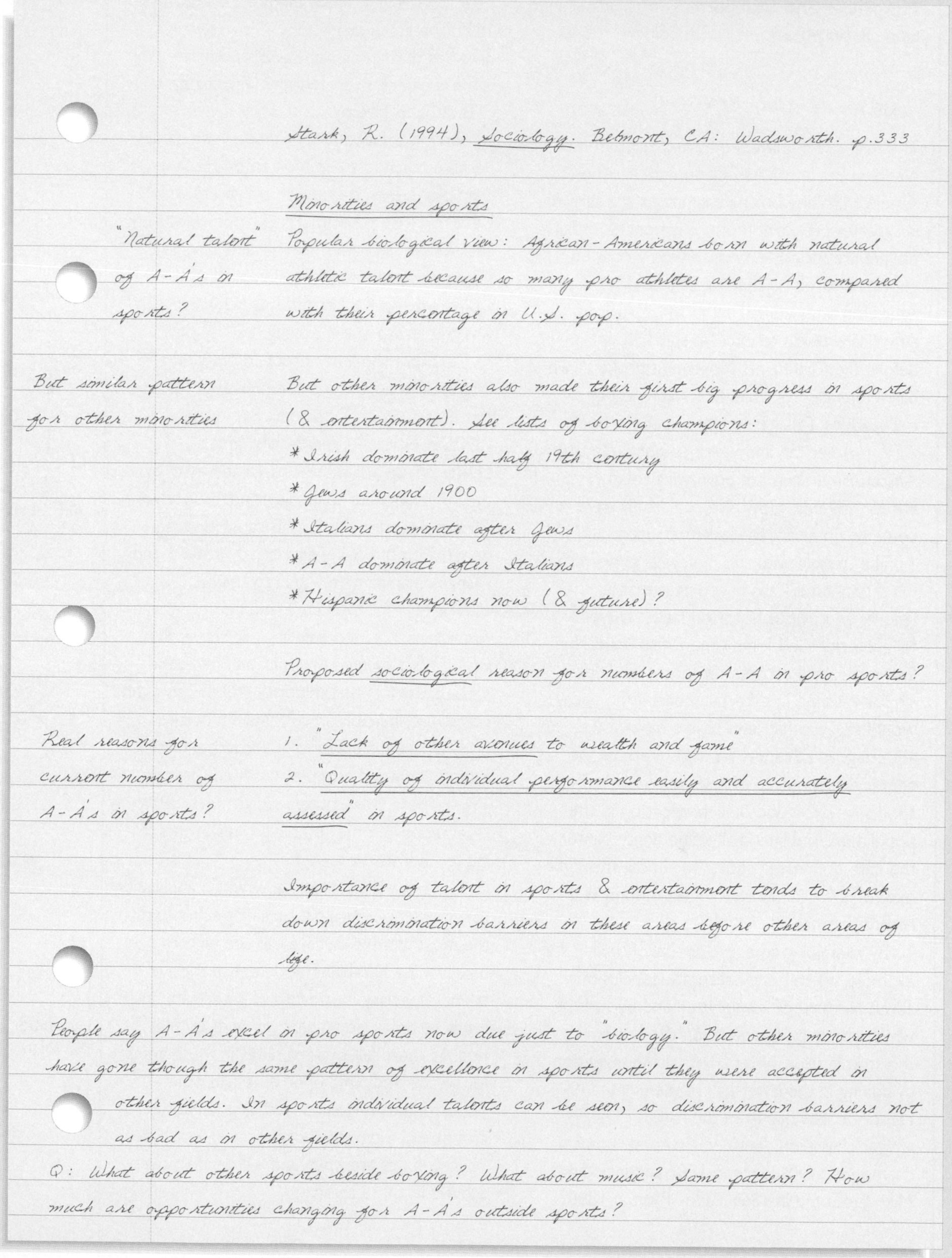

Stark, R. (1994), _Sociology._ Belmont, CA: Wadsworth. p.333

Minorities and sports

"Natural talent" of A-A's in sports? | Popular biological view: African-Americans born with natural athletic talent because so many pro athletes are A-A, compared with their percentage in U.S. pop.

But similar pattern for other minorities | But other minorities also made their first big progress in sports (& entertainment). See lists of boxing champions:
* Irish dominate last half 19th century
* Jews around 1900
* Italians dominate after Jews
* A-A dominate after Italians
* Hispanic champions now (& future)?

Proposed _sociological_ reason for numbers of A-A in pro sports?

Real reasons for current number of A-A's in sports? |
1. "Lack of other avenues to wealth and fame"
2. "Quality of individual performance easily and accurately assessed" in sports.

Importance of talent in sports & entertainment tends to break down discrimination barriers in these areas before other areas of life.

People say A-A's excel in pro sports now due just to "biology." But other minorities have gone though the same pattern of excellence in sports until they were accepted in other fields. In sports individual talents can be seen, so discrimination barriers not as bad as in other fields.

Q: What about other sports beside boxing? What about music? Same pattern? How much are opportunities changing for A-A's outside sports?

- **Explain yourself.** College reading is often complex and abstract. It's easy to read a mass of material and think you understand what you've read when in fact you missed a key idea.

  Imagine that you have a study companion who doesn't read as well as you do and struggles to understand the central ideas in assignments. Regularly explain the key ideas in the reading to your "friend," particularly when the material is harder or less interesting for you than usual. When you can't explain the passage easily, you need to review it. Of course, if you use this strategy, please tell your roommates about it so they won't think you're cracking up!
- **Periodically evaluate the quality of your notes.** Especially after an exam, review your notes to see how well they worked.

Learn with *InfoTrac College Edition*

InfoTrac College Edition

Look up articles and search for more on topics that sparked your interest when reading this chapter.

Brooke Ellison Paralyzed grad leaves Harvard. Nanci Hellmich. *USA Today.* June 9, 2000.

College Classes "No books, please; we're students." John Leo. *U.S. News and World Report.* Sept. 16, 1997. v121, n11, p24.

Listening Six ways to be a better listener. Paul C. Blodgett. *Training and Development.* July 1997. v51, i7, p11.

Information Processing "Ohhh! My brain hurts!" How to avoid the curse of information overload. Dean Rieck. *Direct Marketing.* Nov. 1998. v6, i7, p64.

Summary Strategies for Mastering College

Recognizing and capturing key information from your courses will help you reach your academic goals

1 Commit, Concentrate, Capture, Connect

- Summarize information in ways that fit your learning style.
- To make your strategies successful, you need to make a commitment, concentrate, capture key ideas, and make connections.

2 Take Charge of Lectures

- Commit to attending class to get the most out of lectures.
- Overcome distractions to improve your concentration.
- Adapt your listening skills to the demands of the course and the style of the teacher.

3 Take Great Lecture Notes

- Find a note-taking format that works with your learning style.
- Use your notes strategically to improve your ability to recall information.

4 Take Charge of Your Reading

- Find the right time and space to make your reading effective and efficient.
- Tailor your reading intensity and speed to the course requirements.

5 Mark or Take Notes from Reading

- Experiment with note-taking strategies that will help you identify and retain the most important ideas.
- Use your own words to record ideas from texts in order to learn the material well and avoid plagiarism.

Review Questions

1. What are the four C's of learning new information?

_____
_____
_____
_____

2. How can a person listen most effectively to challenging lectures?

_____
_____
_____
_____
_____
_____

3. What styles of note taking make the most sense for the classes you're currently taking?

_____
_____
_____
_____
_____
_____

4. What are the different reading styles and how can they help students succeed in various types of college courses?

_____
_____
_____
_____
_____

5. How can you change your way of reading to help you remember material better and read more efficiently?

_____
_____
_____
_____
_____

6. What are some good ideas about taking notes on readings?

_____
_____
_____
_____
_____

Learning Portfolio

Reflect and Journal

1. Getting Insights from Success

Think about a course you're taking this semester in which taking notes is easy for you.

- How does the teacher's style contribute to your success?

  _____

  _____

  _____

- How do you make your notes a personal reflection of your learning?

  _____

  _____

  _____

- How might your note taking improve in all your courses if you adopted some of the ideas in this chapter? Which ideas could work for you?

  _____

  _____

  _____

Expand these notes in your journal.

2. Daydream Believer

One of the biggest obstacles to successful listening in class is the tendency to daydream. Monitor your listening in your current courses. In which class do you daydream the most? Speculate in your journal about how this pattern developed and what you can do to focus more on this class.

_____

_____

_____

_____

_____

_____

_____

_____

_____

_____

_____

_____

Learn By Doing

1. Explore Interpretation

Read a newspaper account (a secondary source) of a current scientific project. Then ask a librarian to help you track down the original work (the primary source) in a scientific journal. Compare the length of the reports, the language level difficulty, the order of importance of ideas, and any other contrasting features. Based on your observations, how would you say that primary and secondary sources differ?

_____

_____

_____

_____

_____

_____

_____

_____

_____

_____

2. How Do You Read?

Monitor how you read your assignments for one week. Then rate how regularly you engage in different kinds of reading:

	I do this regularly	I sometimes do this	I rarely do this
Previewing	_____	_____	_____
Skimming	_____	_____	_____
Active reading	_____	_____	_____
Analytical reading	_____	_____	_____
Reviewing	_____	_____	_____

In which categories might you improve your overall performance?

_____

_____

_____

_____

_____

Think Critically

1. A Shared Path to Success

Form a small group in your college success class to compare your strategies for taking notes. Try to select a course that you have in common even if you don't have the same instructor. See whether as a group you can determine which approaches are most effective in capturing the critical ideas and in promoting appropriate learning in that type of course.

_____
_____
_____
_____
_____
_____
_____
_____
_____
_____
_____
_____
_____
_____
_____
_____

2. Analyze the Sixth Sense

Some students seem to have an uncanny ability to figure out what information given in class will show up on the tests. Think about what kinds of cues they're picking up on in class.

- How do the instructor's vocal cues tell you what's important?

_____
_____
_____
_____

- What kinds of words show an instructor's intent?

_____
_____
_____
_____

- What behaviors show an instructor's excitement about concepts?

_____
_____
_____
_____

Think Creatively

1. Taking Advantage

Effective organizational strategies will serve you well not only in college but also throughout life. Think about your future. How will the ability to process information effectively and efficiently influence the quality of your work? Think about the advantages you can gain by developing good information-processing skills now.

_____
_____
_____
_____
_____
_____
_____
_____

2. The Listener's Advantage

As you learned in the chapter, the listener can process language faster than the speaker can speak. In a group brainstorming session, find the most effective uses for that extra time.

_____
_____
_____
_____
_____
_____
_____

Work toward Goals

Review the results of the self-assessments you completed in this chapter. Also review the opening checklist. Based on your review, select a relatively short-term goal that you want to work on now.

1. What is that goal? (*Hint:* Is it challenging, reasonable, and specific?)

_____

_____

_____

_____

_____

2. What strategies will you use to achieve your goal? (*Hint:* Can you organize your strategy into a series of smaller goals?)

_____

_____

_____

_____

_____

3. What obstacles may be in your way as you attempt to make these positive changes?

_____

_____

_____

_____

_____

4. What additional resources might help you achieve your goal? (Use the CD-ROM that comes with this book for access to some useful leads.)

_____

_____

_____

_____

_____

5. By what date do you want to accomplish your goal?

_____

_____

_____

_____

_____

6. How will you know you have succeeded?

_____

_____

_____

_____

_____

Enhance Your Study Skills

6

Hit the Books

Studying will work best if you know how to make the best use of your study time. This chapter explores ways to improve your memory and to get the most from your study of various disciplines. To get a picture of your current strengths and weaknesses in study skills, place a check mark next to only those items that apply to you.

____ I choose appropriate places and times to study.

____ I set reasonable goals for study sessions.

____ I review regularly to learn course information better.

____ I organize materials to make them easier to learn and remember.

____ I use strategies to remember course information.

____ I pursue deeper learning strategies when I can.

____ I adapt my study strategies to suit different disciplines.

____ I take my learning style into account when I study.

____ I form study groups to expand my learning resources.

On the next page, think about how Jay Leno's life illustrates some important features of effective study strategies.

IMAGES OF COLLEGE SUCCESS

Jay Leno

Jay Leno's fifth-grade teacher turned out to be a prophet. School was not exactly Leno's favorite activity. As a comedian in his classroom, he took special pleasure in making his teachers laugh. In retrospect, Leno's humor might have masked his insecurities about his struggles with studying. Of course, the great thing about Leno is that he has developed a successful show business career despite a learning disability.

Leno reports that his childhood in Andover, Massachusetts, was blissful. He may have come by his sense of humor from his parents, who encouraged his spontaneity. His father, Angelo, whom Leno describes as the "funniest guy in the office," managed a successful insurance career. His mother, Catherine, worked in the home. Leno credits his mother with helping him develop the "female side" of his humor. As a consequence, he claims, he especially enjoys making women laugh.

A graduate of Emerson College, Leno began experimenting with stand-up comedy during college. After seeing a dreadful comedian on *The Tonight Show,* he abandoned his career as a Rolls Royce salesman and began to pursue life in the spotlight. Ironically, his greatest success has been as the host of the very show that launched his career.

Leno has been open about his struggles with dyslexia. In this learning disability, words sometimes appear to be scrambled or have backward letters. Leno tends to shrug off verbal misfires with witty, self-deprecating humor. Many people with learning disabilities cite his triumph as an inspiration.

Learning disabilities can be overcome, as shown by the successful career of the comedian Jay Leno.

Reuters/Corbis-Bettmann

Learn more about Jay Leno.

If Jay spent as much time studying as he does trying to be a comedian, he'd be a big star.

From a fifth-grade report card

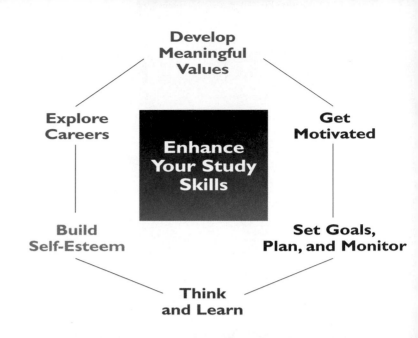

Develop Meaningful Values

Explore Careers

Enhance Your Study Skills

Get Motivated

Build Self-Esteem

Set Goals, Plan, and Monitor

Think and Learn

Effective study flows from solid planning based on your goals. Use your goals to motivate yourself to maximize your study skills and resources.

Plan Your Attack

To do well in college, most of us need concentrated study time with notes we've made from readings and classes. A systematic study strategy will make your investment of time and effort pay off.

Studying accomplishes many objectives. It makes recalling the core material of the course easier. It helps you develop richer insights. It also promotes good work habits that will carry over into your career.

The amount of time students report doing assignments or studying is related to many aspects of college success (Astin, 1993). Students who study more hours say they are more satisfied with college than do students who study less. Also, students who study more report that college improves their cognitive skills and emotional life. But studying *more* is only one way to improve. Studying *more effectively* can also help. Among other benefits, sensible study methods save you time so you have more of it for social life and other interests.

Where to Study

The phone rings. Your downstairs neighbor is throwing a noisy party. The television in the living room is blaring a *Friends* rerun. And your relentless appetite demands a hot fudge sundae. At times the world is so full of distractions that it seems impossible to find the right time and place to study. But your success as a student depends on your ability to conquer these distractions and stick to a good study routine.

The Best Available Space Find the best place you can to work, and study consistently there. The best place is usually private, quiet, and well lit and provides a comfortable temperature. Finding a study space at home is easiest, but you have other options as well.

Some areas of the library are designed to promote concentration. Colleges also usually try to maintain other quiet spaces on campus. Residence halls often set aside quiet rooms away from noisy roommates. Ask other students about good study places on campus.

*F*or a man to attain an eminent degree in learning costs him time, watching, hunger, nakedness, dizziness in the head, weakness in the stomach, and other inconveniences.

Miguel de Cervantes
17th-century Spanish author

Some students can study effectively in uncomfortable postures and distracting environments, but many students prefer to study at a desk or a table. Have you figured out where you study best?

*P*atience and tenacity of purpose are worth more than twice their weight in cleverness.

Thomas Henry Huxley
19th-century English biologist

Stave off the Sleep Invasion

1. **Use your desk *only* for studying.** When you drift asleep at your desk, you learn to associate your desk with napping, a cue you may not be able to afford.

2. **Set an alarm.** Buy a wristwatch that can signal you at reasonable intervals to keep you focused.

3. **Rely on friends or family to keep you awake.** Study with others. Ask a parent or partner to check on you.

4. **Take a five-minute fresh-air break.** A brisk walk can clear your mind so you can focus better when you return to your studies.

5. **Stay involved in your reading.** The more invested you are, the less tempting it is to give in to sleepy feelings.

6. **Get enough sleep to begin with.** You can manage a late night every once in a while, but a steady diet of all-nighters guarantees that you'll be fighting off the sandman.

Commuters can use driving time to review audiotapes of complicated lectures or carpool with someone in class to provide review time. Riding on a bus or train, especially if the commute is long, can also give you blocks of study time.

The Right Conditions Although some students can concentrate in strange places and odd postures, most find that sitting at a desk improves concentration. Desks provide storage for study materials and help you stay organized. If you don't have a desk, use boxes or crates to contain and organize your supplies and books. You may be able to set up a simple filing system.

What if you have to share study space at home with others, even children? Assign desk drawers to everyone who will be sharing the space. Then together figure out how best to share the space. Hang a bulletin board near the work space to display everyone's best work to promote good motivation. If you have to take over the kitchen or dining room table, be sure to tidy up after each study session unless you make other arrangements with your family.

If you must share a computer, develop a schedule for access. Practice saving your work and respect the privacy of others who share your equipment.

Wherever you study, minimize noise. Many people study best when the CD player, radio, and television are off. Some people like music in the background to mask other sounds and give a sense of control over the environment. If you can't control the noise around you, use headphones and soft instrumental music to minimize distraction.

Avoid getting too comfortable. Too much comfort is just an invitation to doze. See "Stave off the Sleep Invasion" for other ways to beat the urge to sleep.

When to Study

Try to allocate several hours outside class for every hour you spend in class. Outstanding students often put in even more time. Although some study strategies can make you a better learner, there is no denying the need to study long hours for academic success. What are some ideas about how to use those hours wisely?

When to Review One of the best study strategies is to review your notes immediately after class. This lets you rehearse new ideas and identify unclear ideas so you can clarify them with your instructor or in your reading. See "After Class Is Over" for tips on how to review.

Reviewing your class notes before the next class, along with your notes on reading assignments, adds another rehearsal session that prepares you to participate in the next class effectively. You'll also remember the concepts better. Successful students often get to class about 10 minutes early to review their notes.

Schedule regular cumulative review sessions. Devote some time to seeing the big picture in each of your courses. Look at how each lecture fits the broader course objective. If you regularly review your notes during the term, you'll need less review time right before exams.

Listen to Your Body Pay attention to your natural rhythms. Research suggests that many young adults undergo developmental changes that predispose them to being night people (Carskadon, 1990). They require more rest to cope with those changes and may not get in sync until later in the day. Sometimes that preference lingers so that even older students may feel more functional later in the day.

If you're a night person, review sessions may be most effective after supper and late into the evening. If you're a morning person, you need to study earlier in the day to maximize your attention and concentration. Complete Self-Assessment 6-1 to evaluate your high- and low-energy periods.

ON-TARGET TIPS

After Class Is Over

1. **Rewrite and reorganize your notes.** This not only allows you to create a neater, clearer set of ideas for study but also provides an immediate review to help you take in and organize information.
2. **Highlight the most important ideas.** Underline or color-code the ideas you think may appear on a test. Write notes in the margins that will make the material more meaningful to you.
3. **Write a summary paragraph of the main ideas.** What were the main points covered in class? How did this class fit into the overall course?
4. **Identify any ideas that are still confusing.** Make notes about what remains unclear so you can look up the answer in your reading. You can also ask other students or the instructor.

What to Study

Use your daily and weekly calendar to decide when your activities must intensify or when you can take a much needed recreation break. Keep your long-term goals posted in your study area so you can have easy access to reminders about what your commitments will require.

Set subgoals for each study session. Plan how long your study session will be as well as what specific tasks you want to accomplish and in what order. Build in some break time to help your concentration stay fresh. Monitor how well you're achieving your subgoals and adapt your planning and resources accordingly. (For detailed suggestions on how to make the best use of your time, refer to Chapter 3.)

Improve Your Memory

Memorizing is a necessary skill in college. Some tests may depend entirely on your ability to memorize. For example, naming the levels of the phylogenetic scale in zoology or recognizing the musical instruments in a symphony requires memorization. Let's explore how memory works before we look at methods for improving memory.

Set Study Goals ⟷ Set Session Subgoals ⟷ Monitor Progress ⟷ Maximize Learning

Early Bird or Night Owl?

To determine your typical energy level, check all the characteristics that apply to you.

How's Your Energy?

_____ I roll out of bed eager to face the day.

_____ I manage to get up without an alarm.

_____ My friends complain that I'm too chipper early in the morning.

_____ I tend to run out of steam in the middle of the afternoon.

_____ I prefer intense activity before noon.

_____ I can't function without a minimum amount of sleep.

_____ I leave parties early.

_____ I drag myself out of bed, sorry the day has started.

_____ I regularly use the snooze button on my alarm clock.

_____ My friends complain that I'm too crabby in the morning.

_____ I tend to start hitting my stride in the middle of the afternoon.

_____ I prefer intense activity after noon.

_____ I can function on little or no sleep.

_____ I leave parties late.

Respect Your Natural Energy

• Schedule classes as early as you can.

• Avoid commitments when your energy dips in the afternoon.

• Consider an afternoon catnap.

• Study your hardest course work before your energy lapses.

• Don't plan to study late at night unless you absolutely must.

• Schedule your classes in the late morning and early afternoon.

• Try night classes. They may be a perfect match for your energy.

• Buy a good alarm clock (maybe even a backup alarm).

• Don't study when you're groggy.

• Study late and fall asleep. It may help you retain information.

Are you an early bird or a night owl? The category with the most check marks reveals your energy profile, which suggests when study strategies and class scheduling will produce the greatest payoff. Early birds should make their most serious efforts before late afternoon. Night owls should avoid making commitments before late morning.

How Memory Works

Two important memory systems are involved in academic learning: *short-term memory* and *long-term memory*.

Short-Term Memory Short-term memory ("working memory") enables us to get some work done without cluttering up our minds. For example, when you look up a new phone number, that number doesn't automatically go into your long-term memory for important numbers. Short-term memory lets you retain it briefly, for 30 seconds or so, just long enough to get the number dialed. Then it vanishes. Besides being brief, short-term memory has other features:

- **It's fragile.** Unless you rehearse the information in short-term memory, it will disappear. If you're interrupted while rehearsing the information—suppose someone asks you a question after you have looked up a phone number—your short-term memory will be disrupted and you'll probably lose the information.
- **It has limited capacity.** Short-term memory can hold approximately seven "chunks" of information before the system becomes overtaxed and information is dumped out of awareness (G. A. Miller, 1956).
- **It can be tricked.** You may be able to trick short-term memory into holding more detail through a process called "chunking": making each memory "chunk" represent more than one piece of information. This is the basis for the *mnemonics,* or memory aids, discussed later.

Long-Term Memory You've already stored a mountain of facts and impressions in your long-term memory from your education and life experience. What is the meaning of *prerequisite*? When did the Great Depression begin? What was the best movie you ever saw? How do you ride a skateboard? Each memory exists in your long term memory store. Ideally, you can *retrieve* it as you need it. What are some other features of long-term memory?

- **It appears to have no limits.** Many long-term memories endure. For example, you may be able to recall the name of your first-grade teacher even though you haven't thought of him or her in a long time. We can also remember vivid information without much practice.
- **It's built through association.** The more you know about a topic, the easier it is to lean more, because you have more ways to make associations between new ideas and what you already know. For example, if you're a fan of old movies, you may devote a lot of memory storage to retaining odd facts about directors, movie locations, and favorite actors. If you're *not* a sports fan, then you'll feel bewildered when your sports-focused friends discuss obscure statistics related to the Super Bowl. People easily store a lot of information in long-term memory on the topics that interest them most.

  If you don't know much about a subject, then your task is harder. You'll be building your concept base from the ground up. This is why some course materials are harder to learn than others. You have to work harder to make associations.
- **It can be tricked.** Memory research suggests that long-term memory can be remarkably creative. In a series of clever experiments, Elizabeth Loftus (1980) demonstrated that people could report vividly recalling events that had never really happened to them. Once we are convinced that we know

something, we may fill in the gaps without realizing how much we've invented.

■ **It can fail.** Unfortunately, no matter how hard you study, you're bound to forget some things you learn. Experts cite two reasons why we forget: *interference* and *decay*.

Interference can crowd out memories, making them difficult to retrieve. For example, when you take a full academic load, the sheer volume of the material may cause interference among the subjects, especially when courses use similar terms.

Memory decay is the disintegration of memory that occurs when the ideas are not kept active through use. If you fail to review regularly or do not practice retrieving information, you may find it impossible to recall it when you want it, such as during a test.

Ideally, your learning strategies should be geared toward building your long-term memory with important and meaningful information. Your goal should be to learn course information so you can recall it not just for tests but well beyond the end of the course.

How to Memorize

There are two general ways to put information into long-term memory (Minninger, 1984): *rote rehearsal* or *comprehensive understanding*. For example, if you're trying to learn a new procedure on your computer, you can either memorize the sequence of things you have to do to accomplish the job or strive to learn what each step accomplishes in relation to your goal. As you can imagine, the first approach leads to superficial learning. Rote learning tends not to last. The next time you have to repeat the procedure on the computer, you'll probably have to relearn it. Learning through understanding initially may require more work, but the learning sticks. What strategies can help?

Adopt the Right Attitude Memorizing new material is a challenge, but a positive attitude helps. Make a serious effort to develop interest in the subject you must study. Think about the potential personal or professional value the course may provide, even if you have to use your imagination a bit. Then study to meet specific learning objectives.

Pay Close Attention Don't allow yourself to be distracted when you're processing information about things you must do or remember. Some absentmindedness is caused not by forgetting but by failing to absorb the information in the first place.

Concentrate on one thing at a time. You may have to study multiple subjects in one session. If so, try to focus your attention on the subject at hand. Study the more difficult subjects first because you need more energy for harder material. Reward yourself at the end by saving the subject you enjoy most for last.

If you're taking two similar subjects, space them apart when you study. This will reduce the amount of interference between the two sets of ideas. Sometimes two courses offer overlapping or conflicting ideas. To help distinguish the ideas, space them apart when you study, to minimize potential interference. If you must study for multiple tests in a short time frame, schedule your final study session in a particular subject as the last thing you do before the test.

Involve Yourself in Your Studies Look for personal connections. This will make learning and recalling unfamiliar or abstract ideas easier (Matlin, 1998), especially if you're a visual learner. For example, in history you may have to learn about periods that seem quite remote to you. Think about how these periods might have involved your own ancestors. For example, would your great-grandmother have been a flapper during the Roaring '20s, or would she have led a different life? Make her the focal point of your learning about this era. If you don't know anything about her, imagine her.

Ask yourself questions about what you've read or what you've recorded about class activities. Expand the number of associations you make with the information, which makes the ideas easier to recall. Add this activity to your rehearsal time. The following questions and others like it can help you create additional links to course concepts:

- Have I ever seen this concept before?
- Do I like or dislike the ideas?
- What are some practical examples of the concept?
- Are there other ways to explain the concept?

This practice will improve not only your memory for course concepts but also your ability to think critically about them.

Create Memory Prompts Organize concepts in a tree diagram or concept map (see Figure 6-1 or other models in Chapter 5) to give yourself additional cues for remembering ideas. For example, suppose you're studying important events in U.S. history in the 1950s. Construct a map that captures the important details of the period to make them easier to remember.

Use mnemonics to expand visual or auditory associations. *Mnemonics* are strategies that provide additional associations to help you learn. They involve linking something you want to remember to images, letters, or words that you

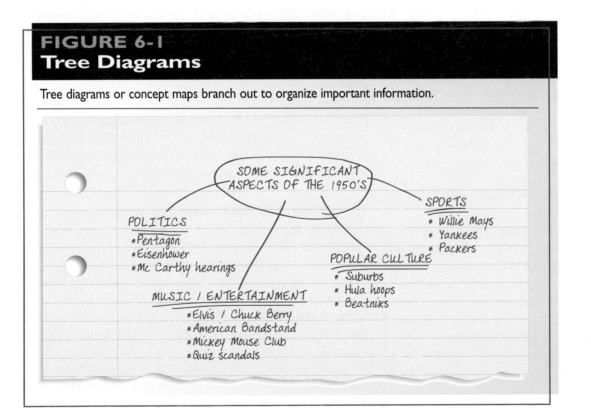

FIGURE 6-1
Tree Diagrams

Tree diagrams or concept maps branch out to organize important information.

SOME SIGNIFICANT ASPECTS OF THE 1950'S

POLITICS
*Pentagon
*Eisenhower
*Mc Carthy hearings

MUSIC / ENTERTAINMENT
*Elvis / Chuck Berry
*American Bandstand
*Mickey Mouse Club
*Quiz scandals

POPULAR CULTURE
*Suburbs
*Hula hoops
*Beatniks

SPORTS
*Willie Mays
*Yankees
*Packers

Thanks for the Memory

Rhymes If you were raised in the United States, you most likely learned when Columbus came to America through rhyme: "Columbus sailed the ocean blue/In fourteen hundred ninety-two." The rhyme leaves an indelible impression. Eventually you do not have to repeat the rhyme to remember the date.

Here's another example from first aid: "When the face is red, raise the head. When the face is pale, raise the tail." Remembering the rhyme allows you make a swift decision about appropriate treatment. See Figure 6-2 for other examples.

Songs Melodies can also produce enduring memories. A generation of U.S. children learned how to spell *encyclopedia* by singing its spelling along with Jiminy Cricket on "The Mickey Mouse Club" in the early days of television. Many children learn their phone numbers or addresses when parents sing the information to them using a familiar melody.

Acronyms Acronyms are special words (or sentences) that you construct using the first letter from each word in the list you wish to memorize. The acronym cues you not only to the items on the list but also to their proper order.

Method of loci. In another mnemonic, you associate the parts of a list with a physical sequence of activities or a specific location that you know well. For example, you can remember a long and difficult speech by thinking about walking through your home and associating a piece of the speech with each of the rooms. Another example of the method of loci can be found in a creative pharmacy major's attempt to remember the path of a red blood cell by imagining an oversized body on a familiar floor and walking her or his way through the heart, arteries, and veins.

Visualization. Using your imagination to come up with provocative images can provide memory cues. Making visualizations ridiculous is the best way to make them memorable (Lorayne & Lucas, 1996). Substitute or combine objects, exaggerate their features, make them disproportionate, or involve action in an image to make it distinctive. For example, you could remember elected representatives by combining symbols that represent them in some outrageous way. The Wisconsin Senators Feingold and Kohl became easy to remember if you picture the Senate filled with coal dipped in 14K (fine) gold.

Drawings or diagrams. You don't have to be artistic to draw pictures, make arrows, or create stars in the margins of books or notes. Adding images can make recalling details easier. Draw pictures of the comparisons that your instructor uses to clarify concepts. For example, if your psychology instructor describes Freud's view of the unconscious as similar to an iceberg, draw a large iceberg in the background of your notes. Drawings are especially helpful for visual learners.

© 2000 by Sidney Harris.

already know or that are easy to recall because of how you've constructed the mnemonic. They can be visual or text based, logical or goofy, complex or simple. As you read "Thanks for the Memory" for some examples, think about which techniques fit your learning style best.

Use props. Create a set of flash cards and carry them with you. Rehearse while you wait in grocery store lines, at laundromats, and at doctors' offices. Consider creating audiotapes of the ideas you want to memorize, and review those while driving or doing chores.

Construct a "cram card." Whenever you can't commit important information to long-term memory through regular study and rehearsal, write down the essential points on a small card (Frank, 1996). Don't overload it with detail. Study the card up to the point when your instructor says to put materials away. Then put away the card but rehearse the information until you can write it down in the margins of your test booklet. In this way, your short-term memory can help you when your long-term memory has not. Be sure to put the card away before the test begins. It could easily be mistaken for a crib note.

Strive for Overlearning

When you feel that you really know your stuff, study just a bit longer to "overlearn" the material. Overlearning improves the integration and the endurance of your learning.

Partial memory occurs when you remember something about a concept but not enough to help you. For example, you may recall where a concept appeared on the textbook page but fail to remember its meaning. Or you may be able to remember that a concept starts with "p" but the rest of the word eludes you. Instances of partial memory suggest that your study strategies need more work.

FIGURE 6-2
Examples of Mnemonics from Various Disciplines

DISCIPLINE	MNEMONIC	MEANING
Business	SWOT	Strengths, weaknesses, opportunities, threats (a technique for analyzing problems)
Physics	ROY G. BIV	Red, orange, yellow, green, blue, violet (visible colors in the light spectrum)
Geography	HOMES	Huron, Ontario, Michigan, Erie, Superior (the Great Lakes)
Music	Every	E
	good	G
	boy	B
	does	D
	fine	F (the lines of the treble clef)
Astronomy	My	Mercury
	very	Venus
	elegant	Earth
	mother	Mars
	just	Jupiter
	served	Saturn
	us	Uranus
	nine	Neptune
	pickles	Pluto (nine planets in order from the sun)

When you partially recall important information, you may be able to retrieve the whole of what you stored in memory if you temporarily change the direction of your thinking. Focusing away from the problem gives your mental circuits more time to "warm up," causing a term or name to surface.

Exploit Situational Cues If you can, when you take an exam, sit in the seat you normally sit in for class. Being in the same place may help you dredge up elusive memories.

Evaluate Your Progress

How skilled are you in using memory-enhancing strategies to achieve your goals? Complete Self-Assessment 6-2 to identify the strategies that you use and the ones that show promise for helping you study more effectively.

Another strategy for evaluating your progress involves examining your test results to determine whether your strategies worked. You may need to study for longer periods or seek new, more efficient methods for learning new ideas. See Chapter 7 for specific help on how to revise study strategies based on test results.

Am I Ready to Learn and Remember?

Review the elements of effective study strategies below and decide whether each is something you already do well or something you need to improve.

	I Do This Well	I Could Improve This
To take advantage of my best energy levels, I purposefully schedule when I will study certain subjects.	_____	_____
I select study environments that have few distractions.	_____	_____
I review course materials regularly to spread my learning out over time.	_____	_____
I try to find some angle in my assignments that will increase my interest.	_____	_____
To ensure my understanding and increase my personal involvement, I question what I read.	_____	_____
I look for ways to add meaning to course ideas during review sessions.	_____	_____
I rehearse key ideas to the point of overlearning.	_____	_____
I use mnemonic strategies for memorization. (List several specific strategies you use):	_____	_____

_____

_____

	I Do This Well	I Could Improve This
When I feel frustrated by partial recall, I divert my attention to recover more details.	_____	_____
I schedule an intensive review session before a test.	_____	_____
I avoid cramming whenever I can.	_____	_____
I use review tests to see whether I need to change my study strategies.	_____	_____

Look over your answers. Could the areas you need to improve mean the difference between a mediocre performance and honor-quality work? What would you need to do to improve? How could you reward yourself for adopting better strategies?

Pursue Deeper Learning

If you prefer memorizing information to other kinds of academic work, you're in good company. Interviews by Marcia Baxter Magolda (1992) revealed that most beginning students prefer well-structured, simple learning tasks. Memorizing basic facts feels like a manageable challenge in most courses. However, college courses will routinely challenge you to go beyond rote memory and learn more deeply. One reason to accept these challenges now is that they can build your confidence for upper-level courses that you'll take later on. Overall, you'll emerge from college with greater pride in what you've accomplished.

College instructors sometimes rely on a framework that helps distinguish *surface* and *deep* learning. Benjamin Bloom and his colleagues (1956) developed a *taxonomy*, or hierarchy, of cognitive skills that describes the kind of work college courses require (see Figure 6-3). In fact, some instructors will introduce *Bloom's taxonomy* as a framework to you to help you understand how to delve more deeply into your studies.

Beginning courses tend to emphasize *lower-order* cognitive skills such as memorization, comprehension (understanding), and application (trying out in new situations what you've learned). Instructors tend to assess lower-order skills using multiple-choice tests. To study for tests of surface learning you may want to rely on memory strategies.

Advanced courses emphasize *higher-order* cognitive skills including analysis, synthesis, and evaluation. Skills in analysis contribute to your effectiveness in reasoning and asking questions. Synthesis involves the integration of ideas into a new creation or perspective. Evaluation requires making decisions or judgments. Higher-order tasks require you to show greater independence and creativity in your thinking.

You can follow the spirit of Bloom's taxonomy in your own approach to study. Challenge yourself to go one level above what the course requires. For example, if your instructor emphasizes knowledge and comprehension in assignments, practice applying course materials to new situations. This will promote learning that endures.

Master the Disciplines

If you're majoring in an area that will train you for a specific profession, you may wonder why you also need to take liberal arts courses. The reason is that each discipline represents a specialized way of thinking about human experience that should help you develop a richer perspective on life and more ways to view and handle problems.

FIGURE 6-3
Bloom's Taxonomy

Highest level of cognitive development

Evaluation

shows ability to judge the value of material for a given purpose based on definite criteria and rationale; includes decision-making and selection; is the highest level in the cognitive domain. It contains elements of all the other categories; e.g., synthesis is critical to evaluation.

Evidence: assessments, critiques, and evaluations

Synthesis

recombines the parts created during analysis to form a new entity, different from the original one.

Evidence: creative behaviors such as development of a research proposal or a scheme for classifying information, and the creation of new patterns or structures.

Analysis

breaks down material into its constituent parts so that its organizational structure may be understood.

Evidence: breaking down, categorizing, classifying, differentiating; requires understanding of the material, its content and its structure.

Application

uses data, principles, theory learned to answer a question in a new environment; shows one can apply what was learned and understood.

Evidence: conceptual activities such as application, classification, development, modification, organization, and prediction.

Comprehension

is an awareness of what the material means; allows one to demonstrate understanding of a work based on one's knowledge of it.

Evidence: activities that indicate comprehension might include comparison and contrast, paraphrasing, extension, and summary.

Knowledge

is the recall of previously learned material; of specific facts or of complete theories; all that is required is the bringing to mind of the appropriate information; the lowest level of learning outcomes in the cognitive domain.

Evidence: definitions, outlines, recall exercises, and requests to reproduce knowledge acquisition.

Source: McNett and others (2000), p. 5.

Courses differ in how much they make you think. Beginning courses in most disciplines are most likely to emphasize memorization and comprehension. Memorizing is hard work, but some courses require a lot more than that.

You may have already noticed that you have to adjust your study strategies to the disciplines that you are studying. Here is a four-part framework to help you adjust to these differences and maximize your results:

■ **The Rules.** Although each discipline requires memorizing new content, each also has sophisticated frameworks and theories that require deeper levels of thinking and understanding.

- **The Risks.** Each discipline tends to have special challenges associated with developing mastery.
- **The Resources.** Your learning style will make some disciplines more successful than others for you. Which elements of your learning style facilitate that success?
- **The Remedy.** If you're studying a discipline that doesn't match your learning style, there are some things you can do to improve your efficiency and effectiveness.

The Humanities

Humanities courses develop your understanding of human experience. Most emphasize exploring your subjective experience as you read literature, examine specific periods in history, or evaluate the ideas of philosophers.

The Rules Typically each humanities course is built around a particular *framework,* or set of concepts or theories, that will help you develop a new perspective or richer appreciation for the human condition. For example, learning about literature will expose you to various frameworks of literary criticism, such as psychoanalytic or feminist criticism. Each framework in turn is built on a distinct set of values and assumptions. Applying the frameworks to literature will probably lead you to different kinds of conclusions. A psychoanalytic framework encourages you to look at unconscious motivations; a feminist framework sensitizes you to social forces that create different options for women and men. You can apply these frameworks to expand your personal insight.

Humanities instructors look to your insights as evidence that you understand the frameworks.

The Risks You may fear that your personal interpretations will get you in trouble in humanities courses. You may assume that there may be only one right answer and may be afraid that you'll look foolish if what you say is "wrong." However, the objective of most humanities courses is to encourage breadth of thinking.

Take the risk of sharing your insights. You may end up offering ideas that your class members have never heard. "Deep Study Strategies for the Humanities" illustrates one helpful approach based on Bloom's taxonomy.

The Resources Because of their learning styles, some students have a natural advantage in humanities courses.

- If you have verbal-linguistic intelligence, you bring a love of words and their meanings to complex humanities assignments.
- If you're skilled in auditory processing, you can track difficult lectures with ease.

ON-TARGET TIPS

Deep Study Strategies for the Humanities

Suppose you've enrolled in a film appreciation class. You've just read a chapter about the works of Steven Spielberg. Asking the following (or similar) questions during your review session will help you probe the material most deeply (questions based on Bloom and others, 1956):

Memorization	What are the names of Spielberg's past films? When did his first film debut?
Comprehension	Name the ways his films could be regarded as successful. What themes does he regularly present in his films?
Application	What other filmmakers tend to borrow from Spielberg's methods? Think about how a different director might have directed the film *E.T.*
Analysis	Why are his films so financially successful? What role has technology played in his productions?
Synthesis	Create a story line that would be intriguing to Spielberg. How might his films be different if he'd been born 20 years earlier?
Evaluation	In what ways do you think his work is unique? Rank order Spielberg's films from best to worst.

Notice that by using your imagination to think about your assignments, you also make new connections to the assigned material. The more connections you make, the easier it will be for you to recall information. This strategy also helps you anticipate and practice for essay tests.

- If you enjoy assignments that emphasize reflection and creative learning styles as well, humanities assignments offer you wide latitude for personal interpretation.
- If you like to think critically, you'll have many opportunities to create and defend your perspective.

The answers you get from literature depend on the questions you pose.

Margaret Atwood
Contemporary Canadian novelist

The Remedy Not everyone has a learning style that makes learning in the humanities easy. What are some strategies you can use to enhance your success in humanities classes?

- Keep a dictionary close. You're bound to run into new terms that will slow down your reading.
- Compare ideas. Exploit any opportunity to discuss central ideas or identify challenging concepts.
- Practice making conclusions. Rehearse aloud or on paper the key ideas and principles you draw from the assignment.
- Read to make connections. The more you read about a topic, the more you'll have to reflect on.

Natural Science and Math

Natural science explains the natural phenomena of the world, including everything from how fast an apple falls from a tree to the mysteries of the cell. Mathematics provides the tools to measure observations and assess change.

The Rules Natural science and math are loaded with theorems, laws, and formulas that you'll probably need to memorize, but comprehension should be your primary objective. Most of the activities that you undertake in science and math give you practice in application—applying the rules to produce a specific outcome or solution. Obviously, the more you practice applying the principles or formulas, the more enduring your learning will be.

The Risks Natural science and math often have an unappealing reputation. The stereotype is that only science and math "geeks" do well in these courses. It will help if you deflate your images about science a little. For example, you regularly act like a scientist does when you figure out how things work, although you may not be as systematic or careful in your observations as scientists are. With some practice, you, too, can do real science.

The Resources The natural sciences and mathematics attract students who have particular strengths in the logical-mathematical and naturalist dimensions of intelligence.

ON-TARGET TIPS

Becoming Better at Science and Math

- **Talk about what you already believe.** Sometimes preexisting notions can interfere with learning new ideas in science (Treagust, Duit, & Fraser, 1996). If you state what you really know or think about a scientific event, it may be easier for you to see where your explanation may not be adequate. Scientific explanations may then offer a clear improvement.
- **Collaborate with others.** Despite the stereotype of the lone scientist, most scientists do not work in isolation. Collaboration is a good model for beginners as well. By talking through problems with other students, you can improve your scientific problem solving.
- **Change representational strategies.** Some students find science and math too abstract. By changing the format of the problem, you may get a clue about how to work with the ideas involved. For example, if a problem is presented in pictures or symbols, translate those to words. If you have a difficult word problem, try using pictures or symbols.
- **Know why you're studying.** Keep the big picture in mind. What will you accomplish by learning the skills involved in any given assignment?
- **If you get confused, find another class section and sit in.** Sometimes it helps to sit through a class twice, which may be possible if your instructor teaches multiple sessions.
- **Be persistent and check your work.** Some problems don't yield a fast answer. Keep working, seeking, and persisting until you gain the insight you need to crack the problem. Be sure to check your answers so you don't lose credit because of carelessness.
- **Don't let anxiety overwhelm you.** Practice the skills and try to relax. If that doesn't work, get counseling or tutoring.

Although the stereotype suggests that scientists do their work alone, progress in science depends on collaboration. Therefore, interpersonal intelligence also facilitates discovering new scientific knowledge.

Visual learners manage the challenges of mathematical formulas and also bring strong observational skills to science problems. Kinesthetic learners function well in laboratory exercises or field applications. Solving problems in natural science and mathematics also offers opportunities to exercise critical and creative thinking, thoughtful reflection, and active learning.

The Remedy If you don't have natural abilities to support your learning in the natural sciences and mathematics, see "Becoming Better at Science and Math" for some ideas that can help.

Social Science

Because the social sciences use scientific methods to understand human experience, they often draw on both the sciences and the humanities.

The Rules The social sciences produce laws and theories to explain the behavior of individuals and groups. Concepts in the social sciences often serve as shorthand for complex patterns of behavior. For example, "social stratification," a sociological concept, refers to how people in a society can be classified into groups according to how much money they make, what types of jobs they have, how much power they wield, and so forth. Much of what students need to memorize in social science courses has to do with learning new terms such as *stratification*.

The Risks Learning in the social sciences can be challenging because what you are expected to learn may conflict with what you previously believed. Say, for example, that you heard on television and from your Uncle Ernie that it's dangerous to wake up a sleepwalker. It made sense to you, so you believe it. In your psychology class, however, you discover that this knowledge is inaccurate, and that it is more dangerous to allow a sleepwalker freedom to walk into trouble. You have to reject some things you thought were true—such as opinions from Uncle Ernie—to make room for new ideas derived from social science research.

Here's an example of another problem faced by social science students. Trudy's really frustrated. "I don't get it," she says. "I asked my psychology teacher why I can't get along with my sister and she says, 'It depends on lots of things.' That isn't the way shrinks answer questions on *Oprah!*" In other words, social scientists draw on multiple theories to explain the same thing. Social science is considered to be a "soft" science because it has to explain many deeply complex problems that depend on numerous circumstances. It can be frustrating to look for a simple answer and end up with five explanations.

© 2000 by Sidney Harris.

The Resources Both interpersonal and intrapersonal intelligence can help you understand the social part of social science. Logical-mathematical and naturalist intelligence support the science part of social science. Both auditory and visual sensory styles help social scientists do what they do. The strong analytic requirements of social science tend to reward critical thinking, although other kinds of processing can also help.

The Remedy

- **Expect complexity.** You're less likely to be disappointed by the limits of social science if you understand that not all your questions will have clean answers. The most interesting topics are complex and do not present simple answers.
- **Use your own experience.** Most of the topics you'll study correspond to things you've already experienced. When you connect concepts to your experiences, you can bring additional associations to the concepts that will make them easier to learn. However, don't restrict yourself to understanding only what you've personally experienced.
- **Stay open to alternative explanations.** Recognize that your experience may not be typical of the systematic observations in science. You'll need to practice staying objective as you evaluate evidence, which may include reevaluating your personal experience.

"I'm a social scientist, Michael. That means I can't explain electricity or anything like that, but if you ever want to know about people, I'm your man."

Foreign Languages

Many colleges require students to study a foreign language. This helps students step outside their own culture to develop a broader perspective.

The Rules The study of a foreign language is loaded with rules. Proper grammar, verb tenses, and noun forms such as "feminine" and "masculine" all represent rules that you must learn to acquire a new language. The rules may also include the norms and practices of the culture in which the language is practiced.

The Risks Many foreign languages have new sounds that may not be natural to you. You may fear revealing any shortcomings in your "ear" for language. The amount of time you have to spend drilling can also be daunting. Overcoming the risks and succeeding in foreign language classes involve understanding and memorizing as much as you can.

The Resources If you're blessed with a good ear for language, the chances are good that you have a strong auditory sensory preference. Your fascination with words and meanings in another language point to verbal-linguistic intelligence. Because learning a new language requires a lot of memorization, the learning process of reflection may be the best tool available to help you learn a new language.

The Remedy

- **Use color-coded materials.** Color-coded flash cards may give you additional cues about the kinds of words you're trying to learn. For example, use blue cards for verbs, yellow for nouns, and so on.

A special kind of beauty exists which is born in language, of language, and for language.

Gaston Bachelard
20th-century French scientist

- **Construct outrageous images.** Construct an image from the sounds of the language that will help you recall the vocabulary. For example, if you want to learn the word for "dinner" in Portuguese (*jantar*), picture John eating a plate full of tar at the dinner table.
- **Talk out loud.** Label objects that you know. Rehearse routine conversations and stage practices with classmates when you can. Read your assignments aloud to improve your ear for the language.
- **Don't get behind.** Keep up, because this sort of classwork will pile up fast.
- **Distribute your practice sessions.** Although using shorter but frequent study sessions to memorize college material is good in general, it's *essential* when you're learning a foreign language. Regular practice sessions make your learning last longer.
- **Immerse yourself.** Try to find some natural exposure to the language you're studying. Get a pen pal. Watch movies or television programs that feature the language you're studying.

Overcome Learning Disabilities

Perhaps nearly one in ten people in the United States experiences complications in learning caused by a learning disability or learning difference. Learning differences can interfere with incoming information by scrambling printed words, garbling spoken words, or causing confusion regarding numbers. As a result of confused input, people show problems in expression, including impaired short-term memory, problematic spelling, confusion about terminology, substandard grammar, and poor math skills.

Clearly, students with learning disabilities face daunting problems, including some unfounded prejudices from professors and students that equate learning disability with low intelligence. However, many find great success in school and afterward, as in the case of Jay Leno.

Famous people with learning disabilities include the investment company owner Charles Schwab and the actors Tracey Gold and Tom Cruise.

One of the most common forms of learning disability, dyslexia, interferes with a person's ability to read. People with dyslexia report that words and sentences are hard to decode. Because they worry about performance and their slower rate of reading, students with dyslexia often feel singled out in classes for "not trying" or "failing to live up to their potential" despite the fact that they try hard to keep up.

Check It Out

Many students think they might have learning disabilities when they really don't. Sometimes they simply don't put in enough study time or their performance; other times their anxiety sabotages them on tests. When you confer with your advisor about your academic struggles, prepare an honest evaluation of how much work you're putting in on your studies. Your problems may lie in bad strategies, not in a learning disability.

If you've experienced criticisms about your performance even though you're trying hard, you may find it helpful to complete Self-Assessment 6-3, which identifies many characteristics of learning disabilities. This inventory will not tell you whether or not you have a learning disability. It merely provides a rough outline of concerns that you can raise with your academic advisor to sort out whether more diagnostic testing is in order.

Know Your Rights

If you have a learning difference, your academic outlook can still be good. Students whose learning difference can be verified by a qualified examiner may apply for special education support through the Education for All Handicapped Children Act of 1975. In addition, the Americans with Disability Act encourages campuses to support the special needs of students with disabilities. Many instructors have developed their own strategies to assist students. For example, they may offer longer test periods for students with language-processing problems. Figure 6-4 offers some questions you might pursue with your instructor to help you stay competitive.

FIGURE 6-4
Talk with Your Instructors about Learning Disabilities

Here are some questions you can ask your instructor to help you stay competitive if you have a learning disability.

Do you mind if I audiotape your lecture?

Have you worked with learning disabled students before?

Do you have any special advice to help me stay current in the course?

May I use a spelling device to help me during testing?

May I arrange for extended time to finish exams? Can we arrange for someone to monitor me?

Can you recommend a tutor in case I run into difficulties in your course?

When would be a good time for me to talk with you to clarify things I've learned in class?

Would you like to have more information about my learning disability?

Compensate

If you do have a learning disability, you'll need to develop a set of strategies to compensate for the challenges your learning style presents. Among other things, you can do the following:

- Set up a study group where you can discuss course material with others.
- Compare your notes with a friend's after each class to see if you've missed any important details.
- Use audio versions of textbooks when available.
- Use a spell-checker.
- Get support from the campus study skill center.
- Ask friends to proofread your written work.
- Alert your instructors to your special needs.

The compensating strategies that you develop in college will continue to serve you throughout life.

Could I Have a Learning Disability?

You may have a learning disability if you have the following difficulties:

Misunderstand simple printed materials _____

Have a lot of trouble working with basic math problems _____

Have difficulty writing and speaking _____

Approach studying in a haphazard manner _____

Get easily distracted _____

Confuse *left* and *right* or other spatial words _____

Arrive late a lot (such as frequent late arrival to class) _____

Struggle with categories and comparisons _____

Have trouble with fine motor skills or finger control _____

Feel awkward in gross motor (body) movements _____

Misinterpret subtle nonverbal cues _____

Have difficulty following instructions _____

Reverse letters in words or words in sentences _____

Hear teachers complain that you "are not living up to your potential" _____

If you feel frustrated in these areas, you may want to see if you have a learning difference. First, talk with your advisor about the nature of your difficulties. She or he can recommend changes in your study strategy or refer you to a specialist on campus who can help you with diagnostic testing. On some campuses this evaluation is expensive, but you're likely to get advice that makes the investment worthwhile.

Join a Study Group

Working in study groups adds a vital element to your education and expands your resources. Besides learning the course content better, study groups can improve your ability to communicate, develop your project skills, and help you deal with conflict. This section describes what you can do to make group work efficient and effective.

ON-TARGET TIPS

Strategies for Study Groups

- Identify the hardest concepts or ideas you've encountered.
- Talk about the problems or ideas you especially like or dislike.
- Discuss which parts of the readings interest you the most.
- Help one another share and clarify everyone's understanding of the material.
- Discuss strategies for remembering course material.
- Generate questions to prepare for tests.

Don't wait for an instructor to convene a study group. Find interested and competent classmates to meet regularly and talk about a challenging course. See "Strategies for Study Groups" to get the most from your study group commitment.

Making Study Groups Work

Whether the group is working on a ten-minute discussion project in class or a challenge that spans several weeks, effective groups usually work in stages. Here are three that work quite well.

1. **Plan the task.** As the group convenes, lay the groundwork for working together efficiently by doing four things:
   - "Introduce group members ("Who are we?")
   - Identify the purpose of meeting by agreeing on goals and objectives ("What tasks do we need to do?")
   - Create a plan for working together ("How can we work together efficiently?")
   - Set criteria for success ("How will we know we've succeeded in our task?")
2. **Come to a consensus.** Once the ground rules have been established, your group can address the specific task at hand. You don't have to choose a formal leader although that might be helpful. Group members who ask questions and move the group along help the group by guiding it informally.
3. **Evaluate the results.** In the final stage of the discussion, summarize what has been accomplished and evaluate how well the group has performed so you can improve its efficiency. Then, plan another meeting.

Overcoming Group Work Obstacles

Muddle is the extra unknown personality in any committee.
Anthony Sampson
Contemporary British social historian

Group work can provide some of your most exciting—and most frustrating—learning. When you join others to solve a problem or explore the meaning of a work of art, your pooled brainpower can result in insights you might never have had on your own. Effective groups tend to bring out the best in their members. However, people regularly have problems working in groups. Figure 6-5 describes some common group work problems and what to do about them.

FIGURE 6-5
Common Problems and Sensible Solutions for Study Groups

PROBLEM	SOLUTION
Failure to do groundwork Group members may be so eager to get on with the task that they jump right into a chaotic and unsatisfying discussion.	**Establish goals** Your group will collaborate more efficiently if you have a clear picture of what the group wants to achieve and how you hope to achieve it.
Conflict avoidance Some groups become disorganized as disagreements emerge. Conflict is valuable because differences of opinion can lead to a better discussion or well-considered solution.	**Legitimize difference of opinion** When conflict emerges, ask group members to support their opinions with evidence. Let the quality of evidence persuade the group.
Unequal participation When groups are large and some members take charge, shy or unprepared members may be less likely to participate.	**Specify useful roles** Ask quiet members to serve the group by taking notes or summarizing the key ideas. Ask them directly about their opinions.
Domination by one member Sometimes leaders push too hard and end up alienating other group members. They may not recognize the value of involving all members to improve the quality of the group's conclusion.	**Ask for space and cooperation** When leaders get too pushy, suggest that other members need more time and space to express their ideas. If this gentle confrontation does not work, be more forceful. Point out what the group may lose when some don't participate.
Off-task behavior Less committed members may engage in behaviors (such as popping gum) that distract the group.	**Ask for concentrated effort** Suggest that the offending person change the behavior to help promote a more favorable, quiet working environment.
Members who coast Some group members may not contribute once they sense that the group will succeed by the work of the more energetic or motivated members.	**Clarify expectations** Express your disappointment and anger about the unfair distribution of work. Propose some consequences for those who aren't doing their fair share.

Learn with *InfoTrac College Edition*

InfoTrac College Edition

Look up these articles and search for more on topics that sparked your interest when reading this chapter.

Jay Leno Building the Leno legend. Peter Bart. *Variety.* May 9, 2000. v379, i2, p2.
Mnemonics How's your memory? Carolyn Gard. *Current Health 2.* March 1998. v24, i7, p22.
Study Strategies Developing powerful study skills leads to success in college. Judy T. Cusimano. *Black Collegian.* Oct. 1998. v29, i1, p136.
Freshman survival tips. *USA Today (magazine)* Nov. 1996. v125, i2618, p7.
Learning Disabilities Resources for people with learning disabilities. http://www.ldresources.com

Summary Strategies for Mastering College

Enhance your study skills by using strategies that match your resources to the demands of the work.

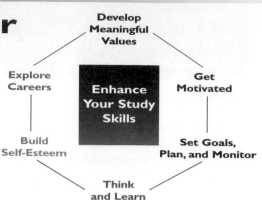

1 Plan Your Attack

- Recognize that study has more positive effects than good grades.
- Find a quiet place and use it consistently.
- Schedule study times that work with your energy level and course demands.
- Set goals for what you want to accomplish in a study session.

2 Improve Your Memory

- Know the differences between short- and long-term memory.
- Approach memorizing with the right attitude.
- Attend, concentrate, and minimize interference among subjects.
- Use mnemonics to build personal connections to your course work.

3 Pursue Deeper Learning

- Recognize how surface and deep learning differ.
- Push yourself to work at deeper levels to help learning endure.
- Consider Bloom's taxonomy.

4 Master the Disciplines

- Prepare to think more abstractly as course work deepens.
- Understand the rules, risks, resources, and remedy for each discipline.
- Know how your learning style fits with a given discipline.
- Share your personal insights in humanities courses.
- Strengthen your logic and math skills to succeed in science.
- Expect complexity and a blend of science and the humanities in social science.
- Memorize rules and terminology to optimize language learning.

5 Overcome Learning Disabilities

- Recognize how confused input affects student performance.
- Undergo special testing if your results don't match your effort.
- Rely on the Disabilities Act to secure the help you need.
- Develop compensating strategies to minimize the effects of a learning difference.

6 Join a Study Group

- Form study groups to learn course concepts.
- Assign roles, plan tasks, set criteria for success, and evaluate your progress to ensure an effective study group.
- Solve routine problems that compromise group progress.

Review Questions

1. What should you do to secure adequate study space and time?

_____

_____

_____

_____

_____

_____

_____

2. What are some good strategies for memorizing academic concepts?

_____

_____

_____

_____

_____

_____

_____

3. How do higher-order thinking skills enhance study success?

_____

_____

_____

_____

_____

_____

_____

4. How do the disciplines encourage different kinds of study?

_____

_____

_____

_____

_____

_____

_____

5. How do learning disabilities influence study success?

_____

_____

_____

_____

_____

_____

_____

Learning Portfolio

 Reflect and Journal

1. Study-Group Savvy

Reflect on what kinds of situations would prompt you to form a study group. In which courses would you benefit from forming a study group? What special talents would you bring that would help the group succeed?

_____
_____
_____
_____
_____
_____
_____
_____
_____
_____
_____
_____

2. Reduce Your Disciplinary Risks

Many people have fears related to disciplines they are required to study to complete their education. Select the discipline with which you are least comfortable and describe the source of your concern. What might you do to get more comfortable with this discipline?

_____
_____
_____
_____
_____
_____
_____
_____
_____
_____

Learn By Doing

1. Conversations with a Difference

Talk with someone who has personal experience with learning disabilities. If you suspect you might have this problem, make an appointment with a learning disabilities specialist on campus to find out about further testing. If you don't think you have a learning disability, talk with a classmate who does. Find out what kinds of compensations seem to be most effective for him or her. Do some of the compensations seem like they might also be useful to you?

_____
_____
_____
_____
_____
_____
_____

2. Deep Study

Pick a topic area from a subject you're currently studying. Develop a question that represents a lower-order level of Bloom's taxonomy. A multiple-choice question that you can answer through rote memory is a good example. Identify a tentative answer to the question. Then develop a higher-order question on the same topic. How much harder do you have to work to come up with a good answer to a higher-order question than a lower-order one?

_____
_____
_____
_____
_____
_____
_____

Think Critically

1. Call Waiting

You're assigned to a discussion group that will meet throughout the semester, but one of the group members brings her cell phone. The phone usually rings five minutes into the meeting. She excuses herself to take the call and usually misses more than half of each meeting. What strategies could you and your group use to address this challenge?

_____

_____

_____

_____

_____

_____

_____

_____

_____

_____

_____

_____

_____

_____

_____

_____

_____

2. Expanding Study Time

Suppose that you've been asked to address the next incoming class of students about the importance of systematic study. How would you attempt to persuade them of the need to develop a sensible study plan? What arguments would you give? List some main points here.

_____

_____

_____

_____

_____

_____

_____

_____

_____

_____

_____

_____

_____

_____

_____

_____

Think Creatively

1. What's in a Name?

Locate one list in any of the content areas you're studying this semester. Develop a mnemonic device for remembering the list. Write it here.

_____

_____

_____

_____

_____

_____

_____

_____

_____

_____

_____

2. Creative Space Management

Identify a place where you have a hard time studying, such as a bus, a noisy dorm room, or a crowded kitchen table. Think of three strategies that would help you make this place better for studying.

_____

_____

_____

_____

_____

_____

_____

_____

_____

_____

_____

Work toward Goals

Review the results of the self-assessments you completed in this chapter. Also review the opening checklist. Based on your review, select a relatively short-term goal that you want to work on now.

1. What is that goal? (*Hint:* Is it challenging, reasonable, and specific?)

_____

_____

_____

_____

2. What strategies will you use to achieve your goal? (*Hint:* Can you organize your strategy into a series of smaller goals?)

_____

_____

_____

_____

3. What obstacles may be in your way as you attempt to make these positive changes?

_____

_____

_____

_____

4. What additional resources might help you achieve your goal? (Use the CD-ROM that comes with this book for access to useful leads.)

_____

_____

_____

_____

5. By what date do you want to accomplish your goal?

_____

_____

_____

_____

6. How will you know that you have succeeded?

_____

_____

_____

_____

Succeed on Tests

Take Your Full Measure

By this point in the term, you've probably already faced one ongoing challenge that all college students face—tests! Happily, some tests match how you've studied and what you've learned. Other tests, however, may have led you to think that you and the instructor weren't on the same planet let alone in the same classroom. To get a current picture of your test-taking skills, place a check mark next to only those items that apply to you.

_____ I pace myself effectively to get ready for a test.

_____ I figure out ahead of time what will be on the test and try to predict the test questions.

_____ I control my nervousness about test performance.

_____ I size up the test to know what I need to do and read all directions carefully before I start.

_____ I know effective strategies for scoring well on multiple-choice tests.

_____ I know how to do well on essay questions.

_____ I regularly complete tests in the allotted time.

_____ I know how to analyze test results to improve my learning and future test performances.

_____ I know the consequences of academic dishonesty at my college.

As the next page will explain, the physicist Albert Einstein was a notoriously poor student and test-taker until the right learning climate helped him to thrive as a learner.

IMAGES OF COLLEGE SUCCESS

Albert Einstein

When he was a small child, no one could have predicted the extraordinary future of Albert Einstein. He was slow in learning to talk and painfully shy. Although he loved science and mathematics, he struggled with the style of his formal education. His teachers at the Luitpold Gymnasium in Munich, Germany, taught by constant drilling, which Einstein found boring. He often skipped classes or was ill prepared, resulting in punishment for his disobedience and scorn from his classmates. Although his teachers thought he was dull, Einstein simply hated the persistent drilling he faced in school. When his father's business failed and the family moved to Italy, Einstein purposefully failed so many tests that he was asked to leave his school. One teacher told Einstein that he was glad to see him go, because the teachers thought he encouraged other students to be disrespectful.

In this situation, failing his tests enabled Einstein to be with his parents in Milan.

When his family later suggested that he needed to prepare for a career, Einstein applied to a technical school in Switzerland. To be admitted, he had to pass rigorous entrance examinations. Although his scores on his math and science exams clearly showed promise, he was a dismal failure in zoology, botany, and language. A remedial year at a relatively creative school, where his questioning was encouraged rather than discouraged, allowed him to catch up. He passed his entrance exams on his second attempt and went on to revolutionize the field of physics. Ironically, the Luitpold Gymnasium, an institution once offended by Albert Einstein's uncooperative and dull academic performance, was renamed in honor of him before he died (Levenger, 1949).

What can we learn from Albert Einstein's experiences in testing?

Corbis-Bettmann

Einstein himself would have been quite amused at the extent to which his own ideas would become the basis for testing millions of physics students struggling to understand his creative conceptualization of energy and matter. When asked to explain the theory of relativity, Einstein once joked, "Put your hand on a hot stove for a minute and it seems like an hour. Sit with a pretty girl for an hour and it seems like a minute. That's relativity!"

Learn more about Albert Einstein.

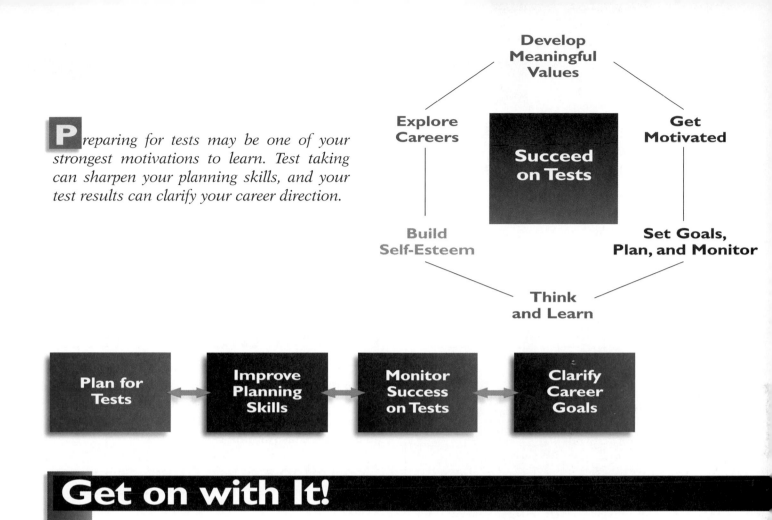

Preparing for tests may be one of your strongest motivations to learn. Test taking can sharpen your planning skills, and your test results can clarify your career direction.

Develop Meaningful Values

Explore Careers — Succeed on Tests — Get Motivated

Build Self-Esteem — Set Goals, Plan, and Monitor

Think and Learn

Plan for Tests ⟷ Improve Planning Skills ⟷ Monitor Success on Tests ⟷ Clarify Career Goals

Get on with It!

No matter what course of study you pursue, you're going to be evaluated. Believe it or not, tests can benefit you. They can help you to

- **Pace your reading.** College reading assignments can feel overwhelming, so it's easy to get behind. Tests throughout the term push you to do the work on time.
- **Consolidate your learning.** Tests encourage you to study the course material more intensively and retain the ideas longer. Your effort in preparing for tests can produce insights you might not have made without the pressure of the test.
- **Improve your thinking.** Tests sharpen your critical-thinking skills. Whether you're figuring out which multiple-choice alternative to eliminate or determining how to structure an essay, tests give you practice in careful observation, analysis, and judgment.
- **Get feedback.** Test results tell you whether your study strategies have worked. Good results confirm that you're on the right track. A string of poor scores suggests that you need to improve your motivation or study skills.
- **Achieve special status.** As demonstrated in the introductory story about Albert Einstein, test results can confer special status. For example, good results might qualify you for a scholarship or allow you to skip preliminary courses and move on to more advanced ones.

Difficulties, opposition... there is a special joy in facing them and in coming out on top.

Vijaya Lakshmi Pandit
20th-century Indian diplomat

"You're kidding! You count S.A.T.s?"

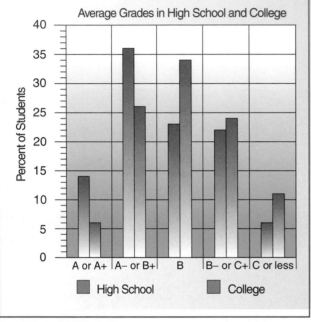

FIGURE 7-1
How Grades Can Change

As you can see in the graph, grades drifted downward from high school to college. This means that you have to study harder to maintain the same grade point average in college.

Average Grades in High School and College

(bar graph, Percent of Students vs. grade categories)

- A or A+: High School 14, College 6
- A– or B+: High School 36, College 26
- B: High School 23, College 34
- B– or C+: High School 22, College 24
- C or less: High School 6, College 11

Legend: ■ High School ■ College

Source: Astin (1993).

You know that instructors are going to test you. What can you do to show them you've got the right attitude to succeed?

First, recognize that there are important differences between tests in high school and tests in college. Most students regularly take more tests and quizzes in high school than in college. But most students also say that tests in college are harder. See Figure 7-1 to see how grades tend to drift downward as testing intensifies. Then, use the following systematic approach to do your best on future tests.

Plan for the Long Term

Pace Yourself Don't count on cramming! Eleventh-hour learning is fragile. It may crumble under pressure. The strategies offered in "How Not to Cram" will help you pace yourself so you won't have to go through a last-minute rush to learn.

Commit to a Study Group Studying with others will motivate you to do your reading and help you to identify trouble spots. Ask other students who seem to understand the course—at least as well as you do if not better—to join a study group. This screening process helps to ensure that the group will be productive and not slowed down by students who don't reliably do their work. To improve testing success, study group members can compare notes to create the most comprehensive understanding, share hunches about likely test material, create practice questions, and challenge fuzzy explanations.

ON-TARGET TIPS

How *Not* to Cram

- **Concentrate on the big picture.** Keep a master calendar for the term. Put all your scheduled tests on it. Post the calendar in your study area.
- **Design your test preparation across courses.** Plan how you'll read, study, and review assigned materials and class notes according to the test demands in all your courses. Wherever possible, distribute your study sessions over time to minimize interference among courses.
- **Keep up with your reading.** If you keep up with your reading, class experiences will reinforce your learning. Avoid trying to do massive catch-up reading the night before the test—there will probably be too much ground to cover, understand, and remember.
- **Reward yourself for staying on target.** A shiny "A" would be a powerful reward for strong test-preparation habits. However, that reward may come too far in the future to help you sustain better test preparation. Reward yourself on a regular basis for sticking to your study plan. For example, after you've studied hard each evening, watch a tape of a favorite TV show, listen to some music that you really like, or talk with someone you like.
- **Schedule a concentrated review session.** If you've kept up, a solid review session the night before your test should be adequate.

Protect Your Health If you stay healthy throughout the term, you'll have fewer problems in managing your study schedule and fewer distractions at test time than if you don't. You can't do your best if you're fighting off the urge to nap, feeling bad from a hangover, or coming down with a cold.

Learning is such a very painful business.

May Sarton
Contemporary American writer

Adopt the Right Attitude Examinations can be emotional events. Nearly everyone feels some test anxiety, but some are overwhelmed by it. We address this problem further later in the chapter. Others view testing as doing battle. They cast the instructor as a villain out to expose them. The student gets distracted into "outfoxing" the instructor rather than learning the material. Facing the test with the confidence that comes from good planning and systematic study is the best way to overcome negative attitudes and emotions.

Plan for the Short Term

Know What to Expect Test conditions vary. In large lecture classes, security issues may be intense. For example, you may be required to sit in alternate seats to reduce cheating. Proctors may roam the aisles and retrieve all materials after the test. Your instructor may not even be present, so you might want to get all of your questions answered before the day of the test. On the other hand, in smaller classes with the instructor present you may be able to clarify issues as they come up.

Either during the class or in the syllabus, most instructors describe the kinds of tests they are planning. Some even make sample tests from prior semesters available. Many welcome questions about how to prepare. "Will This Be on the Test?" suggests questions you can ask your instructor to clarify the nature of the exam.

You may know some students who have completed the course before you. Find out what they did to succeed or what strategies didn't work. Don't be afraid to research your instructor's test-construction practices.

"Psych out" the Teacher Some students seem psychic when guessing what will be on a test. How do they do it? They size up the instructor by identifying what concepts have been stressed enthusiastically during class lectures and discussions. As you've seen, instructors often use specific cues to communicate what they have said is important and *testable* (Appleby, 1997). They may be signaling test material when they

- Repeat or emphasize certain concepts
- Illustrate key ideas with examples
- Stop pacing back and forth behind the lectern
- Intensify eye contact
- Use gestures in more dramatic ways
- Change the tone of their voices
- Say "in conclusion..." or "to summarize..."
- Pause to allow you time to write your notes
- Write on the board or point to ideas on an overhead transparency
- Highlight ideas in their introductory remarks or conclusion

ON-TARGET TIPS

Will This Be on the Test?

Some instructors don't offer many clues about the tests they give. If you have one of these instructors, you might ask these questions:

- How long will the test be?
- What types of questions will be on it?
- Are there any particular aspects of the work we've been doing that you'll emphasize?
- What topics *won't* be on the test?
- Are there penalties for wrong guesses?
- Will this material also be covered on a cumulative exam at the end of the term?

Design Your Study Strategy Your success depends on developing a study strategy that takes into account the kind of thinking the test will require and how that relates to your learning style. Find out as much as you can about what the test will involve, then plan a suitable study strategy. Keep track of your progress as you prepare for the test.

Many tests, especially in the beginning of college, focus on memorization. If you're a visual learner, your preparation strategy should include visualizing key elements of the content and rehearsing that imagery. Auditory learners may prefer to rehearse key ideas out loud. Tactile learners may try role-play or other hands-on strategies to add cues that help them recall information.

Other types of tests may focus on more sophisticated kinds of thinking. Find out what the format of the test will be ahead of time. Know how points will be distributed across the test. This knowledge may help you decide where to spend your time if it's clear you won't be able to finish the test. Find out whether there are penalties for guessing.

Objective Tests. Memorizing facts is usually a good strategy for answering simple objective test questions. These include tests with multiple-choice, matching, true-false, and fill-in-the-blank items. As discussed in Chapter 6, successful memorizing strategies include using flash cards, making a concept vocabulary list, reviewing a text's study guide, and reorganizing your notes. Find the memorizing strategy that works best for your learning style.

At the college level, instructors ask objective questions that require more than just rote memory. When you have to do more than recall facts, your study strategy will also be more complex. Draw organizational charts or diagrams to identify relationships. Design some practice questions that show your ability to reason.

To succeed on tests, you need to review your notes to think about how the ideas can be incorporated in designated test formats.

Essay Tests. Digesting a whole term's worth of material for an essay can be a challenge. If you know the specific topics ahead of time, scan the notes you've made and highlight all related ideas in a specific color. This will let you concentrate on those ideas as you think about questions or practice answers. If you don't know the essay topics ahead of time, go back over your course and reading notes. Write a paragraph for each entry, such as a text chapter or course lecture, into your notes that summarizes the key ideas in the passage.

Procedural Tests. Some types of tests ask you to demonstrate specific procedures such as applying a formula to solve a math problem, demonstrating an interviewing technique in nursing, or solving for an unknown in chemistry. To prepare for procedural tests, go through the procedure until you're comfortable with it. If test time will be limited, build time limits into your practice.

Protect Your Study Time Classmates may request your help at the last minute, especially if you live with them. You may happily accept. Helping others can make you

> *You have to accept whatever comes and the only important thing is that you meet it with the best you have to give.*
>
> Eleanor Roosevelt
> *20th-century American humanitarian and lecturer*

FIGURE 7-2
A Timetable for Sensible Study Strategies

After each assignment	Write a summary paragraph of what you learned and how it relates to the course objectives.
After each class	Review your notes to consolidate your learning.

During the last class before the test	Find out about the test:
	    What will be and won't be in the test
	    The format of the test
	    The contribution of the test to your grade
	
	Clarify any confused ideas from past classes.

After the last class before the test	Plan your final review session.

The night before the test	Organize your notes for systematic review.
	
	Study the test material exclusively—or last—to reduce interference
	
	Practice the kind of thinking the test will require:
	    Rehearsal and recital for objective tests
	    Critical analysis for subjective tests
	
	Identify any fuzzy areas and confer with classmates to straighten out your confusion.
	
	Get a good night's sleep.

The day of the test	Organize your supplies Eat a good breakfast/lunch/dinner Review your notes, chapter summaries, course glossary.
The hour before the test	Review your notes. Go to the classroom early and get settled. Practice relaxing and positive thinking.

feel good and also can help you rehearse material. Or you may need to use the time alone to master the material yourself. If giving help does not appeal to you, explain that you've planned out your study strategy and need every minute to concentrate.

What if a loved one makes demands on your time that interfere with your study schedule? Explain to partners or family members, including children, that you need extra help from them before a test to make it as easy as possible to study. Promise them that you will spend time with them after the test. Then keep your promise.

If you practice good long-term and short-term strategies, your work is much easier as the test gets closer. Figure 7-2 summarizes strategies for pacing yourself for the least stressful test preparation.

If You Need to Salvage

It's a bad idea to depend on cramming, but sometimes it can't be helped. You may have too many courses to manage any other way. What are some ideas for last-minute, concentrated study?

- **Clear the decks.** Dedicate your last study session before the test to only that test. Studying anything else can interfere with the test at hand.
- **Skim for main ideas.** Scan each paragraph in relevant readings for the key ideas. Topic sentences that capture the central idea of each paragraph are usually the first or the last sentences in the paragraph. Skim the entire assignment to improve your chances of remembering the material.
- **Divide and conquer.** Once you've skimmed the entire body of study materials, size up how much you have to learn in relation to your remaining time. Divide the information into reasonable sections and make your best guess about which will have the largest payoff. Master each section in turn with whatever time you have left. Even if you don't get to the lower-priority material, your test performance may not suffer much.
- **Set the stage.** Study in good light away from the lure of your bed. Take regular breaks and exercise mildly to stay alert through your session. Caffeine in moderation and regular snacks may also help.
- **Use study aids.** Some textbooks include summaries. Use them if you can't master the entire chapter. Use professional summaries of great works if you can't complete a full reading. If you rent a film version of great work of literature, be aware that films often depart from the original in ways that may reveal your shortcut.
- **Learn from your mistakes.** When you enter a test feeling under-prepared, you've undermined your ability to succeed. Even if you luck out and do well, this strategy won't serve your learning over the long term. Think about what factors left you in such desperate study circumstances. Commit yourself to doing all you can not to get stuck in a situation where you have to cram.

> *Sixty minutes of thinking of any kind is bound to lead to confusion and unhappiness.*
>
> James Thurber
> *20th-century American cartoonist*

As the Moment Draws Near

It's almost here. Whether you're filled with dread or eager to show what you know, the following strategies give you the best chance of doing well.

- **Get a good night's sleep.** If you're well-rested, you have a better shot at sounding smart.
- **Bring supplies for your spirit.** A bottle of water or cup of coffee may keep up your spirits (and your caffeine level). Instructors usually specify what comforts you can bring to class. Avoid causing distractions, such as unwrapping noisy candy wrappers; other students are likely to be as nervous and distractible as you are. If you get stress headaches, don't forget to pack your aspirin.
- **Bring required academic supplies—and spares.** You may need to bring a blue book (a standard lined essay book for handwritten responses). Bring a sharpened pencil or pen and a backup, a calculator, scratch paper, or whatever other supplies the instructor allows. Make sure you have a watch or can see a classroom clock so you can pace your work.
- **Organize your resources.** In some cases, instructors may let you bring a summary of notes to jog your memory during the test. They even may let you have open access to your books and notes (a sure sign that the test will

be hard). Write your summaries clearly so that you don't lose time trying to decode your own writing. Attach some tabs, use marked index cards, or highlight your resources in other ways that will make them easy to navigate under pressure.

If you struggle with writing and spelling, bring a dictionary or a spell-checker if they are permitted. Many instructors will let you use them because it shows your desire to do good work. Some instructors will refuse because of concerns about security.

In Case of Emergency

What happens if you can't make it to the test? Most instructors have strict regulations about taking scheduled tests on time to ensure fair treatment for all students. However, sick children, car accidents, and deaths in the family can interfere with your plans to be present for a test.

If you can't report at the scheduled time, call your instructor *before* the test. Explain your situation. Ask whether you can take a makeup exam. Being courteous encourages your instructor's cooperation. Instructors may ask you to document your absence (for example, with a doctor's excuse) before they'll let you make up a test. Do all you can to take tests on schedule to avoid this kind of complication. See "The World's Toughest Test" to see how "crime doesn't pay" when it comes to arranging retests.

Control Your Test Anxiety

Just moments before your instructor hands out an exam, you may feel as if you're in the first car of a roller coaster about to hurtle down the first drop. Your heart pounds. You're sweating. The butterflies just won't go away.

A few butterflies are okay. A little anxiety even can be a good sign. It signals you to prepare for the test and can motivate you to do your very best.

Too many butterflies, though, can cripple your test performance. Nervousness and worry activate the emergency systems in your body. Your pulse increases. Your heart beats faster. Your hands perspire. These responses prepare you to flee or to fight. In stressful circumstances, they help you survive. But in the quiet of the classroom, they interfere with your ability to focus on the test.

Test-anxious students sabotage their own efforts because they focus on themselves in negative ways (Kaplan & Saccuzzo, 1993). Preoccupied with the certainty of their own failure, they can't free up the energy to perform well. This reaction increases their chances of failure. Test-anxious students interpret even neutral events as further proof of their own inadequacy. For example, if a test monitor looks troubled, the test-anxious student may assume that

"Hello, you've reached the office of Professor Arte. If your excuse for not turning your paper in on time is that your computer broke down, press '1.' If your excuse is that you had psychological problems, press '2.' If your excuse is that your grandmother died, press '3.' If your excuse is ..."

AMAZING BUT TRUE COLLEGE STORIES

The World's Toughest Test

Whatever your complication in taking the test on time, it pays to be honest when trying to negotiate alternate arrangements, as the unusual saga of one college instructor illustrates.

Two of the instructor's first-year students became overconfident about their course performances so they partied heavily at another campus instead of preparing for the final. They returned to campus late with major hangovers. When they contacted their instructor, they "explained" that they had been away for the weekend but got a flat tire on the way home and couldn't get help. They begged for mercy and asked if they could reschedule the final. The instructor thought about it and then agreed. At test time, he sent the students to separate rooms. The problem on the first page was worth 5 points and dealt with a simple application about molarity and solution. When they turned the page, they were surprised by the second and final question:

(95 points) Which tire?

Anxiety is the interest paid on trouble before it's due.

William R. Inge
20th-century American playwright

her or his own behavior somehow caused the troubled look. Test-anxious students also are more likely to experience stress-related physical symptoms, such as an upset stomach or a stiff neck, that further hinder performance.

If you have anxiety about tests, you need to do two things: cope with your anxiety and improve study skills to build your competence and confidence (Zeidner, 1995). If you learn to cope with anxiety but don't improve your study skills, you'll feel calmer and more in control but won't improve your performance. On the other hand, if you improve your study skills but don't master your anxious feelings, the results may be eroded. It will take some effort to do both things, but consider the long-term rewards.

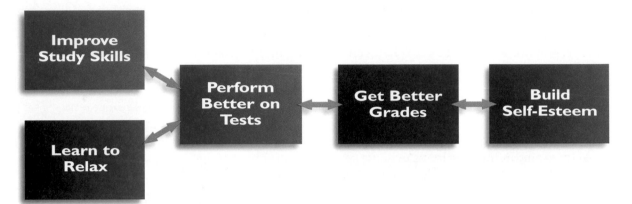

What are some specific things you can do to master test anxiety?

- **Invest your time properly.** Think about it. If you haven't spent as much time preparing for a test as you should, it makes sense to be frightened about performing poorly. Test jitters may only mean that you need to invest more time.
- **Relax.** One simple strategy is to neutralize your anxious feelings by relaxing. Breathe from your diaphragm. Visualize the tension flowing out of your body. Picture how good you'll feel when the tension is gone.
- **Talk positively to yourself.** Test-anxious students often make their anxieties worse by predicting their own failure. Instead of tormenting yourself with criticism and dire predictions, substitute positive statements, such as "I will overcome this challenge: or "I feel confident I will do well." Practice a positive outlook.
- **Exercise regularly.** Many students find relief from their anxieties by building a regular exercise program into their busy schedules. Exercise is a great stress reliever. It also promotes deeper, more restful sleep.
- **Avoid drugs.** Monitor your caffeine intake. Too much can compound agitated feelings. But this is a minor problem compared with problems that result from using harder drugs to ward off anxiety of stay alert. See "Just Say 'Whoa'" to learn more about the cost of drug abuse.
- **Find support.** Most campuses offer support groups for test anxiety. These groups emphasize study strategies, anxiety management techniques, and moral support.

Self-Assessment 7-1 will help you determine whether you need help conquering test anxiety.

STAYING OUT OF THE PITS

Just Say "Whoa"

Gary stared at his test paper and realized that what he had written didn't make sense. But he couldn't stay focused long enough to fix it. His hands were starting to shake. He looked at the clock and prayed for the hour to be over.

Under the pressure of trying to meet the demands of multiple courses, some students turn to drugs to sustain a higher level of energy and attention. Stimulants can stave off sleep, but at a cost. You may feel out of control when the drug kicks in. You may "crash" after using stimulants. This will just put you further behind and maintain the incentive to keep using the drugs. It's a losing proposition. Don't even start.

Do I Have Test Anxiety?

Check the category that best describes the way you feel when you take tests:

	Never	Occasionally	Regularly
I feel physically ill just before a test.	_____	_____	_____
I fail to complete tests, because I fret about what will happen when I fail.	_____	_____	_____
I can't seem to organize my time to prepare well for exams.	_____	_____	_____
I know I could do better if I could ignore how nervous I feel during tests.	_____	_____	_____
I struggle with stomach pain and bathroom urges just before a test.	_____	_____	_____
My mind has gone completely blank during the middle of an exam.	_____	_____	_____
I fear that I'll end up turning in the worst performance on the test in the entire class.	_____	_____	_____
I have difficulty getting a good night's sleep before a test.	_____	_____	_____
I'm very concerned about what my instructor will think of me if I don't do well on a test.	_____	_____	_____
I get more distracted during the test than other students seem to do.	_____	_____	_____
I start to panic when other students finish their exams while I'm still working.	_____	_____	_____
I know the material better than my exam score indicates.	_____	_____	_____
I know I won't be able to have the kind of future I want unless I can get a better grip on my testing fears.	_____	_____	_____

These items give you a general idea about how seriously test anxiety may be interfering with your test performance. If you marked any items "regularly" or marked several "occasionally," you might benefit from a more in-depth assessment of your test anxiety. Contact the study skills center on your campus. After evaluating the nature of your difficulty, the study skills specialists can make specific recommendations to help you master your anxiety. If you're seriously troubled by test anxiety, seek counseling.

Meet the Challenge

The test is just moments away. You take your seat. The class quiets down as the instructor hands out the questions. What can you do during the test to maximize your performance?

General Strategies

- **Relax.** Take a deep breath. The calmer you stay during a test, the better you'll do. Take relaxing breaths at the start and continue breathing calmly throughout the test. Concentrate on breathing slowly from your diaphragm. When you do this right, your stomach will move out as you breathe in and in as you breathe out.

- **Look at the entire test.** Examine the structure. Count the pages. Think about how you should divide your time, given your strengths and weaknesses. If the test includes different types of questions (such as multiple choice and short essay), begin with the type you do best on to build your confidence. As you plan how to allot your time, leave more time for parts that require more effort or that make up more of your total score. Plan some time at the end to review your work.

- **Read the instructions ... twice!** You'll be very upset if you discover near the end of the exam time that you were supposed to answer only certain questions rather than all the questions on the test. Read the instructions carefully. Then read them again.

- **When you get stuck, identify the problem and move on.** You'll be taking most exams under time pressure, so you can't afford to spend much time probing the depths of your memory. If time is left over after you've finished the parts of the exam that you could answer with confidence, return to the parts you skipped.

- **Concentrate despite distractions.** If you start daydreaming, circle the item that got you off task and come back to it later. Avoid getting caught up in competition with any students who complete the test early. Do the test at your pace—don't worry about who gets done first.

- **Ask for clarification.** When you're confused, ask your instructor or proctor for help. Most instructors try to clarify a question if they can without giving away the answer. An instructor may even decide that the question doesn't work and will throw it out.

- **Learn from the test.** The test itself may jog your memory. One area of the test may hold clues that can help you with other areas.

- **Proofread your work.** Whether it's a series of math problems or an extended discussion on Japanese haiku, review your work. Under pressure, it's easy to misspell, miscalculate, and make other errors even on things you know well. Using clear editing marks on your test paper demonstrates that you were being as careful as possible about your work.

Multiple-Choice Strategies

You'll probably face many tests that are mainly multiple choice: "question stems" or incomplete statements, followed by possible answers from which to choose. Figure 7-3 provides an example. To improve your scoring on multiple-choice questions,

- **Read the test items carefully and completely.** Cover up the alternatives and read just the stem. See whether you can answer the question in your head before you look at the alternatives. Then read *all* the alternatives before you identify the best one. This is especially important when your instructor includes "All of the above" or "A and C only" types of choices.
- **Strike out wrong answers.** When the correct answer is hard to identify, eliminate the wrong choices so you can concentrate only on real contenders.
- **Mark answers clearly and consistently.** Use the same method of marking your choices throughout the test. This may be important if questions arise later about an unclear mark. If your test is machine scored, avoid having extra marks on the answer sheet. They can be costly.
- **Change your answers cautiously.** Make sure you have a good reason before you change an answer. For example, change your answer if you mismarked your exam, initially misread the question, or clearly know you're moving to the correct alternative. If you aren't certain, it's best not to change. Your first impulse may be best.
- **Guess!!** Some tests subtract points for incorrect answers. In this case, answer only the questions that you know for certain. However, most multiple-choice tests give credit for correct answers without extra penalty for wrong answers. In this situation, guess. If the question has four alternatives, you have a 25 percent chance of being correct.
- **Look for structural clues.** When the item involves completing a sentence, look for answers that read well with the sentence stem (see Figure 7-4). Sometimes instructors don't pay close attention to how the wrong alternatives read. If a choice does not work grammatically with the stem, it's probably not the right choice. In complex questions, the longest alternative may be the best one. The instructor may simply require more words to express a complex answer.

FIGURE 7-3
Multiple-Choice Format

The best way to succeed on multiple-choice tests is	[question stem]
A. Read the question carefully	[contender]
B. Check on the weather	[distracter]
C. Look for language cues to throw out choices	[contender]
D. Cry like a baby	[distracter]
E. A & C	[correct contender]

True-False Strategies

True-False questions ask you to make judgments about whether propositions about the course content are valid or truthful. For example, consider this item: "True or False: It is always a bad idea to change your answer." This would be a good true-false question to assess your understanding of the last section on multiple-choice questions. (The answer is "False.")

To maximize your performance on true-false items,

- **Go with your hunch.** When you don't know the answer on a true-false question, you have a 50 percent chance of being right when you guess. Choose the alternative with the intuitive edge.
- **Don't look for answer patterns.** Instructors generally strive to make the order of true-false answers

FIGURE 7-4
Using Grammar Tools to Find Multiple-Choice Answers

In this example, spot the grammar clue that can help you determine the correct answer.

Don't change your multiple-choice answers unless you can find an
A. Error in how you marked your test booklet
B. Typo in the sentence stem
C. Justification from peeking at your lecture notes
D. Clues from cloud formation out the classroom window

Final page of the Medical Boards

random. This means there is no particular pattern to the true and false answers. Selecting "False" on question 35 should have no bearing on how you answer question 34 or 36. Focus your energy on the questions themselves rather than on trying to detect nonexistent patterns.

■ **Honor exceptions to the rule.** If you can think of exceptions to the statement, even one exception, then the statement is probably false. In the earlier example, if you can think of even one circumstance in which changing your answer is a good idea, then the statement should be marked "False."

■ **Analyze qualifying terms.** Words that specify conditions, such as *always, usually,* and *never,* usually identify an item that is false. Those terms suggest an unlikely or unwarranted generalization. Notice in our example, "It is always a bad idea to change your answer," the word *always* makes the statement invalid because there are some times when changing your answer makes sense.

Fill-in-the-Blank Strategies

Like multiple-choice questions, fill-in-the-blank questions test how well you recall information. An example of a fill-in-the-blank format is "Instructors try hard to make a _____ pattern of answers on true-false tests." (The answer is "random.") You probably either know or don't know the answers to these kinds of questions.

Short-Answer Strategies

Short-answer questions demonstrate how well you can explain concepts briefly. For example, a short essay question about the last section might be "Describe some strategies for doing well on true-false questions."

To maximize your score on short-answer questions, write clear, logical, and brief answers. Writing a lot more than asked or including information not asked for suggests that you do not understand the concepts. When you skip a short essay question because it stumps you, look for cues in the rest of the test that may help you go back and answer it later.

Essay-Question Strategies

Essay questions evaluate the scope of your knowledge and your ability to think and write. They tend to be much more demanding than objective test questions. What are some steps you can take to do your best on essays?

■ **Anticipate possible questions.** If you were in your teacher's shoes, what questions would you ask? If you practice predicting and answering questions, your performance is likely to improve even if your predictions aren't on target. For example, an essay question that you could predict about the material in this section could be "Compare and contrast multiple-choice and essay question strategies as a way of measuring your learning."

- **Read the question carefully.** A well-developed answer won't help you capture points if you don't answer the right question.
- **Highlight the requested action.** For example, in our earlier sample question you could underline <u>compare and contrast</u> to keep you focused on the most successful approach. See Figure 7-5 for help.
- **Outline the key ideas.** A systematic blueprint can help you capture the most important ideas in your answer as shown in the following example:

    I. How are multiple-choice and essay questions alike?
        A. They're constructed from same material.
        B. You start with remembering concepts.
        C. You demonstrate your mastery of material.
   II. How are multiple-choice and essay questions different?
        A. Multiple-choice usually relies more on rote memory—recognition or recall of terms. Essays usually involve higher-order thinking skills.

To talk without thinking is to shoot without aiming.

English proverb

FIGURE 7-5
Decode Essay Questions

Look carefully at the verbs your instructor uses in essay questions. This chart offers some hints about how your instructor wants you to construct your answer.

When your instructor wants you to ...	Your answer should ...
ANALYZE	break into smaller parts and interpret importance
APPLY	extend a concept or principle to a new situation
COMPARE	identify similarities between two concepts
CONTRAST	distinguish important differences between two concepts
CRITICIZE	judge the positive and negative features of a concept
DEFINE	offer the essential idea behind a concept
DESCRIBE	provide sufficient details to establish key ideas in a concept
DESIGN	develop a new strategy to accomplish a goal
EXPLAIN	clarify the meaning of a concept through detail or example
EVALUATE	make a well-reasoned judgment about value or worth
GENERALIZE	apply a principle to make predictions about a new problem
HYPOTHESIZE	develop a specific prediction about a complex situation
IDENTIFY	designate the key elements involved
ILLUSTRATE	provide examples or details to clarify
INTERPRET	offer your distinctive point of view about concept's meaning
LIST	identify factors in a systematic or comprehensive manner
PREDICT	offer your best guess about an outcome
PROVE	create your best argument using examples or reasoning
RECOMMEND	put forward a preferred course of action with a rationale
RELATE	draw connections among ideas
REVIEW	discuss the most important aspects of the concept
SUMMARIZE	briefly identify the most critical ideas

PEANUTS reprinted by permission of United Feature Syndicate, Inc.

B. Multiple-choice questions can be answered more quickly.

C. Multiple-choice questions usually have crisper right answers.

D. Essay questions are usually harder to answer.

E. Essay questions are probably harder to grade.

F. Well-written essays require planning and outlining.

- **Represent the question in your opening sentence.** Don't waste time rewriting the question. Set the stage for the information that will follow:

  Multiple-choice and essay questions are often used to demonstrate how much you have learned from a course. These strategies share some similarities, but each offers some strategic advantages over the other.

- **Develop the main body of the essay.** Each paragraph should address an element required in the question:

  The common characteristics of multiple-choice and essay questions include . . .

  Multiple-choice and essay questions also differ in what information they impart about a student's learning . . .

- **Summarize only if you have time.** If you write like a reporter—you present key ideas first and follow with details—you increase the likelihood that you'll cover the most important and point-scoring information before you run out of time.

  - **Write legibly.** If your handwriting gets worse under stress—slow down. Instructors can't give credit for what they can't decipher. For some other pointers about good essay format, see "Get Your Essay Points."

  - **Proofread your work.** Under time pressure, your written language can easily escape your control. Go back over your work and make any corrections the instructor will need in order to understand you clearly. Don't worry about the mess. Your own editing marks show that you care about the quality of your thinking.

  - **Don't bluff.** The longer your write and the more you ramble, the more you expose what you really don't know.

  - **Use humor carefully.** Unless you have clear cues from your instructors that they would appreciate a light-hearted response, don't substitute humor for an effective answer.

Self-Assessment 7-2 provides a review of many points that we've just covered. Use it to evaluate your current test-taking methods and to identify areas that need improvement.

*D*o not on any account attempt to write on both sides of the paper at once.

W. C. Sellar
20th-century British writer

ON-TARGET TIPS

Get Your Essay Points

- Use dark ink or pencil
- Carefully cross out parts that you no longer want evaluated.
- Avoid drawing numerous arrows to redirect your instructor's attention.
- Write on just one side of the paper.
- Use organizing notations, headings, or subpoints to clarify the order of your thoughts.
- Leave space between answers so your instructor can give you feedback or you can add ideas that you think up later.

How Well Do I Test?

Rate how often you use these skills.

	Always	Usually	Sometimes	Never
As part of my general test-taking strategy				
I stay relaxed during the exam.	____	____	____	____
I look at the entire test before I start.	____	____	____	____
I read the instructions carefully.	____	____	____	____
I concentrate even when distracted.	____	____	____	____
I ask the instructor for help when I'm confused.	____	____	____	____
I move on when I get stuck.	____	____	____	____
I look for clues in other parts of the test.	____	____	____	____
I proofread my work.	____	____	____	____
In multiple-choice questions				
I read the test items carefully and completely.	____	____	____	____
When I'm uncertain which answer is right, I take steps to rule out the alternatives that are wrong.	____	____	____	____
I mark the correct answer clearly and consistently.	____	____	____	____
I change my answers only when I'm certain I should do so.	____	____	____	____
When I don't know an answer, I guess.	____	____	____	____
When stumped, I look for cues in the question's structure.	____	____	____	____
On true-false items				
I go with my hunches.	____	____	____	____
I avoid looking for patterns on the answer sheet.	____	____	____	____
I analyze qualifying terms (such as *always, never*).	____	____	____	____
I try to find exceptions to the rule.	____	____	____	____
On fill-in-the-blank questions				
I don't loiter when stumped.	____	____	____	____
In short essay questions				
I write brief, logical answers.	____	____	____	____
In essay questions				
I underline the verbs in the question to help figure out what kind of thinking I need to do.	____	____	____	____
I think and outline before I write.	____	____	____	____
I reflect the question in my opening sentence.	____	____	____	____
I write main ideas first and fill in details and examples later.	____	____	____	____
I don't bluff when I don't know.	____	____	____	____
I write for readability.	____	____	____	____
I'm careful about using humor.	____	____	____	____

Now go back over the list and circle the test-management skills that you marked "rarely" or "never."
Check your calendar for the date of your next exam. Use your goal-setting skills to make improvements
for that exam.

Make the Grade

Grades don't change what you learned for the test, but grades can affect your self-esteem and motivation to study in the future. For example, good grades make you feel proud. They encourage you to stick with the study strategies that worked. Bad grades prompt you to make changes in order to succeed. But bad grades can also harm your self-esteem.

Recover Your Balance

The chances are very good that at some point in your college career you won't perform as well on a test as you hoped you would. Sometimes instructors don't design tests effectively. At other times, you simply may be pushed in too many directions to be able to concentrate and do your best. Or the course may be a bad match to your natural skills and interests.

Don't let yourself become undone by one failure. Frame this disappointment as an opportunity to do some good critical thinking to figure out the causes of poor performance and to craft some new strategies to improve your situation. That approach can start by a careful review of your test results.

Review Your Work

Some reviewing will help you do better on the next test, including reviewing to consolidate your learning, reviewing to analyze what worked and what didn't work in your study strategy, and reviewing to make sure that the grade was accurate.

Review all items, not just ones on which you made mistakes. Review and rehearse one more time the material that your instructor thinks you need to learn in the course. This can help you in the long run, especially if you have a cumulative exam at the end of the term. Even without a comprehensive final, test review consolidates your learning.

Your test review should tell you whether your study strategy worked. Did you spend enough time studying for the test? Did you practice the right kinds of thinking to match the particular demands of this teacher? How can you use your study time more efficiently for the next test? Talk with the instructor about better ways to prepare.

What if your instructor doesn't allow extensive time for review of your exam during class—or worse, doesn't return the exams at all but only posts the grades? Visit your instructor during office hours and ask for the chance to review your work. This visit also allows you to clarify any questions you have about your instructor's testing or grading practices.

Know When to Challenge

Check the grading. Instructors easily can make errors when applying test keys or counting up point totals. Also identify questions that were not clearly written. Even if your critique of a question does not persuade an instructor to change your grade, your review may give you insight into how the instructor constructs tests, which can help you on the next one.

Instructors are unlikely to change a grade without good reason. Most construct tests carefully and grade them as fairly as possible. However, if you believe the instructor misunderstood you or made an actual error in calculating your score that affects your grade, by all means ask for a grade change. Remember, though, that instructors can't give you extra points if it gives you an unfair advantage over others in the class.

If you view grades as a key to the future, you may want to fight for the grade you deserve. Some strategies for getting maximum consideration from your instructor are shown in "How to Get an Instructor to Consider Changing Your Grade."

Understand Grading Systems

What systems of grading do most colleges use?

Traditional Grades Most schools use the traditional A–F grading system. Many also include plus (+) and minus (–) judgments to make even finer distinctions in quality of work. Schools that use the traditional system convert grades into a grade point average, or GPA. In this system, A = 4 points, B = 3 points, C = 2 points, and D = 1 point. The point values of grades in all your courses are added up then averaged to create your GPA.

For example,

American history	C	2 points
College algebra	A	4 points
Intro to business	A	4 points
Sociology	B	3 points

GPA = 13 points divided by 4 courses = 3.25

A higher GPA improves your chances of getting a good job after college and getting into graduate school.

A GPA has special meaning at some colleges. For example, GPAs over 3.5 may qualify you for the Dean's List, the roster of students recognized for academic excellence. Some academic honor societies, such as Phi Beta Kappa and Phi Kappa Phi, invite students to join on the basis of GPA.

If your GPA falls below 2.0, you may be placed on academic restrictions or probation. On some campuses, this may limit the number of courses you can take in the next term and slow down your progress in your major. Because GPA is averaged across terms, a bad term's GPA will exert a heavy weight on your GPA even if your performance improves in later terms. If your GPA remains low, you can flunk out.

Instructors sometimes assign test or course grades by using a curve. The overall results of the test for the class are tied to the strongest performance in the class. Other students' scores are judged in relation to that strongest score. For example, suppose that on a test with 100 points the highest score was 85. An instructor who is grading on a curve might give As to scores of 76–85, Bs to scores of 66–75, and so on. Instructors may do this when a test turns out to be much harder than originally intended. However, even when most of the class performs poorly, some instructors don't curve the grades.

ON-TARGET TIPS

How to Get an Instructor to Consider Changing Your Grade

- **Ask for time after class to present your case.** Most instructors will not spend class time on the challenges of one student.
- **Develop your argument.** Point to evidence, such as an interpretation in the book that conflicts with something said in lecture, to support your request.
- **Explain your interpretation.** If you misinterpreted a question, describe your interpretation. Instructors will sometimes grant partial credit for a well-argued but off-base interpretation.
- **Avoid labeling a question as "bad."** Placing blame on the instructor will probably not encourage a helpful response.
- **Be gracious, whether you win or lose.** Most instructors remember and admire students who effectively advocate for themselves.

THE MARKS OF ZORRO

Pass-Fail Systems Some schools determine progress on a pass-fail basis: They don't give grades A through F, only pass (P) and fail (F) grades. When this is the only grading system a college uses, students often get extensive feedback about what they have achieved. Instead of grade point average, students graduate with other indicators of the quality of their work, such as a *narrative transcript*. In this document, their instructors describe their academic work and how well they achieved their goals.

Some colleges use both A–F and pass-fail grading. For example, students might get A–F grades in most of their courses but be allowed to take a certain number of credits outside their majors on a pass-fail basis. This dual system allows students to take some courses that they otherwise might avoid because of a potential mediocre grade.

Build Your Character

Character is destiny.

Heraclitis
Greek philosopher, 500 B.C.E.

Each test that you take actually tests you twice, once on the content and once on your character. Every test gives you an opportunity to demonstrate your personal integrity, and integrity matters a lot.

How Widespread Is Cheating?

Unfortunately, cheating is widespread in college. A comprehensive survey of 6,000 college students showed how big the problem is (S. F. Davis and others, 1992). Although more than 90 percent said that it was wrong to cheat, 75 percent said that they themselves had cheated in college or high school or both.

Most students won't report other students' cheating. In one survey, three-fourths of the students witnessed cheating by others but only one in a hundred informed the instructor (Jendrick, 1992). Many of the students ignored the situation even though they were angered or upset by the cheating. One-third of the students said they weren't bothered by the cheating.

Why Cheat?

Cheating in college has many causes (Keith-Spiegel, 1992). Often students who cheat feel pressure to succeed. They feel overwhelmed by the demands of so many deadlines and can't see any other way. Cheating gives students better grades with less effort.

Many students and instructors simply expect people to cheat if they have the opportunity. Some students reason that because other students cheat, it's okay for them to cheat, too. Instructors sometimes make it easy to cheat by not monitoring tests closely.

Often students who cheat do not get caught or aren't punished when they are caught. Most students recognize that cheating involves some risk. However, they report that they have seen students cheat and get away with it. Many instructors don't feel confident in challenging students who cheat, so they overlook suspicious acts. Inaction by the instructor encourages others to cheat.

Some students who cheat may not recognize when they are cheating. Some students "work together" and share answers either before or during a test. They believe that there is nothing wrong with sharing answers as long as both parties agree to collaborate. These students don't recognize that how they arrive at answers is just as important as the answers themselves.

Why Not Cheat?

Would you want to be cared for by a physician who cheated her way to a medical license? When the outcome of education involves life-and-death decisions, we clearly want to be cared for by someone with sound knowledge and skills.

Even if you don't plan to become a physician, you'll benefit from direct and accurate measurements of what you know. For example, your survival in more difficult, advanced courses may depend on your learning from an earlier course. By cheating, you increase the likelihood of serious academic problems in the future.

In their mission statements, most colleges pledge to foster moral and ethical behavior. Some colleges have a stringent honor code. These principles, usually described in the student handbook, recognize that students will have plenty of opportunities to cheat. When you exercise integrity, however, you demonstrate not just to your instructor but also to your classmates that you're a trustworthy, moral person.

Cheating can have ugly consequences. Even if they get away with cheating, some students struggle with a nagging conscience. The relief they initially feel in escaping a bad grade can be replaced by self-doubt, dissatisfaction, and guilt. These students suffer because they have fallen short of their own ideals. Further once they cheat and get away with it, they may be tempted to do it again the next time they aren't as prepared as they should be.

When cheaters do get caught, they face multiple risks. Being accused of cheating in front of others is humiliating. Being found guilty of cheating means that they may have to explain this judgment to their friends or parents. Worse, some instructors will turn them over to a student court for punishment, spreading their humiliation even further. Penalties for cheating differ. An instructor may give cheaters a "0" on the exam or an automatic F in the course. On campuses that practice a strict honor code, one episode of cheating leads to expulsion.

On some occasions, cheating students have received surprising consequences. Randy was appalled to discover that when his only episode of cheating surfaced, all of his instructors refused to write reference letters for him. This outcome ruined his plans for graduate school.

Under what circumstances do you think most students might be inclined to cheat?

When it's unlikely that they would be caught   _____

When they feel desperate to get a better grade   _____

When a lot is riding on a particular grade   _____

If they haven't managed their time well enough to study effectively   _____

When they might be teased by their peers if they refused to cheat   _____

Other: _____

If someone is caught cheating, which consequence do you think is the most appropriate?

Expulsion from school   _____

Failure in the course where the cheating occurred   _____

Failure of the assignment on which the cheating occurred   _____

Review by the school's honor board   _____

Public censure   _____

Repeating the assignment without cheating   _____

Depends on the cheater's history   _____

Other: _____

Rank order the things that discourage you from cheating:

I would lose my self-respect.   _____

I would be frightened of getting caught.   _____

I want my test results to reflect my learning accurately.   _____

I consider it my honor to uphold academic integrity.   _____

I don't want to give in to group pressure to do things that I don't believe in.   _____

Other: _____

Will you be able to withstand the temptation to take the easy (but risky) way out of making the grade?

What Will You Do?

You've now heard the arguments about why students cheat and why they resist cheating. If your assessment of values in Chapter 1 demonstrated that honesty was an important value for you, then you may have already committed yourself to making sure that you take no shortcuts to success. But what if you're not persuaded? Perhaps you've seen dishonest people get away with too much. After all, if 75 percent of students report that they have cheated, how wrong can it be?

Cheating is not a victimless crime. Students who cheat potentially rob themselves of learning that may be useful to them in the future. If you aspire to true excellence, you can't really do so by being a fraud. If you can't be a trustworthy student, how can you be a trustworthy partner or friend?

To explore your own perspective about cheating, complete Self-Assessment 7-3.

Learn with *InfoTrac College Edition*

InfoTrac College Edition

Look up these articles and search for more on topics that sparked your interest when reading this chapter.

Albert Einstein (1879–1955). Frederic Golden. *Time*. Dec. 31, 1999. v154, i27, p62.

Studying for Tests Study habits and test taking tips. Donna Gloe. *Dermatology Nursing.* Dec. 1999. v11, i6, p439.

Essay Tests How to write an essay. Gareth Affleck. *History Review*. March 1997. n27, p26.

Cheating Students are pulling off the big cheat. Carol Innerst. *Insight on the News*. March 9, 1998, v14, n9, p41.

Summary Strategies for Mastering College

Tests can help you refine your skills in planning and achieving goals as you build your knowledge base and your personal integrity.

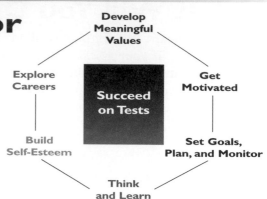

1 Get on with It!

- Accept that tests are a fact of life in college. They offer feedback for how well you're learning and give you a sense of accomplishment when you succeed.

2 Get in Gear

- Use long-term strategies: pacing yourself, protecting your health, and getting in the right frame of mind.
- Use short-term strategies: knowing what to expect, sizing up the teacher, and designing study strategies that suit your learning style.
- Cramming happens. Concentrate your efforts in the home stretch if you haven't had time to prepare.
- Reduce your test anxiety through positive self-talk, appropriate preparation, and relaxation strategies.

3 Meet the Challenge

- Plan how to use your time in each testing challenge.
- In objective tests look for clues to help you determine the best answer.
- Do your best on essay questions by planning, expressing yourself precisely, and writing legibly.

4 Make the Grade

- Review your results to consolidate your learning and to plan better study strategies.
- Use good judgment when you challenge your instructor's judgment about the fairness of a grade.
- Don't waste a semester. A bad semester will have a whopping impact on your cumulative GPA.

5 Build Your Character

- Demonstrate your academic integrity by resisting cheating.
- Avoid the ugly personal outcomes of cheating, including possible expulsion from school if you are caught.

Review Questions

1. How does a positive attitude influence your success on tests?

_____

_____

_____

_____

_____

_____

2. How do your study strategies vary by the kind of test you'll be facing?

_____

_____

_____

_____

_____

_____

3. What are some ways to overcome test anxiety?

_____

_____

_____

_____

_____

_____

4. Why should you review your test results carefully when the instructor returns your work?

_____

_____

_____

_____

_____

_____

5. What advantages does avoiding the temptation to cheat on tests offer?

_____

_____

_____

_____

_____

_____

Learning Portfolio

Reflect and Journal

1. Then and Now

Think about the grades you made in high school. How much time did you put into studies to achieve your high school grades? Now contrast your high school pattern to the work you're investing in your college grades. Are you managing the same levels of achievement? Have you had to increase your effort just to hold your ground? Are you now studying harder than you ever have? Is that effort resulting in the achievement you're aiming for?

_____
_____
_____
_____
_____
_____
_____
_____
_____

2. Reflect on Cheating

You've probably experienced a situation in which you could easily have cheated but you resisted the opportunity.

- Describe what would have made the cheating easy.

  _____
  _____
  _____

- Identify the feelings and values that were involved in resolving this problem.

  _____
  _____
  _____

- Were you satisfied with the resolution?

  _____
  _____

- What actions, if any, did you take to feel comfortable with the outcome?

  _____
  _____

Learn By Doing

1. Construct Your Own Exam

Construct a sample test for the next real test you'll face. If you were the teacher, what would be the most important concepts to test for? How would you go about assessing them?

_____
_____
_____
_____
_____
_____
_____
_____
_____
_____
_____

2. What's the Risk?

Locate a copy of your school's honor code or procedures that govern academic integrity. Review it to determine the risks involved in cheating. In most cases, the outcomes of being caught and punished for cheating are fairly severe. How can you reconcile this outcome with the fact that 75 percent of college students report cheating at some point in high school or college or both?

_____
_____
_____
_____
_____
_____
_____
_____
_____

Think Critically

1. Decode Essay Instructions

Find some examples of essay questions, preferably ones from tests you took this term. Circle the verbs that represent the kind of thinking the instructor has asked you to do in completing the essay. Think about what kind of question is being asked.

_____
_____
_____
_____
_____
_____
_____
_____
_____
_____
_____
_____
_____
_____
_____
_____
_____
_____
_____

2. Grades: Carrots or Sticks?

Many students thrive in graded systems. They like the clear-cut messages they get when their efforts are rewarded by good grades. However, other students find grades less rewarding. They think competition for grades undercuts meaningful learning and feel stressed out by the process. With a group of students, discuss the advantages and disadvantages of using grades to evaluate learning.

_____
_____
_____
_____
_____
_____
_____
_____
_____
_____
_____
_____
_____
_____
_____
_____

Think Creatively

1. Promote Better Test Preparation

Create a 60-second public service announcement either about the hazards of cramming or offering six bits of good advice about how to succeed on tests. See if it could be aired over the campus radio station during midterms or final exams.

_____
_____
_____
_____
_____
_____
_____
_____
_____

2. Find Your Quiet Place

Imagine your favorite peaceful place. Where would it be? What would you be doing there? Think of this calming refuge to help you ward off anxiety during testing. What would you need to do to make this image one you can rely on during stress to restore your peace? Also try the exercise "Learn to Relax" on the CD-ROM that comes with this book.

_____
_____
_____
_____
_____
_____
_____

Work toward Goals

Review the results of the self-assessments you completed in this chapter. Also review the opening checklist. Based on your review, select a relatively short-term goal that you want to work on now.

1. What is that goal? (*Hint:* Is it challenging, reasonable, and specific?)

_____

_____

_____

_____

2. What strategies will you use to achieve your goal? (*Hint:* Can you organize your strategy into a series of smaller goals?)

_____

_____

_____

_____

3. What obstacles may be in your way as you attempt to make these positive changes?

_____

_____

_____

_____

4. What additional resources might help you achieve your goal? (Use the CD-ROM that comes with this book for access to some useful leads.)

_____

_____

_____

_____

5. By what date do you want to accomplish your goal?

_____

_____

_____

_____

6. How will you know you have succeeded?

_____

_____

_____

_____

Expand Your Thinking Skills

Sharpen Your Saw

This chapter describes how you can use your college experience to become a better thinker. You'll explore ways to move beyond memorization to refine your thinking skills, including developing strong arguments, solving problems, making sound decisions, and being more creative. To get a current picture of your thinking skills, place a check mark next to only those items that apply to you.

_____ I can tell the difference between critical and uncritical thinking.

_____ I know how to ask good questions.

_____ I argue well.

_____ I use systematic strategies to solve problems.

_____ I regularly make sound decisions.

_____ I can avoid routine thinking problems that prevent good decisions.

_____ I strive to be creative in numerous ways.

_____ I practice mindful thinking to improve my options.

Consider the unusual story of Temple Grandin on the next page. Her distinctive problem-solving skills demonstrate many dimensions of the thinking abilities that this chapter explores.

IMAGES OF COLLEGE SUCCESS

Temple Grandin

"I think in pictures. I don't think in words," says Temple Grandin, a professor at Colorado State University. "I translate both spoken and written words into full-color-movies, complete with sound, which run like a VCR tape in my head.... In my job as an equipment designer for the livestock industry, visual thinking is a tremendous advantage" (Grandin, 1995, p. 19).

Grandin has become world famous for her problem-solving skills in managing livestock. She has specialized in methods that help livestock handlers herd cows more peaceably by thinking about the challenge from the "cow's eye view." She has constructed holding areas that provide physical supports that calm agitated livestock, making them easier to handle. As she studies a problem at hand, pictures develop in her mind about how to solve the problem. Grandin's accomplishments are all the more remarkable because she has a rare form of autism called Asperger's syndrome.

Asperger's syndrome has a profound impact on how people think and relate to others. One problem is supersensitivity of the senses. Grandin suggests that having almost "bionic ears" means that she is easily distracted by sounds that other people would ignore. For example, a school bell would literally hurt her ears.

This type of autism also causes her to behave eccentrically, with repetitive actions, abrupt shifts in conversation, and very limited social skills. In her book, *Thinking in Pictures,* Grandin claims that she doesn't seem to possess the basic brain wiring that most people have to comprehend and react to social situations.

Temple Grandin's autism has not hindered her success in resolving problems in livestock management.

© Rosalie Winard

For example, she never could understand or relate to what was going on between Romeo and Juliet. She often compares her existence with the emotionless character Data on *Star Trek.*

However, Grandin's intellectual gifts are dazzling. Her exceptional visualization skills, careful observations, and well-developed spatial and critical-thinking skills combine with her knowledge of animal behavior to produce many creative solutions that have advanced the humane treatment of animals.

Learn more about Temple Grandin.

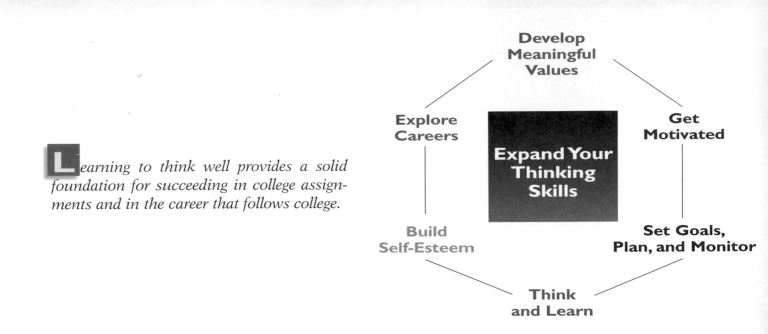

earning to think well provides a solid foundation for succeeding in college assignments and in the career that follows college.

Think Critically

You've probably heard the term _critical thinking_ used in many different contexts. It refers to the use of purposeful, reasoned thinking to reach your goals (Halpern, 1997). Among other benefits, when you think critically you improve your ability to learn and retain new learning. Clearly, this will benefit you in college and beyond.

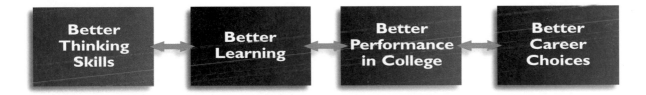

The complexities of life in the twenty-first century underscore the need for critical-thinking skills. Conserving the environment, managing nuclear energy, and staying a competitive economic force are just a few of the tasks that require our best collective thinking. Such concerns have prompted national discussions about the role of colleges in helping citizens develop better thinking skills.

Many colleges have created courses specifically on critical thinking. One aim of a liberal arts education is to help you develop broad critical-thinking skills by sampling the various ways of thinking required in different disciplines (Beyer, 1998). Different disciplines tend to approach critical thinking in distinctive ways. For example, the natural sciences often emphasize thinking skills as they relate to problem solving. The humanities focus on the critical analysis of expressive works. Your own knack for critical thinking will depend on your learning style and the successes you've had in various thinking challenges.

Figure 8-1 summarizes the general qualities of both passive and critical thinkers. Self-Assessment 8-1 gives you an opportunity to evaluate how well your characteristics match those of good critical thinkers.

Change your thoughts and you change your whole world.

Norman Vincent Peale
20th-century American philosopher

The Critical Difference

Review your general approach to intellectual challenges. Check the category that most closely corresponds with your usual pattern of critical thinking.

	Always	Usually	Sometimes	Rarely
I like to talk about topics that I know a lot about.	_____	_____	_____	_____
I don't pretend to know more than I really do.	_____	_____	_____	_____
I feel energized by differences in opinion.	_____	_____	_____	_____
I get more enthusiastic as ideas get more complicated.	_____	_____	_____	_____
I regularly need to revisit what I think to correct errors.	_____	_____	_____	_____
I like to look more deeply into things to get greater insight.	_____	_____	_____	_____
I'm not afraid to change my mind.	_____	_____	_____	_____
I prefer evidence over intuition as a way to persuade others.	_____	_____	_____	_____
I can spot flaws in arguments.	_____	_____	_____	_____

If you marked most of the columns "always" or "usually," you demonstrate the characteristics of a good critical thinker. Those marked "sometimes" show some room for improvement. Work on items marked "rarely" to maximize your ability to think critically.

FIGURE 8-1
Two Types of Thinkers

Critical Thinkers ...

Are honest with themselves. They acknowledge what they don't know and watch for their own errors.

Regard problems and controversies as exciting challenges. They don't shrink from complexity.

Strive for understanding. They stay curious and invest time to overcome confusion.

Base judgments on evidence rather than personal preference. They deter judgment when evidence is insufficient and revise judgment when justified.

Show interest in other people's ideas. They read and listen attentively, even when they disagree with others.

Recognize that extreme views are seldom correct. They practice fair-mindedness.

Practice restraint. They control their feelings and think before acting.

Uncritical Thinkers ...

Pretend to know more than they do. They ignore their limitations and assume their views are error-free.

Regard problems and controversies as nuisances. They get annoyed if things aren't as simple as possible.

Show impatience. They would rather remain confused than make an effort to understand.

Base judgments on first impressions and gut reactions. They show no concern about evidence and cling steadfastly to earlier views.

Preoccupy themselves with their own opinions. They are unwilling to pay attention to others' views, and they argue out of reflex, not merit.

Ignore the need for balance. They prefer ideas that support their own point of view.

Act on impulse. They follow their feelings before thinking.

Source: Adapted from Ruggerlo (1996).

Ask Questions

One sign of a good critical thinker is the ability to ask on-target questions. But you sometimes may feel discouraged about asking questions in college. You may have acquired passive learning habits in earlier years of school. Yet when you were little, you were probably constantly asking questions. If you don't ask questions often, your questioning skills may be in hiding.

The problem may be fear of embarrassment. You may think of good questions to ask but worry about what others will think of you. Perhaps the instructor will think your question comes from left field. Or maybe other students will think you are showing off what you know. The problem with worrying so much about

Reprinted with permission of the artist, Carol Cable.

what others think is that you sacrifice your chances to improve your own thinking and speaking skills. It's *your* education. If you don't take risks, you won't get to develop your mind as much as you deserve.

Although instructors may reassure you that "there's no such thing as a stupid question," there are *unwelcome* questions. These include questions that detract from the momentum of the class, focus more on self-concerns than on the needs of the class, or demonstrate that the questioner has failed to pay attention.

Get your curiosity out in the open. If you recapture your enthusiasm for asking questions, your college years will be more interesting and more fun than if you don't. A special kind of thrill occurs when your mind works well. "I Have a Question" gives some tips on how to ask good questions.

ON-TARGET TIPS

I Have a Question

You can improve your analytic skills by learning to ask questions that will help you break open the ideas you're studying (Browne & Keeley, 1990). Here are some questions that can help you strengthen these important skills.

- What are the issues and the conclusion?
- What are the reasons?
- What words or phrases are ambiguous?
- Are there value conflicts?
- What assumptions are being made?
- What is the evidence?
- Are there other ways to explain the results?
- Are there flaws in the reasoning?
- Is any information missing?
- Do the conclusions fit the reasons?
- How do the results fit with my own values?

Offer Criticism

Dr. Gray shuts off the videotape of the president's State of the Union address, then turns to the class and says, "What do you think?" Jeff dreads moments like this because the question feels so open-ended. He's never sure what instructors want.

When a teacher offers you a chance to practice the higher-order skill of thinking critically and evaluating, it's easy to feel intimidated. However, some strategies can help you handle it.

1. **Decide whether you like what you're being asked to judge.** Your general reaction can set the stage for detailed analysis later on. For example, were you smiling or frowning during most of the State of the Union address?

2. **Look for both positive and negative attributes.** Some people unnecessarily limit their thinking by looking only for flaws or highlights. If you were thrilled by what the president said, try to find some weaknesses in the address. If you were dissatisfied, look also for positive features in what you heard.

Questions posed to you by instructors can show how you're thinking. Many instructors expect you to ask questions to indicate your interest and improve your grasp of course concepts.

Gary A. Conner/PhotoEdit

3. **Use criteria to stimulate your thinking.** To what degree is the work you are evaluating

effective?	*sufficient?*
efficient?	*adequate?*
reasonable?	*logical?*
beautiful?	*sensitive?*
practical?	*accurate?*
thought provoking?	*stimulating?*
justifiable?	*comprehensive?*
understandable?	*relevant?*

Which of the criteria would apply to a presidential address? A work of art? A symphony? A public policy?

4. **Use examples to support your judgment.** Expect to explain your judgment. Which phrases or examples in the State of the Union stayed with you? What made the examples compelling?

Reason

Good critical thinkers can make inferences, use logic, and create and defend arguments (Beyer, 1998). Great reasoning isn't always easy, but it can be learned.

Make the Right Inferences

As you head for class early in the morning during finals week, suppose you came across a student who was out cold, sprawled across the sidewalk, his books scattered on the ground (Halonen & Gray, 2001). What would you think? There are many inferences you might draw based on what you observed. *Inferences* are interpretations that you derive from processing cues in a situation.

For example, you might infer that your fallen campus colleague might be

1. Exhausted from studying for finals
2. Suffering from a serious health problem
3. A poor, book-loving traveler from another culture
4. A psychology major doing an experiment

All of the inferences are *plausible*, meaning that they are logical, potentially accurate ways to explain what you saw. However, it's likely that one explanation is better than others.

You constantly make inferences. Your roommate is scowling so you infer she failed a test. You find the dishes piled up so you infer that you'll have to do them. You get an unsigned note asking you to go out for coffee and you infer who was the most likely to have invited you.

Your interpretations of the events around you are based on your collected experiences. Therefore, your inferences will reflect that experience and sometimes produce biases in interpretation. Go back to the example of the fallen colleague. If you inferred that the individual might be recovering from a hangover, your past experiences may have created a predisposition or bias in how you make sense of what you see in this situation. To test this proposition further, imagine that the fallen colleague is female, not male. How does simply changing the sex of the person change your interpretive bias? You can see how bias can shape and possibly distort the reality that you experience.

The chances are that your ability to make accurate inferences is very good. However, inferences can be tricky. Notice in the examples given how easy it is to be wrong. In fact, think about a recent situation in which you jumped to the wrong conclusion. A faulty inference was probably to blame.

Sometimes inferences become *assumptions,* an inference that we accept as the truth. You may not recognize that you're operating from a faulty assumption until you learn otherwise.

Learn How to Handle Claims

Instructors may challenge you to sort fact from fiction. They may ask you to judge the *validity* (truthfulness) of a *claim* (a statement that can be either true or false but not both) (Epstein, 2000). Claims are different than *facts,* which are truths that can't be disputed.

Fact: The moon is full at least once a month.
Claim: The full moon makes people a little crazy.

Notice how the claim is debatable and requires evidence before we can determine its validity; the fact cannot be challenged.

When you evaluate a claim, you have three choices:

1. Accept the claim
2. Reject the claim
3. Suspend judgment until you have more information

How will you rise to this challenge?

When to Accept a Claim There are three circumstances in which it's reasonable to accept a claim:

- **Personal experience.** Trust your personal experience *only* if your confidence level is high and there isn't a good contradictory explanation. Human memory can be faulty; human perception can sometimes introduce distortions that can lead you to endorse a claim that simply isn't true. For example, you may claim that Spike Lee's most recent movie is the best film ever made. Your claim will be bolstered if he wins an Oscar and weakened if you've seen only Spike Lee movies.
- **Trustworthy expert.** If a claim is made by someone with a trustworthy track record or other similar credentials such as expertise, it's reasonable to accept the claim as true. This includes claims made in reputable journals and references. For example, claims about damage from smoking that are reported in the *New England Journal of Medicine* are usually trustworthy. Claims by your next-door neighbor about the value of vitamin B may not be trustworthy.
- **Reliable media sources.** Unless the media source is going to profit from the claim presented, it's reasonable to accept the claim from it. For example, local weather forecasters regularly make claims about future weather patterns that generally are accurate. Some newscasters demonstrate their reliability over time with the accuracy of their predictions.

When to Question a Claim
Question claims that do the following:

- **Come from "unnamed sources."** If you can't verify the source, you shouldn't readily accept the claim.
- **Confer an advantage.** Experts sometimes make big money by supporting certain claims. Be suspicious of claims that can be linked to payoff.
- **Offer personal experience as "proof."** Just as your own personal experience can be unreliable, so can the personal experience of others.
- **Appeal to common beliefs and practice.** Just because "everybody does it" doesn't make it right or truthful.
- **Use language in misleading ways.** Politicians are often accused of putting a "spin" on their claims. For example, they might report that the "vast majority" of Americans believe in vouchers for private school, when the actual statistic in favor is 51 percent at the time. Beware of overblown language that can disguise the truth.

See Self-Assessment 8-2 for practice in spotting shaky claims.

Form Strong Arguments
In formal reasoning, an *argument* is a set of claims. The argument begins with *premises,* initial claims that lead to a final claim called the *conclusion* of the argument (Epstein, 2000).

A good argument is one in which the premises (1) are true and (2) lead logically to the truth of the conclusion. Good arguments are also called *strong* or *valid* arguments. Here's an example of a good argument:

> *Premise:* All healthy dogs have fur.
> *Premise:* Spot is a healthy dog.
> *Conclusion:* Therefore, Spot has fur.

Some good arguments are reasonable because the premises and conclusion are sound, even though the conclusion may not be as absolute as the one in the example. In most cases, these plausible arguments deal with probable outcomes instead of definitive ones.

> *Premise:* Most dogs who live outside have fleas.
> *Premise:* Spot lives outside in a doghouse.
> *Conclusion:* Therefore, Spot probably has fleas.

Spot could be the rare exception, but the conclusion is logical if the first two premises are true.

Here are some simple suggestions that will help you develop the most persuasive arguments.

1. Be sure that the conclusion follows logically from the premises.
2. Leave out faulty or dubious premises.
3. Use precise language to pinpoint your claim. (Vague or ambiguous language makes your position easier to challenge).
4. Avoid making claims you can't prove. See Figure 8-2 on page 200 for examples.

Form Counterarguments
In many classes you may be asked to find flaws in an argument. A counterargument challenges an argument by showing (1) a premise is false, (2) the conclusion is false, or (3) the reasoning is weak or faulty.

However, some counterargument strategies are ineffective. For example, ridicule is not a good way to counterargue. Making fun of someone disrupts communication without improving anyone's understanding.

Claim Check

Would you accept (+), reject (–), or suspend judgment (0) on the following claims?

On what basis?

_____ 1. NASA officials claim that increased spending on moon
exploration will produce enormous scientific gains.

_____

_____ 2. The Smithsonian Institution claims to house rocks that
were taken off the surface of the moon.

_____

_____ 3. Aunt Fanny claims that "dancing in the light of the full
moon will make you fall in love with your partner."

_____

_____ 4. *Discover Magazine* reports the current claim that
the moon may have been separated from earth by
a comet's strike.

_____

_____ 5. The moon is made of green cheese.

_____

Answers to Claim Check

1. *Reject* (−). Although NASA officials claim that increased spending on moon exploration will produce enormous scientific gains, the claim must be rejected since their successes in making the claim will increase the funds that pay their salaries. Therefore, the claim is suspect because it confers an advantage.

2. *Accept* (+). The Smithsonian Institution's claims that they house rocks taken from the surface of the moon should be accepted because it is a trustworthy organization and the moon walks were covered thoroughly by reliable media, so you could easily look this up.

3. *Reject* (−). Aunt Fanny's expertise about the connection between dancing and the full moon is a good example of personal experience that probably should not be trusted.

4. *Suspend Judgment* (0). *Discover Magazine's* claim that the moon may have been separated from earth by a comet's strike is credible because *Discover* makes a practice of reporting emerging scientific theory and is well-respected in the scientific community. However, because this is just one of many theories about the origin of the moon, it's best to suspend judgment until you examine the competing views.

5. *Reject* (−). Although this belief was once shared by many people, contemporary science has demonstrated that the moon is mineral, not dairy, in composition.

See if you can spot ways to challenge the following arguments.

© 2000 by Sidney Harris.

Example 1

Premise: All cats have four legs.
Premise: I have four legs.
Conclusion: Therefore, I am a cat.

Both premises are true, but together they do not produce a logical conclusion, because the first premise does not state that *only* cats have four legs. The conclusion must follow logically from the premises.

Example 2

Premise: All birds have fur.
Premise: Tweetie is a bird.
Conclusion: Tweetie has fur.

The first premise is false, so the conclusion is implausible.

Example 3

Premise: Good dogs sit on command.
Premise: Spot sits on command.
Conclusion: Spot is a good dog.

Although the premises may both be true, the conclusion isn't supported. Spot may engage in lots of other behavior that makes him a bad dog.

Example 4

Premise: The dog show winner is the best dog in the country.
Premise: Spot won first place in the dog show.
Conclusion: Spot is the best dog in the country.

The conclusion follows logically, but what exactly is meant by "best"? And is the first claim likely to be true? There are lots of dog shows every year. Was the show that Spot won really the Super Bowl of dog shows? In other words, the first premise is suspect, so the conclusion is as well.

Another ineffective strategy is restating the original argument in a distorted way and then disproving the distortion. To be effective, your counterargument must accurately represent the original argument and defend against only that argument.

Deduction versus Induction

There are two types of argument: induction and deduction. *Induction* involves generalizing from specific instances to broad principles (see Figure 8-3). For example, perhaps you really enjoyed your first college foreign language class. Based on that experience, you might reason inductively that *all* language classes in college are great. Notice that your conclusion or rule—your *induction*—might be incorrect, because your next course may turn out to be disappointing. Inductive arguments are never 100 percent certain. They can be weak or strong.

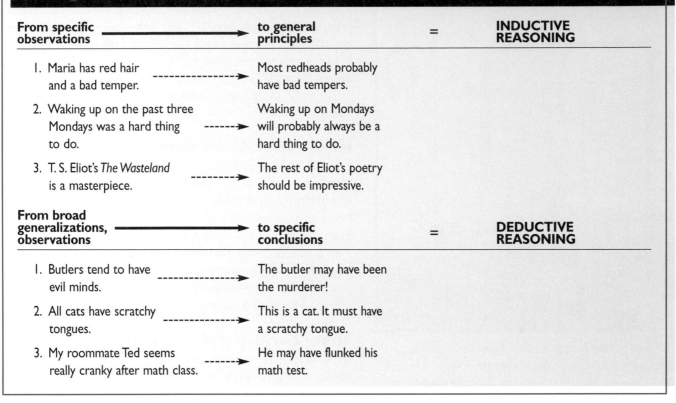

FIGURE 8-3
Using Induction and Deduction

From specific observations ———→	to general principles	=	INDUCTIVE REASONING
1. Maria has red hair and a bad temper. ------→	Most redheads probably have bad tempers.		
2. Waking up on the past three Mondays was a hard thing to do. ------→	Waking up on Mondays will probably always be a hard thing to do.		
3. T. S. Eliot's *The Wasteland* is a masterpiece. ------→	The rest of Eliot's poetry should be impressive.		

From broad generalizations, observations ———→	to specific conclusions	=	DEDUCTIVE REASONING
1. Butlers tend to have evil minds. ------→	The butler may have been the murderer!		
2. All cats have scratchy tongues. ------→	This is a cat. It must have a scratchy tongue.		
3. My roommate Ted seems really cranky after math class. ------→	He may have flunked his math test.		

In contrast, *deduction* moves from general situations or rules to specific predictions or applications. Deductive reasoning parallels the hypothesis-testing procedures used in the sciences. For example, your chemistry professor may ask you to identify an unknown substance. By applying specific strategies of analysis, you narrow the possibilities until you know what the substance is. A deductive argument is 100 percent true if the premises are true and the reasoning is sound. When the premises are untrue or the logical connection between the premises and the conclusion is shaky, a deductive argument may be false. Look at the deductive examples in Figure 8-3. Is any one of these arguments completely convincing? Why or why not?

Refine Your Reasoning

You can improve your reasoning skills in the following ways.

Be Willing to Argue   You may have to present a position in a term paper, in a speech, or in answer to a complex question in class. Reasoning is studied as a formal science in logic classes, but you'll certainly have opportunities to create and defend arguments in many other formal and informal situations. Don't shrink from those opportunities, even if you have negative feelings about the word *argument* based on the tension that you've felt when in conflict with a friend or loved one.

Check Your Assumptions   It's easy to reach wrong conclusions from wrong assumptions. For example, the satirist Jonathan Swift caused a stir in the eighteenth century when he proposed one solution for two serious

$$\frac{4\,(Wr)^2}{\sqrt{(8-y)^2+(y-}} = r$$

"Yes, yes, I know that, Sidney . . . everybody knows that! . . . But look: Four wrongs squared, minus two wrongs to the fourth power, divided by this formula, do make a right."

problems facing British society: too many orphaned children and not enough food. Swift proposed that both problems could be solved if the orphans were eaten! Those who *assumed* Swift was putting forward a serious position were outraged. Those who carefully examined Swift's real purpose and discovered that he meant to bring serious attention to these social problems were amused by his wit and sensitized to the problem.

Identify your assumptions. Do your best to verify them.

Know Your Own Bias We all have strong preferences and prejudices that may prevent us from evaluating an argument fairly. By knowing your own assumptions and prejudices, you can increase the likelihood of coming up with more effective arguments. For example, if you know that you feel strong sympathies for single parents, you can take this bias into account when you evaluate government policies that affect their lives. Good reasoners guard against their own "soft spots" to increase their objectivity.

Take Time before Concluding Sometimes we short-circuit our reasoning. It's easy to get excited about a bright idea and stop the hard analytic work involved in thinking the problem through to the end. A premature judgment may work out, but it tends to make us even less exacting the next time we analyze a problem. Careful reasoners resist impulsive judgments. They thoroughly review an argument to make sure they have addressed all questions.

Solve Problems the "IDEAL" Way

It's tempting to go on hoping that a problem can be solved without giving it much thought. Good problem solving begins by reaching back and clarifying your motivation to bring the problem to an end. One motivation can be to reduce the number of things that you always worry about.

| Motivation to Solve the Problem | Reliable Method | Best Solution | Higher Self-Esteem |

Temple Grandin demonstrated elegant problem-solving skills when she figured out how to manage livestock by looking at the problem from a cow's point of view. After careful examination of all the contributing factors, she discovered that applying some form of pressure made cows less agitated when herded from one area to another. She redesigned entry ramps to provide pressure points, experimenting with different design strategies until she successfully produced a design that reduced the herds' agitation. Her ideas were so successful that the livestock industry widely adopted them for more humane care.

But her problem solving didn't stop there. She adapted the same technique that calmed livestock to her own struggles to stay calm when she felt overstimulated by social activity. She developed a "human squeeze box," which provides gentle pressure on her when she climbs into it. She uses this device regularly to restore her feelings of control.

Grandin's problem solving illustrates a systematic approach to solving problems. Many people find it helpful to use a specific problem-solving system, such as the five-step IDEAL method (Bransford & Stein, 1984):

1. **Identify the problem.** Grandin recognized that herding livestock was challenging under usual conditions.
2. **Define the problem.** She comprehended the relationship between pressure and calmness after analyzing the relevant factors.
3. **Explore alternative approaches.** She applied different strategies to find an approach that would calm the herd.
4. **Act on the best strategy.** Grandin synthesized the best ideas to come up with a squeezing device that worked to calm cows.
5. **Look back to evaluate the effects.** Grandin was so satisfied with the results of her experimental designs that she tried out the same squeeze-box principles to calm agitated humans.

How might this approach work to solve common problems in a college setting? Let's look at a typical case.

1. **Identify the problem.** Bernita discovered when she arrived at her first art appreciation class that her instructor had already started. The instructor looked distinctively displeased as Bernita took a seat in the back of the class. When she looked at her watch, Bernita discovered that she was two minutes late. Obviously, she didn't want to annoy her instructor by arriving late to class each day. How could she avoid being late?
2. **Define the problem.** Be as specific and comprehensive as you can in defining a problem. Outline the contributing factors. What made Bernita late to class? Was her watch broken? Was she carrying 60 pounds of books? Did she walk too slowly? Probably the main factor was the distance between the art class and the English class that Bernita had on the other side of the campus in the prior period. Even if she walked at top speed, she couldn't get to the art class on time.
3. **Explore alternative approaches.** Systematically gather and explore alternative solutions to isolate the best approach. Assuming that arriving late to class makes her uncomfortable enough to take action, what are some reasonable alternatives that Bernita could pursue? She can drop either class, transfer into another section that prevents the conflict, or ask the instructor to wait until she gets there (maybe not). Or perhaps she can talk to both instructors and explain her situations. "Coming up with Alternatives" suggests ways to generate solutions.
4. **Act on the best strategy.** Take specific action to resolve the problem. Include more than one strategy. Bernita decided to explain to her art instructor why she would be a few minutes late to class, added that she would do her best to get there on time, and

ON-TARGET TIPS

Coming up with Alternatives

These approaches may help you generate new ideas for resolving problems:

- Examine how you feel about the situation.
- Collect opinions about possible approaches.
- Research what the experts would do.
- Break the problem up into smaller pieces.
- Think through the consequences of leaving the problem alone.
- Work backward from the preferred outcome.

asked for her instructor's support. The instructor verified that Bernita would be late only by two minutes and asked that she sit near the door to minimize disruptions. She also thanked Bernita for her courtesy.

5. **Look back to evaluate the effects.** The final step is to evaluate whether or not your solution works. You might be thrilled with how well it works and feel free to move on to your next challenge. Or you might discover that the solution didn't work. In this instance, Bernita's problem solving was successful. Her solution not only saved her from the trouble and expense of dropping the class but also gave her a better personal connection with her instructor.

To evaluate how systematic you are in problem solving, complete Self-Assessment 8-3. Look for ways to make your problem-solving skills more systematic.

What are some other ways you can maximize your problem-solving skills (Whimbey & Lochhead, 1991)?

*Y*ou see, but you do not observe.

Sherlock Holmes
19th-century fictional detective

- **Observe carefully.** Try to identify all the relevant factors in a problem from the outset. Superficial observation misses factors that hold keys to ultimate solutions. Careful observation involves analysis—identifying the relationships among the elements of the problem.
- **Stay positive and persistent.** Don't be beaten by frustration. Search for ways to make the struggle invigorating rather than frustrating.
- **Show concern for accuracy.** Pay attention to detail. It's easy to let small errors occur in moments of inattention. Take care not to leave out crucial information. Proofread statements and recheck calculations before submitting your work for review.

Make Good Decisions

Some decisions have far-reaching consequences. For example, you decided where to go to college. To make that decision, you may have used some systematic criteria. Perhaps you wanted a college close to home with low tuition costs and specific majors. Or you may have decided to go to the campus you liked best when you visited. How satisfied you are now with your college experience may reflect how carefully you made that decision.

Making decisions involves not only using higher-order thinking skills but also integrating those skills with your own values and your knowledge about yourself. Good decisions solve problems and make your life better. Bad ones often make a mess. See "We're Only Human" for some tips on avoiding bad decisions.

Think Creatively

*D*on't be afraid to go on a wild goose chase. That's what wild geese are for.

Anonymous

College abounds with opportunities for you to build self-esteem by expanding your creative abilities. Start to become more creative by motivating yourself to exercise your creativity whenever you can. Figure 8-4 on page 207 spotlights recent winners of the Collegiate Inventors Competition sponsored by the National Inventors Hall of Fame.

How Systematically Do I Solve Problems?

Think about the problems you've faced in your academic and personal life in the last month. Review how regularly you went through each of the stages of the IDEAL model.

	Usually	Not Usually	Explain
Identification: I accurately identify when something needs attention.	_____	_____	_____
Definition: I describe problems comprehensively, including all factors that might influence the problem.	_____	_____	_____
Evaluation: I figure out different approaches to take and decide on the best alternative.	_____	_____	_____
Action: I put my plans into action.	_____	_____	_____
Looking back: I purposefully examine how effective my chosen solutions are.	_____	_____	_____

As you examine the results of your review, which aspects of problem solving are your strengths? What elements do you need to practice to become more systematic in your problem solving? What ideas do you have for incorporating these skills into your problem-solving style?

We're Only Human

All of us make bad decisions from time to time. How can you avoid everyday errors that produce bad decisions? See the following for some helpful answers (Halpern, 1997).

- **Avoid overconfidence.** We tend to be overconfident about the correctness of our past decisions. Usually we neglect to notice that a path not taken might have been better than the one we chose. For example, you may be convinced that you chose exactly the right place to start your college education. However, you can't be completely positive, because you won't have any way to compare how you might have felt starting on other campuses. Be a little skeptical when you evaluate how wise your past decisions have been.

- **Look for disconfirming evidence.** We tend to look for evidence to support the outcome that we prefer. We also tend to ignore information that might change our minds. For example, when buying a new car, we may pay close attention to consumer reports on what a great buy the car is but still ignore the reports that discuss the car's safety problems. Good decisions makers actively look for disconfirming evidence so that their final decisions cover all the bases.

- **Distinguish wishes from reality.** If you believe that things are always going to turn out positively, you're in for some surprises! People who expect only positive outcomes are sometimes referred to as "Pollyannas." Pollyanna is a fictional character who always finds something to be chipper about no matter how ugly her circumstances. In the throes of optimism, we can mistakenly assume that we can will what we want to happen. For example, you may think that because you worked so hard your instructor couldn't possibly hand out the grade that your test scores predict. Think again. Good decision makers recognize that merely wishing for positive outcomes won't make it so.

- **Abandon sunken costs.** Once you've embarked on a course of action, especially if you've had to invest time or money, it may be hard to recognize a bad decision and choose a different course. For example, if you've worked your hardest and just can't seem to do well in a particular class, don't stay there just because of the time you have already invested unless you have a good strategy that could make things change positively. Forget the time and energy you've already sunk—they're gone!

- **Don't overreact to forceful positions.** Most Americans hate to be told what to do. Even if we might actually like a course of action, our preferences get squashed when someone tells us we *must* take that course of action. Suppose your older brother forcefully tells you to major in political science. You might think, "Not on your life!" and begin to look for other majors just to show him your independence. Despite the way he told you, your brother might be right. Good decision makers don't choose a lesser-quality alternative just to demonstrate their freedom of choice. They evaluate the quality of the suggestion apart from the manner of the person making the suggestion.

- **Overcome hindsight bias.** Suppose you're in a class where the instructor seems a bit erratic. Toward the end of the term, he fails to show up for class and another instructor reports that he quit for mental health reasons. You might think, "I knew it all along." This pattern is referred to as *hindsight bias*. One anonymous observer reported that "hindsight bias is 20/20." It's easy to claim that we could have predicted something *after* it has already happened. Good decision makers don't waste time claiming they predicted what has become obvious.

"You take all the time you need, Larry—this certainly is a big decision."

Creative people tend to have some common characteristics (Perkins, 1984). They actively pursue experiences that are aesthetically pleasing. For example, they enjoy experiencing beauty in art or elegance in a scientific theory. They also enjoy taking a unique approach to research, choosing new and exciting topics rather than going over more familiar territory that other students might address.

Creative people love the process of creating. For example, creative students may feel as good when they turn their work in as when they get back a successful grade.

FIGURE 8-4

Winners of the 1999 Collegiate Inventors Competition

Amy B. Smith developed an incubator that can run without electricity, which will be helpful in remote areas or developing countries in medical work and water-quality testing.

William C. W. Chan developed an ultrasensitive dye that will help in the detection of a variety of diseases, including cancer, AIDS, or Down syndrome.

Tobin J. Fisher designed a new hull shape that can increase the mid- to high-wind speed performance of catamarans because it incorporates some of the design features of windsurfing.

Jennifer E. Davis produces the "Twistmaster," a device that can help people with limited dexterity or arthritis open any kind of twist-off cap, including prescription containers.

Source: http://www.invent.org/induction99/collegiate.html

Creative thinkers are flexible and like to play with problems. Although creativity is hard work, the work goes more smoothly when taken lightly; humor greases the wheels (Goleman, Kaufmann, & Ray, 1992). Playing helps you stay open to more possibilities and disarms the inner censor that often condemns your ideas as off-base.

Creative people take risks and learn from their mistakes. Picasso created more than 20,000 paintings; not all of them are masterpieces. Your learning will be limited if you don't stick out your neck once in a while. If you're considering a particularly creative approach to an assignment, however, share your plan ahead of time with your instructor.

Despite the stereotype that creative people are eccentric, most creative people strive to evaluate their work fairly. Whether they use an established set of criteria or generate their own, they themselves ultimately judge the value of what they have created. Creative students thrive when they think of guidelines for assignments as a launching point for their imagination.

To evaluate your own creative style, complete Self-Assessment 8-4, "My Creative Profile."

Break the Locks

Many people believe that they can't lead creative lives. Despite childhoods filled with imaginative play, most of us surrender our sense of curiosity over time, harming our capacity for creativity.

Roger Von Oech (1990) lists numerous "mental locks" that prevent us from pursuing creative responses (see Figure 8-5). A flexible attitude sets the stage for creativity in school and throughout your life.

FIGURE 8-5
Some "Mental Locks" that Reduce Your Creativity—and What to Do about Them

Mental Lock	The Creative Key
I have to have the right answer.	Sometimes the "right" answer isn't as much fun or as satisfying as an alternative.
I must be logical.	But I need to get in touch with my emotional side.
I must follow the rules.	But breaking the rules can be really liberating!
I have to be practical.	But not in every situation.
Play is frivolous and wastes time.	And I miss it! I want those feelings back!
That's not my area.	But it could be!
I must avoid ambiguity.	But ambiguity can open new doors.
I can't appear to be foolish.	Until I remember that foolishness can be fun.
To err is wrong.	And I'm designed to derail from time to time.
I'm not creative.	But I could be!

Source: Von Oech (1998).

Practice Mindfulness

Developing the right frame of mind about possibilities is an essential ingredient in improving your creative potential. The psychologist Ellen Langer (1989, 1997) demonstrated how practicing a "mindful" approach to life can improve not only the quality of your life, but also its length.

Langer and her colleague, Judith Rodin, recruited residents of a home for the elderly to participate in an experiment (Roden & Langer, 1977). They randomly assigned residents to one of two groups. Staff members encouraged

My Creative Profile

To get some measure of your creative potential, answer the following:

1. If you were managing a rock group, what original name would you give them?

2. You've been asked to plan a birthday party for your 5-year-old nephew. How would you make it different from other parties his friends have attended?

3. How many uses can you think of for a pencil?

4. What kind of musical instrument could you make out of the contents of the junk drawer in your family's kitchen?

5. You've just been invited to a costume party. What will you wear?

6. What theme would you propose for a sales campaign for your favorite shoe?

7. What business could you set up that would make the lives of your classmates easier? What would you call the business? How would you promote and develop it?

8. What is one strategy you could develop that would make people less afraid of failure?

9. You have to negotiate a late deadline for a paper with your professor. How might you do that creatively?

10. How many creative uses can you think of for a remote control unit?

This assessment highlights flexible thinking. If you found yourself stumped by most of the items, then you may not have developed the flexible mindset that helps creative people. If you answered a few of the questions, then you can probably point to a few creative areas in your life. If you felt exhilarated by the questions, chances are good that you're often creative.

the members of the first group to exercise more personal responsibility. For example, those people decided who could visit them and what movies they wanted to see. The members of the second group did not get the same opportunities to exercise personal control. Langer compared the activities of the two groups and came to a surprising conclusion. Not only did the group exercising personal choice report being happier, they also lived longer. Eighteen months after the experiment began, only half as many in the personal responsibility group than in the second group had died. The responsibility created a new mindset about their usefulness and contributed to their longer lifespan.

There are many ways to practice mindfulness. Here are several that are particularly helpful in a college setting.

- **Create new categories.** We often dismiss things by categorizing them in a global way. For example, you might dismiss a "bad" instructor as not worthy of attention. However, if you look more closely at the various aspects of teaching, your perceptions will be richer. For example, perhaps the instructor's delivery is plodding but his choice of words is rich. Or his ideas are delivered without enthusiasm but his precise examples always make things easier to understand. A closer look can make us less judgmental and more tolerant.
- **Take control over context.** The Bird Man of Alcatraz overcame a narrowed context. When an injured bird found its way into his prison cell, the Bird Man nursed it to health. This act began a love of learning about birds that helped him to transcend confinement. When you feel like your own options have been constrained, reexamine your circumstances to see whether you have overlooked some aspect of the situation that could make it more palatable or more rewarding.
- **Welcome new information.** We tend to disregard information that does not fit with what we already know. This is an especially important tendency to overcome when you do research. Staying open to new information maximizes your pool of ideas. You may begin with one idea of what you want to prove, but find that another possibility is actually more exciting.
- **Enjoy the process.** It's easy to become so single-minded about achieving a goal that you forget to pay attention to the process of achieving it. Remember that the process is just as important as the outcome. At times the task before you may seem too large to finish. By taking a large project and breaking it into smaller, achievable deadlines and goals, you'll also stay mindful of the learning that occurs along the way.

Discover "Flow"

Creative people regularly experience a heightened state of pleasure from being completely absorbed in mental and physical challenges. Mihaly Csikszentmihalyi (pronounced ME-high CHICK-sent-me-high-ee) (1995) coined the term *flow* to describe this special state. He interviewed ninety prominent people in art, business, government, education, and science for his study.

Csikszentmihalyi (1997) believes that everyone is capable of achieving flow. What are some practices that can facilitate flow?

- **Seek a surprise every day.** Maybe the surprise will be something you see, hear, or read about. Become absorbed in a lecture or a book. Be open to what the world is telling you. Life is a stream of experiences. If you swim widely and deeply in it, your life will be enriched.

- **Surprise at least one person every day.** In many tasks and roles you have to be predictable and patterned. Do something different for a change. Ask a question you normally would not ask. Invite someone to go to a show or a museum you've never visited. Buy a bagel for someone who shares your commute.

- **Write down each day what surprised you and how you surprised others.** Most creative people keep a diary, notes, or lab records to ensure that their experiences are not fleeting or forgotten. Start with a specific task. Each evening record the most surprising event that occurred that day and your most surprising action. After a few days, reread your notes and reflect on the past experiences. After a few weeks, you might see a pattern of interest emerging in your notes, one that may suggest an area to explore in greater depth.

- **When something sparks your interest, follow it.** Usually when something captures our attention, it's short-lived—an idea, a song, a flower. Often we're too busy to explore the idea, song, or flower further. Or we think we can't because we're not experts. It's none of our business. But the world *is* our business. We can't know which part of it is best suited to our interests until we make a serious effort to learn as much about as many aspects of it as possible.

- **Wake up in the morning with a specific goal.** Creative people wake up eager to start the day. Why? It's not necessarily that they are cheerful, enthusiastic types but because they know that there is something meaningful to accomplish each day and they can't wait to get started.

- **Take charge of your schedule.** Figure out which time of the day is your most creative time. Some of us are most creative late at night, others early in the morning. Carve out some time for yourself when your creative energy is greatest.

Learn with *InfoTrac College Edition*

InfoTrac College Edition

Look up these articles and terms for more on topics that sparked your interest when reading this chapter.

Temple Grandin Beyond the rain man: A singular woman changes the cattle industry and our image of autism. Joseph P. Shapiro. *U.S. News and World Report.* May 27, 1996. v120, n21, p78.

Creative Thinking Four steps toward creative thinking. Michael Michalko. *The Futurist.* May 2000. v34, n3, p18.

Thinking like a genius: Eight strategies used by the supercreative, from Aristotle and Leonardo, to Einstein and Edison. Michael Michalko. *The Futurist.* May 1998. v32, n4, p21.

Mindfulness In the Ozarks, the dark of night offers a lesson in mindfulness. Rich Heffern. *National Catholic Reporter.* April 14, 2000. v36, i24, p27.

"Flow" A creative dialog. *Psychology Today.* July 1999 v32, i4, p58.

Summary Strategies for Mastering College

Motivate yourself to expand and deepen your thinking skills by taking advantage of all the opportunities you'll have in and out of the classroom.

1 Think Critically

- Know why college faculty have focused on improving critical-thinking skills in their graduates.
- Recognize the common features of good critical thinkers.
- Ask questions and offer criticism to hone critical-thinking skills.

2 Reason

- Make accurate inferences by attending to the proper cues.
- Reject claims that mislead, give an advantage, or have no source.
- Evaluate arguments by looking at the logic of the premises and conclusion.

3 Solve Problems the "IDEAL" Way

- Recognize how problem-solving involves many critical-thinking elements.
- Demonstrate good observational skills, strategic approaches, persistence, and attention to detail.
- Evaluate the consequences of your solutions.

4 Make Good Decisions

- Practice decision-making skills that integrate your knowledge, values, and thinking skills.
- Work systematically to create the most effective decisions.
- Overcome personal biases.

5 Think Creatively

- Understand and imitate people with creative characteristics.
- Adopt the attitude that creativity is possible.
- Practice "mindfulness" to help you improve the quality of your life.
- Live creatively to produce a state of "flow."

Review Questions

1. What distinguishes good critical thinkers from bad ones?

2. How can you improve your ability to ask good questions?

3. What steps can you take to construct a good argument?

4. What are some good problem-solving strategies?

5. What tactics could you use to make better decisions?

6. How can you improve your creativity?

Learning Portfolio

Reflect and Journal

1. No Regrets

Think about a decision you made that was very satisfying to you. What about the process helped to ensure that your decision would be right? What aspects of this process can you practice regularly in making sound decisions? Make notes here to expand in your journal.

_____
_____
_____
_____
_____
_____
_____
_____
_____
_____
_____
_____
_____
_____

2. Going with the Flow

By the time they reach college, many people have formed some firm ideas about whether they're creative. Do you consider yourself creative? In what respects? Explain your judgment. If you don't feel creative, describe what advantages you could gain by practicing strategies to improve your "flow."

_____
_____
_____
_____
_____
_____
_____
_____
_____
_____
_____
_____
_____

Learn by Doing

1. A Question a Day

Sometimes it's hard to overcome the impression that if you ask questions, other people will think you don't know what's going on. Good questions show just the opposite—that you're alert, thoughtful, and invested. For at least one week, make a point to ask a good question in each of your classes. Bring it up in class or else ask your instructor after class or e-mail your question. Then analyze how you feel about being more actively involved in this way.

_____
_____
_____
_____
_____
_____
_____
_____

2. Claims Detector

Record the claims you hear in the media for one day. Commercials are especially good targets for this activity. See if you can convert the commercial claims into premises and conclusions. Should you accept the claim, reject the claim, or suspend judgment based on the evidence offered?

_____
_____
_____
_____
_____
_____
_____
_____
_____
_____

Think Critically

1. The Great Debate

Think about an issue or controversy that stirred your feelings in one of your classes. Perhaps it was a political concern or a strong reaction you had to a poem or painting. Briefly map your position on this issue by providing the key ideas that support it. Now assume you've been assigned to argue the opposite side in a debate. Map this position as well. Did careful mapping of the opposing side do anything to weaken your commitment to the original position?

_____

_____

_____

_____

_____

_____

_____

_____

_____

_____

_____

_____

_____

_____

_____

2. A Critical Rationale

Educators often contrast an emphasis on teaching critical-thinking skills with one on teaching the basics. Which of these approaches do you think will make the most adaptable citizens in the twenty-first century? In a paragraph, forge your best argument. Underline your premises and circle your conclusions. Is your argument convincing, or have you left room for a more compelling counterargument?

_____

_____

_____

_____

_____

_____

_____

_____

_____

_____

_____

_____

_____

Think Creatively

1. "I Wonder…."

Here is a simple exercise to increase your creative thinking. Each day for a week, take a few minutes to ask yourself a question that begins with "I wonder…." Ask this question about a particular aspect of your life. It's important not to censor yourself, no matter how impractical or outlandish the question sounds. After you practice doing this, pose your questions to your friends. Focus on something that you're sincerely curious about and that matters to others. Listen carefully to your friends' responses. You'll probably discover that your questions have some assumptions that deserve to be challenged or fine-tuned (Goleman, Kaufman, & Ray, 1993).

_____

_____

_____

_____

_____

2. Creative Surfing

Find out what the Internet has to say about being creative. Enter "creativity" into a search engine and visit at least three sites that address the issue. What did you learn about creativity? How creative were the Internet sites themselves?

_____

_____

_____

_____

_____

_____

_____

_____

_____

_____

_____

Work toward Goals

Review the results of the self-assessments you completed in this chapter. Also review the opening checklist. Based on your review, select a relatively short-term goal that you want to work on now.

1. What is that goal? (*Hint:* Is it challenging, reasonable, and specific?)

_____

_____

_____

_____

_____

2. What strategies will you use to achieve your goal? (*Hint:* Can you organize your strategy into a series of smaller goals?)

_____

_____

_____

_____

_____

3. What obstacles may be in your way as you attempt to make these positive changes?

_____

_____

_____

_____

_____

4. What additional resources might help you achieve your goal? (Use the CD-ROM that comes with this book for access to some useful leads.)

_____

_____

_____

_____

_____

5. By what date do you want to accomplish your goal?

_____

_____

_____

_____

6. How will you know you have succeeded?

_____

_____

_____

_____

Refine Your Expression

9

Have Your Say

One exciting aspect of college is the opportunity to develop poise in how you express yourself. In this chapter you'll explore ways to improve your expression in writing and speaking. You'll also read about strategies for overcoming common problems in assignments that involve communication. To get a picture of your current strengths and weaknesses in expression, place a check mark next to only those items that apply to you.

_____   I pursue opportunities to practice effective communicational skills.

_____   I can design and execute projects involving research.

_____   I can create a thesis statement that helps me stay focused on my goal.

_____   I prepare writing or presentational projects well in advance.

_____   I avoid problems with plagiarism.

_____   I seek criticism from other people to improve the quality of my work.

_____   I use strategies to engage the audience during speeches.

_____   I can control jitters while communicating.

_____   I can rebound when my communicational efforts don't succeed.

Now read how the writer Amy Tan demonstrates combining rich personal experience with good communicational strategies to produce writing and speaking that makes an impact.

IMAGES OF COLLEGE SUCCESS

Amy Tan

When she won her first essay contest at age 8, Amy Tan knew she wanted to write fiction. However, her mother wanted her to follow a different dream. In the late 1940s Tan's parents had emigrated from China to Oakland, California. They were eager for their only daughter both to enjoy the advantages of their adopted land and to honor her Chinese heritage. After her father's unexpected death from a brain tumor, Tan decided to major in pre-med at Linfield College in Oregon. But the lure of the liberal arts proved too strong. Despite her mother's protests that her father would have been disappointed in her decision, she chose English as her major. Tan completed her education at San Jose City College and San Jose State University.

Writing was not easy for Tan. Living with her pessimistic mother had undermined her ability to express herself. She was even advised by a former employer to go into accounting because her writing skills were so poor. Despite these obstacles, she began doing freelance writing. This developed into a successful career in business writing, including projects with companies such as IBM. As Tan acquired clients, she struggled with 90-hour weeks and a growing sense of feeling unfulfilled. She joined a writer's group and began to write fiction. Tan published her insights as a series of interrelated stories about the struggle between Chinese mothers and Chinese-American daughters. Published in seventeen languages, including Chinese, *The Joy Luck Club* has sold more than three million copies and became a successful film. Tan not only achieved her childhood dream of writing fiction professionally but often speaks to enthusiastic audiences on promotional tours.

When she delved deeply into her relationship with her mother, Amy Tan launched a successful writing and speaking career.

Reuters/Corbis-Bettmann

Tan uses her writing to make sense of her life. "Life is a continual series of bumps and crises. You think you're never going to get over a hurdle, and you get over it.... You can look back on what's just happened and you make sense of it and grow, or you stagnate and you go back down. The hurdles and conflicts are really momentary" (Tan, 1996). Learning to express yourself can be an important means of finding your balance in difficult times and making the very best of good times.

Learn more about Amy Tan.

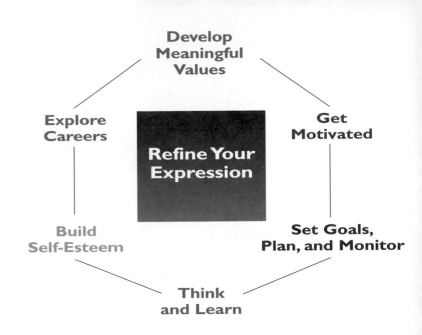

Motivate yourself to practice your communication skills whenever you can. Setting and achieving communication goals will help you succeed in college and prepare you for your career.

Express Yourself!

Imagine where you might be ten years from now. If you enter the world of business or a profession, part of your work will probably involve communicating with others regularly. If you choose your college opportunities carefully, you'll learn to express yourself in writing and speaking with precision, poise, and polish.

Communication-oriented projects sharpen skills that employers value (Appleby, 1994). Writing projects help you learn to develop effective memos, proposals, and reports. They improve your attention to detail through practice in editing and proofreading. They also encourage the kind of creativity that might secure jobs in advertising, publishing, and marketing. Classroom speaking provides practice for interviewing, supervising, persuading, negotiating, selling, and other aspects of working with the public.

You're a natural communicator if you connect well with others and can usually think of the right thing to say at the right time. College requires you to build on those skills to develop more formal writing and speaking skills. Bringing personal expression under your control through a variety of projects in college will give you great flexibility in the challenges you'll face after graduation.

Your college will likely provide you with many opportunities to express yourself. Introductory communications courses usually begin with assignments that allow you to write or speak about your personal experiences. As you go further into your major, the communicational requirements will

Good communication is as stimulating as black coffee, and just as hard to sleep after.

Anne Morrow Lindbergh
20th-century American poet

Strong Writing and Speaking Skills ⟷ **Confidence** ⟷ **Self-Esteem**

become more challenging. With some practice, you can significantly improve your skills by graduation. How much you improve will depend on your own ingenuity in making the most of your opportunities.

Do Your Research

Whether your project involves writing or speaking, you'll need to pursue certain predictable goals to produce your best effort.

Get Started

Review the Directions Make sure you understand the goal of the assignment. Ask questions to clarify anything that is unclear. Compare your ideas with your classmates' perceptions.

Select a Topic Many instructors will select your topic, at least in a general way. However, you still may have to narrow it down. What strategies can help?

1. Look through your notes. What concepts stand out as the most interesting to you?
2. Examine your textbook and course readings, explore the encyclopedia, or cruise the Internet to spark your imagination.
3. Explore your personal experience. Try to think about aspects of the assignment that naturally connect to your own life. For example, Amy Tan's troubled relationship with her mother became the basis of her remarkable fiction.

As you explore possible topics, avoid ones that are too large, too obscure, too emotional, or too complicated for you to work with in the allotted time. Do not write or speak about areas where you have little knowledge. Do research or redesign the project until you have the knowledge you need to succeed.

Dig In There are two schools of thought on how to begin a communication-oriented project. One school suggests that you think through your intentions carefully, make maps or outlines of your writing objectives, and then begin writing. The other school suggests that you just start writing. Roughing out your ideas on paper gives you material that you can then reorganize and improve.

Locate Helpful Resources

Once you have an idea, it's time to begin collecting new insights about it to create the backbone of your research paper.

Notice Good Ideas Carry a small notebook or maintain a separate file in which you can capture ideas that come to you. Thinking often about your topic will sensitize you to ideas that might strengthen the development of your argument. Although popular media resources, such as magazines and television programs, may not be acceptable resources for a formal research paper, they can suggest interesting directions for more formal research.

Conduct a Key Word Search Whether you use the library or the Internet, your search will begin with a key word or two that you'll enter into an appropriate database.

For example, if your environmental science class requires a paper on effective recycling strategies, you could start with the word *recycling*. You may need to narrow your search to something more specific such as *newspaper recycling* to find more targeted information. Narrowing will be especially helpful if your preliminary key word search produces too many "hits." If your search produces too few hits, broaden the concept until you find some resources that will help you.

Gather Sources How many sources should you include in your paper? Sometimes instructors will specify a minimum number; sometimes they won't. It may help to think about how many sources you'll need in order to develop the most effective argument.

Plan to look at more materials than you ultimately will refer to in your work. You may not have a clear idea about what will help you until you have done some research. Not every resource you read will be relevant in the end. Choose those that help you develop a sound argument. Quality of evidence, not quantity, will impress your instructor.

Write down the complete reference for each source *as you go*. It's frustrating to assemble a reference list at the end of your work only to discover that you forgot to write down the year a book was published or an important page number.

Master the Library Become familiar with your library's resources so you can locate information quickly. Take a tour if you haven't already done so. Approach the librarian who appears friendliest and most helpful so that you can feel comfortable asking questions.

Library searches often start in the reference room, which usually houses both paper and electronic databases. From there you may be routed to other areas of the library where you can locate original or *primary* sources (e.g., books, journal articles), *secondary* sources (e.g., textbooks and other sources that review primary works), or popular press items. References to research or expert opinions that you use in your research are called *citations*.

Your research assignment may specify which types of sources you can use. Most instructors prefer original sources to others. They also are more impressed by journal articles that are "peer reviewed." This means that the article was critically analyzed and then approved by other experts in the field.

Once you've collected several sources, scan each one. Discard the unhelpful ones. Read those with potential more carefully, taking notes that will help you represent the author's ideas. Chapter 5 offers some good tips on how to take notes from text.

If you have trouble locating what you need, ask! Most librarians enjoy helping students.

Use the Internet The Internet can help you come up with and refine ideas for research. Do key word searches on several search engines to see what the nature of the discussion might be on the topic you have in mind. Cruising the Internet may help you narrow or broaden your topic. You may spy something that will point you in an entirely new but more interesting direction.

Relying on the Internet, however, can be risky. Most instructors still favor library research that will help you locate printed publications and peer-reviewed sources. One reason for this is that the information on the Internet isn't always reliable. Anyone can post anything, making it hard to sift out the gold. As such, don't assume that an Internet source will be acceptable.

When is an Internet resource acceptable? Instructors may be willing to accept Internet citations that are

1. Written by a recognized authority in the field
2. Supported by a reputable host group
3. Peer reviewed

Develop Your Ideas

Good researchers find and carefully show persuasive evidence. They use various forms of it but stick with evidence that is appropriate to the project and the discipline. For example, you can include statistics in a political science essay because numerical evidence communicates information about voting trends. However, citing statistical evidence in an expressive essay about literary criticism in a humanities class probably won't work. The point of any formal communicational assignment is to demonstrate your learning of course-related ideas.

As you develop your ideas, discuss sources that argue against your assertions. When you anticipate criticisms that the reader might have and defend against them in your writing, you make your overall argument stronger.

Know Your Audience

Be sure you strike the right tone for your audience. For example, some tasks require an objective and precise presentation of the facts. Other projects may require you to be exploratory and imaginative. Some projects work best with a casual tone; others may require a polished professional presentation. Knowing your audience can help you make the right decisions.

Consider a Research Stream

Good students see the value of an ongoing focus for their college papers (Hansen & Hansen, 1997). They develop a "research stream" that begins with the first paper they write and builds with each new project. This way they don't have to start from scratch, and it allows them to manage greater depth in each new assignment.

For example, Paulo enjoys thinking about environmental issues. He looks for opportunities in his writing assignments to read what he enjoys. He writes about literature with ecological themes, evaluates ecology-related legislation in social science classes, and explores environmental crises in natural science term papers. As a result, Paulo knows his material very well and builds a collection of focused writing that may serve his job-hunting future better than a hodgepodge of unrelated essays. When you choose topics for papers and other projects, keep your long-term goals in mind.

Write with Impact

Over time, writing projects will help improve your writing skills and develop your confidence as a writer and self-esteem as a student.

Master the Types of Writing Projects

If you're lucky, you'll get to write in a variety of formats that will prepare you for the writing demands in professional life. Strong writing skills are a great asset in most professional careers.

Writing is easy: all you do is sit staring at the blank sheet of paper until the drops of blood form on your forehead.
Gene Fowler
20th-century American biographer

Essays and Theses Instructors assign essays when they want you to develop your writing and reasoning skills. Essays demonstrate your ability to think analytically about the subject you're learning. Your essay should reflect the content of the course in which the essay was assigned.

Typically, you state a problem or question at the beginning of an essay. Your *thesis statement* conveys your general position on the topic and should guide the direction of your research. Then you support your thesis with evidence, such as the opinions of experts. Each paragraph should develop a separate but connected point that helps support your thesis.

For example, in an art history class you might be asked to contrast the work of two impressionist painters. Your thesis statement might read as follows: "Both Manet and Monet are important impressionist artists, but Monet's work has achieved wider popularity." Subsequent paragraphs could address the following elements of the thesis statement:

- What is impressionism?
- Why are the artists considered important?
- What distinguishes the work of each?
- What evidence suggests that one artist is more highly regarded than the other?

To answer each of these questions, your essay will need to reflect expert opinions found in your research.

A *thesis* is a longer, more carefully developed essay, often written as part of completing the special requirements of a major. For example, honors programs may require an extensive position paper called an *honors thesis*. Getting a graduate degree also usually requires a thesis.

Project Reports Some course requirements combine writing and problem-solving skills. In the social sciences, business, and nursing classes you may be asked to work independently or collaborate on solving a problem.

For example, nursing students might collaborate to make recommendations for improving the quality of care under short-staffed conditions. Projects like this benefit from the following:

- A clear definition of the problem and its impact
- A description of the origin of the problem
- An identification of any other relevant factors
- A proposed solution
- A prediction about the impact of the solution
- A plan for follow-up

Notice how research could bolster any of these elements.

Lab Reports In science classes, you may work independently or collaborate on a lab report that describes a specific scientific procedure. Lab reports are usually highly structured, based on a set of conventional headings. For example, a botany instructor might ask you to experiment with how different nutrient levels affect plant growth. The lab report will contain the following sections:

- **Introduction:** The nature of the problem, including relevant research
- **Methods:** The procedure used to investigate the problem
- **Results:** The findings
- **Discussion:** The significance of the results; improvements to the procedure

Reflective Writing Some classes will involve sharpening your reflective writing skills. For example, literature instructors may assign creative writing projects, such as poetry and short stories, to help foster an appreciation of these genres. Don't rule out doing research in reflective assignments. Try to locate authors whose style you admire. Do some background reading on a topic that might serve as the focus of your work.

Another reflective writing assignment, journal writing, lets you explore the personal significance of the material. For example, when you take courses that require fieldwork, a journal will help you capture what was most important about that experience. Journals are usually not graded in a traditional way. The instructor will give you feedback about the seriousness or insight your writing shows. Although research may not be required in such projects, it's a good idea to connect with course concepts to show what you have learned.

Learn the Habits of Effective Writers

Regardless of the writing task, writers must develop effective strategies for various stages of their work.

A #2 pencil and a dream can take you anywhere.

Joyce A. Myers
20th-century American businesswoman

Get Ready Curiously, not all of the activity involved in preparing to write is logical. Some students report that they go through some specific writing rituals to bring them good luck. For example, Jim does not feel confident about his writing unless he uses his "lucky" pen, a scratched-up, medium-point Papermate he has had since tenth grade. Alicia must have her beagle resting his head in her lap before she can be creative. Ernest Hemingway sharpened a certain number of pencils before he wrote each morning. As long as they don't take too much time, such rituals are fine. As your abilities and confidence grow, you probably won't need them to bring out your best.

FIGURE 9-1
The Well-Equipped Reference Shelf

These resources will help you find facts, abide by conventions, and answer questions as you revise your work.

Type	Function
Dictionary	Word definitions, pronunciation, and spelling
Thesaurus	Synonyms
Atlas	Geographic facts
Style manual	Grammar and writing conventions
	American Psychological Association
	Modern Language Association
Book of quotations	Proverbs and memorable quotations organized by topic, author, or key phrases

Establish a place to write where you keep your writing resources and works in progress (Figure 9-1). Most writers say that they need uninterrupted time to think about their writing. Find a quiet place where you won't be interrupted. Hang a "Do Not Disturb" sign on your door to reduce distraction.

Starting a paper the night before it's due is not a sound strategy. Set some intermediate goals for completing the task so that the assignment will not seem so overwhelming. Figure 9-2 offers a sample timetable.

FIGURE 9-2
A Sample Timetable for a Writing Deadline

1–2 months before the deadline	Select your topic.
	Map your ideas.
	Develop your writing plan.
	Begin to develop a thesis statement.
	Start your research.
Two weeks before the deadline	Develop individual sections of your paper.
	Revise with vigor.
	Complete your research.
	Finalize your thesis statement.
The week before the deadline	Polish the individual sections of the paper.
	Create an interesting title.
	Check your references for accuracy.
	Get some feedback from a friend.
The night before the deadline	Combine the parts of the paper.
	Print the final draft.
	Proofread your paper.
	Assemble the paper.
The morning of the deadline	Proofread your paper one more time.

Organize Your Argument Formal papers usually have three parts: introduction, body, and conclusion. The introduction lays a foundation for the rest of the piece. Good writers establish the context or the purpose for writing, even when the instructor is the audience. They state their intentions early and anticipate the kinds of information readers might want to know to help them understand the motive in writing. Throughout the paper, keep in mind what your audience already knows and what they need to know.

The body of the paper should include your opinions and the evidence that supports your argument. Each paragraph in the body should develop a separate idea and follow logically from the one before. All paragraphs must relate to the thesis of the paper.

The end of your paper should summarize your argument. Make sure that your conclusions fit with the thesis statement you established at the beginning. You can say more about its implications for action or further study.

PEANUTS reprinted by permission of United Feature Syndicate, Inc.

Draft, Revise, and Revise Again The blank page can be daunting, but a few helpful ideas may get you started and help you monitor your progress.

Free Write. Spontaneous writing may help you uncover new ideas, questions, and connections regarding your topic. Simply write whatever you think about the topic. Save the parts that have potential.

Talk It Out. You may find it easier to write a first draft by pretending that you're talking to a friend or an imaginary audience. Once you have some ideas to work with, you can jot down the parts of the conversation you liked and proceed with the formal aspects of writing. Or you can talk to real friends and colleagues and use the most interesting parts of that conversation to launch your own perspective.

Set Your Goal. Draft a "working" thesis statement to establish a formal objective for your project. To accomplish your goal, generate an outline that allows you to incorporate your research and make your best argument. Set subgoals for how much writing you want to accomplish in any given sitting. For example, it may help to draft the introduction one day, the conclusion the next, and key paragraphs on other days.

Monitor Your Quality. Effective writing rarely takes only one draft. As you plan your schedule, allow time for rewriting and revising so you can take advantage of new ideas. A good piece of writing usually takes several drafts.

Beginning writers sometimes struggle with knowing how much to write. Typically, beginners write too little rather than too much. Check your writing to see that you explained your intentions to the reader. Provide good examples. Make sure that the parts connect to each other with good transitional sentences. All the elements of the writing should follow logically from your original thesis statement.

Blot out, correct, insert, refine,

Enlarge, diminish, underline,

Be mindful, when invention fails,

To scratch your head, and bite your nails.

Jonathan Swift
18th-century English satirist

Some writers have the opposite problem. Their writing contains nonessential elements and long-winded sentences. For example, phrases such as "It is well known that" or "There are many things that" are unnecessary. Using a lot of adjectives and adverbs also slows down your writing. Review your writing carefully to pare it down.

Frustrated by being unable to persuade his students about the importance of revising, one writing teacher posted this sign on his office door:

> *First draft:*
>
> *"I think about you all the time and admire you for all your many qualities.*
>
> *I probably even love you. I could go on and on...."*
>
> *Final draft:*
>
> *"How do I love thee? Let me count the ways."*
>
> *—Elizabeth Barrett Browning, 19th-century poet*

Follow the Rules Effective writers are careful about following the rules or *conventions* of good writing. Conventions include standards in grammar and spelling. In general, these are essential elements of a successful paper. There are many *style manuals* you can choose from, depending on your class. The American Psychological Association (APA) offers the standard for writing in the natural and social science disciplines. Another common set of guidelines is published by the Modern Language Association (MLA). Ask your instructor which style manual is best.

Instructors vary in how much they care about whether you follow the guidelines. Some simply reject papers that include substantial problems with spelling, grammar, and sentence structure. Others overlook these matters if the ideas are good. Some are sticklers about learning and implementing APA or MLA format. They may provide a *style sheet* that states how the paper must be written. Others may not specify guidelines but expect you to observe the principles of good writing that you've learned in composition class.

Avoid the common problems that easily surface in but tend to weaken the quality of formal writing. Even seasoned writers have questions about punctuation or grammar in their writing. Have a reference manual handy during polishing and proofreading.

Consult with Colleagues The stereotype is that writers lead a solitary life. However, most writers benefit from reviews by others who know good writing. When your draft is almost finished, get feedback from others who write well. Ask them to point out places where you're not clear or identify points that need further development. For example, despite her successful publishing record Amy Tan still uses her writing support group to help her in

The Saving Grace

Using a word processor can help your writing, but some precautions are in order.

1. Save your writing as you go.
Nothing is more frustrating than having the power go down after you've been working on your computer for hours. In this situation you'll lose everything that has not been saved. Develop a habit of frequently saving what you write. For example, save your work every time you complete a section or a page of writing. Or, turn on the automatic save function so you won't have to think about doing it manually.

2. Make a backup copy—just in case. Computer viruses can wreak havoc with your hard drive. By making a backup copy on a floppy disk, Zip drive, or CD, you'll still have your complete work if your hard drive crashes. Label your disks so you don't have to waste time searching every disk you own to find your paper.

3. Avoid eating and drinking around your computer. A spilled soda can foul up your computer and lead to expensive repairs. Move away from your computer when you eat and drink.

4. Have a backup plan. Even the most reliable computer can fail when you need it most. If you've duplicated your work on a portable medium, make sure you know where you can find a compatible system to use in a pinch. Your campus computer center may provide some backup machines.

Word processors can save you time on your writing projects. They are especially helpful for rewriting and revising. If you don't own a computer, find out when you can use your school's computers.

refining her work. Find a writing partner and exchange services. Your campus may have a writing center where experts can help you improve your writing.

Finish in Style Many assignments require a title. Some writers wait until the project is almost completed before creating a title that captures the appeal of the work. Strive to create a title that compels the reader to read further.

Your writing is an extension of you. Your final product not only reveals your ability to construct an argument but also communicates your pride about your own work. Smudge-free, easy-to-read writing also tends to please the grader.

Most instructors expect you to type your paper. Use a word processor to make the best use of your writing time. You can revise easily on a computer. Although word processors can save time, they can also frustrate you if you overlook some simple precautions. See "The Saving Grace" for some good advice.

Include a cover page that shows the title of the paper, your name, your instructor's name, the course, and the date unless your instructor requires a different format. Be sure to number the pages. Ask your instructors for other format preferences, including whether they like fancy covers. Many look on plastic folders or binders as a waste of money. On the other hand, some think a cover gives a more professional look. It's probably best to ask.

Proofreading can be tricky. You may be so close to what you've created that you can't spot errors. A break can help. For example, Bret likes to get a good night's sleep before he proofreads and prints his final draft. By returning to the paper after a good sleep, he feels more confident about catching the subtle errors that he might miss when he is tired.

Proofreading your paper aloud may help you catch more errors. Some experts even recommend reading your paper sentence by sentence from back to front (Axelrod & Cooper, 1996). Altering your usual method of reading may help you see weak sentence structure. When you think that you've caught all errors, proofread one more time.

When the paper is finished, good writers perform one more task. They assess the quality of their work. Complete Self-Assessment 9-1 to explore review skills that will lead to better papers. If you evaluate the quality of your work early enough, you still may have time to revise it and earn a better grade.

Turn projects in on time or negotiate an exception with an instructor *before* the deadline. Even if you've written the best paper in the history of the class, many instructors penalize late submissions. Some even refuse to accept them.

Myrleen Ferguson/PhotoEdit

What Are My Writing Strengths and Weaknesses?

Once you've completed at least one formal college writing assignment, examine your work using the guidelines here (after Alverno College, 1995). The feedback or grade you received from your instructor may provide some clues about areas that you need to improve. Keep the writing criteria handy to help guide your future writing projects.

Writing Criteria	Completely	Partially	Barely or Not At All
I followed the instructions.	_____	_____	_____

	Effectively	Partially	Barely or Not At All
I established *appropriate context* and kept this focus throughout.	_____	_____	_____
I crafted the *style* of the paper and selected *words* carefully to suit the purpose.	_____	_____	_____
I showed conscientious use of appropriate *conventions*, including spelling and grammar.	_____	_____	_____
I *structured* the paper, including an introduction, main body, and conclusion.	_____	_____	_____
I included *evidence* to support my thesis.	_____	_____	_____
I added *content* that reflected learning specific to the course.	_____	_____	_____

Review your responses to these criteria and answer the following:

• *What are your writing strengths?*

• *What do you need to improve?*

• *Is this pattern typical of your writing projects?*

• *What strategies will help you improve?*

• *Would it be useful to consult with the campus writing center?*

Learn from Feedback Instructors vary in the methods they use to evaluate papers. Some simply assign a grade that captures the overall quality of your work. Others provide detailed feedback. When you get feedback, read it carefully so you can learn something that will help in future assignments.

A river of red ink can be hard to take. Read extensive criticisms quickly, then take some time to recover before you try to learn from the feedback. Let yourself be disappointed. Maybe even mope a little. Then return with the intention of learning what to do to improve your writing. Remember, we all often learn more from mistakes than from successes.

Ask for feedback if you don't understand the grade. Many instructors believe students are willing to settle for a summary judgment—a grade—with little or no justification. However, when you don't understand how a grade was derived, ask. Specific feedback on your strengths and weaknesses is essential to becoming a good writer.

Watch your growth as a writer by keeping track of how your papers are improving. Review this record now and then, especially when you're disappointed by an evaluation. Many students retain their papers so they can review their progress. In some college programs, you may be asked to construct a portfolio of your work to track your growing skill.

Solve Writing Problems

Even the best writers sometimes run into problems that can keep them from achieving their goals. Common problems include procrastination, writer's block, plagiarism, and difficulty developing a distinctive voice.

Procrastination Like many writers, you may struggle with starting on time. Sometimes delay is caused by distraction or by other more pressing projects. In any case, you may suddenly find yourself with a deadline pressing down on you and end up submitting an assignment that you dashed off at the last minute. A rough draft may make your instructor think that you weren't taking the task seriously. To combat procrastination, plan a reasonable schedule that breaks your research and writing into manageable parts. Then stick to it. Reward yourself for completing each phase. To remind yourself of other strategies to help reduce procrastination, refer to Chapter 3. Also see "Good Intentions."

STAYING OUT OF THE PITS

Good Intentions

Katie knows that she needs to get started on her term paper, due the next day, but she can't concentrate. She decides to do some laundry first. She notices that the laundry area needs straightening. "Looks like the washer could use a wipe-down," she thinks. Before she knows it, two hours slip away. The laundry room is squeaky clean, but all she has to show for her term paper are good intentions. At least she will have a clean T-shirt when she has to explain to her instructor where her paper is.

Writer's Block Sometimes you have nothing to say. Don't panic. All writers face times when words don't come easily and inspiration fails. Interestingly, one good response is to write about your writer's block. Write about how it feels to be empty and the nature of your blocks. You may gain insight into your resistance and find ideas that will get you going.

Another good step is asking for a conference with your instructor. By talking about the assignment, you may find a new twist that unleashes your creativity. Ask whether your instructor has any model student papers. By observing how others tackled related problems, you may be able to spark some ideas of your own.

You can also try a creativity-generating computer program that provides a systematic approach to helping you plumb your ideas. IdeaFisher and Inspiration are two popular programs.

Plagiarism *Plagiarism* means presenting someone else's words or ideas as your own. This is a serious academic offense. Experienced instructors, who have read many student papers, easily notice plagiarism, whether intentional or careless. Instructors may have different ideas about what constitutes plagiarism. For instance, many frown on being given a paper you have previously written for a different class, while other instructors don't mind so much. It's always best to ask about the acceptability of any sort of duplication, even of your own work.

Ironically, Any Tan reports a miserable experience related to plagiarism. Her brother was caught and punished for allowing a friend to copy a paper in college. He later developed a terminal illness which their mother swore was caused by the shame of committing this dishonorable act. Although no one has proven that plagiarism is fatal, it can shortchange your learning and severely risk your academic health.

How can you avoid plagiarism? "Prevent Plagiarism" offers a few good ideas.

Exercise Your Creativity

Most instructors give high marks to writing that is logical and uncluttered. However, there is also room for originality. Consider what it must be like for the instructor to grade one essay after another that strives merely to meet a narrow set of criteria. Like most other people, instructors generally appreciate variety, creativity, and even some humor.

You can be creative in various ways. Find out what approaches students typically take, then do something different. Consider a unique slant for the project. Create an engaging title. Use a thesaurus to expand your word choice. Add interesting quotations.

ON-TARGET TIPS

Prevent Plagiarism

- **Paraphrase when you do research.** As you take notes from various resources, translate the ideas of others into your own words. Compare what you have written with the original source to make sure that your paraphrase captures the spirit of the ideas written, not the actual words and phrases themselves.
- **Give proper credit.** When you directly quote or refer to the ideas of another writer, provide source information in the format required by your instructor.
- **Make your own observations stand out in your notes.** Put your own ideas in the margin or print them so that they look physically different from the ideas you received from others. Later you can use your own observations without fear of committing plagiarism.
- **Use quotations sparingly.** Rely on the words of experts only when their writing is so elegant that your paraphrase will not do it justice. Using many or long quotations is a sign that you're uncomfortable expressing your own ideas.
- **Don't help others plagiarize.** Lending others your papers when you suspect the borrowers plan to submit something based closely on your work implicates you in plagiarism. If the borrower's submission is questioned, you may find yourself in the unpleasant situation of explaining why you lent your paper for an unethical purpose.
- **Guard against others plagiarizing your work.** If you use a community-based computer, do not store your work on the computer's hard drive. Others who use the computer can easily download your writing and submit it as their own without your knowledge or permission.

Speak!

If you're both a capable writer and a confident, reliable speaker, you have the basic tools to succeed in most organizational careers. Although both speaking and writing give you an opportunity to express yourself, speaking differs from writing in significant ways. In most writing tasks, you can refine your work until it says exactly what you want. However, in most speaking experiences, even though you can practice to a fine point, the reality of live performance adds a whole new challenge.

Engage in Speaking Opportunities

College should offer several opportunities for you to improve your speaking skills in the contexts of working individually and collaborating with others. For instance, you may be asked to address the class formally by delivering a carefully researched position, or you may have to give an extemporaneous speech on a topic given just moments beforehand. Some courses offer the opportunity to do expressive reading of dramatic works. All of these opportunities will help you refine your public-speaking skills, including pacing, voice quality, and connecting to the audience.

Group speaking projects include case presentations, panel discussions, and debates. These projects are most successful when group members can coordinate their individual pieces and practice together.

You can also learn a lot about speaking by watching good speakers. College campuses often host dynamic speakers who can show you how it's done. In addition, you can get experience in the spotlight by asking questions at the end of the speech. If that option feels overwhelming at first, approach the speaker with your questions or comments when the speech is over. Most speakers want your feedback. By being an active audience member, you can learn a great deal about good speaking skills.

Learn the Habits of Good Speakers

Formal speeches must first be written. Therefore, the skills involved in preparing good papers also apply to preparing good speeches. What additional strategies can help you make good speeches?

Plan for Success Know your goal. Are you supposed to persuade? Inform? Entertain? Debate? Your purpose will determine how to use resources and structure your speech so you can satisfy the criteria for success. It will also help you avoid running too short or too long.

To enhance your success, talk with your instructor about your intentions. Submit a topic sentence, an outline, or a map before your scheduled presentation time. Ask for comments to help you stay close to the goal of the assignment.

Rehearse The time put into rehearsal often makes or breaks a speech. If you know your speech well enough, you'll need your notecards only for cues about what you intend to say. Otherwise, you may be tempted to read what you've written, which disconnects you from the audience. Because effective speakers know their own intentions and order of ideas, they don't need to rely heavily on their notes or a memorized script. They give the impression of connecting with the audience by talking with them rather than reciting from memory or reading directly from a prepared text.

Practice working with an overhead projector, the cue cards, or a computer. By training yourself to look up and out as you speak, you can develop good speaking habits such as eye contact.

THE FAR SIDE   By GARY LARSON

The Far Side, © FarWorks, Inc. All Rights Reserved.

Engage the Audience Most college audiences will be sympathetic. After all, your peers are likely to be in your shoes before the term is over. This usually provides a uniquely supportive environment in which to learn to give a speech. If you assume that your audience is supportive, you may feel less apprehensive about giving the speech.

Start your speech with a personal experience or a joke. You can introduce an interesting news item, quotation, or event that the audience will remember. In all cases, your opening should conclude with a statement of your objective and a description of where you intend to go.

Identify your purpose and scope early in your speech. Keep in mind what your audience knows already and what they need to know. However, never omit your purpose, even if the audience already knows it. It's best to be brief but clear in this case.

Effective speakers address the audience on its level. For example, if your college recruits you to talk to high school students about college life, your vocabulary and examples might be different than those in the same kind of speech given to their parents. Good speakers also try to understand the values of their audience so they appeal to them more effectively.

Polish Your Delivery Some speaking opportunities are formal, while others are more casual. But even casual speeches benefit from the polish that comes from practice. Minimize the number of pauses, "ums" and "ahs," or other interruptions that invite your audience to stop listening. Strive to make eye contact with audience members and pace your speech to draw their attention. Stand straight, breathe in a controlled manner, and harness other nervous mannerisms that might distract from your message. Effective speakers also project their voices to reach people at the back of the room and put life in their voices to keep people's attention.

Nothing can harm good ideas more than bad grammar and sloppy sentence structure. When you practice giving your speech to a friend, ask for specific feedback on grammar and language.

Build Your Message An anonymous speech instructor once recommended the perfect structure for public presentations, "Tell 'em what you are going to tell 'em, tell 'em, then tell 'em what you told 'em." Although this approach might sound boring, repeating the key ideas of a speech really counts. As in good writing, the main pint of the speech serves as the backbone, and each portion of the speech must support it. Many speakers like to hand out a printed outline of a speech so the audience can follow it better.

As you construct the body of your talk, pay attention to the kinds of support that appeal most to the audience. You don't have to overwhelm your audience with statistics and stories to make your point. Choose your evidence carefully to create both emotional and logical appeal.

Class speeches should reflect what you've learned from the course. You can draw ideas from the textbook, class notes, or other readings that relate to what you're studying. However, if you give a speech that shows no evidence that you've learned from the course, your grade will probably suffer.

Use Media Effectively Speakers can use a variety of means to make their ideas believable, including stories, video clips, quotations, statistics, charts, and graphs. Every element should play a meaningful role in the development of the speaker's position.

If you use an overhead projector, make the lettering large and easy to read. (To test the size of your lettering, put the transparency on the floor and stand over it. If you can read it from this position, the font is probably large enough.) Prepare typed overheads; handwritten ones suggest a lack of pride in your work. If you use audio- or videotapes to support your presentation, be sure to wind the tape to the appropriate starting point ahead of time. If you plan to use a computerized presentation, check the lighting conditions beforehand to be sure people will be able to see it.

Finish Gracefully When you conclude your speech, return to the key themes that began it. Summarize what you've covered and identify any actions you expect the audience to take as a result of your speech. If you've given a long speech, repeat your objectives. Then smile and prepare to receive your applause.

Many instructors include a question-and-answer period following a student's speech. Such activity encourages you to think on your feet and to learn how to manage unexpected events. See "Winning in the Home Stretch" for how to manage the question-and-answer period.

Evaluate Your Work Good speakers check the quality of their speaking as they rehearse as well as during and after the actual performance. Complete Self-Assessment 9-2 to examine your speaking strengths and weaknesses.

Remember that trying to reduce anxiety with tranquilizers or other drugs is not a good idea. Altering your feelings chemically may reduce your capacity to respond to unexpected events or to answer questions.

Solve Delivery Problems Many students face choking, tearing up, and other obvious signs of nervousness when they speak to a group. These can undermine your effectiveness. However, there are several strategies that can put you at ease.

Diagnose your problem carefully. If you routinely choke during oral presentations, identify when the problem occurs and if there are any consistent causes. Contrast those situations to others in which you have been more satisfied with your performance. This analysis will help you find ways to improve your delivery.

Anticipate what your body needs. Breathe deeply and stretch your muscles to give your body signals about your intention to control your nervousness. Take a bathroom break before your talk begins. Have a glass of water handy to relieve parched lips and give you time to regain your composure.

ON-TARGET TIPS

Winning in the Home Stretch

When your classmates ask questions that stump you after you've given a speech, consider these strategies for coping with the strain:

- **Ask for a restatement of the question.** This can give you clues to help you answer the question or provide extra time to think through your response.
- **Say "I don't know."** Sometimes it's best to admit that the questioner poses a new topic for you, then move on. No one expects a speaker to have all the answers.
- **Ask the questioner for an opinion.** Many people who ask questions have their own ideas about what constitutes a satisfying answer. Your willingness to share the stage will be seen as gracious, and the gesture gives you more time to respond.

What Are My Speaking Strengths and Weaknesses?

Even if you haven't already had a speaking assignment in college, you've probably developed a sense of your strengths and weaknesses in giving presentations. Review the following, based on Alverno College's *Writing and Speaking Criteria* (1995), to determine how effective you are as a public speaker. Keep these speaking criteria available to help you in future speaking assignments.

Speaking Criteria	Routinely	Often	Rarely
I connect with the audience by talking directly to them rather than reading my notes or delivering a memorized script.	_____	_____	_____
I state my purpose and keep this focus throughout.	_____	_____	_____
I craft the style of the speech and select words carefully to suit the purpose.	_____	_____	_____
I effectively deliver the speech, using eye contact, supportive gestures, and effective voice control.	_____	_____	_____
I follow appropriate conventions, including grammar.	_____	_____	_____
I organize the speech well, including the introduction, main body, and conclusions.	_____	_____	_____
I include evidence that supports and develops my ideas.	_____	_____	_____
I use media effectively to help the audience grasp key ideas.	_____	_____	_____
I include content that reflects my learning from the course.	_____	_____	_____

Review your accomplishments in speaking.

• What are your strengths in speaking?

• What criteria show that you need to improve?

• Is this pattern typical of your speaking projects?

• What strategies should you pursue to improve?

"I could have been a big celebrity but for my fear of public speaking."

Reprinted with permission of United Media.

Organize in order to maintain control. You can prevent losing your place if you use well-organized, easy-to-read note cards. Number the cards so that you can restore their order quickly if you drop the stack.

Use technology strategically. A tape or video recorder during rehearsal can provide clues about where your delivery suffers. Note any mannerisms or gestures that may turn off or distract your audience. Practice reducing these problems until you're satisfied that you can perform smoothly. If you use technology during your presentation, rehearse blending these elements with your talk. Pausing to show an overhead display can divert your attention from your own anxiety.

Enlist audience support, but don't admit that you're nervous. If you announce that your hands are shaking or your knees are knocking, your audience will think about your hands or knees and not your ideas. If you lose your place, however, admit the problem to the audience, then stop and regain your control. If you lose your composure because you feel overwhelmed, tell the audience that this topic is hard for you. They'll appreciate your candor and support you.

Seek a Second Chance All great speakers suffer an occasional bad performance. Recognize your potential to learn from experiences that don't go well. Then commit yourself to better preparation, goal-setting, and performances in the future.

You may be able to work out a second chance with your instructor. Sometimes your speech can be videotaped in the college media facilities so the instructor can review it at a convenient time. Whether this second chance improves your grade or not, your positive practice will help you turn in a performance in which you have greater pride.

It is no sin to attempt and fail. The only sin is not to make the attempt.
SuEllen Fried
20th-century American social activist

Learn with *InfoTrac College Edition*

InfoTrac College Edition

Look up these articles and search for more on topics that sparked your interest while reading this chapter.

Amy Tan Amy Tan: Author of *The Joy Luck Club*. Hazel Rochman. *Booklist*. June 1, 1996. v92, il9–20, p1690.

Internet Sources Web research: Ten steps to find what you need. Jenny M. McCune. *HR Focus*. Sept. 1998. v75, n9, p7.

Effective Writing Pick up best sellers' writing secrets. Sam Harrison. *Marketing News*. Feb. 15, 1999.

Writer's Block Dissolving Writer's Block. Jack Rawlins. (1992). *The Writer's Way*. Boston: Houghton Mifflin, pp68–73.

Plagiarism Avoiding plagiarism. *The Writing Place*. http://www.writing.nwu.edu/tips/plag.html

Effective Speaking Keeping up public appearances: Master the fine art of public speaking and give a great presentation every time. Audrey Arthur. *Black Enterprise*. July 1997. v27, il2, p54.

Summary Strategies for Mastering College

Refine your expressive skills by seizing every opportunity to practice communication, prepare properly, and evaluate how well you've met your goals.

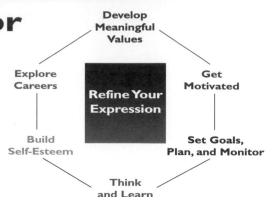

1 Express Yourself!

- Recognize why future employers place great value on communicational skills.
- Seek opportunities for practice and feedback.

2 Do Your Research

- Get familiar with the library.
- Select the best evidence to support the positions you'll develop.
- Use key word searches at the library or on the Internet.
- Consider developing a research stream to maximize your efficiency.

3 Write with Impact

- Get familiar with the formal and informal types of writing.
- Imitate the habits of good writers, especially in starting early, revising regularly, and meeting deadlines.
- Practice the appropriate use of conventions.
- Through careful planning avoid writer's block, procrastination, and accusations of plagiarism.
- Bounce back from disappointing performances by revising your plan.

4 Speak!

- Explore all the speaking opportunities you can find to hone your oral presentation skills.
- Work for success in speeches through careful rehearsal, strong organization, and polished deliveries.
- Use technology and multimedia to produce professional results.
- Overcome speaking jitters and delivery problems through self-control and practice.

Review Questions

1. Why are communicational skills important for life after graduation?

_____

_____

_____

_____

_____

_____

2. What are the most important elements of doing good research?

_____

_____

_____

_____

_____

_____

3. What are some strategies that can produce effective writing?

_____

_____

_____

_____

_____

_____

4. What are some typical problems faced in giving formal speeches and how can these be overcome?

_____

_____

_____

_____

_____

5. What are some ways to recover from disappointing performances in communication?

_____

_____

_____

_____

_____

Learning Portfolio

Reflect and Journal

1. The View from the Audience

Recall a time when you observed someone making a bad speech.

- At what point did you recognize the speech would be unsatisfying?

_____

_____

- Did the speaker make any attempts to correct the failing outcome during the speech?

_____

_____

- How did you feel as you watched the speech flop?

_____

_____

- What advice could you have offered the speaker to turn the speech around?

_____

_____

2. Exploiting Your Life

Amy Tan explored a turbulent theme in her personal life—the challenging relationship between mother and daughter—that resonated with her audience. Make a list of important events in your own life that might become a resource for future expressive writing projects.

1. _____

_____

2. _____

_____

_____

3. _____

_____

_____

4. _____

_____

5. _____

_____

_____

Learn By Doing

1. Lucky Charms

Write down any "magical" rituals you may be using to help you write. Then in a group discussion, explore the significance of such rituals. Describe the range of these activities and share your list. Discuss what would have to happen before you could abandon these practices.

_____

_____

_____

_____

_____

_____

_____

_____

_____

_____

_____

_____

_____

_____

_____

2. Evaluating History

Find a videotape of a famous speech. For example, your college may own a video of Martin Luther King's "I Have a Dream" or other famous speeches. Watch the speech and evaluate its effectiveness using the criteria in Self-Assessment 9-2. What feedback would you give the speaker? Why was the speech so well regarded?

_____

_____

_____

_____

_____

_____

_____

_____

_____

_____

_____

_____

_____

_____

_____

Think Critically

1. The Cost of Plagiarism

Identify reasons why students may plagiarize. Once you have a list of reasons, think about what the consequences of plagiarism may be, whether the student is caught or not.

_____
_____
_____
_____
_____
_____
_____
_____
_____
_____
_____
_____
_____
_____
_____
_____

2. Debate Savvy

In some courses you may be asked to debate in order to show what you know. What learning styles would help make this challenge easier? Think of some ways to help people whose learning style is not well suited to debating.

_____
_____
_____
_____
_____
_____
_____
_____
_____
_____
_____
_____
_____
_____
_____

Think Creatively

1. Entitlement

If you happen to be working on a writing assignment, brainstorm with classmates some high-interest titles for the paper that you're currently developing.

_____
_____
_____
_____
_____
_____
_____
_____
_____
_____

2. Creating a New Role

Elizabeth picked the perfect role model to help her overcome her speaking fears. By pretending to be Auntie Mame, she was able to master her fears until she could own her own success as a speaker. Whom would you select as a good role model for speaking? What characteristics do you particularly admire? How challenging would role-playing be if you needed help managing your fears?

_____
_____
_____
_____
_____
_____

Work toward Goals

Review the results of the self-assessments you completed in this chapter. Also review the opening checklist. Based on your review, select a relatively short-term goal that you want to work on now.

1. What is that goal? (*Hint:* Is it challenging, reasonable, and specific?)

_____

_____

_____

_____

_____

2. What strategies will you use to achieve your goal? (*Hint:* Can you organize your strategy into a series of smaller goals?)

_____

_____

_____

_____

_____

3. What obstacles may be in your way as you attempt to make these positive changes?

_____

_____

_____

_____

_____

4. What additional resources might help you achieve your goal? (Use the CD-ROM that comes with this book for access to some useful leads.)

_____

_____

_____

_____

_____

5. By what date do you want to accomplish your goal?

_____

_____

_____

_____

6. How will you know you have succeeded?

_____

_____

_____

_____

_____

Communicate and Build Relationships

10

More Than Just Grades

Success in college isn't just about grades. Total college success involves mastering communication and developing positive relationships with many kinds of people. Being skilled in these areas will make your college years more enjoyable and productive.

To see where you stand right now regarding communication and relationships, place a check mark next to only those items that apply to you.

____ I am a good listener.

____ I am a good communicator

____ I have strategies for resolving conflicts.

____ I have good relationships with my family and friends.

____ If I get lonely, I can usually find ways to remedy this.

____ I get along well with people from other cultural and ethnic groups.

____ I get along well with the opposite sex.

As you read about Oprah Winfrey on the next page, think about how central good communication skills have been to her life and career.

Don Smetzer/Stone

IMAGES OF COLLEGE SUCCESS

Oprah Winfrey

Oprah Winfrey hosts one of the most watched TV shows in America. She also received an Oscar for her role in *The Color Purple*, in which she played a proud, assertive woman. Oprah was born on a Mississippi farm and spent her early years there, reared by her grandmother. When Oprah was 6, she was sent to live with her mother in a Milwaukee ghetto. Beginning at the age of 9, she was sexually abused by a series of men she trusted. She began committing delinquent acts as a young adolescent. Then her father had Oprah come live with him in Nashville.

At that point, her life improved dramatically. As a high school senior, while raising money for charity, Oprah visited a local radio station and talked her way into a part-time job broadcasting the news. On a scholarship at Tennessee State

A master communicator smiles.

UPI/Corbis-Bettmann

University, she started a major in speech and drama. At age 19 she switched from radio to local television, broadcasting the evening news. Still, she continued college until a Baltimore TV station lured her away in her senior year. A few years later, she moved to Chicago to host a local talk show that eventually became *The Oprah Winfrey Show*.

The millions of dollars Oprah has earned have not decreased her motivation to achieve. She continues to seek new ways to use her tremendous energy and talent productively. As Oprah says, "I have been blessed, but I create the blessings."

Success has not spoiled her. Oprah spends many nights lecturing, often for free, at churches, shelters, and youth organizations. She established the Little Sisters program in a poverty-stricken area of Chicago. She continues to spend some of her Saturdays working with young girls to improve their lives.

When she finally finished college, Oprah was a multimillionaire. In 1987, invited to speak at TSU's commencement, she insisted on finishing the last bit of coursework for her degree. Then, because her father had always urged her to finish college, she endowed ten scholarships in his name.

Learn more about Oprah Winfrey.

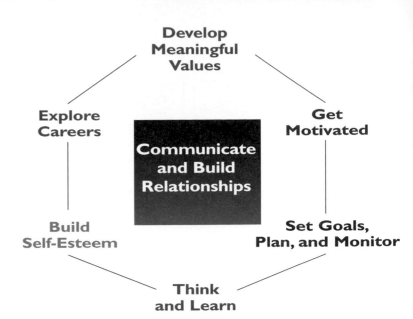

When employers are asked what skills they seek most in college graduates, they consistently say "communication skills." Thus, mastering communication skills will benefit you in college and thereafter in careers and many other aspects of your life. So will building good relationships with many different kinds of people.

Communicate Effectively

Oprah Winfrey's communication skills are admirable. She listens attentively, shows interest, and asks appropriate questions. She also knows how to get people to open up, talk, and feel good about themselves.

It's hard to do much in life without communicating. We communicate when we ask an instructor a question and listen to a student give an explanation of a concept. We communicate in the warmth of an intimate exchange, the heat of an intense conflict, even the chill of a faded relationship.

Communication skills are powerful. Being a good communicator can help you think and learn, gain high self-esteem and elevate the self-esteem of others, achieve your goals, and succeed in careers. For example, asking good questions and listening carefully can stimulate your thinking and lead you to advanced learning. When you communicate well, other people tend to like you, which can increase your self-esteem. By being a supporting communicator you can also help others feel good about themselves. Good communication skills also can help you reach your goals and attain career success. As mentioned, employers rate communication skills as the most important skills they look for in the people they want to hire. Let's explore some of the characteristics of good communication.

> **"We** live to have relationships with other people."
>
> Albert Camus
> *20th-century French-Algerian philosopher*

Communication Skills ⟷ Better Learning Better Grades ⟷ Higher Self-Esteem ⟷ Reach Short-Term and Long-Term Goals

PEANUTS reprinted by permission of United Features Syndicate, Inc.

Develop Good Listening Skills

In the third century B.C.E., the Greek philosopher Zeno of Citum said that the reason people have two ears and one mouth is so they can listen more and talk less. But you can hear what another person is saying without really listening. As one college student put it, "My friends *listen* but my parents only *hear* me talk." Listening is a critical skill for making and keeping relationships. If you're a good listener, others will be drawn to you. Bad listeners hog conversations. They talk *to* rather than *with* someone. Good listeners actively listen. They can't just passively absorb information. "Develop Active-Listening Skills" provides some good tips.

ON-TARGET TIPS

Develop Active-Listening Skills

- **Pay careful attention to the person who is talking.** This shows the person you're interested in what he or she has to say. Maintain good eye contact and lean forward slightly when another person is saying something to you, at least in U.S. culture.
- **Paraphrase.** This means to state in your own words what someone just said. You can start your paraphrase with words like "Let me se, what I hear you saying is…" or "Do you mean…?" Paraphrase when someone says something important.
- **Synthesize themes and patterns.** Conversations can become strewn with bits and pieces of disconnected information. A good active listener summarizes the main themes and feelings the speaker has expressed in a long conversation. The following sentence stems can help get you start synthesizing the themes of a conversation:
  - □ "One theme you seem to be coming back to is…"
  - □ "Let's go over the ground we've been covering so far…"
- **Give good feedback.** Verbal or nonverbal feedback gives the speaker an idea of how well he or she is getting a point across. Good listeners give feedback quickly, honestly, clearly, and informatively.

Avoid Barriers to Effective Verbal Communication

Mike says, "I blew it again. When I went home last weekend, I vowed I wouldn't let my older brother get to me. We were only with each other for about ten minutes when he started in on me. I couldn't take his criticism any more. I started yelling at him and calling him names."

Like Mike we all too often want to communicate better with others but run into barriers we just can't seem to get around. Barriers to communicating include the following (Gordon, 1970):

- **Criticizing** (making negative evaluations), as in "It's your own fault—you should have studied."
- **Name-calling and labeling** (putting down the other person), as in "You're such an idiot, for not planning better."
- **Advising** (talking down to the other person while giving a solution to a problem), as in "That's so easy to solve. Why don't you just…?"
- **Ordering** (Commanding the other person to do what you want), as in "Get off the phone, right now!"
- **Threatening** (trying to control the other person), as if "If you don't listen to me, I'm going to make your life miserable."

- **Moralizing** (preaching to the other person what he or she should do), as in "You know you shouldn't have gone there tonight. You ought to be sorry."
- **Diverting** (pushing the other person's problems aside), as in "You think *you* have it bad. Let me tell you about my midterms."
- **Logical arguing** (trying to convince the other person with logical facts without considering the person's feelings), as in "Look at the reasons why you failed. Here they are.... So, you have to admit I'm right." It's good to use logic to try to persuade someone, but if you lose sight of the person's feelings, no matter how right you are, the other person won't be persuaded and may be hurt.

Tune in to Nonverbal Communication

How do you behave when you talk with others? Does the way you fold your arms, cast your eyes, move your mouth, cross your legs, or touch someone send a message? Communications experts believe it does. You might

Lift an eyebrow for disbelief

Clasp your arms to isolate or protect yourself

Shrug your shoulders for indifference

Wink one eye for intimacy

Tap your fingers for impatience

Slap your forehead for forgetfulness

> **W**hat you are speaks so loudly I cannot hear what you say.
>
> Ralph Waldo Emerson
> 19th-century American poet and essayist

These are conscious, deliberate gestures people make in the course of communicating. Are there also unconscious nonverbal behaviors that offer clues about what a person is feeling? Hard-to-control facial muscles especially tend to reveal emotions that people are trying to conceal. Lifting only the inner part of your eyebrow may reveal stress and worry. Eyebrows raised together may signal fear. Fidgeting may reveal anxiety or boredom.

Many communications experts believe that most interpersonal communication is nonverbal. Even if you're sitting in a corner silently and reading a book, your nonverbal behavior communicates something—perhaps that you want to be left alone. It might also communicate that you're intellectually oriented.

You'll have a hard time trying to mask or control your nonverbal messages. True feelings usually express themselves, no matter how hard we try to conceal them. So it's good to recognize that your nonverbal behavior communicates how you truly feel.

Resolve Conflicts with Others

Conflicts are inevitable in our everyday interactions, especially in an intense college environment. Developing skills to resolve these conflicts can make your life calmer and more enjoyable. Strategies for reducing interpersonal conflict include being assertive and negotiating effectively.

Be Assertive Assertive expression has become a communication ideal. However, not everyone acts assertively.

We can deal with conflict in our lives in four main ways: aggressively, manipulatively, passively, and assertively. That is, when faced with conflict you can blow up, get down and dirty, cave in, or speak up.

The Boyfriend and the Dumpster 💿

A first-year student, Jeanette decided to visit her boyfriend at his apartment without notice. She entered without knocking and found him in bed with another woman. She lost it. She grabbed everything she had ever bought for him, including the TV and some clothes. She threw everything in the dumpster but the TV, which she kept for herself. She returned to his apartment and began embarrassing him in front of his roommates. What do you think? Did her boyfriend get what he deserved? Was Jeanette too aggressive or was she just being assertive?

Become More Assertive

- **Evaluate your rights.** Determine your rights in the situation at hand.
- **Designate a time for discussing what you want.** Unless you need to be assertive on the spot, find a mutually convenient time to discuss the problem with the other person involved.
- **State the problem to the other person in terms of its consequences for you.** Clearly outline your point of view, even if it seems obvious to you. This allows the other person to get a better sense of your position. Describe the problem as objectively as you can without blaming or judging. For example, you might tell someone you live with, "I'm having a problem with your music playing so loud. I need to study for a test tomorrow, but the stereo is so loud I can't concentrate."
- **Express your feelings about the particular situation.** When you express your feelings, even others who completely disagree with you can tell how strongly you feel about the circumstance.
- **Make your request.** This is an important aspect of being assertive. Simply ask for what you want (or don't want) in a straightforward way.

- **Aggression.** People who respond aggressively to conflict run roughshod over others. They communicate in demanding, abrasive, and hostile ways. Aggressive people often are insensitive to the rights and feelings of others.
- **Manipulation.** Manipulative people try to get what they want by making other people feel sorry for them or feel guilty. They don't take responsibility for meeting their own needs. Instead, manipulative people play the role of the victim or martyr to get others to do things for them. They work indirectly to get their needs met.
- **Passivity:** Passive people act in nonassertive, submissive ways. They let others run roughshod over them. Passive people don't express their feelings and don't let others know what they want or need.
- **Assertion:** Assertive people act in their own best interests. They stand up for their legitimate rights and express their views openly and directly. Assertiveness also builds equal relationships (Alberti & Emmons, 1995).

Of the four styles of dealing with conflict, acting assertively is clearly the most appropriate. Assertiveness is an attitude as well as a way of acting. Be assertive in any situation in which you need to express your feelings, need to ask for what you want, or want to say "no" to something you don't want.

To determine your dominant style, take Self-Assessment 10-1. The strategies advocated by the behavioral expert Edmund Bourne (1995) are described in "Become More Assertive."

Negotiate Effectively

Everybody negotiates. You negotiate when you apply for a job, dispute a grade with a teacher, buy a car, ask your landlord to paint your apartment, or try to get your roommate or partner to do something. Whenever you want something from someone whose interests are at odds with your own, you can choose to negotiate.

Some negotiation strategies are better than others. Negotiating effectively helps you to get what you want from others without alienating them. Negotiation experts often describe three main ways of solving problems with others: win-lose, lose-lose, and win-win.

- **Win-lose strategy.** In this type of negotiating, one party gets what he or she wants and the other comes up short. This strategy often goes like this: "Either I get my way or your get your way." For example, a couple has a specific amount of money they can spend, but they totally disagree on how to spend it. Most of the time a win-lose strategy is not wise. Why? Because the loser may harbor bad feelings for a long time.

Do You Blow Up, Get Down and Get Dirty, or Speak Up?

Think about each of the following situations. Check which style you tend to use in each.

	Assertive	Aggressive	Manipulative	Passive
You're being kept on the phone by a salesperson trying to sell you something you don't want.	_____	_____	_____	_____
You want to break off a relationship that no longer works for you.	_____	_____	_____	_____
You're sitting in a movie and the people behind you are talking.	_____	_____	_____	_____
Your doctor keeps you waiting more than 20 minutes.	_____	_____	_____	_____
You're standing in line and someone moves in front of you.	_____	_____	_____	_____
Your friend has owed you money for a long time and it's money you could use.	_____	_____	_____	_____
You receive food at a restaurant that is over- or undercooked.	_____	_____	_____	_____
You want to ask your friend, romantic partner, or roommate for a major favor.	_____	_____	_____	_____
Your friends ask you to do something that you don't feel like doing.	_____	_____	_____	_____
You're at a large lecture. The instructor is speaking too softly and you know other students are also having trouble hearing her.	_____	_____	_____	_____
You want to start a conversation at a gathering, but you don't know anyone there.	_____	_____	_____	_____
You're sitting next to someone who is smoking, and the smoke bothers you.	_____	_____	_____	_____
You're talking to someone about something important to you, but they don't seem to be listening.	_____	_____	_____	_____
You're speaking and someone interrupts you.	_____	_____	_____	_____
You receive an unjust criticism from someone.	_____	_____	_____	_____

Total up the number of your aggressive, manipulative, passive, and assertive marks. Whichever style has the most marks is your dominant personal style of interacting with others in conflicts. If you did not mark the assertive category ten or more times, you would benefit from working on your assertiveness.

- **Lose-lose strategy.** This strategy usually unfolds when both parties initially try a win-lose strategy that does not work. As a result of the struggle, both end up unsatisfied with the outcome.
- **Win-win strategy.** The goal in this strategy is to find a solution that satisfies both parties. They avoid trying to win at each other's expense. They believe that by working together they can find a solution that satisfies everyone.

Some compromises approach this win-win ideal. You and the seller settle on a price for a used car. The price is between what the seller was asking and you wanted to pay. Neither of you got exactly what you wanted, but the outcome left each of you happy. Similarly, you and your companion each want to see a different movie. In order to spend the evening together, you might choose another movie that you both agree on.

The best solutions of all, though, are not compromises. Rather, they are solutions in which all parties get what they want. For example, Andrea and Carmen are roommates with different study habits. Andres likes to study in the evening. This leaves most of her day free for other activities. Carmen thinks that evenings should be for relaxation and fun. They arrived at the following solution. On Monday through Wednesday, Andrea studies at her boyfriend's; Carmen does anything she wants. On Thursday and Sunday Carmen agrees to keep things quiet where she and Andrea live. On Friday and Saturday they both have fun together.

The win-win strategy gives you a creative way of finding the best solution for a problem among two or more parties. You can use it to solve conflicts with others and make everyone involved feel better.

Develop Good Relationships

Relationships play a powerful role in college. As you think about your relationships with the people in your life, such as family members, partners, roommates, friends, and dates, keep in mind that the strategies for communication, assertiveness, and negotiation we just discussed will serve you well.

With Parents

For college students who still depend on their parents financially and in other ways, relationships can vary considerably. Some parents treat their first-year students as if they are still completely under their wing. Some college students remain too dependent on the security of their parents. They don't tackle enough new challenges on their own. Some parents have little contact and provide little support for first-year students. Some students break off communication with their parents.

Let Your Parents Know You Haven't Fallen off the Planet No matter how much independence you want, it is a good idea not to break off communication with your parents. You'll likely need them at some point, possibly for money, a place to live, or emotional support.

Maintaining communication with the folks back home doesn't mean you have to write them a letter three times a week or call every night. You don't have to tell them everything you do. However, if they don't hear from you for a couple of weeks, they may fear that something really bad has happened to you. In most cases parents regularly want to know how you are getting along and that you haven't been kidnapped by aliens.

What is regular contact? If you're away from home, a phone conversation once a week should do. One first-year student didn't want his roommates to kid him about calling home regularly, so he wrote a coded reminder on his calendar once a week, "E. T.," from the movie where E. T. phones home. E-mail is cheap, convenient, and easy—another great way to keep in touch.

If you're a young adult student in your first year, your parents are probably concerned about your increased independence. They may ask questions that seem intrusive. "How much are you studying?" "How come you didn't get an A on your English test?" "What's your roommate like?" "Are you dating anyone?" "Have you been going to religious services?" Try to listen politely to their questions. Realize that they have your best interests at heart. You don't have to tell them all the details of your life. They usually will accept your answers if you tell them a few general things and contact them weekly.

What Your Parents Can't Find out without Your Approval Your parents know only what you choose to tell them about your college experiences. According to the Family Education Responsibility and Privacy Act, the college cannot release your records to anyone but you. Instructors can discuss your progress or problems only in your presence or with your permission. This legal constraint encourages your family members to let you resolve your own problems. Use this control responsibly and wisely.

With Spouse or Partner

Students who are married or have a partner face special challenges. Here are some strategies keeping relationships with a partner positive (Sternberg, 1988):

- **Don't take your relationship for granted.** The seeds of a relationship's destruction are planted if you or your partner take the other for granted. Continue to nourish the relationship, giving it high priority along with your studies. You don't want to get a degree and lose your partner. Schedule time with your partner just as you schedule time for classes and study. Don't expect your partner to take over all of the household duties or pamper you.
- **Develop a positive identity.** Don't seek in your partner what you lack in yourself. Feel good about your pursuit of education—it will enhance your identity. When both partners have positive identities, their relationship benefits, and both are likely to have high self-esteem.
- **Share your college life with your partner.** Let your partner know what you're doing in college. Discuss your schedule, what you're learning, and what your day is like. Look for campus activities or events—such as lectures, sporting events, and plays—that you can attend with your partner. Remember to ask about your partner's activities to avoid being too self-focused.

- **Be open with your partner.** Sometimes it seems easier in the short run to lie or hold back the truth. The problem is that once omissions, distortions, and flat-out lies start, they tend to spread and ultimately can destroy a relationship. Talk becomes empty because the relationship has lost its depth and trust.
- **See things from your partner's point of view.** Ask yourself how your partner perceives you. This helps you to develop the empathy and understanding that fuel a satisfying, successful relationship.
- **Be a friend.** Researchers have found that one of the most successful factors in a successful marriage is the extent to which the partners are good friends (Gottman & Silver, 1999). Friendship acts as a powerful shield against conflict.

With Children

If you're a parent as well as a student, you also face special challenges. Here are some helpful strategies.

- **Be an authoritative parent.** The psychologist Diana Baumrind (1991) wanted to know whether one type of parenting style is linked with having a child who is well-adjusted and competent. She found that the best parenting style is authoritative, which involves being nurturing, engaging in verbal give-and-take with the child, and exercising some control but not in a punishing way. That is, authoritative parents don't let children run wild and they give children feedback to help them develop self-control. By contrast, being either permissive and uninvolved or punitive and cold are ineffective parenting styles. Children reared by these types of parents often have trouble controlling their behavior.
- **Communicate.** If your children are old enough, talk with them about how important they are to you. Discuss with them how important your education is to you. Each day set aside time to listen to your children.
- **Be a good time manager.** At times, you may feel overwhelmed with juggling a family and school. Planning can be an important asset in your effort to balance your academic and family time. Check into child-care and community agencies for services and activities for your children before and after school.
- **Set aside time for your children and yourself.** It's not going to be easy, but be sure to block out at least some time each week for activities you enjoy or for relaxation. You might have a hobby, like to exercise, or enjoy going to movies. Set aside time every day for your children's interests as well.

With Roommates

Relationships with roommates vary. You might become best friends. You might grow to hate each other. You might be indifferent and simply live in the same place.

In many cases, a first-year student's roommate is a total stranger. You're asked to live in close quarters for nine months with someone you know little or nothing about. That's enough to cause apprehension in anyone.

What are some good strategies for getting along with this total stranger who is now your roommate? See "Getting Along with a Roommate." But what if, after trying hard to reconcile problems, you still hate your roommate? What if your roommate difficulties are lowering your grades? What can you do?

If you live in a college dorm, you probably have an RA (resident advisor) with whom you can discuss your roommate problems. Take the initiative. Go to the RA and ask for advice about what to do. Try out the advice and give it a chance to work. Then, if things are still intolerable, go to the campus housing office. Courteously and clearly state your roommate problems. Campus housing offices usually don't like to change roommates. However, if your problem is severe enough, they might help you.

With Dates

Dating can involve wonderful, happy times. It also can be a source of unhappiness, anxiety, and turmoil, including sexual assault.

The Dating Scene Some first-year students date a lot, others very little or not at all. Some students view dating as a way to find a spouse. Others see it as an important part of fitting into the social scene. Some students date for romantic reasons, others for friendship or companionship.

Dating can detract from or enhance your college success. It's clearly not a good idea to get so head-over-heels in passionate love that all you can think about is your romantic partner. If that happens to you, you'll probably spend too little time studying. On the other hand, some people who date someone regularly or live with a partner feel more settled down and freer to work.

It's not unusual for many first-year students to have a high school boyfriend or girlfriend back home. Also, many commuter students have a romantic partner who does not go to college or goes to college somewhere else. You do not necessarily have to give up this romantic relationship. However, it's important to evaluate how much time you think about a distant romance at the expense of your academic work and relationships on your campus.

Too many first-year students get caught up in wanting to date an ideal person rather than a real person. They search for the stereotypical jock, person with movie-star looks, or punk rocker. Some first-year students also look at every date as a potential girlfriend or boyfriend, someone they eventually might marry. College counselors say that such students would probably be better adjusted and happier if they broadened their perspective on dating. Don't look at every date as a potential Mr. or Mrs. Perfect. Dates can be potential friends as well as romantic partners.

Rape and Unwanted Sexual Acts Rape is sexual intercourse that is forced on a person. A special concern in college is date or acquaintance rape. One-third to one-half of college men admit that they have forced sexual activity on women (Koss & Boeschen, 1998).

Rape is a traumatic experience for victims. They initially feel shocked and numb. Recovery is easier with the support of parents and friends. Professional

ON-TARGET TIPS

Getting Along with a Roommate

Here are some suggestions for getting along with a roommate:

1. **Cut off problems early.** Whenever two people live together, problems appear. Don't let them fester. Detect and resolve them early.
2. **Use good communication skills.** Good communication skills include being an active listener and avoiding barriers to communication. If you have a roommate problem, review these strategies and use them with your roommate.
3. **Be responsible.** You may have gotten into the habit of not keeping your room clean before you came to college. Old habits are hard to break. Do your share of keeping the room clean. Make your bed. Pick up your clothes.
4. **Show respect.** You can learn a lot about the importance of give-and-take in relationships by living with a roommate. To get along, you have to show respect for each other. It's not a good idea to come in at 2 A.M., flip the lights on, and wake up your roommate. It's also not a good idea to rev up the stereo when your roommate is trying to study.
5. **Be assertive.** If you think that you're doing more than your fair share of the giving in your roommate relationship, be more assertive. Stand up for your rights. Use the strategies for being assertive outlined earlier in the chapter.

Strategies for Avoiding Settings in Which Rape Most Often Occurs

THINGS TO DO:

Go places with other people.

If you go alone, tell someone your plans.

Walk briskly, with purpose.

Stay in well-lighted, populated areas.

Limit your drug and alcohol intake; these can make you vulnerable.

Exercise good judgment about sharing your private information.

Have your keys ready when going to your car or residence.

Lock all doors and windows in your car and residence.

Do not open doors for strangers.

Carry a whistle or other alarm.

If someone is following you or you feel threatened, go to a public place, call the police, run, scream, or blow a whistle.

THINGS TO REMEMBER:

No one has the right to rape you.

Rape is not the fault of the person who was raped.

Rape is a criminal act of violence for the purpose of power.

Date or acquaintance rape is rape.

Rape is a sexual assault. Assault is a crime.

---

counseling also can help. See "Strategies for Avoiding Settings in Which Rape Most Often Occurs" for some safety precautions.

Some people engage in unwanted sexual acts when not physically forced to do so. Why would they do this? They might be

- Turned on by their partner's actions and later regret it
- Fearful that the relationship will end if they don't have sex
- Intoxicated
- Feeling obligated because of the time and money spent by a partner

In sum, monitor your sexual feelings and make good sexual decisions. As in other aspects of communication and relationships, being aware of people's motives and acting assertively rather than aggressively, manipulatively, or passively are good strategies.

So far in our discussion of relationships we have talked about ways to improve relationships with parents, a spouse or partner, children, roommates, and dates. Next, we explore another important aspect of relationships that hangs over many college students—loneliness.

Deal with Loneliness

Loneliness can be a dark cloud over a person's everyday life. But don't confuse loneliness with being alone. Time spent alone can be meaningful and satisfying. However, when we feel isolated and long to be with others, we need to do something to become more connected.

Leaving Home When young college students leave the familiar world of their hometown and family to go to college, they often face loneliness (Perlman & Peplau, 1998). Many first-year college students feel anxious about meeting new people and developing new social lives. One student comments,

> My first year here at the university has been pretty lonely. I wasn't lonely at all in high school. I lived in a fairly small town. I knew everyone and they knew me. I was a member of several clubs and played on the basketball team. It's not that way here. It is a big place. I've felt like a stranger so many times. It has taken a while but I'm finally adapting better. In the past few months I've been making a special effort to meet people and get to know them. It has not been easy.

As the passage indicates, first-year students rarely carry their high school popularity and social standing into college. Especially when students attend college away from home, they face the challenge of forming new social relationships. In one study, two weeks after the college year began, 75 percent of the first-year students felt lonely at least part of the time after arriving on campus (Cutrona, 1982). Loneliness is not reserved for younger first-year students, though. Older first-year students can be lonely as well. The demands of school, work, and family may leave little time to feel replenished through contacts with friends.

Are You Lonely? If you feel like you aren't in tune with the people around you and you can't find companionship when you want it, you're probably lonely. If you've recently left an important relationship, you'll likely feel lonely until you rebuild your social network.

Strategies for Reducing Loneliness If you feel lonely, how can you become better connected with others? Here are some ideas:

- Get involved in activities with others through college, work, community announcements, or religious organizations. Join and volunteer time with an organization you believe in. You'll probably meet others who share your views. One social gathering can lead to new social contacts. This is especially true if you introduce yourself to others and start conversations. Meeting new people and developing new social ties always involves risk, but the benefits are worth it. Consider joining a new group at dinner, sitting with new people in class, or finding a study or exercise partner.
- Recognize the warning signs of loneliness. People often become bored or alienated before loneliness sinks in. Take action to head it off. Planning new activities is easier than struggling to get out of loneliness once it has set in.
- Practice certain qualities when interacting with friends or potential friends. Be kind and considerate. Be honest and trustworthy. Share and cooperate. Use active listening skills. Have a positive attitude. Be supportive. Comment on something special about the other person.
- If you can't shed your loneliness and make friends on your own, contact the student counseling center at your college. A counselor can show you ways to connect with others on your campus and reduce your loneliness. Also, see the resources section on this book's Web site.

So far we have explored ways to communicate more effectively, to improve relationships with many individuals in our lives, and to reduce loneliness. As we'll see next, relationships with diverse others can also contribute positively to college life.

> *Where you used to be, there is a hole in the world, which I find myself constantly walking around in the daytime, and falling into at night.*
> Edna St. Vincent Millay
> 20th-century American poet

Appreciate Diversity

Ana Bolado de Espino came to Dallas, Texas, from Mexico in 1980. She did not speak a word of English, but she did have a dream. Ana wanted to become a medical doctor. She worked as a maid, scrubbing floors and doing laundry for fifteen years to earn enough money to get through college. Divorced, she raised two children while attending college and working.

She feared that she would never make it to medical school. She also hit a major snag. As a young teen, her daughter began to hang out with a gang, ran away, and became pregnant. Ana thought about dropping out of college to spend more time with her daughter, but her daughter told her to stay in college. Since then, the daughter at age 15 has started to turn her life around.

Ana was 38 years old when she obtained her college degree with a GPA of almost 4.00. She worked as an outreach AIDS counselor for a year after graduating from college. Recently she was accepted into medical school.

Ana Bolado de Espino represents the increased diversity in U.S. college campuses. Diversity can come into our lives in many ways, both in terms of our own characteristics and the diverse others we interact with. In some cases,

> *We need every human gift and cannot afford to neglect any gift because of artificial barriers of sex or race or class or national origin.*
> Margaret Mead
> 20th-century American anthropologist

the diversity is very welcome, in others it may involve conflict and uneasy feelings. Let's explore some aspects of the diversity you may encounter in your college life and some strategies for improving relationships with diverse others.

Culture and Ethnicity

We should be accustomed to thinking of the United States as a country with many different cultures. Our population is diverse and comes from many different places. Some college campuses are among the most diverse settings in this country, although smaller colleges tend to be more homogeneous, with most students and faculty sharing a predominant ethnic or religious heritage. Larger campuses tend to be more diverse; most have international students and U.S. students, as well as faculty and staff, from many ethnic backgrounds.

Despite the opportunities to mix, people often associate with their "own kind." Think about where you eat lunch. Commuters often hang out with other commuters. Fraternity and sorority members sit off by themselves. Faculty and students tend not to mix. Our fear of the unknown may keep us close to those whose background we share. This can prevent us from taking advantage of the rich opportunities on campus to meet and learn about people who differ from us. Let's explore some factors that can help us understand cultural diversity better.

Ethnicity, Stereotypes, and Prejudice on Campus

College campuses present many issues and concerns related to diversity. According to a survey of students at 390 colleges and universities, ethnic conflict is common on many campuses (Hurtado, Dey, & Trevino, 1994). More than half of the African Americans and almost one-fourth of the Asian Americans said that they felt excluded from college activities. Only 6 percent of Anglo Americans said that they felt excluded.

Many of us sincerely think that we are not prejudiced. However, experts on prejudice believe that every person harbors some prejudices (Sears, Peplau, & Taylor, 2000). Why? Because we naturally tend to do several things that pro-

An increasing number of college students are from ethnic minority groups. It's important to keep in mind that each ethnic group is diverse. Not taking this diversity and individual variation into account leads to stereotyping. A good strategy is to think of other students as individuals, not as members of a majority or minority group.

Rob Gage/FPG International

mote stereotyping and prejudice. For example, we tend to identify with others who are like us. We tend to be *ethnocentric*, favoring the groups we belong to and tending to think of them as superior. We also tend to fear people who differ from us.

Reduce Prejudice and Stereotyping To explore prejudice on campus, think about these stereotypes: the blonde cheerleader; the computer nerd; the absent-minded professor; the rigid, snarly librarian; the female basketball star; and the class clown. Notice that with merely a simple label we can conjure up an image and expectations about what a person will be like. Now imagine that you get to know these people. You discover that

- The "blonde" cheerleader has a 4.0 average.
- The computer "nerd" plays in a hot new jazz band at a local club on weekends.
- The "absent-minded professor" never misses a class.
- The "rigid, snarly" librarian gives freely of her time to local charities to help improve the lives of children.
- The "female basketball star" is dating a man in his second year of law school.
- The "class clown" recently organized a campuswide initiative to decrease the pollution coming from a nearby chemical plant.

Clearly, stereotypes lead us to view others in limited and limiting ways. There's so much more to people than the social roles they play or the groups to which they belong.

Prejudice is ugly and socially damaging. Many people believe that college campuses should demonstrate leadership in reducing it. Recently, various diversity initiatives have been enacted to work toward this goal: on-campus celebrations of ethnic achievements, festivals that highlight different traditions or beliefs, required coursework to promote the explorations of traditions other than one's own, and inclusion of examples from a broader range of human experience in required readings. In spite of diversity initiatives, we still have a long way to go to reduce discrimination and prejudice.

How unpleasing to the eye if all the flowers and plants, the leaves and blossoms, the fruits, the branches, and the trees were all the same shape and color. Diversity of hues, forms, and shape enriches and adorns the garden.

Allah Baha'
19th-century Persian founder of the Baha'i faith

International Students Most colleges have students from a wide range of countries. These students bring with them customs, values, and behaviors that may be quite different from those of U.S. students (Lin & Yi, 1997). If you're a U.S.-born student, consider getting to know one or more international students. It will expand your education.

If you're an international student, even if you were well-adjusted at home, adapting to college in the United States may bring confusion and problems. You now have to cope with a whole new set of customs and values. In some cases, you have to learn a new language and new rules for special conduct. "International SOS" provides some tips.

Gender

Gender refers to our social and cultural experiences as a female or a male person. We live in a world where

ON-TARGET TIPS

International SOS

- **Be patient.** Give yourself time to adapt to your new life. Things may not be easy at the beginning. Over time, you will develop greater comfort with U.S. culture.
- **Create or join a support system.** Most campuses have international student clubs where you can meet and get to know other international students.
- **Make new friends.** Get the most out of your international experience by reaching out to others to learn about their cultures.
- **Share your culture.** Look for opportunities to share your background so your teachers and classmates can learn about your culture.
- **Keep your own goals in mind.**

If you're a student from the United States, respect the differences between yourself and international students. Value diversity. If you're from another country, create a support system and get involved in campus life. Be patient in adjusting to this new culture.

gender roles are changing, and these changes have affected campus life. For example, first-year student Gina is the first woman in her family to attend college. Her grandmother did not go, because it was not an option. Neither did her mother, who still believed that her place was in the home. However, her mother supported Gina's desire for a different kind of life.

Women now attend college and seek careers outside the home in greater numbers than ever before. In 1966, 57 percent of first-year college students agreed that a married woman should be confined to the home and family; in 1999, that figure had dropped to 28 percent (Sax & others, 2000).

The Controversy Not long ago, virtually all American boys were expected to grow up to be "masculine" and girls to be "feminine." The gender blueprints seemed clear-cut. The well-adjusted man should be independent, assertive, and dominant. The well-adjusted woman should be dependent, nurturing, and submissive.

These beliefs and stereotypes led to *sexism*, the negative treatment of women and girls because of their sex. Some examples of sexism are

- Thinking that women are not as smart as men
- Not being equally comfortable with a woman or man as a boss
- Thinking that a woman's only place is in the home

Today's society is generally more flexible than before, but this produces confusion and uncertainty for many people. Although they have gained greater influence in several professional spheres, many women still experience "glass ceilings" that limit their access to the most powerful positions. In contrast, women who choose more traditional roles sometimes think that other women criticize them unfairly for "selling out."

Some men are confused by the changes in gender expectations. They struggle to grasp what life is really like for women. Some women are angry at men in general for their historic abuse of privilege. Some men, especially white men, are angry—they don't like losing privilege in the job market because of policies that put women on a more equal footing.

Improving the Lives of Women College offers many opportunities for women to explore their lives and set out on a course to improve their opportunities.

Examine Competencies and Needs. In her study of women's lives, Jean Baker Miller (1986) concluded that a large part of what women do is active participation in the development of others. Women help others emotionally, intellectually, and socially. For example, Ana Bolado de Espino supported her daughter while pursuing her dream of going to medical school, and her daughter supported her. Miller argues that women need to retain their relationship skills but become more self-motivated as well by focusing more on themselves and their own needs.

Another gender expert, Harriet Lerner (1989), echoes these beliefs. She states that competent women can stay emotionally connected with others ("YOU-ness"). They also need to focus on improving themselves ("I-ness").

"So according to the stereotype, you can put two and two together, but I can read the handwriting on the wall."

© Joel Pett. All Rights Reserved.

In *The Mismeasure of Woman*, Carol Tavris (1992) wrote that no matter how hard women try, they can't measure up. They are criticized for being too female or not female enough. Tavris argues that women are judged by how well they fit into a man's world, which tends to fixate on the beauty of a woman's body. Tavris said that we need more emphasis on a woman's *soul* as the key indicator of competence and worth.

The message to women is this. Women are certainly not inferior to men. Start evaluating yourself in terms of female competencies, not male ones. For example, women (and society) need to place a higher value on relationship skills. To be leaders, women do not need to stop caring for others. Developing positive relationships with others and developing ourselves are both important for both sexes.

Don't Put up with Sexual Harassment. Improving women's lives also requires reducing and eventually eliminating sexual harassment. Sexual harassment in colleges and the workplace is a major barrier to women's progress. Two million women currently enrolled in college will experience some form of sexual harassment in their student lives (Paludi, 1998).

Sexual harassment includes

- **Gender harassment.** Sexist remarks and behavior that insult and degrade women, a problem apart from harassment for sex.
- **Seductive behavior.** Unwanted, inappropriate, and offensive advances.
- **Sexual bribery.** Harassment for sex, with the threat of punishment for refusal. For example, a woman might be fired or demoted by her boss if she doesn't go along with the sexual demand.

Every college is required by law to take action against sexual harassment. Many colleges and communities have resources to protect women from this harassment. If you are sexually harassed, report it to your school's administration.

Improving the Lives of Men

What can men do to improve their lives? Should they become more masculine and virile? Should they become more sensitive and tuned in to relationships?

Have Today's Men Become too Wimpy? Some men believe that men today have become soft and vulnerable, letting women run their lives. One such man

Gender-Based Strategies for Self-Improvement

Women:

- ■ Don't use male standards to judge your competence.
- ■ Retain strengths in building relationships and staying in touch with emotions. Be proud of them.
- ■ Improve your self-motivation. Be more self-assertive. Focus on knowing your own needs and meeting them. Go beyond the idea that this is selfish. It is self-assertive.
- ■ Don't put up with sexual harassment. Know what qualifies as sexual harassment. Report it when it happens.

Men:

- ■ Retain your strengths. Be self-motivated and achievement-oriented.
- ■ Do a better job of understanding your emotions and self. Explore yourself. Ask yourself what kind of person you want to be. Think more about how you want others to perceive you.
- ■ Work on your relationship skills. Give more consideration to the feelings of others. Make relationships a higher priority in your life.
- ■ If you're aggressive and hostile, tone down your anger. Be self-assertive but not overly aggressive. That is, control yourself and your emotions. Work toward better understanding of your own emotions and the feelings of other people.

is Robert Bly (1990), the author of *Iron John*. Iron John is a mythological creature with a deep masculine identity. He is spontaneous, sexual, and aggressive. He has untamed impulses and thoughtful self-discipline. Will Bly's proposal of a return to the virile, forceful man of yesterday make today's world a better place to live in? Many critics say that Bly's strategy only creates more turmoil between men and women and will not promote cooperation between them.

Be in Tune with Your Emotions and Build Good Relationships. If heightened masculinity isn't the answer for men, what is? One gender expert, Herb Goldberg (1980), says that a huge gulf separates the sexes: Women sense and articulate feelings; men tend not to because of their masculine conditioning. Men's defensive armor causes them to maintain self-destructive patterns. Men become effective work machines, but they suffer emotionally. As a result men live about eight years less than women, have higher hospitalization rates, and have more behavior problems. Goldberg believes that men are killing themselves when they strive to be "true" men like Iron John. That is a heavy price to pay for masculine "privilege" and power.

How can men live more physically and psychologically satisfying lives? Goldberg argues that men need to become better attuned to their emotional makeup and relationships with others. He believes that men can retain their self-assertiveness while doing this.

For more recommendations on how women and men can lead more competent lives, see "Gender-Based Strategies for Self-Improvement."

Sexual Orientation

A large majority of people are heterosexual. Although for many years it was estimated that about 10 percent of the U.S. population are homosexual (attracted to people of the same sex), more recent surveys put the figure at about 2–5 percent (Michael & others, 1994). About 1 percent are bisexual (attracted to both men and women).

Homosexuality and Bisexuality Sexual orientation is not necessarily a fixed decision made once in life. For example, it is not unusual for a person to experiment with homosexual behavior in adolescence but not as an adult.

In most ways the college goals of homosexual and bisexual students are not different from those for heterosexual students. However, their minority status does bring some difficulties. Many heterosexual students still consider them as abnormal rather than simply different. Even the American Psychiatric Association once labeled homosexuality as abnormal behavior and a mental disorder. That is no longer the case, but the stigma remains, along with discrimination. Homosexual and bisexual students encounter physical abuse, hostile comments, and demeaning jokes. Heterosexuals may feel

Be tolerant of others' sexual orientations.

Jonathan Novrok/PhotoEdit

uncomfortable around them. For example, when he found out that one of his fraternity brothers, Bob, was gay, Jim said he felt uncomfortable and increasingly avoided Bob. Several years later, Jim said that he regrets treating Bob the way he did. He realized that nothing prevented a heterosexual from being friends with a homosexual.

Improving the Lives of Gay, Lesbian, and Bisexual College Students
How can gays, lesbians, and bisexual students improve their lives in college? What positive role can heterosexuals play in this?

- Many campuses have organizations for gays, lesbians, and bisexuals. If you are a homosexual or bisexual student, you may want to join one. Some of them include not only the campus gay and lesbian population, but also their friends and family, as well as other students with questions, regardless of sexual orientation. These organizations provide a safe place for students to voice their thoughts and feelings about sexual orientation.

- If you are homosexual or bisexual and your campus does not have a related organization, consider starting one. This may require following procedures that your student activities office has established for starting a campus organization. If you feel uncomfortable on your own campus, consider joining an organization on a nearby campus or in the local community.

- Some good books written by and for homosexual and bisexual people cover many practical issues. See the list in the resources on the Web site for this book.

- Be tolerant of the sexual orientation of others. If you are a heterosexual and harbor negative feelings toward homosexuals, consider taking a course on human sexuality. You'll learn not only about homosexuality but about yourself as well. Researchers have found that college students who take a course in human sexuality gain positive views of homosexual and bisexual people (Walters, 1994).

Improve Your Relationships with Diverse Others

How can you get along better with people who differ from you? Here are some helpful strategies.

Assess Your Attitudes One of the first steps in improving relations with people who are different from you is to understand your own attitudes better. Most of us sincerely think that we are not prejudiced. Are there people you don't like because of the group they belong to? Honestly evaluate your attitudes toward people who

- Are from cultures different from your own
- Are from ethnic groups different from your own
- Are of the other sex
- Have a different sexual orientation

Take the Perspective of Others You can improve your attitude toward others by clarifying your perspective. Ask yourself,

- "What is this person feeling and thinking?"
- "What is she or he really like?"
- "What about their background and experiences makes them different from me?"
- "What kinds of stress and obstacles are they facing?"
- "Is the fact that they are different reason enough for me not to like them or to be angry with them?"
- "How much do I really know about the other person? How can I learn more about him or her?"

Seek Personal Contact Martin Luther King once said, "I have a dream that my four little children will one day live in a nation where they will not be judged by the color of their skin but by the content of their character." How can we reach the world Martin Luther King envisioned, a world beyond prejudice and discrimination? Mere contact with people from other ethnic groups won't do it. However, a particular type of contact—personal contact— often is effective in improving relations with others (Brislin, 1993).

Personal contact here means sharing one's worries, troubles, successes, failures, personal ambitions, and coping strategies. When we reveal information about ourselves, we are more likely to be perceived as individuals than as stereotyped members of a group. When we share personal information with people we used to regard as "them," we begin to see that they are more like "us" than we thought.

Respect Differences but Don't Overlook Similarities
Think how boring our lives would be if we were all the same. Respecting others with different traditions, backgrounds, and abilities improves communication and cooperation.

When we perceive people as different from us, we often do so on the basis of one or two limited characteristics. Maybe it is skin color or sex, age, or a disability. When someone seems different, do you ever try to see how the two of you might be similar? Think about the many similarities between you and someone you regard as totally different because of skin color or national heritage. Both of you might be shy and anxious, fearful of speaking in public. Both of you might feel overwhelmed by all the demands you need to juggle. If the person attends your college, you've both chosen the same campus to pursue your education. You might have similar achievement standards, both hoping to make the Dean's List. You may share a keen interest in a certain sport or both be passionate about Ben and Jerry's ice cream. And so on. You probably have a lot more in common than you imagine.

Search for More Knowledge In many instances, the more you know about people who are different from you, the better you can interact with them. Learn more about the customs, values, interests, and historical background of such people. Take a course on cultures around the world, for example.

Treat People As Individuals In our culture, we want to be treated as individuals. We each want to be unique. You will get along much better with others who seem different if you keep in mind that they are individuals than if you think of them as members of a group. Talk with different others about their concerns, interests, worries, hopes, and daily lives. Avoid stereotypes.

Resolve Conflicts No matter how well-intentioned people are, conflicts with different others can arise. Learn more about ways to resolve conflicts. Too often we get into a mode of treating conflicts as win-lose situations: We want to win and want them to lose. It's best to look at conflict as a win-win situation and a chance for creative cooperation.

Learn with *InfoTrac College Edition*

InfoTrac College Edition

Look up these articles and search for more on topics that sparked your interest while reading this chapter.

Oprah Winfrey The courage to dream. Pearl Cleage, Oprah Winfrey. *Essence.* Dec. 1998. v29, i8, p81.

Effective Communication

Nonverbal Communication It's not what you say, it's how you say it. James P.T. Fatt. *Communication World.* June–July 1999. v16, i6, p37.

Being Assertive

Conflict Resolution/Negotiating

Relationships

Loneliness

Diversity

Prejudice Can't we all get along? Overcoming prejudice. Jan Farrington. *Current Health 2.* Jan. 1997. v23, i5, p6.

Is racism increasing in America? Dobie Holland. *Jet.* April 29, 1996. v89, i24, p4.

Stereotyping

Men's Issues

Summary Strategies for Mastering College

Master communication skills and build relationships.

1 Communicate Effectively

- Develop active-listening skills. Pay attention to the person who is talking. Paraphrase. Focus on the themes and patterns you hear. Give feedback.
- Avoid barriers to effective verbal communication, such as talking down to others and giving orders.
- Tune in to nonverbal communication.
- Resolve conflicts with others by being assertive and negotiating effectively.

2 Develop Good Relationships

- Keep in touch with your parents.
- If you have a partner or spouse, use good communication skills to have a positive relationship with him or her during your college years.
- If you have children, be an authoritative parent, communicate well, be a good time manager, and don't forget to reserve some time for yourself.
- If you have a roommate, cut off problems early, use good communication skills, be responsible, show respect, and be assertive.
- When dating, remember that dates can be potential friends as well as romantic partners. Show respect for your date. Avoid settings in which rape occurs most often. Monitor your sexual feelings and make good sexual decisions.
- If you're lonely, recognize it early on. Get involved in activities with others.
- If you can't shed your loneliness and make friends on your own, contact the counseling center at your college for help.

3 Appreciate Diversity

- Appreciate cultural and ethnic diversity.
- Recognize and reduce any prejudice and stereotyping you might engage in.
- If you're an international student, be patient, create or join a support system, make new friends, and share your culture to improve your adjustment to college.
- Appreciate diversity in gender. If you're a woman, examine your competencies and needs. Retain your strengths in building relationships and emotional skills. Improve your self-motivation. Don't put up with sexual harassment. If you're a man, retain your strengths related to self-motivation and achievement. Do a better job of understanding your emotions and self. Work on your relationship skills. If you're aggressive and hostile, tone down your anger.
- Appreciate diversity in sexual orientation. Homosexual and bisexual individuals can join campus organizations that have been created for them. Whether you are homosexual, bisexual, or heterosexual, be tolerant of the sexual orientation of others.
- To improve your relationships with diverse others, assess your attitudes, take the perspective of others, seek personal contact, and share information. Respect differences but don't overlook similarities. Seek more knowledge about people who differ from you. Treat people as individuals rather than stereotyping them. Resolve conflicts.

Review Questions

1. What are some basic strategies for improving communication skills?

_____

_____

_____

_____

_____

_____

2. If you get involved in a conflict, what might serve you best in resolving it?

_____

_____

_____

_____

_____

_____

_____

3. How can you get along better with the people you spend a lot of time with?

_____

_____

_____

_____

_____

_____

_____

4. What can you do if you get lonely?

_____

_____

_____

_____

_____

_____

5. What are some good strategies for improving relationships with diverse others?

_____

_____

_____

_____

_____

_____

Learning Portfolio

Reflect and Journal

1. Reflect on Conflict with Others

Think about the conflicts you've had with others that you do not feel good about. How could you have behaved more assertively to achieve a more satisfactory outcome?

_____
_____
_____
_____
_____
_____
_____
_____
_____
_____
_____
_____
_____

2. Your Own Experience with Discrimination and Prejudice

What life experiences have you had with discrimination and prejudice? The discrimination might have been directed at you, or perhaps you saw someone else experience it. What were the consequences? If the discrimination took place in school, did anyone do anything about it? The discrimination doesn't have to be about race or gender. You might have been discriminated against because of the part of the country you're from, the way you dress, the way you wear your hair. When you were discriminated against, how did you feel?

_____
_____
_____
_____
_____
_____
_____
_____
_____

Learn By Doing

1. Observe Interaction Styles

Identify someone who comes from a different cultural and ethnic background from yours. It might be a classmate, someone who lives in your neighborhood, or someone in an interest group you attend. Ask him or her to sit down and talk with you for 15 minutes. Tell them this involves a requirement for a college class you're taking. Your conversation objective: Establish how similar you are in as many ways as you can. Describe the identity of the person and discuss your similarities in your learning portfolio.

_____
_____
_____
_____
_____
_____
_____
_____

2. Seek Common Ground

Good observation is an important skill. In the next few days, observe the people you interact with—your roommate, partner, classmates, friends, teachers, and so on. How would you describe their interactional style: aggressive, passive, manipulative, or assertive? How do you think they would classify your interactional style?

_____
_____
_____
_____
_____
_____
_____
_____

Think Critically

1. What Does Touch Communicate?

Touch and posture can be important forms of communication. What are some different ways they can communicate information? How might the same touch or posture be interpreted differently depending on the identity of a person being touched—a friend, a romantic partner, a teacher, a person of a different age, or a stranger, for example?

_____

_____

_____

_____

_____

_____

_____

_____

_____

_____

_____

_____

_____

2. Evaluate Your Attitudes toward Diverse Others

No matter how well intentioned we are, life circumstances produce some negative attitudes toward others. Think about people from cultural and ethnic backgrounds different from yours, people of the other sex, and people with a sexual orientation different from yours.

- Do you have any negative attitudes toward these people?

_____

- Did the attitude come from a bad encounter with someone you decided was representative of the group?

_____

- Have you learned any prejudices by modeling the attitudes of others you admire?

_____

- What will it take for you to eliminate your negative attitudes toward this group or person?

_____

Think Creatively

1. Listen and Laugh

Gathering accurate information is important in the early part of creative thinking. The more good information you have, the better chance you have of devising a creative solution. When the creative challenge involves other people, the art of careful listening is even more important.

Other important ingredients of creativity are playfulness and humor. Although creativity takes hard work, the work goes more smoothly if you take it lightly. Having fun helps you to disarm the inner critic that all too quickly condemns your ideas as bizarre or off-base.

Get together with a group of students and brainstorm some creative way to resolve conflicts with a roommate, partner, friend, or family. In the group work, focus on becoming a better listener and on letting your playfulness emerge.

_____

_____

Work toward Goals

Review the results of the self-assessment you completed in this chapter. Also review the opening checklist. Based on your review, select a relatively short-term goal that you want to work on now.

1. What is that goal? (*Hint:* Is it challenging, reasonable, and specific?)

_____

_____

_____

_____

_____

2. What strategies will you use to achieve your goal? (*Hint:* Can you organize your strategy into a series of smaller goals?)

_____

_____

_____

_____

_____

3. What obstacles may be in your way as you attempt to make these positive changes?

_____

_____

_____

_____

_____

4. What additional resources might help you achieve your goal? (Use the CD-ROM that comes with this book for access to some useful leads.)

_____

_____

_____

_____

_____

5. By what date do you want to accomplish your goal?

_____

_____

_____

_____

6. How will you know you have succeeded?

_____

_____

_____

_____

_____

Be Physically and Mentally Healthy

Work Out and Stay Fit

No getting around it—college has many stressful moments. Cherish your physical and mental health. Motivating yourself to be physically and mentally healthy will help you stay on track as you pursue your academic goals.

To evaluate how you take care of your health, place a check mark next to only those items that apply to you.

_____ I live a healthy lifestyle.
_____ I exercise regularly.
_____ I get enough sleep.
_____ I eat right.
_____ I don't smoke.
_____ I don't take harmful drugs.
_____ I make good sexual decisions.
_____ I cope effectively with stress.
_____ I am not depressed.
_____ I know where to seek help for mental health problems.

As you read about Arnold Schwarzenegger on the next page, think about the importance he places on physical health in his life and how strongly he is motivated to exercise regularly.

IMAGES OF COLLEGE SUCCESS

Arnold Schwarzenegger

One of the world's most popular movie stars is the bodybuilder Arnold Schwarzenegger. After graduating from high school in Austria, Arnold joined the Austrian army. At age 20 he became the youngest man to win the Mr. Universe contest.

When he moved to the United States, Schwarzenegger founded a bricklaying business called Pumping Bricks. With money saved and borrowed, he also started a mail-order business in fitness books and videocassettes.

Arnold wanted to become better educated. At age 26, he attended college part-time. His regular study routine included time for working out and eating right. He stayed with his rigorous exercise program through periods of intense study. Arnold said that working out helped him to blow off steam and clear his mind; when he studied, he could concentrate better.

Arnold Schwarzenegger

Reuters/Corbis-Bettmann

Seven years later he earned his bachelor's degree in business and international economics from the University of Wisconsin at Superior. Along the way, Arnold took English lessons, developed a rehabilitation-through-weight-training program at California prisons, and was a national weight-training coach for the Special Olympics. He said that until you help someone like the people with disabilities who participate in the Special Olympics, you have no idea how good it can make you feel.

In addition to parlaying his bodybuilding prowess into movie stardom, Schwarzenegger has been the chairman of the President's Council on Physical Fitness and Sports. How does he keep in shape now that his bodybuilding contest days are over? He works out for an hour each day with weights and does a cardiovascular activity such as rowing, running, or hiking.

 Learn more about Arnold Schwarzenegger.

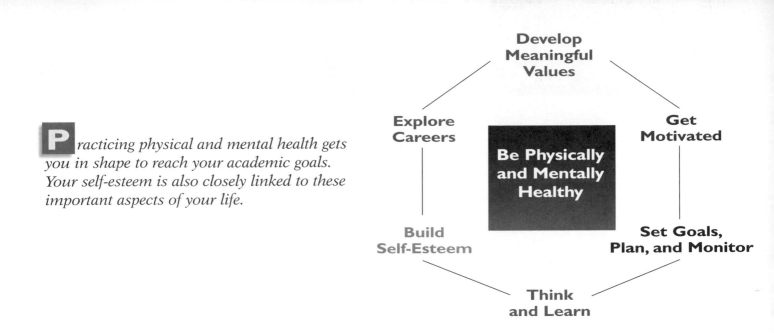

Practicing physical and mental health gets you in shape to reach your academic goals. Your self-esteem is also closely linked to these important aspects of your life.

Link Values, Motivation, Goals, and Self-Esteem

How much do you value your physical and mental health? Like other achievements, strong physical and mental health are supported by setting goals, planning how to achieve them, and monitoring progress. Like everything worthwhile, your vigor and health depend on your values and motivation. Self-esteem also follows from physical and mental health, and vice versa. If you have high self-esteem you're more likely to embark on a program of improvement than if you have low self-esteem. If you're fit, you'll tend to have high self-esteem.

Nothing can be changed until it is faced.

James Baldwin
20th-century American novelist

| Value Physical and Mental Health | ⟷ | Get Motivated to Practice Physical and Mental Health | ⟷ | Set Physical and Mental Health Goals, Plan, and Monitor Progress | ⟷ | Build Self-Esteem |

Consider having a healthy body weight. Individuals who place a high value on this are likely to be motivated to eat balanced, healthy meals. If they begin to become overweight, they are likely to set goals, plan, and monitor their progress toward the goal of returning to a healthy weight. Further, setting and reaching weight goals, getting motivated, and valuing a healthy weight tend to increase self-esteem. Conversely, high self-esteem increases the likelihood that people will actually put forth the effort to reach a more healthy level of weight.

Pursue and Maintain Physical Health

If you're like a lot of college students, you're not nearly as healthy as you could be. In a recent national survey of first-year college students, half said their health could be improved (Sax & others, 2000).

Good health requires good health habits. By making some lifestyle changes, you may be able to live a much longer, healthier, happier life. In fact, as many as seven of the ten leading causes of death (such as heart disease, stroke, and cancer) can be reduced by lifestyle changes, yet most of us tend to deny that the changes we think *other* people need to make also apply to us. Consider that in one study most college students said that they never would have a heart attack or a drinking problem but that other college students would (Weinstein, 1984).

Young adults have some hidden health risks. Ironically, one risk stems from the fact that they often bounce back quickly from physical stress and abuse. This can lead them to push their bodies too far and neglect their health. The negative effects of abusing one's body do not always show up immediately. However, at some point later one may pay a stiff price.

The following lifestyle patterns have been linked with poor health in college students: Skipping breakfast or regular meals, relying on snacks as a main food source, overeating, smoking, abusing alcohol and drugs, avoiding exercise, and not getting enough sleep. Do you have any of these habits?

Know Your Health Style and Your Body

To evaluate your health style, complete Self-Assessment 11-1.

How did you fare on the health style test? Are you putting your health knowledge to work by developing good health habits? If you had low scores on the test, ask yourself some frank questions. You're probably not doing all you can to be healthy.

However well or poorly you scored, be sure to seek medical help promptly when you have a detectable problem. For example, seek medical attention without delay if you do any of the following (Vickery & Fries, 2000):

- Develop a lump in your breast
- Have unexplained weight loss
- Experience a fever for more than a week
- Cough up blood
- Encounter persistent or severe headaches
- Have fainting spells
- Develop unexplained shortness of breath

In some circumstances, these symptoms can signal a cancer or other problems. In many cases, though, a thorough medical exam will confirm that nothing serious is wrong.

Bette Reflects

After 30, a body has a mind of its own.
Bette Midler
Contemporary American actor

Exercise Regularly

In a national survey of first-year college students, regular exercise was linked with good health, and heavy TV viewing was related to poor health (Astin,

What Is My Health Style?

The following brief test was developed by the Public Health Service. Its purpose is to help you gauge how well you're doing in your effort to stay healthy. The behaviors covered in the test are recommended for most people, although some of them may not apply to people with chronic diseases or disabilities or to pregnant women.

Instructions: For each item, check one box:

A = Almost always
S = Sometimes
N = Almost never

Exercise/Fitness

	A	S	N
1. I maintain a desired weight, avoiding overweight and underweight.	3 ☐	1 ☐	0 ☐
2. I do vigorous exercises for 15 to 30 minutes at least three times a week (examples include running, swimming, brisk walking).	3 ☐	1 ☐	0 ☐
3. I do exercises that enhance my muscle tone for 15 to 30 minutes at least three times a week (examples include yoga and calisthenics).	2 ☐	1 ☐	0 ☐
4. I use part of my leisure time participating in individual, family, or team activities that increase my level of fitness (such as gardening, bowling, golf, and baseball).	2 ☐	1 ☐	0 ☐

■ Exercise/fitness score: _____

Eating Habits

	A	S	N
1. I eat a variety of foods each day, such as fruits and vegetables, whole-grain breads and cereals, lean meats, dairy products, dry peas and beans, and nuts and seeds.	4 ☐	1 ☐	0 ☐
2. I limit the amount of fat, saturated fat, and cholesterol I eat (including fat in meats, eggs, butter, cream, shortenings, and organ meats such as liver).	2 ☐	1 ☐	0 ☐
3. I limit the amount of salt I eat by cooking with only small amounts, not adding salt at the table, and avoiding salty snacks.	2 ☐	1 ☐	0 ☐
4. I avoid eating too much sugar (especially frequent snacks of candy or soft drinks).	2 ☐	1 ☐	0 ☐

■ Eating habits score: _____

Alcohol and Drugs

	A	S	N
1. I avoid drinking alcoholic beverages or I drink no more than one or two drinks a day.	4 ☐	1 ☐	0 ☐
2. I avoid using alcohol or other drugs (especially illegal drugs) as a way of handling stressful situations or the problems in my life.	2 ☐	1 ☐	0 ☐
3. I am careful not to drink alcohol when taking certain medicines (for example, medicine for sleeping, pain, colds, and allergies), or when pregnant.	2 ☐	1 ☐	0 ☐
4. I read and follow the label directions when using prescribed and over-the-counter drugs.	2 ☐	1 ☐	0 ☐

■ Alcohol and drugs score: _____

(continued)

What Is My Health Style?

(continued)

Cigarette Smoking	A	S	N
If you never smoke, enter a score of 10 for this section and go the next section on stress control.			
1. I smoke only low-tar and low-nicotine cigarettes *or* I smoke a pipe or cigars.	2 ☐	1 ☐	0 ☐

■ Smoking score: _____

Stress Control	A	S	N
1. I have a job or do other work that I enjoy.	2 ☐	1 ☐	0 ☐
2. I find it easy to relax and express my feelings freely.	2 ☐	1 ☐	0 ☐
3. I recognize early and prepare for events or situations likely to be stressful for me.	2 ☐	1 ☐	0 ☐
4. I have close friends, relatives, or others whom I can talk to about personal matters and call on for help when needed.	2 ☐	1 ☐	0 ☐
5. I participate in group activities (such as church and community organizations) or hobbies that I enjoy.	2 ☐	1 ☐	0 ☐

■ Stress control score: _____

Safety	A	S	N
1. I wear a seat belt while riding in a car.	2 ☐	1 ☐	0 ☐
2. I avoid driving while under the influence of alcohol and other drugs.	2 ☐	1 ☐	0 ☐
3. I obey traffic rules and the speed limit when driving.	2 ☐	1 ☐	0 ☐
4. I am careful when using potentially harmful products or substances (such as household cleaners, poisons, and electrical devices).	2 ☐	1 ☐	0 ☐
5. I avoid smoking in bed	2 ☐	1 ☐	0 ☐

■ Safety score: _____

Total your score separately for each of the six health styles and then evaluate your scores as follows:

9–10   Your health style in this area is excellent. You not only are aware of the importance of this area to your health but also are practicing good health habits in this area.

6–8   Your style in this area is good but you have room for improvement. Look at the items you answered with "Sometimes" or Almost Never." What changes can you make in this area to improve your health style?

3–5   Your health is at risk in this area. Seek help for your health problems in this area.

0–2   Your health is at serious risk in this area. You need to change your health-compromising behaviors. Go to your health or counseling center for help.

1993). In recent research, exercise has been shown to actually generate new brain cells (van Praag, Kempermann, & Gage, 1999).

Exercise ← → **Generate New Brain Cells** ← → **Boost Thinking Power** ← → **Reach Academic Goals**

Clearly, exercise alone is not going to make you reach your academic goals. But it can help you generate new brain cells, which are linked with thinking and learning.

Exercise can certainly do you good. It can be aerobic or anaerobic. *Aerobic exercise* is moderately intense, sustained exercise that stimulates your heart and lungs. Jogging, cycling, and swimming are aerobic. Many health experts recommend that you raise your heart rate to 60 percent of its maximum. Your maximum heart rate is calculated as 220 minus your age, times .6. Thus, if you're 20, aim for an exercise heart rate of 200 times .6, which is 120. If you're 45, strive for an exercise heart rate of 175 times .6, or 105. What exercise heart rate should you aim for?

$$(220 - \text{your age}) \times .6 = \underline{\hspace{3cm}}$$

Anaerobic exercise involves quick or intense movement such as doing push-ups or running a 100-yard dash. In contrast, running a long distance is mainly aerobic. Aerobic exercise has significant cardiovascular benefits and burns fat (what you want for weight loss) (King, 2000). Anaerobic exercise builds muscle tissue but does not help you lose weight as much. Many exercise activities are both aerobic and anaerobic, such as tennis, basketball, and circuit training (circulating among different exercise machines and stations).

Here are some common aerobic and anaerobic exercises:

Aerobic	**Anaerobic**
Walking, Jogging, Biking, Swimming, Rowing, Aerobics, Cross-Country Skiing	Weight Lifting, Sprinting (Running or Swimming) Calisthenics (Push-ups, Sit-ups, Pull-ups)

If you don't exercise, how can you motivate yourself to get going? "Motivate Yourself to Exercise" gives some tips.

Get Enough Sleep

Most of us have occasional sleepless nights. Maybe we feel a lot of stress and can't sleep soundly. In this case, we don't deliberately lose sleep. However, many college students deliberately choose a sleepless night now and then when they pull an all-nighter to cram for a test. In a national survey, more than 80 percent of first-year college students said they stayed up all night at least once during the year (Sax & others, 1995).

ON-TARGET TIPS

Motivate Yourself to Exercise

- **Make exercise a high priority in your life.** Give exercise a regular place in your schedule. Don't let unimportant things interfere with your exercise routine. Don't make excuses.
- **Chart your progress.** Record each of your exercise sessions in a systematic way. Use a notebook or a calendar, for example. This practice can help you to maintain the momentum you need to work out regularly.
- **Make time for exercise.** It's easy to sabotage your own commitment to exercise with excuses. If your excuse is, "I don't have time," find it. Ask yourself, "Am I too busy to take care of my health? What do I lose if I lose my health?"
- **Learn more about exercise.** The more you know about exercise, the more you're likely to continue it. Examine the resources on the Web site for this book to read more about exercise.

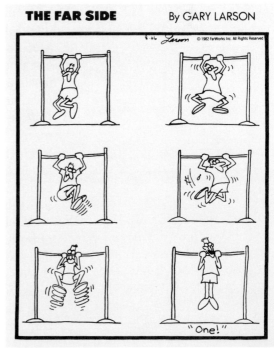

THE FAR SIDE By GARY LARSON

"One!"

© 1982 FarWorks, Inc.

How to Sleep Better

- **Get into a regular daily routine.** This lets you go to sleep and wake up at approximately the same time each day.
- **Do something relaxing before you go to bed.** Maybe listen to some soft music.
- **Avoid discussing stressful problems before you go to bed.** This includes money or dating problems.
- **Make sure your sleeping area is good for sleeping.** It should have minimum light, minimum sound, and a comfortable temperature.
- **Engage in regular exercise.** However, don't exercise just before going to bed, because exercise increases your energy and alertness.
- **Manage your time effectively.** You can get 7–8 hours of sleep every night.
- **Manage your stress.** Learn how to relax and cope with stress effectively.
- **Contact your college health center.** If the above strategies don't work, get some help from health professionals.

How Much Sleep Do You Need? The amount of sleep needed varies from person to person. Most students need at least eight hours of sleep to function competently the next day (Dement & Vaughn, 2000; Maas, 1998).

Why Might You Be Having Sleep Problems? As many as one in five students have *insomnia*, a sleep disorder that involves an inability to sleep. Alcohol, nicotine, and caffeine can interfere with your sleep. For example, drinking before you go to sleep keeps you from getting a full night of restful sleep, because it dehydrates you. Stress also can cause sleep problems. For more on good sleep, see "How to Sleep Better."

Eat Right

One of the best sources of nutritional advice *Dietary Guidelines for Americans*, issued by the U.S. Department of Health and Human Services. These guidelines are revised every five years. The most recent ones support these six principles:

1. ***Eat a variety of foods.*** Use the four basic food groups to evaluate your diet:

   - The milk group (cheese, yogurt, milk)
   - The fruit and vegetable group
   - The grain group (cereals, bread, noodles)
   - The meat group (poultry, fish, red meat, and nuts)

   Healthy adults need to eat at least three servings of vegetables, two of fruit, and six of grain products every day. Megadose supplements of vitamins are no substitute for a healthful diet, and they can be harmful. Avoid them.

2. ***Maintain a healthy weight.*** Some college students are overweight, others underweight. Preoccupation with dieting can lead to dangerous loss/gain cycles that are hard on your body. Strive to maintain a reasonable, manageable weight.

3. ***Follow a diet low in fat, saturated fat, and cholesterol.*** Unfortunately, many of the best-tasting foods are the worst for you. Fat is big in fried foods (fried chicken, doughnuts), rich foods (ice cream, pastries), greasy foods (spare ribs, bacon), and many spreads (butter, mayonnaise). In contrast, yogurt is low in saturated fat. Cholesterol, a key contributor to heart disease, is found only in animal products.

   The fitness expert Covert Bailey (1991) says that if you throw a pound of butter in a swimming pool, it will float just like a cork. The fat in your body will float in the same way, so the fatter you are, the more you'll float. Bailey says that he once had a friend who floated so well he could read a book while coasting along on top of the water in a swimming pool.

   If you have more than 25 percent body fat, you'll float easily. At 13 percent or lower, you'll sink quickly. Healthy body fat percentages vary for women and men. The highest healthy body fat content is 22 percent for women, 15 percent for men. Unfortunately, the average woman has 32 percent body fat, the average man 23 percent.

4. ***Substitute plenty of vegetables, fruits, and grain products for unhealthful foods.*** Replace fatty foods with more healthful sources of starch and fiber. This involves eating grain products, legumes (dried beans, peas), fruits, and vegetables not cooked in fat.

5. ***Use sugar only in moderation.*** In addition to table sugar, other common sugar products include brown sugar, syrups, honey, jams, jellies, ice cream, cookies, cakes, and most other desserts. If you eat dessert, try eating fresh fruit instead of foods with sugar added. Replace soft drinks with water.

6. ***Use sodium in moderation.*** Some people are sensitive to sodium and are at risk for hypertension (persistent high blood pressure). To reduce the sodium in your diet, eat less salt. Flavor your food with lemon, spices, herbs, or pepper.

Dieting and the "Freshman 15"

The "freshman 15" refers to the approximately 15 pounds that many first-year students gain. The weight often shows up in the hips, thighs, and midsection. Why do first-year students gain this weight? During high school many students' eating habits are monitored by their parents, so they eat more balanced meals. Once in college, students select their own diets, which often consist of chips, chips, and more chips, fast food, ice cream, late-night pizza, and beer. Once the extra 15 pounds arrive, what do first-year students do? They diet.

Dieting is a way of life for many college students. Do diets work? Some work in the short run. Over the long haul, most fail (Brownell, 2000).

Does exercise lead to weight loss? Yes! Exercise burns up calories as you do it and raises your metabolic rate (the rate at which your body burns its fuel) for several hours after the workout.

What are some bad dieting strategies? Crash dieting and skipping meals keep you from getting adequate nutrients. Don't jump on every dieting fad that comes along. Poor diets can harm your kidneys and other internal organs. See the resources on this book's Web site for more about healthful dieting.

*E*at, drink, and be merry, for tomorrow ye shall diet.
Lewis Henry
20th-century American writer

Anorexia Nervosa and Bulimia

Nineteen-year-old Andrea gradually eliminated foods from her diet to the point at which she lived on jello and yogurt. She spent hours observing her body. She wrapped her hands around her waist to see whether it was getting any thinner. She fantasized about becoming a fashion model. Even when her weight dropped to 80 pounds, Andrea still felt fat. She continued to lose weight and was hospitalized for *anorexia nervosa*, an eating disorder that involves the relentless pursuit of thinness through starvation. Anorexia nervosa can eventually lead to death.

Most anorexics are white female adolescents or young adults from well-educated middle- and upper-income families. They have a distorted body image, perceiving themselves as overweight even when they become skeletal. Numerous causes of anorexia nervosa have been proposed (Mussell & Mitchell, 1998). One is the current fashion image of thinness, reflecting in the saying, "You can't be too rich or too thin." Many anorexics grow up in families with high demands for academic achievement. Unable to meet these high expectations and control their grades, they turn to something they can control: their weight.

Bulimia is a disorder that involves binging and purging. Bulimics go on an eating binge then purge by vomiting or using a laxative. Sometimes the binges alternate with fasting. However, they can also alternate with normal eating. Anorexics can control their eating; bulimics cannot. Bulimia can produce gastric and chemical imbalances in the body, as well as long-term dental damage. Depression is common in bulimics. If you have anorexic or bulimic characteristics, go to your college health center for help.

Don't Smoke

Some stark figures reveal why smoking is called suicide in slow motion:

- Smoking accounts for more than one-fifth of all deaths in the United States.
- It causes 32 percent of coronary heart disease cases in the United States.
- It causes 30 percent of all cancer deaths in the United States.
- It causes 82 percent of all lung cancer deaths in the United States.
- Passive smoke causes as many as 8,000 lung cancer deaths a year in the United States.

More than fifty million people in the United States smoke cigarettes. Through most of the 1990s, cigarette smoking in first-year college students increased. However, by the year 1999, this trend had started to reverse. For example, in 1998, 15.8 percent of first-year students said they smoke frequently, but in 1999 this figure had dropped to 14.2 percent (Sax & others, 1999).

Most smokers want to quit. Can they? Unfortunately, the survey just mentioned offers some more bad news. About half of the smokers had seriously tried to quit smoking but had lost the battle. The immediate addictive, pleasurable effects of smoking are extremely difficult to overcome. There was some good news, though. About half of people in the United States who ever smoked have quit.

If you're a smoker, how can you quit? Many different strategies have been tried to help people quit smoking. They include drug treatments, hypnosis, and behavior modification (Pomerleau, 2000). Drug treatments include *nicotine gum*, a prescription drug that smokers chew when they get the urge. Another drug treatment is the *nicotine patch*, a nonprescription adhesive pad that delivers nicotine through the skin. The dosage is gradually reduced over 8–12 weeks. Some smokers, usually light smokers, can quit cold turkey. The resources on the Web site for this book include good information about ways to quit smoking.

Avoid Drugs

We are a drug-using society. Hardly a day goes by when most of us do not take a drug, although we don't always call it that. For example, many cola beverages contain the drug caffeine.

Why Do People Take Drugs? People are attracted to drugs because they help them adapt to or escape from an ever-changing, stressful environment. Smoking, drinking, and taking drugs can reduce tension and frustration, relieve boredom and fatigue, and help us to ignore the world's harsh realities. Drugs can give us brief tranquility, joy, relaxation, kaleidoscopic perceptions,

The real reason dinosaurs became extinct

and surges of exhilaration. They sometimes have practical uses; for example, amphetamines can keep you awake all night to study for an exam. We also take drugs for social reasons. We hope they will make us feel more at ease and happier at parties, on dates, and in other anxious social contexts.

However, the use of drugs for personal pleasure and temporary adaptation can be dangerous. The use can lead to drug dependence, personal distress, and in some cases fatal diseases. What initially was intended for pleasure and adaptation can turn into pain and maladaptation. For example, on a short-term basis, a few drinks help some people to relax and forget about their problems. However, drinking can become an addition that destroys relationships, careers, minds, and bodies. Ruptured lives and families, permanent liver damage, and depression are common outcomes of alcoholism.

The Increase of Drug Use in College Students
Many college students take drugs (including alcohol) more than they did in high school (Johnston, O'Malley, & Bachman, 1996). Among the reasons for the increased use of drugs among first-year college students are

- Greater freedom from parental supervision
- High levels of stress and anxiety associated with academic and financial concerns
- Peer use of drugs for recreational purposes

Alcohol
Alcohol abuse is a special concern. Alcohol is the most widely used drug in our society. More than 13 million people in the United States call themselves alcoholics. Alcoholism is the third leading killer in the United States. Each year about 25,000 people are killed, and 1.5 million injured, by drunk drivers. More than 60 percent of homicides involve the use of alcohol by either the offender or the victim. About two-thirds of aggressive sexual acts toward women involve the use of alcohol by the offender.

Almost half of U.S. college students say they drink heavily (Johnston, O'Malley, & Bachman, 1996; Wechsler & others, 1994). The drinking takes its toll on them. In a recent national survey of drinking patterns on 140 campuses (Wechsler & others, 2000), almost half of the binge drinkers reported problems that included missed classes, injuries, troubles with police, and unprotected sex (see also Figure 11-1). Binge-drinking college students were eleven times more likely to fall behind in school, ten times more likely to drive after drinking, and twice as likely to have unprotected sex than were college students who did not binge drink. Self-Assessment 11-2 can help you judge whether you are a substance abuser.

If you have a substance abuse problem, what can you do about it?

- **Admit that you have a problem.** This is tough. Many students who have a substance abuse problem won't admit it. Admitting that you have a problem is the first major step in helping yourself.
- **Listen to what others are saying to you.** Chances are that your roommate, a friend, or someone you've dated has told you that you have a substance abuse problem. You probably denied it. They are trying to help you. Listen to them.

Alcohol is a good preservative for everything but brains.

Mary Poole
20th-century American writer

STAYING OUT OF THE PITS

"Let's Get Wasted"

Art tells his friend, "It's been a bummer of a week. I blew two tests. I'm depressed. Let's get wasted." And they do. They drink a fifth of gin and pass out. Sound common? Sound harmless?

It's common. It often is not harmless. When students get wasted, they can get arrested and go to jail, have car wrecks, accidentally set dorm rooms on fire, flunk out of school, damage property, and make bad sexual decisions.

Avoid being friends with someone who likes to get wasted. Stay away from parties where getting wasted is the main objective. If you get tempted, keep in mind all of the things that can go wrong when you lose control and consciousness. Also, keep thinking about how you'll feel the next day.

Do I Abuse Drugs?

Check Yes or No.

	Yes	No
I have gotten into financial problems because of using drugs.	_____	_____
Using alcohol or other drugs has made my college life unhappy at times.	_____	_____
Drinking alcohol or taking other drugs has been a factor in my losing a job.	_____	_____
Drinking alcohol or taking other drugs has interfered with my preparation for exams.	_____	_____
Drinking alcohol or taking drugs is jeopardizing my academic performance.	_____	_____
My ambition is not as strong since I started drinking a lot or taking drugs.	_____	_____
Drinking or taking other drugs has caused me to have difficulty sleeping.	_____	_____
I have felt remorse after drinking or using other drugs.	_____	_____
I crave a drink or other drugs at a definite time of the day.	_____	_____
I want a drink or another drug the next morning.	_____	_____
I have had a complete or partial loss of memory as a result of drinking or using other drugs.	_____	_____
Drinking or using other drugs is affecting my reputation.	_____	_____
I have been in a hospital or institution because of drinking or taking other drugs.	_____	_____

College students who responded Yes to these items from the *Rutgers Collegiate Abuse Screening Test* were more likely to be substance abusers than those who answer No. If you responded Yes even to just one of the thirteen items on this drug-abuse screening test, you're probably a substance abuser. If you responded Yes to any items, go to your college health or counseling center for help with your problem.

FIGURE 11-1
The Hazardous Consequences of Binge Drinking in College

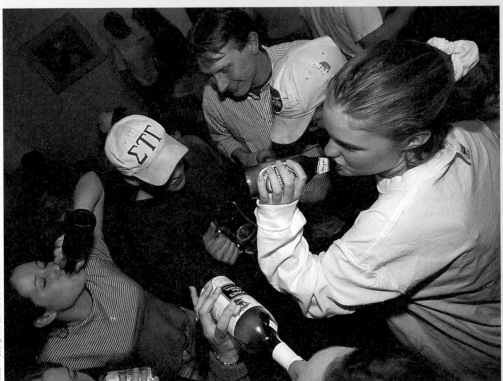

Paula A. Scully/The Gamma Liaison Network

The Troubles Frequent Binge Drinkers Create for...

Themselves[1] (% of those surveyed who admitted having had the problem)		and Others[2] (% of those surveyed who had been affected)	
Missed a class	61	Had study or sleep interrupted	68
Forgot where they were or what they did	54	Had to care for drunken student	54
Engaged in unplanned sex	41	Were insulted or humiliated	34
Got hurt	23	Experienced unwanted sexual advances	26
Had unprotected sex	22	Had serious argument	20
Damaged property	22	Had property damaged	15
Got into trouble with campus or local police	11	Were pushed or assaulted	13
Had five or more alcohol-related problems in school year	47	Had at least one of above problems	87

[1]Frequent binge drinkers were defined as those who had had at least four or five drinks at one time on at least three occasions in the previous two weeks.
[2]These figures are from colleges where at least 50% of students are binge drinkers.

■ **Seek help for your problem.** There are lots of resources for students who have a substance abuse problem. These include Alcoholics Anonymous, Cocaine Anonymous (CA), Al-Anon, and Rational Recovery Systems. Most towns have one or more of these organizations, which are confidential and are led by people who have successfully combated their substance abuse problem (Bennett & Miller, 1998). They can help you a great deal. Also, the health center at your college can provide help.

■ **Use the resources on this book's Web site.** Examine the resources for reducing drug use. They include phone numbers, information about organizations that can help you overcome your problem, and links to other relevant Web sites.

Make the Right Sexual Decisions

Making the right sexual decisions never has been more important than today. AIDS, other sexually transmitted diseases, and unwanted pregnancy pose life-altering challenges (Crooks & Bauer, 1999).

Avoid Sexually Transmitted Diseases *Sexually transmitted diseases (STDs)* are diseases contracted primarily through sex. This includes intercourse as well as oral-genital and anal-genital sex. STDs affect about one of every six adults.

With certain STDs you may be showing no immediate symptoms and yet still pass the disease on to someone else who will suffer. Here are some symptoms for which you should certainly see a doctor or visit a clinic as soon as you can.

Men:
■ Foul-smelling, cloudy discharge from the penis
■ Burning sensation while urinating
■ Painless sore on the penis
■ Painful red bumps in the genital region, usually on the penis, turning into tiny blisters containing clear fluid
■ Warts in the genital area, either pink/red and soft or hard and yellow/gray

Women:
■ Yellow-green discharge from the vagina
■ Painless sore on the inner vaginal wall or cervix
■ Burning sensation during urination
■ Painful red bumps on the labia, turning into tiny blisters containing clear fluid
■ Warts in the genital area, either pink/red and soft or hard and yellow/gray

No single STD has had a greater impact on sexual behavior or created more fear in the last decade than HIV-AIDS. Experts say that AIDS can be transmitted only by sexual contact, sharing hypodermic needles, blood transfusion, or other direct contact of cuts or mucous membranes with blood or sexual fluids (Kelly, 2000).

It's not who you are but what you do that puts you at risk for getting AIDS. *Anyone* who is sexually active or uses intravenous drugs is at risk. No one is immune.

Protect against Unwanted Pregnancy Most college students want to control whether and when they have children. That means either abstaining from sex or using effective contraception. Students who feel guilty and have negative attitudes about sexuality are less likely to use

If you have sex, be proactive rather than reactive. Use effective contraception and protect yourself against STDs. Promiscuity greatly increases your chances of contracting AIDS and other STDs. Think before you act. Too often enchanted evenings are followed by disenchanted mornings.

Bachmann/PhotoEdit

contraception than are students who have positive attitudes about sexuality. Following are the main contraceptive choices:

- **Abstinence.** This is the only strategy that is 100 percent effective in preventing unwanted pregnancy.
- **Oral contraceptives.** Advantages of birth control pills are a high rate of effectiveness and low interference with sexual activity. However, the pill can have adverse side effects for some women, such as blood clots, nausea, and moodiness.
- **Condoms.** A main advantage is protection against STDs. A small proportion of condoms break. Improve protection by using a spermicide with condoms.
- **Diaphragm.** This consists of a latex dome on a flexible spring rim that is inserted into the vagina with contraceptive cream or jelly. The diaphragm must be fitted by a skilled medical practitioner. The diaphragm has few negative side effects and a high effectiveness rate when used properly. A cervical cap is like a miniature diaphragm that fits over the cervix.
- **Spermicides.** These include foam, suppositories, creams, and jellies that contain a chemical that kills sperm. Advantages include a lack of serious side effects. Disadvantages include potential irritation of genital tissues and interruption of sexual activity. Most experts on sexuality say not to rely on spermicide alone for contraception.
- **IUD.** The intrauterine device (IUD) is a small, plastic device that is inserted into the vagina. The IUD's advantages include uninterrupted sexual activity and simplicity of use. Possible disadvantages include pelvic inflammation and pregnancy complications.
- **Norplant.** Norplant consists of six thin capsules filled with a synthetic hormone that are implanted under the skin of a woman's upper arm. In 1991 it became the first new contraceptive system approved in the United States in thirty years. The implanted capsules gradually release the hormone into the bloodstream over a five-year period to prevent conception. Working like a mini birth control pill, Norplant provides highly effective contraception. Its negative effects include potential bleeding and hormone-related side effects.
- **Depo-Provera.** Depo-Provera is an injectable contraceptive that lasts three months. Users have to get a shot every 12 weeks. Depo-Provera is a very effective contraceptive method but can cause menstrual irregularities.
- **Tubal ligation.** This is the most common sterilization procedure done for women. It involves severing or tying the fallopian tubes.
- **Vasectomy.** This is a male sterilization procedure that involves cutting the sperm-carrying ducts.

Figure 11-2 summarizes the effectiveness of these contraceptive methods and lists some other, ineffective choices. As it indicates, using no contraceptive method, trying to withdraw the penis just before ejaculation, and periodic abstinence are not wise strategies. If you're sexually active, compare the

FIGURE 11-2
Effectiveness of Contraceptive Methods

The following are birth control methods and their failure rates in one year of average use.

Method	Unintended-pregnancy rate*
No Method (Chance)	85.0
Spermicides	30.0
Withdrawal	24.0
Periodic Abstinence	19.0
Cervical Cap	18.0
Diaphragm	18.0
Condom	16.0
Pill	6.0
IUD	4.0
Tubal Ligation	0.5
Depo-Provera	0.4
Vasectomy	0.2
Norplant	0.05

*Figures are based on women of reproductive age, 15 to 44. Rates vary with age. Failure rates with perfect use are lower, but people rarely use methods perfectly.

various contraceptive methods and choose the method that is the safest and most effective for you.

What can you do to reduce the likelihood of contracting an STD? First, recognize that the only completely effective strategy is abstinence. But if you do choose to have sex, here are some ways to reduce your chances of being infected (Crooks & Bauer, 1999):

1. **Assess your and your partner's risk status.** If you've had previous sexual activity with others, you may have contracted an STD without knowing it. Have you been tested for STDs in general? Remember that many STDs don't produce detectable symptoms. If you care enough to be sexually intimate with a new partner, you should be willing to be open with him or her about your own physical sexual health.

   Spend time getting to know a prospective sexual partner before you have sex with him or her. Ideally, this time frame is at least 2–3 months. Use this time to convey your STD status and inquire about your partner's. Keep in mind that many people are not honest about their sexual history.

2. **Obtain prior medical examinations.** Many experts on sexuality now recommend that couples who want to begin a sexual relationship abstain from sexual activity until both undergo medical and laboratory testing to rule out the presence of STDs. If cost is an issue, contact your campus health service or a public health clinic in your area.

3. **Use condoms.** When correctly used, condoms help to prevent the transmission of many STDs. Condoms are most effective in preventing chlamydia, gonorrhea, syphilis, and AIDS. They are less effective against the spread of genital herpes and genital warts. Recommendations for the effective use of condoms include the following: Put on a condom before any genital contact has occurred; make sure the condom is adequately lubricated; don't blow up the condom or fill it with water to test it for leaks (this stretching weakens the latex); don't unroll the condom first like a sock and then put it on but instead unroll it directly onto the erect penis; twist the end of the condom as it is rolled onto the penis to leave space at the tip; if the condom breaks, immediately replace it; never reuse a condom.

4. **Avoid having sex with multiple partners.** One of the strongest predictors of getting AIDS, chlamydia, genital herpes, and other STDs is having sex with multiple partners.

Be Mentally Healthy

As we said at the beginning of the chapter, an important factor in being mentally healthy is having high self-esteem. This section describes several strategies for improving mental health, all of which are linked with building self-esteem.

Cope with Stress

According to the American Academy of Family Physicians, two-thirds of all medical office visits are for stress-related symptoms. Stress also is a major contributor to heart disease, accidental injuries, and suicide.

What are the most common stressors for college students? In one study (Murphy, 1996), the academic circumstances creating the most stress for students were tests and finals, grades and competition, professors and class environment, too many demands, papers and essay exams, career and future success, and studying.

In this same study, the personal circumstances that created the most stress for students were intimate relationships, finances, parental conflicts and expectations, and roommate conflicts. In another study, the first year was by far the most stressful year of college for students (Sher, Wood, & Gotham, 1996).

Coping with stress is essential to making your life more productive and enjoyable. Coping means managing difficult circumstances, solving personal problems, and reducing stress and conflict. Not everyone responds the same way to stress; some of us have better strategies than others. The good news is that if you don't currently cope with stress effectively you can learn to do so (DeLongis & Newth, 1998). Before we talk about the positive ways to cope with stress, let's look at some typically unsuccessful ways of dealing with a stressful problem:

"I think we can rule out stress."

- Repress it so you won't have to think about it.
- Take it out on other people when you feel angry or depressed.
- Keep your feelings to yourself.
- Tell yourself the problem will go away.
- Refuse to believe what is happening.
- Try to reduce tension by drinking and eating more.

Fortunately, there are successful coping strategies as well.

See Stress As a Challenge Rather Than a Threat

Consider how first-year students view stress differently. Antonio sees an upcoming test as stressful; Anna sees it as a challenge. Greta views a D on a paper as a disaster; Dion views the same grade as a challenge to improve his writing. To some extent, stress depends on how we interpret events.

To cope successfully, it helps a lot to (1) see the circumstances as a challenge to overcome rather than an overwhelming, threatening stress and (2) have good coping resources such as friends, family, a mentor, and the counseling center at your college (Lazarus, 1993, 1998).

Develop an Optimistic Outlook and Think Positively
How important is it to be optimistic? In one study, college students were initially identified as optimists or pessimists (Peterson & Stunkard, 1986). Then their health was monitored over the next year. The pessimists had twice as many infections and doctors' visits as the optimists did.

How can you develop a more optimistic outlook? One way is to use positive thinking to challenge self-defeating

© 1995, Ziggy and Friends, Inc./Dist. by Universal Press Syndicate

thoughts (Seligman, 1991). This strategy helps you avoid ruminating and wallowing in self-pity when bad things happen. Another good strategy is to dispute your negative thoughts (Ellis, 1996). Pessimists tend to use absolute, all-encompassing terms to describe their defeats. They often use words like *never* and *always*. If this sounds like you, talk back to these negative thoughts in a self-confident, positive way that will get rid of self-blame and negative feelings.

Thinking positively helps to put you in a good mood and improves your self-esteem. It also gives you the sense that you're controlling your environment rather than letting it control you. Thinking positively improves your ability to learn. A negative outlook increases your chances of getting angry, feeling guilty, and magnifying your mistakes.

Talk positively to yourself. It can help you reach your full potential. Monitor your self-talk, because unchallenged negative thinking has a way of becoming a self-fulfilling prophecy. That is, if you tell yourself you can't do something well, you won't. How can you monitor your self-talk? At random times during the day, ask yourself, "What am I saying to myself right now?" Potentially stressful moments are excellent times to examine your self-talk. You also can ask friends to give you feedback on your negative or positive attitudes.

Seek Emotional Support

In stressful times, family members, friends, classmates, and co-workers can help by reassuring you that you're a valuable person who is loved. Knowing that others care about you can give you the confidence to tackle stressful circumstances.

Consider Juan, who was laid off from three jobs in three years. By all accounts he should be depressed. Yet he says he is a happy person. When asked his secret in the face of adversity and stress, Juan says it stems from the support of a wonderful family and great friends.

Recognize the potential support in your own life. Learn how to draw on these resources in times of stress. Sometimes you can improve your ability to cope by joining community groups, interest groups, or informal social groups that meet regularly (Taylor, 1999).

Relax

We usually think of relaxation as unwinding in front of the TV, taking a quiet walk in the evening, and so forth. These activities can be relaxing. However, a different form of relaxation can also help college students cope with anxiety and stress. It's called *deep relaxation*.

Try the following to attain a deeply relaxed state (M. Davis, Eshelman, & McKay, 1995):

The time to relax is when you don't have any.

Sydney J. Harris
20th-century American newspaper writer

1. In a quiet place, either lie down on a couch or bed or sit in a comfortable chair with your head supported.
2. Get into a comfortable position and relax. Clench your right fist tighter and tighter for about five seconds. Now relax it. Feel the looseness in your right hand. Repeat the procedure with your left hand. Then do it with both hands. When you release the tension, let it go instantly. Allow your muscles to become limp.

3. Bend your elbows and tense your biceps as hard as you can. After a few seconds, relax and straighten out your arms. Go through the procedure again. Tighten your biceps as hard as you can for a few seconds and then relax them. As with your biceps, do each of the following procedures twice.

4. Turn your attention to your head. Wrinkle your forehead as tightly as you can, then relax it. Next, frown and notice the strain it produces. Close your eyes now. Squint them as hard as you can. Notice the tension. Now relax your eyes. Let them stay closed gently and comfortably. Now clench your jaw and bite hard. Notice the tension throughout your jaw. Relax your jaw.

5. Shrug your shoulders. Keep the tension as you hunch your head down between your shoulders. Then relax your shoulders.

6. Breathe in and fill your lungs completely. Hold your breath for a few seconds. Now exhale and let your chest become loose. Repeat this four or five times. Tighten your stomach for several seconds. Now relax it.

7. Tighten your buttocks and thighs. Flex your thighs by pressing your heels down as hard as you can. Relax and feel the difference. Next, curl your toes downward, making your calf muscles tight. Then relax. Now bend your toes toward your face, creating tension in your shins. Relax again. To avoid muscle cramping, don't overtighten your toes.

Some students have limited success when they first try deep relaxation. With practice, though, it usually works. Initially you may need 20–30 minutes to reach a deeply relaxed state, but eventually many students can become deeply relaxed in 2–3 minutes. The resources section on this book's Web site provides further information about deep relaxation. *Note:* If you have high blood pressure and are taking medication for it, do not do the deep relaxation exercise, because it could lower your blood pressure too far.

Get Rid of Depression

Depression is all too common among college students. In one study, depression was linked with poor academic performance (Haines, Norris, & Kashy, 1996). Consider Sally, who was depressed for several months. Nothing seemed to cheer her up. Sally's depression began when the person she planned to marry broke off their relationship. Her emotional state worsened until she didn't feel like getting out of bed most mornings. She started missing a lot of classes and got behind in all of them. One of her friends noticed how sad she was. She got Sally to go to the counseling center at her college.

Each of us feels blue or down in the dumps some of the time. These brief bouts of sad feelings or discontent with the way our life is going are normal. If sad feelings last for only a few hours, a few days, or a few weeks, you won't be classified as depressed. But if the sad feelings linger for a month or more, and you feel deeply unhappy and demoralized, you probably are in a depression. A person with depression often has the following symptoms:

Changes in sleep patterns

Changes in appetite

Decreased energy

Feelings of worthlessness

Difficulty concentrating

Feelings of guilt

It is hard to make people miserable when they feel worthy of themselves.
Abraham Lincoln
19th-century U.S. president

Depression is so widespread that it's called the "common cold" of mental disorders (Nolen-Hoeksema, 2001). More than 250,000 people in the United States are hospitalized every year for depression. Students, professors, and laborers get depressed. No one is immune to it, not even great writers such as Ann Sexton and Ernest Hemingway, or famous statesmen such as Abraham Lincoln and Winston Churchill.

A man's lifetime risk of having depression is 10 percent. A woman's lifetime risk is much greater—almost 25 percent. Many people with depression suffer unnecessarily, because depression can be treated effectively. To evaluate whether you may be depressed, complete Self-Assessment 11-3.

What to Do When Someone Is Thinking about Suicide

- **Stay calm.** In most cases, there is no rush. Sit and listen, *really* listen, to what the person is saying. Be understanding, and emotionally support the person's feelings.
- **Deal directly with the topic of suicide.** Most people have mixed feelings about death and are open to help. Don't be afraid to ask or talk directly about suicide.
- **Encourage problem solving and positive actions.** Remember that the person in the crisis is not thinking clearly. Encourage the person to refrain from making any serious, irreversible decisions while in the crisis. Talk about the alternatives that might create hope for the future.
- **Get help.** Although you want to help, don't take full responsibility by being the sole counselor. Seek out resources, such as your college counseling center, for help. Do this even if it means breaking confidence. Let the troubled person know that you're so concerned that you're willing to get help beyond what you can offer.
- **Emphasize getting through it.** Say that the suicide crisis is temporary. Unbearable pain can be survived.

Understand Suicide

The rate of suicide in the United States has tripled since the 1950s. Each year about 25,000 people in this country take their own lives. As many as two of every three college students say they have thought about suicide on at least one occasion. Immediate and highly stressful circumstances can produce suicidal thoughts. These include the loss of a partner, a spouse, or a job; flunking out of school; and unwanted pregnancy. In many cases, suicide or its attempt has multiple causes (Maris, 1998).

Consider Brian, who just flunked two of his college courses. When the grades came in, his father harshly criticized Brian and told him he had not put enough effort into his classes.

This past week, Brian's girlfriend broke off their long-standing relationship. He became depressed and began to think about putting an end to his life.

If you know someone like Brian, what can you do? Some guidelines are offered in "What To Do When Someone Is Thinking about Suicide."

Seek Help for Mental Health Problems

When should you seek professional help? There is no easy answer to this question. However, as a rule, seek psychological help

- If you're psychologically distressed
- When you feel helpless and overwhelmed
- If your life is seriously disrupted by your problems

Various mental health professionals can help students. They include clinical psychologists, counselors, social workers, and psychiatrists. Clinical psychologists, counselors, and social workers use psychotherapeutic strategies to help students, but they do not prescribe drugs. Psychiatrists are medical doctors who often prescribe drugs in treating students' emotional problems. They also can conduct psychotherapy.

The counseling or health center at your college is a good place to go if you think that you have a mental health problem. The center will probably have

Am I Depressed?

Below is a list of the ways you might have felt or behaved in the *past week*. Indicate what you felt by checking the appropriate box for each item, as follows: Column A for "Rarely or None of the Time (Less Than 1 Day)"; column B, "Some or a Little of the Time (1–2 Days)"; column C, "Occasionally or a Moderate Amount of the Time (3–4 Days)"; or column D, "Most or All of the Time (5–7 Days)."

During the Past Week:	A	B	C	D
1. I was bothered by things that usually don't bother me.	____	____	____	____
2. I did not feel like eating; my appetite was poor.	____	____	____	____
3. I felt that I could not shake off the blues even with help from my family and friends.	____	____	____	____
4. I felt that I was just as good as other people.	____	____	____	____
5. I had trouble keeping my mind on what I was doing.	____	____	____	____
6. I felt depressed.	____	____	____	____
7. I felt that everything I did was an effort.	____	____	____	____
8. I felt hopeful about the future.	____	____	____	____
9. I thought my life had been a failure.	____	____	____	____
10. I felt fearful.	____	____	____	____
11. My sleep was restless.	____	____	____	____
12. I was happy.	____	____	____	____
13. I talked less than usual.	____	____	____	____
14. I felt lonely.	____	____	____	____
15. People were unfriendly.	____	____	____	____
16. I enjoyed life.	____	____	____	____
17. I had crying spells.	____	____	____	____
18. I felt sad.	____	____	____	____
19. I felt that people disliked me.	____	____	____	____
20. I could not get going.	____	____	____	____

Scoring: *After completing the Depression Scale, for items 1, 2, 3, 5, 6, 7, 9, 10, 11, 13, 14, 15, 17, 18, 19, and 20 give yourself a 0 each time you checked A, 1 each time you checked B, 2 each time you checked C, and 3 each time you checked D. Then for items 4, 8, 12, and 16, give yourself a 3 each time you checked A, 2 each time you checked B, 1 each time you checked C, and a 0 each time you checked D. Total your score for all 20 items.*

Interpretation: *A score of 7 is average for men, of 8–9 for women. If you scored 16 or more, you might benefit from professional help.*

staff to help you or will refer you to a mental health professional in the community. Figure 11-3 shows the reasons college students on one campus sought counseling.

Some students may not admit their problems or seek help for them, because they fear others will think they are weak. It takes courage to face your problems. Instead of a weakness, consider it a strength to admit that you have a problem and are willing to seek help for it. You'll be doing something about a problem that stands between you and your goals.

Making changes can be hard. Be patient and allow some time for professional help to work. Part of the success of therapy involves developing a positive relationship with the therapist, so it may take several sessions for you to notice a change. Also, if you do seek professional help, continue to evaluate how much it is benefitting you. Not all therapists and therapies are alike. If you become dissatisfied, ask to be referred to someone else. More information about mental health professionals is provided in the resource section on the Web site for this book.

FIGURE 11-3
College Students' Main Reasons for Seeking Counseling

Reason	Percent
Stress/Anxiety/Nervousness	51%
Romantic Relationships	47%
Lack of Self-Confidence/Self-Esteem	42%
Depression	42%
Family Relationships	37%
Academic Performance	29%
Career Choice or Future	25%
Loneliness	25%
Financial Matters	24%

Learn with *InfoTrac College Edition*

InfoTrac College Edition

Look up these articles and search for more on topics that sparked your interest while reading this chapter.

Arnold Schwarzenegger True myths: The life and times of Arnold Schwarzenegger. Mike Tribby. *Booklist.* Sept. 15, 1996. v93, i2, p199.

Healthy Lifestyle Teens who turned bad habits into good health. Janice Arenofsky. *Current Health 2.* May 1997. v23, n9, p6.

Exercise

Eating Disorders

Smoking Using tobacco: Why you need to quit. *American Family Physician.* Sept 15, 2000. v62, n6, pNA.

Drinking College-age drinking problems. Ralph W. Hingson. *Public Health Reports.* Jan.–Feb. 1998. v113, p152.

AIDS

Stress

Depression

Summary Strategies for Mastering College

Value and practice physical and mental skills to get you in shape to reach your academic goals.

Develop Meaningful Values

Explore Careers | **Be Physically and Mentally Healthy** | Get Motivated

Build Self-Esteem | | Set Goals, Plan, and Monitor

Think and Learn

▮1 Link Physical and Mental Health Values, Motivation, Goals, and Self-Esteem

▮2 Pursue and Maintain Physical Health

- Know your health style and your body.
- Exercise regularly. It will help your physical and mental health.
- Get enough sleep, which for most college students means eight hours or more each night to maximize alertness and productivity the next day.
- Eat right, which means eating a variety of foods, maintaining a healthy weight, and not going on extreme, unhealthy diets. Watch out for the "freshman 15," and avoid anorexia nervosa and bulimia.
- Don't smoke, Smoking is difficult to quit once started. Seek help from the health center of your college if you have a smoking problem.
- Don't take drugs. Alcohol abuse is a major problem on college campuses and it can seriously undermine success. If you have a substance abuse problem, admit it and listen to what others are saying about you. Seek help for your problem, and use the resources on the Web site for this book.
- Make the right sexual decisions. Increase your understanding of sexually transmitted diseases and protect yourself against them by assessing your and your partner's risk status, obtaining prior medical exams, using condoms, and avoiding sex with multiple partners. Protect yourself against unwanted pregnancy by abstaining from sex or by using effective contraceptive methods.

▮3 Be Mentally Healthy

- Cope with stress. Some strategies for coping with stress include perceiving stress as a challenge rather than a threat, establishing an optimistic outlook and thinking positively, seeking emotional support, and learning how to engage in deep relaxation.
- Get rid of depression.
- Know what to do when someone is contemplating suicide.
- Seek help for mental health problems at the counseling or health center at your college. Making changes can be hard. Be patient and allow some time for professional help to work.

Review Questions

1. What can people do to exercise, sleep, and eat better?

_____

_____

_____

_____

_____

_____

_____

2. If a person has a drug problem, what strategies can help him or her deal with it?

_____

_____

_____

_____

_____

_____

_____

3. What can you do to protect yourself from sexually transmitted diseases and unwanted pregnancy?

_____

_____

_____

_____

_____

_____

_____

4. What are some ineffective ways of coping with stress? What are some effective ways?

_____

_____

_____

_____

_____

_____

5. How can you tell if you have a mental health problem? If you think you have one, what should you do?

_____

_____

_____

_____

_____

_____

_____

Learning Portfolio

Reflect and Journal

1. Make Good Sexual Decisions

Think about the kinds of sexual decisions you've made.

- What was the best one?

  _____
  _____
  _____

- What was the worst one?

  _____
  _____
  _____

- What do you predict will be the most important sexual decision you'll have to make in the next year? What will your choice be?

  _____
  _____
  _____
  _____
  _____

2. Examine Your Coping Style

This is good time to take stock of your coping style. Think about your life in the last few months. When stressful circumstances have come up, how have you handled them in general?

- Did you appraise them as harmful, threatening, or challenging?

  _____
  _____

- Did you repress the stress or did you consciously make an effort to solve your problems?

  _____
  _____

- Did you refuse to believe what was happening?

  _____
  _____

- Did you try to reduce the stress by eating and drinking more?

  _____
  _____

Learn By Doing

1. Keep an Eating Journal

Write down everything you eat for a week. Include when you eat (time of day), how much you eat, where you eat, whom you're with when you eat, and the mood you're in when eating. At the end of the week, rate how good your nutritional style is (based on what you read in the chapter) on the following scale:

1 2 3 4 5 6 7 8 9 10

Bad Nutritional   Good Nutritional
Style   Style

If you do not have a good nutritional style, map out a plan that you're willing to carry out.

  _____
  _____
  _____
  _____
  _____
  _____
  _____
  _____

2. Visit the Health and Counseling Centers at Your College

Find out where the health and counseling centers are at your college. Record their addresses. Stop by and find out what services and materials are available. Describe the services in your learning portfolio. Ask for copies of any health or mental health brochures that interest you.

  _____
  _____
  _____
  _____

3. Use the Resources on the Web Site for This Book

The Web site for this book has a large number of helpful resources related to this chapter. Go to the Web site, look them over, then do the following:

- Call one or more of the telephone numbers listed and find out what services, brochures, and advice are available.
- Read one of the books and write a summary of what you learned from it.

Think Critically

1. What Should You Tell Your Date?

If someone has a sexually transmitted disease, should the person tell his or her date ? Does the date have the right to know? If you think the person should tell his or her date, what is the best way to do this?

_____

_____

_____

_____

_____

_____

_____

_____

_____

_____

_____

_____

_____

_____

_____

_____

_____

2. Increase Awareness of Problems

Too many people are not aware that they have personal problems. How can we help people become more aware of their problems? What thinking strategies would you recommend to someone for becoming more aware of problems they need to cope with? How can you improve your awareness of your own problems?

_____

_____

_____

_____

_____

_____

_____

_____

_____

_____

_____

_____

_____

_____

_____

_____

Think Creatively

1. Become a Movie Producer

Imagine that you're a screenwriter with a major studio. Your task is to create a movie on coping and mental health. Describe the movie by writing a short treatment of it. Give it a title.

_____

_____

_____

_____

_____

_____

_____

_____

_____

2. Make Your Own Graphic

Using the graphic of linked ideas on page 271 as a model, create a graphic to remind yourself of other connections that are central to your own physical and/or mental health.

_____

_____

_____

_____

_____

_____

_____

_____

_____

_____

Work toward Goals

Review the results of the self-assessments you completed in this chapter. Also review the opening checklist. Based on your review, select a relatively short-term goal that you want to work on now.

1. What is that goal? (*Hint:* Is it challenging, reasonable, and specific?)

_____

_____

_____

_____

_____

2. What strategies will you use to achieve your goal? (*Hint:* Can you organize your strategy into a series of smaller goals?)

_____

_____

_____

_____

_____

3. What obstacles may be in your way as you attempt to make these positive changes?

_____

_____

_____

_____

_____

4. What additional resources might help you achieve your goal? (Use the CD-ROM that comes with this book for access to some useful leads.)

_____

_____

_____

_____

_____

5. By what date do you want to accomplish your goal?

_____

_____

_____

_____

6. How will you know you have succeeded?

_____

_____

_____

_____

Explore Careers and Majors

Forge a Bright Future 💿

Pinpoint careers and majors that fit your values and interests. The time you spend exploring careers and majors will help anchor your college work and your success after college.

To evaluate where you are now in relation to careers and majors, place a check mark next to only those items that apply to you.

_____ I have begun to explore career options and know of at least one that matches up with my values and interests.

_____ I have chosen a major or specialization.

_____ I have made a coursework plan toward a degree or certificate.

_____ I have a mentor.

_____ I have talked with a career counselor.

_____ I know what makes a person valuable in the working world.

_____ I have ideas about work experiences during college that might help me with my long-term goals.

As you read about Bernard Shaw on the next page, think about how his part-time job in college provided him with experience in his future career.

IMAGES OF COLLEGE SUCCESS

Bernard Shaw

As the principal Washington anchor for CNN, Bernard Shaw is one of the nation's most distinguished journalists. Shaw was born in Chicago, where his father was a housepainter and his mother a housekeeper. His high school grades were good, and he was considered to be a bright student. However, his parents could not afford to send him to college, so he entered the U.S. Marine Corps.

When he was a 21-year-old marine stationed in Hawaii, he heard that Walter Cronkite, the famous news anchor for CBS, was coming to Hawaii to film a news special. As a young boy, Shaw had always dreamed of being a major news anchor. He found out where Cronkite was staying and called his room "about 34 times," as he recalled. According to Cronkite, Shaw was the most persistent person he had ever encountered. Cronkite finally relented and planned to give Shaw five minutes of his time. They ended up spending half an hour talking.

Erica Lansner/Black Star

Bernard Shaw's **persistence helped him launch an award-winning career in journalism.**

At 23, Shaw left the Marines and entered the University of Illinois, choosing history as his major. While carrying a full load of classes, he took an unpaid position at a rhythm-and-blues radio station. Within a few months, the station switched to an all-news format. Later in the year, when Martin Luther King, Jr., came to Chicago, Shaw talked the management of the radio station into hiring him for $50 as a reporter on the scene. He continued to work hard in college and at the radio station, which finally put the relentless young man on their paid staff.

Shaw still abides by the advice his mentor Walter Cronkite gave him early in his career: Read prolifically and remain open and curious about all facets of human existence. Shaw has donated more than $130,000 to the Bernard Shaw Endowment Fund, which he established at the University of Illinois. Shaw has also earned many awards and honors, including a medallion from the University of Kansas for distinguished service.

Learn more about Bernard Shaw.

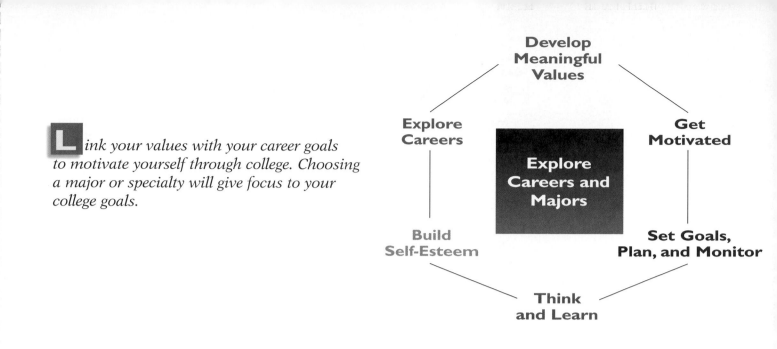

ink your values with your career goals to motivate yourself through college. Choosing a major or specialty will give focus to your college goals.

Get Motivated to Explore Careers

A good mentor can both help you choose a fulfilling major or specialization and give you good career advice. Exploring different careers and making the right career choices are critical steps in our lives. This is a good time to get motivated to look at several different career paths.

Where Am I in Exploring Careers?

How far along are you in exploring careers? Here are some activities that can benefit your career exploration. To what extent have you done the following?

- Examined what your values are and how they link up with career choices
- Explored the occupational outlook for the next decade to determine which jobs are likely to grow the fastest and pay best
- Engaged in personal networking about career options and job opportunities
- Spent time with a career counselor to explore career options
- Taken an interest inventory to see which types of careers match up with your interests
- Checked out and read books on careers from the library
- Scoped out Internet networks and resources on careers and jobs
- Found out what employers want in an ideal job candidate
- Explored some good strategies for performing well in a job interview
- Checked out potential work experiences in college that could help you in future careers

*W*hatever you can do, or dream you can, begin it. Boldness has genius, power, and magic.

> Johann Wolfgang von Goethe
> 19th-century German playwright and novelist

Choose Career Options That Match Your Values

An important first step in choosing career options is to know your values. Knowing what you value most—what is important to you in life—will help you refine your career search and choice.

Some people want to pursue a career in which they help others. Some desire a career that is prestigious. Others seek one in which they will make a lot of money. Yet others want one that will give them plenty of time for leisure and family interests. Complete Self-Assessment 12-1 to examine your values in relation to your career pursuits.

When you clarify your values, it helps you to zero in on the careers that will likely be the most meaningful and rewarding to you. Once you've decided on a career, you need to set goals, plan how to reach them, and monitor your progress toward them. When your values, career choice, and career goals are established and aligned, your internal motivation to think and learn will be strengthened.

Monitor the Occupational Outlook

Keep up with the occupational outlook for various fields. Get to know which ones are adding jobs and which ones are losing them. An excellent source is the *Occupational Outlook Handbook*, which is revised every two years. The following information comes from the 2000–2001 handbook.

In the near future, service-producing industries will provide most new jobs. Among service occupations, business, health, and professional services are projected to account for 75 percent of job growth from 1998 to 2008. Employment in computer and data processing services is projected to grow 117 percent in this time frame, ranking it as the fastest-growing industry.

Jobs that require college degrees will be the fastest-growing and highest-paying ones. Jobs that require an associate degree are projected to increase more than 30 percent from 1998 to 2008; those that require a bachelor's degree or doctoral degree more than 25 percent; and those that require a master's degree more than 20 percent. Almost all of the highest-paying occupations require a college degree.

Map Out an Academic Path

Later in the chapter we explore ways to find the right career. Now that you've thought about your values and which careers you might want to pursue, give some thought to designing an academic path. A good way to start this is to study your college catalog.

My Values and My Career Pursuits

Place a check mark next to those values you consider important in a career.

_____ Work with people I like.

_____ Feel powerful.

_____ Have peace of mind.

_____ Make a lot of money.

_____ Be happy.

_____ Have self-respect.

_____ Contribute to the welfare of others.

_____ Not have to work long hours.

_____ Be mentally challenging.

_____ Be self-fulfilling.

_____ Have opportunities for advancement.

_____ Work in a setting where moral values are emphasized.

_____ Have plenty of time for leisure pursuits.

_____ Have plenty of time to spend with family.

_____ Work in a good geographical location.

_____ Be creative.

_____ Work where physical and mental health are important.

_____ Other: _____

_____ Other: _____

_____ Other: _____

As you explore careers, keep the values you checked off in mind. How do those values match the careers you've thought about pursuing? Explain.

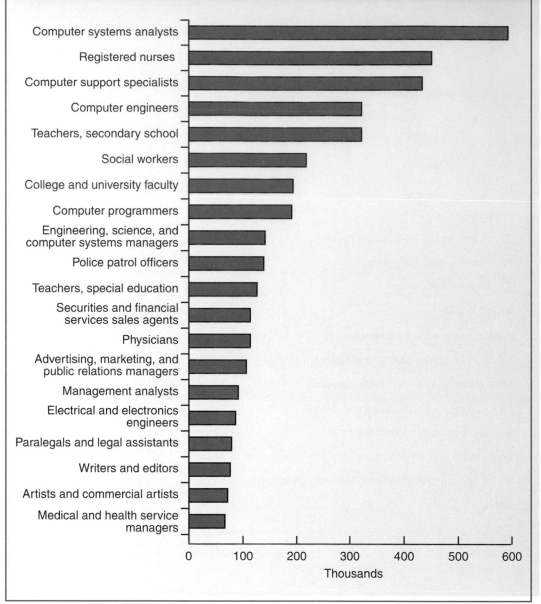

FIGURE 12-1

Occupations with Fast Growth and High Pay Expected to Show the Largest Numerical Growth in Jobs from 1998 to 2008

Computer systems analysts
Registered nurses
Computer support specialists
Computer engineers
Teachers, secondary school
Social workers
College and university faculty
Computer programmers
Engineering, science, and computer systems managers
Police patrol officers
Teachers, special education
Securities and financial services sales agents
Physicians
Advertising, marketing, and public relations managers
Management analysts
Electrical and electronics engineers
Paralegals and legal assistants
Writers and editors
Artists and commercial artists
Medical and health service managers

0   100   200   300   400   500   600
Thousands

Source: Occupational Outlook Handbook. (2000–2001). Chart 4. Washington, DC : U.S. Department of Labor.

Get to Know Your College Catalog

A college catalog is a valuable resource. If you don't have one, check with your advisor or the admissions office to obtain one. College catalogs usually are published every one or two years. Be sure to save the catalog that is in effect when you enroll for the first time. Why? Because requirements for specific programs sometimes change, and you usually will be held to the degree plan that was in place then.

If you've decided on a field or have several fields in mind, turn to the part of the catalog that describes those areas of study and the courses required for graduation. The catalog should tell you what the core requirements are, whether there are any prerequisites for the programs, and whether there is a sequence of courses you should follow.

Explore Majors and Specializations

Whether you are in a two-year or a four-year college, you'll need to select a major or specialization. The major or specialization that you select should match up with your career goals and values.

Two-Year Colleges Some students enter a community college with a clear idea of what they want to major or specialize in, but many enter with no clear idea. Some students plan to obtain an associate degree, others to pursue a certificate in a specialty field.

The Associate of Arts (AA) degree includes general academic courses that allow students to transfer to a four-year institution. If you plan to transfer, you'll need to select a college and study its degree requirements as soon as possible. You should consult regularly with an advisor at your community college and the four-year institution to ensure that you're enrolling in courses appropriate to your major.

In addition to a core of general education courses, obtaining an AA degree means taking either a concentration of courses in a major (or area of emphasis) such as history, English, psychology, and so on or taking a required number of electives. In most community colleges, a minimum of 60 or more credit hours is required for an AA degree. A typical breakdown might be 45 credits in general education and 15 in your major, area of emphasis, or electives. Some community colleges also offer an Associate of Science (AS) degree that requires a heavy science concentration.

Many community colleges also offer certificate programs designed to help people reenter the job market or upgrade their skills. There are many specializations: food and hospitality, graphic communication, press operation, medical record coding, word processing, building-property management, travel management, vocational nursing, and others.

The coursework in certificate programs does not include general education requirements, as Associate of Arts and Science programs do. Certificate programs focus specifically on the job skills needed in a particular occupation. The number of credits required varies but is usually fewer than the number required for an associate's degree.

If you're a community college student, whether you're enrolled in an associate's or certificate program, it's a good idea to map out a plan that lists each of your courses until graduation. Study your college's catalog and become familiar with the requirements for your degree. With your college catalog in hand, complete Self-Assessment 12-2. Use this self-assessment as a starting point in discussing your plans with your academic advisor.

Coursework for an Associate Degree or Certificate

Examine the requirements for the major or certificate you're considering. Then fill in the blanks with the courses you plan to take. Use this self-assessment to discuss your decisions with your academic advisor.

Fall	Spring	Summer
First Year		
Second Year		
Third Year		

Four-Year Colleges A college major, or field of concentration, is a series of courses that provides a foundation of learning in an academic discipline. Majors vary in the number of courses required. For example, engineering requires more courses than does history or psychology. They allow you to choose more electives.

Some graduate programs may prefer a specific undergraduate degree. Others may not. For example, law schools admit students from many different undergraduate majors. In contrast, graduate schools in physics require a physics undergraduate degree or a large concentration of physics classes. If you want to be an English teacher in a public high school, you probably need to major in secondary education with a concentration in English.

"Well, we've finally done it. We've listed two courses, each of which is a prerequisite for taking the other."

© Harald Carl Bakken.

Many first-year students take several general education courses before they invest in courses in their specialty or major. This allows them to broaden their education and have more time to choose their focus.

If you're not sure what you want to focus on, you're not alone. More than two-thirds of first-year college students change their intended majors in the first year. Don't panic. When college administrators have you fill out forms during your first year, most let you write "undecided" or "exploring" in the column for a college major. Some four-year institutions have a one- or two-year general curriculum you can follow before you choose a major. But if you're in a four-year program and aren't sure about a major after two years, you'll find yourself taking extra courses that you may not need when you graduate.

Some students don't major in a specific area but instead pursue a broad range of college courses. Many four-year institutions have individualized majors that allow this. Even individualized majors, though, usually require one or two concentrations of courses to keep the coursework somewhat unified, not totally disconnected.

Create a Four- or Five-Year Plan Even though many first-year students don't know what to major in, or they find themselves changing majors in their first year, it's still a good idea to map out a four- or five-year plan that lists each of your courses every term until graduation. Study your college's catalog and become familiar with requirements in a major that interests you. You'll need to know the general education requirements, required courses in the major, prerequisites for courses, restricted electives, free electives, and other requirements. In this way, you can take control of your academic planning and give yourself the most flexibility toward the end of your four or five years of college.

The risk in not doing a four- or five-year plan is that you'll end up in your junior or senior year with too many courses in one area and not enough in another, which will extend the time needed to get your bachelor's degree. The four- or five-year plan also lets you see which terms will be light and which will be heavy, as well as whether you'll need to take summer courses.

Of course, it's unlikely that you'll carry out your plan exactly. As you make changes, the plan will allow you to see the consequences of your moves and what you have to do to stay on track to complete your degree.

The four- or five-year plan is an excellent starting point for sessions with your academic advisor. The plan can be a springboard for questions you might have about which courses to take this term, next term, and so on. If you're considering several different majors, make a four- or five-year plan for each

"Hmm, summa cum laude—very impressive. But what exactly is a Bachelor of Arts & Leisure?"

one and use the plans to help you decide which courses to take and when. If you're in a four-year institution, begin your planning with Self-Assessment 12-3.

How Do You Know Whether a Major Is Right for You?

Make a realistic assessment of your interests and abilities. Are you getting Cs and Ds in biology and chemistry, though you've honestly put your full effort into those courses? Then pre-med or a science area may not be the best major for you. If you hate the math or computer science class you're taking, you may not be cut out for a career that requires that kind of background.

But be patient. The first year of college, especially the first term, is a time of exploration and learning how to succeed in college. Many first-year students who don't do well at first in courses related to a possible major adapt, meet the challenge, and go on to do extremely well in that major. A year or two into your college experience, you should have a good idea of whether the major you've chosen is a good fit. At that point, you will have had enough courses and opportunities to know whether you're in the right place.

A good strategy is to seek out students who are more advanced in the field you're considering. Ask them what it's like to specialize in that particular area, and ask them about various courses and instructors.

Unfortunately, too many students choose majors for the wrong reasons: to please their parents, follow their friends, or have a light course load.

What really interests you? It's your life. You have the right to choose what you want to do with it. Go back to your own values and long-term goals. What do you really want to major in? The courses in your major can be challenging and still be right for you, but you should have a good feeling about your match with the major program. You should be enthusiastic about it and motivated to learn more about the field.

What Do You Need to Know to Transfer to Another College?

If you decide that you want to transfer to another college, you'll want to know whether the credits you've earned at your current college will transfer to the new one. How well your credits will transfer depends on the schools and on your major. Check the catalog for the new college and see how its requirements match up with those of your current college. The catalog will also describe transfer requirements. Next, be sure to talk with an advisor at the new college about which of your courses will transfer. Here are some questions you might ask the admissions advisor (Harbin, 1995):

- What are the minimum admission criteria that I have to meet in order to transfer to your college?
- Do I need a minimum grade point average for admission? If so, what is it?
- What are the application deadlines for transfer admissions?
- Where can I get a transfer application?
- What else can you tell me about transferring to your college?

If you want to change colleges but aren't sure where you want to go, consult some general guides to colleges such as *Peterson's National College Data Bank* or *Barron's Profiles of American Colleges*. Try to visit several campuses that might meet your needs. Talk with students there, as well as an academic advisor. Walk around and get a feel for how you like it. Be clear about what aspects of your current life are unsatisfying and why the new school will be better.

A Four- or Five-Year Academic Plan

Study your college catalog to find out what courses you need to graduate in a particular major. If you have not selected a major, examine the requirements for one you're considering. Then fill in the blanks with the courses you plan to take. Use this self-assessment to discuss your decisions with your academic advisor. The plan here is for schools on a semester schedule. If your school has a quarterly system, create your own plan by listing the quarters for each of the four or five years and then filling in the courses you plan to take.

Fall	Spring	Summer
First Year		
Second Year		
Third Year		
Fourth Year		
Fifth Year		

Get the Right Courses

With a little effort, you can learn how to select courses that both fulfill your requirements and are enjoyable. Some strategies for making sound selections:

- **List your constraints.** You might have child care responsibilities or an inflexible work schedule. If so, block out the times you can't take classes.
- **Study your options.** Colleges have lists of classes required for various specialty diplomas or majors. Examine the college catalog to determine which courses are required for both general education requirements and specific courses in the specialty or major you want to pursue.
- **Register for a reasonable course load.** Many colleges do not charge for additional courses beyond those needed for full-time status. You might be tempted to pile on extra courses to save time and money. But think again. By taking too many courses. you may spread yourself too thin.
- **Take the right mix of courses.** Don't load up with too many really tough courses in the same term. Check into how much reading and other time is required for specific courses. If you can't find anyone else who can tell you this, make appointments with the instructors. Ask them what the course requirements are, how much reading they expect, and so on.
- **Talk with your advisor.** Get an appointment with your academic advisor to discuss the courses you prefer. Prepare a tentative schedule and questions beforehand. Ask the advisor's recommendations about various courses and instructors.

Many academic counselors are specially trained to advise you about selecting the program that is right for you. They can help you examine a wide range of specialties or majors. They can talk with you about your abilities and interests and help you find the one that matches what you want to do. Before you see your advisor, make up a list of questions such as:

- ☐ What classes should I take this term and next?
- ☐ What sequence of classes should I take?
- ☐ Am I taking too many difficult classes in one term?
- ☐ What electives do you recommend?
- ☐ What career opportunities are there if I study mainly ___ or ___?

- **Ask the pros.** The "pros" in this case are students already in your preferred program. Ask their advice about which courses and instructors to take. On many campuses, academic departments have undergraduate organizations you can join. If you want to be a biology major, consider joining something like the Student Biology Association. These associations are good places to get connected with students more advanced than you are in a major. "Get What You Want" provides more tips on getting the right courses.

Find a Mentor

A mentor is an advisor, coach, and confidant. A mentor can help you become successful and master many of life's challenges. He or she can also advise you on career

---

ON-TARGET TIPS

Get What You Want

1. **Register as soon as you can.** Early registration improves your chances of getting the courses you want.

2. **Use computer registration.** Many campuses encourage students to register directly by using the campus computer system. This gives you immediate feedback about your scheduling. It may even suggest alternatives if you run into closed courses.

3. **Have a backup plan.** Anticipate the courses that might close out (for example, preferred times or popular instructors). Have alternatives in mind to meet your requirements.

4. **Explore the wait list option.** If you want to get into a closed class, find out your chances for getting into a class if you agree to be put on the waiting list. If the odds aren't good, explore other options.

5. **Plead your case.** If you get closed out of a class you really want, go directly to the instructor and ask for an exception. Base your request on your intellectual curiosity for the course content, not on scheduling convenience. Some instructors may reject your request, but others will listen and try to help you.

pursuits, suggest ways to cope with problem situations, and listen to what's on your mind. A mentor might be

- A student who has successfully navigated the first-year experience
- A graduate student
- An instructor
- Someone in the community you respect and trust

If you don't have a mentor, think about the people you've met in college so far. Is there a person you admire whose advice might benefit you? If you don't have anyone in mind right now, start looking around for someone. As you talk with various people and get to know them better, one person's competence and motivation can start to rub off on you. This is the type of person who can be a good mentor.

Examine Career and Job Skills

Is the career you want to enter a good match for your skills? What skills do many of today's employers look for in job candidates?

Find the Right Career Match

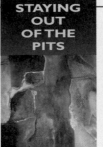

A Mentor Saves the Day

Carla did not have much academic guidance while growing up. Neither of her parents went to college. Her grades in high school were okay but not great. She went to college mainly because her friends were going.

The first semester in college was eye opening. Poor study habits and lack of motivation landed her in academic probation. At the beginning of the second term, she was talking with Marta, a third-year student. Marta told Carla that she also had low grades in her first year. She said that what turned college around for her more than anything else was finding a mentor.

Marta explained to Carla what a mentor is. She told Carla that she would like to mentor her. They hit it off well and began studying together. Marta kept Carla on the right track. She convinced Carla that she needed to manage her time better and set some goals. Marta got Carla to begin thinking about what she wanted to do with her life.

One day Carla was sick and missed a test. Carla just was going to blow off the course and not even talk with the professor about making up the test. Marta had Carla call the professor at his office and explain her illness. He allowed her to take a makeup exam.

The mentoring paid off. Carla's second term grades were not terrific, but they were good enough to get her off probation. Carla says that if she hadn't met Marta, she would have dropped out of college.

When you're seeking the right career, it's good to have several careers in mind rather than just one in your first year. In a recent national survey of first-year college students, only 12 percent believed that they were likely to change their major field of interest or career choice (Sax & others, 2000). In reality, far more than this will change. Thus, it pays to be knowledgeable about more than just one career field. It also pays to develop a wide variety of general skills, such as communication, that will serve you well in various fields.

Network Check with people you know—your family, friends, people in the community—about career information. They might be able to answer your questions themselves or put you in touch with people who can.

Networking can lead to meeting someone who can answer your questions about a specific career or company. This is an effective way to learn about the type of training necessary for a particular position, how to enter the field, and what employees like and don't like about the work.

See a Career Counselor You might want to talk with a career counselor at your college. This professional is trained to help you discover your strengths and weaknesses, evaluate your values and goals, and help you figure out what type of career you want. The counselor will not tell you what to do. You might be asked to take an interest inventory, which the counselor can interpret to help you explore various career options.

Scope out Internet Networks and Resources The dramatic growth of Web sites has made instantly available almost countless resources for job possibilities and careers. Most companies, professional societies, academic institutions, and government agencies maintain Internet sites that highlight their latest information and activities.

The range of career information on the Internet provides much of the same information that is available through libraries, career centers, and guidance offices. However, no single network or resource is likely to contain all of the information you're searching for, so explore different sources. As in a library search, look through various lists by field or discipline or by using keywords.

Be sure to scan the resources on the Web site for this book. You'll find some helpful books and Web links that explore many aspects of careers.

Be the Ideal Job Candidate

You might think it's too early to start considering how you'll fare in the job market when you graduate. It's not. If you know what employers are searching for, you can work on developing those qualifications during college.

Communication Skills The National Association of College Employers conducted a survey of its members. The employers ranked skills in oral communication, interpersonal relations, and teamwork as the three most important skills of a prospective job candidate (Collins, 1996). All of these skills involve communicating effectively. Employers also look for candidates to be proficient in their field, having leadership and analytical abilities, and show flexibility. Figure 12-2 summarizes the skills that employers want in a job candidate.

An employer will look for evidence of your accomplishments and experiences. This might include

- Leadership positions
- Activity in campus organizations or extracurricular activities
- Relevant experiences in co-ops, internships, or part-time work
- Good grades

Employers look for a combination of these characteristics. The more of them you have when you graduate from college, the better.

In the survey just mentioned, employers also said that first-year students need to realize that it's later in the job search than they think. Graduation and job hunting are only a few years away. Much of what employers look for in top job candidates (such as relevant experience) takes time to acquire. The employers especially recommend that first-year students get

- Work-related experience
- Experience in campus or extracurricular activities
- Good grades
- Computer skills

Computer Skills The employers point out that no matter what your career aspirations, you'll likely need computer skills to perform your job competently. These days computer skills are a must.

FIGURE 12-2
Desired Skills of an Ideal Job Candidate As Described by Employers

Speaking Skills	Leadership Skills
Interpersonal Skills	Proficiency in Field of Study
Analytical Skills	Writing Skills
Teamwork Skills	Computer Skills
Flexibility	

Self-Management Skills Many people think of work-related skills as engineering, writing, speaking, and computer skills, to name a few. These skills often are important in many jobs. However, self-management skills are also extremely important to career success (Farr, 1999). By completing Self-Assessment 12-4, you can evaluate your self-management skills.

The skills and qualities you checked off in Self-Assessment 12-4 are among the most important things a prospective employer should learn about you. They have to do with your ability to be a competent worker in many different situations and adapt to challenging tasks. Even so, most job seekers don't understand how important they are and don't mention them during interviews. Don't make this mistake.

"I threw in a couple of paragraphs about my love life to make my résumé interesting."

© Engleman/Rothco Cartoons.

Knock 'em Dead in a Job Interview

A key step in getting the job you want is to perform well in an interview. Here are some strategies for succeeding in a job interview (Yate, 2000):

- Interviewers ask for detailed examples of your past experience. They figure you'll do as well on the new job as the old one, so the examples you give can seal your fate.
- Résumés are important. Employers use them to decide whether they want to interview you in the first place. Organize your résumé, write it clearly, and avoid jargon.
- Don't wing the interview. Do your homework. Find out as much about your prospective employer as possible. What does the company do? How successful is it? Employers are impressed by applicants who have taken the time to learn about their organization. This is true whether you are interviewing for a part-time job at your college library or for a full-time job in a large company after you graduate.
- Anticipate what questions you'll be asked. Do some practice interviews. Some typical interview questions include
    "What is your greatest strength?"
    "What interests you the most about this job?"
    "Why should I hire you?"
  Also be prepared for some zingers. For example, how would you respond to
    "Tell me something you're not very proud of."
    "Describe a situation where your idea was criticized."
  These are examples of questions some interviewers ask to catch you off guard and see how you handle the situation.
- Ask appropriate job-related questions. Review the job's requirements with the interviewer.
- Keep your cool. Always leave in the same polite way you entered.
- As the interview closes, decide whether you want the job. If so, ask for it. Tell the interviewer that you're excited about the job and that you can do it competently. If the job isn't offered on the spot, ask when the two of you can talk again.
- That's not all. Immediately after the interview, type a follow-up letter. Keep it short, less than one page. Mail the letter within 24 hours after the interview. If the decision is going to be made in the next few days, hand deliver the letter or send a telegram. If you do not hear anything within five days, call the organization and ask what the status of the job is.

SELF-ASSESSMENT 12-4

My Self-Management Skills

To explore your self-management skills, place a check mark next to any skills and qualities that you believe you have.

____ accept supervision	____ flexible
____ complete assignments	____ well organized
____ get along with co-workers	____ friendly
____ learn quickly	____ helpful
____ get things done on time	____ humble
____ take pride in work	____ imaginative
____ good attendance	____ intelligent
____ sense of humor	____ loyal
____ hard working	____ mature
____ honest	____ motivated
____ productive	____ open-minded
____ punctual	____ optimistic
____ able to coordinate	____ patient
____ ambitious	____ persistent
____ assertive	____ responsible
____ cheerful	____ self-confident
____ conscientious	____ sincere
____ creative	____ trustworthy
____ dependable	____ other _____
____ eager	____ other _____
____ energetic	____ other _____

Now go back through the list and select your five strongest self-management skills. Number them 1–5.

Are there any items you did not place a check mark next to that you think would help you in the careers you might pursue? If so, what can you do to develop these self-management skills and qualities?

Source: After Farr, J. M. (1999). American's top jobs for college graduates (3rd ed., pp. 365–366). Indianapolis, IN: JIST Works.

Get Positive Work Experiences during College

Students can participate in cooperative education programs, internships, or part-time or summer work relevant to their field of study. This experience can be critical in helping students obtain the job they want when they graduate. Today's employers expect job candidates to have this type of experience. In the recent national survey of employers, almost 60 percent said their entry-level college hires had co-op or internship experience.

More than 1,000 colleges in the United States offer co-op (cooperative education) programs. A co-op is a paid apprenticeship in a career field that you're interested in pursuing. You may not be permitted to participate in a co-op program until your junior year.

A wide range of life experiences during college may help you explore your values in areas related to careers. One aspect of these experiences might be *service learning*, which involves engaging in activities that promote social responsibility and service to the community (Stukas, Clary, & Snyder, 1999). In service learning, you might tutor, help the elderly, volunteer in a hospital, assist in a day care center, or clean up a vacant lot to make a play area.

Why should you participate in service learning during your college years? Researchers have found that when students participate in service learning,

- Their grades improve, they become more motivated, and they set more goals (Johnson & others, 1998).
- Their self-esteem improves (Giles & Eyler, 1998; Hamburg, 1997).
- They increasingly reflect on society's moral order (Yates, 1995).

"Uh-huh. Uh-huh. And for precisely how long were you a hunter-gatherer at I.B.M.?"

Learn with *InfoTrac College Edition*

InfoTrac College Edition

Look up these articles and search for more on topics that sparked your interest while reading this chapter.

Bernard Shaw *Broadcasting and cable.* Bernard Shaw. Nov. 8, 1999. v129, i46, p529.

Exploring Careers Tapping the internet's job search resources. Jerome Curry. *Business Communication Quarterly.* June 1998. v61, i2, p100.

Majors Information technology: Big major on campus. Leslie Goff. *Computerworld.* June 16, 1997. v31, i24, p100.

Academic Plans Nontraditional education: Alternative ways to earn your credentials. Kathleen Green. *Occupational Outlook Quarterly.* Summer 1996. v40, n2, p22.

Ideal Job Candidate

College Work Experience

Summary Strategies for Mastering College

Link your values with your career goals to motivate yourself through college.

1 Get Motivated to Explore Careers

- Examine where you are now in exploring careers.
- Choose career options that match your values.
- Link values, career choices, goals, motivation, and thinking and learning.
- Monitor the occupational outlook to find out about the fastest-growing careers and how things will change in occupations in the future.

2 Map out an Academic Path

- Study the college catalog.
- Explore majors and plan your coursework for a degree or certificate.
- Know some good strategies for transferring to another college if this is on your mind.
- Get the right courses by listing your constraints, studying your options, registering for a reasonable course load, taking the right mix of courses, talking with your advisor, and checking in with advanced students.
- Find a mentor who can advise you on mastering college and being successful in life.

3 Examine Career and Job Skills

- Find the right career match by networking, seeing a career counselor, and scoping out the Internet and other resources.
- Know about the characteristics that employers look for in an ideal job candidate. Especially important are communication, computer, and self-management skills.
- Know some good strategies for succeeding in a job interview.
- Explore work experiences during college that could benefit your future career options.
- Consider engaging in service learning activities.

Review Questions

1. How can you determine how far along you are in exploring careers?

   _____

   _____

   _____

   _____

   _____

   _____

2. What are some key aspects of designing an academic path?

   _____

   _____

   _____

   _____

   _____

   _____

   _____

3. How do you know whether a major is right for you?

   _____

   _____

   _____

   _____

   _____

   _____

   _____

4. What are some good strategies for finding the right career?

   _____

   _____

   _____

   _____

   _____

   _____

5. What characteristics do many employers seek in an ideal job candidate?

   _____

   _____

   _____

   _____

   _____

Learning Portfolio

⊙ Reflect and Journal

1. My Ideal Job

- Write down your ideal occupation choice.

_____
_____
_____
_____
_____

- Describe the degree you'll need for your ideal job, such as an AA, BA, MA, or PhD. How many years will this take?

_____
_____
_____
_____
_____
_____
_____
_____
_____
_____

- On a scale of 1 to 10, estimate your chances of obtaining your ideal job.

1	2	3	4	5	6	7	8	9	10
Poor									Excellent

- Discuss these answers further in your journal.

_____
_____
_____
_____
_____
_____
_____
_____
_____
_____
_____

⊙ Learn By Doing

1. Examine Your College Catalog

Look at your college's catalog. If you don't have one, your academic advisor can tell you where to get one. In most cases the admissions or registrar's office has copies.

- If you're not doing well in a particular class, you may want to consider dropping it. Look up the procedure for dropping a class and the latest date in the term you can do this.

_____
_____
_____
_____

- Look up the specialty or major you've chosen or that you're considering. What are the degree requirements for it? Is there a particular sequence of courses you should take?

_____
_____
_____
_____

2. Current Résumé and Future Résumé ⊙

Create a current résumé. List your education, work experience, high school or college campus organizations, and extracurricular activities. List any honors or awards you have achieved. Then write down what you would like your résumé to look like when you apply for your first job after college. By going to the Web site for this book, you can read about and see some examples of résumés.

_____
_____
_____
_____

3. Visit Your College's Career Center

Visit the career center at your college. Find out what materials and services are available. Get brochures about the careers that you're interested in. Consider making an appointment with a career counselor.

_____
_____
_____

Think Critically

1. Why Do People Choose Particular Careers?

Get together with several other students. Critically analyze what influences people to pursue a particular career.

- Are some people born to be engineers or nurses?

_____

_____

- Do their parents shape their career interests?

_____

_____

- Do teachers?

_____

_____

- What kind of an impact can mentors have on career choice?

_____

_____

_____

_____

- Are economic factors important?

_____

_____

_____

- Are values important?

_____

_____

_____

2. How Good Are Your Communication Skills?

Among the skills that employers want college graduates to have, communication skills are the most important. Honestly examine your communication skills. Rate yourself from 1 to 5 (with 1 being weak and 5 being strong) on the following:

	1	2	3	4	5
Speaking skills					
Interpersonal skills					
Teamwork skills					
Writing skills					
Listening skills					

- What are your strengths and weaknesses?

_____

_____

- Find out how important each of these skills is in the job you want when you graduate from college.

_____

_____

_____

Think Creatively

1. Collect Inspirations

Many creative people write down daily impressions, events, and feelings on index cards or in notebooks. These notes can be the raw material out of which creative ideas spring. Some artists tear out dozens of interesting images from magazines and newspapers, put them in boxes, and then return to them for creative inspirations. Start keeping a special box to store your impressions, feelings, and images related to your career interests and dreams. Come back to them from time to time for inspiration.

_____

_____

_____

_____

_____

_____

2. Beyond the Given

Imagine a dream career—not a paying job that you already know exists, but something else that you've dreamed of doing. Describe that ideal in your journal. Then look around to see whether that sort of career actually exists in some form. Use your career center and the Internet to explore possibilities.

_____

_____

_____

_____

_____

_____

_____

Work toward Goals

Review the results of the self-assessments you completed in this chapter. Also review the opening checklist. Based on your review, select a relatively short-term goal that you want to work on now.

1. What is that goal? (*Hint:* Is it challenging, reasonable, and specific?)

_____

_____

_____

_____

_____

2. What strategies will you use to achieve your goal? (*Hint:* Can you organize your strategy into a series of smaller goals?)

_____

_____

_____

_____

3. What obstacles may be in your way as you attempt to make these positive changes?

_____

_____

_____

_____

4. What additional resources might help you achieve your goal? (Use the CD-ROM that comes with this book for access to some useful leads.) 💿

_____

_____

_____

_____

5. By what date do you want to accomplish your goal?

_____

_____

_____

_____

6. How will you know you have succeeded?

_____

_____

_____

_____

Putting It All Together

How has the term or year gone so far? Are you mastering college? Have you put to good use many of the strategies we have described?

It's always good to take stock periodically where you are now, how things have gone, and where you're headed. This is a good time to reflect on the main themes of this book.

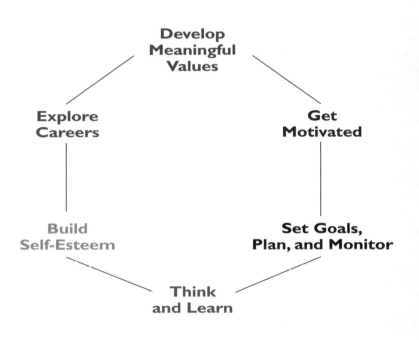

Develop Meaningful Values

Go back to Self-Assessment 1-2, "What Are My Values?" on page 7. Now that you've almost finished your first college term or year, are your values the same as they were at the beginning of the term or have they changed? Look at what you listed as your five most important values. Are those five still the most important today? If you're still a little uncertain about your values, follow the recommendations in "Clarify Your Values" on page 6.

Get Motivated on Behalf of Your Values

How has your motivation been this term? Has your confidence been high and have you enthusiastically put your heart and mind into mastering college? Have you made a great effort and been persistent in your work? Have you been internally motivated and viewed yourself as responsible for your achievement?

Set Goals, Plan, and Monitor

Are being well-educated and academically successful important values for you? Have you been motivated this term on behalf of these values? Or are there other values that are more important to you? Have you linked your motivation to setting actual goals, planning, and monitoring your progress this term? Have you set goals that are challenging, reasonable, and specific? Have you set long-term and short-term goals? Have you been a great manager of time, and has this helped you reach your goals?

Go back to Self-Assessment 1-3, "What Are My Goals?" on page 13. Where are you now regarding your main goals in life? Are they the same now as they were at the beginning of the term? In Self-Assessment 1-3, you listed four goals you wanted to achieve this term. How have you done? If you have not reached your goals, why? What things could you have done better?

Think and Learn

How has your thinking and learning gone this term? Do you understand your learning style and have you successfully mastered how to use this knowledge effectively? Have you developed effective work skills? Are you using computers to help you reach your goals? Did you keep a learning portfolio this term? If so, this is a good time to look back over it and reflect on your development as a thinker and learner. How have you changed over the course of the term? What improvements have you made in your learning and thinking skills?

Build Self-Esteem

How has your self-esteem been this term? Has it gone up and down a lot or has it stayed at about the same level most of the term? Have you believed in yourself this term? If you have low self-esteem, do you know what is causing it? Have you linked your self-esteem with your values and the areas of your life that are important to you? Have you achieved what you wanted to this term and how has this affected your self-esteem? How effectively have you coped with stress this term?

Explore Careers

Thinking about which career(s) you want to pursue reflects long-term goals. Do you now have one or more careers that you want to pursue? Are your college classes and major or specialization adequately linked to your career interests? Have you improved some of the skills this term that many employers seek in the employees they want to hire, such as communicational skills?

This book has emphasized the importance of these six areas in mastering college. Place a check mark next to the areas that you feel you have mastered this term:

_____ I have developed meaningful values.

_____ I am highly motivated.

_____ I have set goals, planned how to reach them, and regularly monitored my progress toward these goals. I have also reached the goals I set for myself at the beginning of the term.

_____ I am a good thinker and learner.

_____ I have high self-esteem.

_____ After exploring careers I have found one or more I want to pursue that match up with my values.

Besides these overarching factors, many specific areas are also important for college success, as you saw in particular chapters. Now that you're near the end of the term, look back and reflect on how you've done in applying the general strategies for college success in these areas. Place a check mark next to the areas that you feel you have mastered.

_____ I understand my learning style and know how to use it to help me master college.

_____ I have been a great time manager this term.

_____ I have effectively managed money this term.

_____ I am well connected with the campus and use its resources effectively.

_____ I have excellent computer skills and have used them to my advantage in reaching my academic goals this term.

_____ I have good reading skills.

_____ I am a great note taker.

_____ I have outstanding study skills.

_____ I have very good test-taking skills.

_____ I have excellent writing skills.

_____ I have excellent speaking skills.

_____ I have outstanding communicational skills.

_____ I have good social relationships.

_____ I am physically healthy.

_____ I am mentally healthy.

Where Are You Now?

You've just done quite a bit of reflecting about some important aspects of life. How do you feel about where you are now? Did you place a check mark next to most of the areas—both the six general ones and the fifteen specific ones? Or did you leave a lot of these blank, feeling that you need to improve?

Your Future

If you checked off most of the twenty-one areas, you're likely well on your way to mastering college and developing critical skills that will help you in life after college. If you left many of the spaces blank, this is a good time to reevaluate what your values are and what you want to do with your life.

You have a lot of change ahead of you. Developing meaningful values, getting motivated, setting goals, planning, monitoring, thinking and learning, building self-esteem, and exploring careers will continue to be very important themes for you in mastering the remainder of your college years and thereafter. Write a summary of these themes in your own words to post on the wall above your desk, in your time-management tools, or in another visible place so that you can refer to them from time to time. Another good strategy is to keep the self-assessments, strategies, on-target tips, and checklists in a convenient place so that you can refer to them if you run into obstacles in the remainder of your college journey. A good place for them is a learning portfolio that you can continue to update.

We wish you all the best. We have enjoyed communicating with you this term and hope that as a result of this course and book you feel well on your way to mastering college success.

References

A

Alberti, R., & Emmons, M. (1995). *Your perfect right* (7th ed.). San Luis Obispo, CA: Impact.

Alverno College. (1993). *Writing and speaking criteria*. Milwaukee, WI: Alverno Productions.

Appleby, D. (1990). Faculty and student perceptions of irritating behaviors in the college classroom. *Journal of Staff, Program, and Organizational Development, 8,* 41–46.

Appleby, D. (1994). *Liberal arts skills at work* [Career Currents]. Hanover, IN: Hanover College.

Appleby, D. (1997, February). *The seven wonders of the advising world*. Invited address at the Southeastern Teachers of Psychology Conference, Kennesaw State University, Marietta, GA.

Armstrong, W. H., & Lampe, M. W. (1990). *Pocket guide to study tips* (3rd ed.). Hauppage, NY: Barron's Educational Series.

Astin, A. (1993). *What matters in college: Four critical years revisited*. San Francisco: Jossey-Bass.

Axelrod, R. B., & Cooper, C. R. (1996). *The concise guide to writing* (2nd ed.). Boston: Bedford/St. Martin's Press.

B

Bailey, C. (1991). *The new fit or fat* (Rev. ed.). Boston: Houghton-Mifflin.

Bandura, A. (2000). Self-efficacy. In A. Kazdin (Ed.), *Encyclopedia of psychology*. Washington, DC, and New York: American Psychological Association and Oxford University Press.

Baumrind, D. (1991). Parenting styles and adolescent development. In J. Brooks-Gunn, R. Lerner, & A. C. Petersen (Eds.), *The encyclopedia of adolescence*. New York: Garland.

Baxter Magdola, M. B. (1992). *Knowing and reasoning in college*. San Francisco: Jossey-Bass.

Bednar, R. L., Wells, M. G., & Peterson, S. R. (1995). *Self-esteem* (2nd ed.). Washington, DC: American Psychological Association.

Bennett, M. E., & Miller, W. R. (1998). Alcohol problems. In H. S. Friedman (Ed.), *Encyclopedia of mental health: Vol. 1*. San Diego, CA: Academic Press.

Beyer, G. (1998). *Improving student thinking*. Boston: Allyn and Bacon.

Bloom, B. S., Englehart, M. D., Furst, E. J., & Krathwohl, D. R. (1956). *Taxonomy of educational objectives: Cognitive domain*. New York: David McKay.

Bly, R. (1990). *Iron John*. New York: Vintage Books.

Bourne, E. J. (1995). *The anxiety and phobia workbook* (2nd ed.). Oakland, CA: New Harbinger.

Bransford, J. D., & Stein, B. S. (1984). *The ideal problem solver*. New York: Freeman.

Brislin, R. W. (1993). *Understanding culture's influence on behavior*. Fort Worth, TX: Harcourt Brace.

Browne, M. N., & Keeley, S. M. (1990). *Asking the right questions: A guide to critical thinking* (3rd ed.). Englewood Cliffs, NJ: Prentice-Hall.

Brownell, K. (2000). Dieting. In A. Kazdin (Ed.), *Encyclopedia of psychology*. Washington, DC, and New York: American Psychological Association and Oxford University Press.

C

Canfield, J., & Hansen, N. V. (1995). *The Aladdin factor*. New York: Berkeley.

Carskadon, M. A. (1990). Patterns and sleep and sleepiness in adolescence. *Pediatrics, 17,* 5–12.

Collins, M. (1996, Winter). The job outlook for '96 grads. *Journal of Career Planning*, pp. 51–54.

Covey, S. R. (1989) *The seven habits of highly effective people*. New York: Simon & Schuster.

Covey, S. R., Merrill, A. R., & Merrill, R. R. (1994). *First things first*. New York: Simon & Schuster.

Crooks, R., & Bauer, K. (1999). *Our sexuality* (7th ed.). Pacific Grove, CA: Brooks/Cole.

Csikszentmihalyi, M. (1995). *Creativity*. New York: HarperCollins.

Csikszentmihalyi, M. (1997). *Finding flow*. New York: Basic Books.

Cutrona, C. E. (1982). Transition to college: Loneliness and the process of social adjustment. In L. A. Peplau & D. Perlman (Eds.), *Loneliness: A sourcebook of current theory, research, and therapy*. New York: Wiley.

D

Davis, M., Eshelman, E. R., & McKay, M. (1995). *The relaxation and stress reduction workbook* (4th ed.). Oakland, CA: New Harbinger.

Davis, S. F., Grover, C. A., Becker, A. H., & McGregor, L. N. (1992). Academic dishonesty: Prevalence, determinants, techniques, and punishments. *Teaching of Psychology, 19,* 16–20.

DeLongis, A., & Newth, S. (1998). Coping with stress. In H. S. Friedman (Ed.), *Encyclopedia of mental health: Vol. 1*. San Diego, CA: Academic Press.

Dement, W. C., & Vaughn, C. (2000). *The promise of sleep*. New York: Dell.

E

Edelman, M. W. (1992). *The measure of our success*. Boston: Beacon Press.

Ellis, A. (1996). A rational-emotive behavior therapist's perspective on Ruth. In G. Corey (Ed.), *Case approach to counseling and psychotherapy*. Pacific Grove, CA: Brooks/Cole.

Epstein, R. L. (2000). *The pocket guide to critical thinking*. Belmont, CA: Wadsworth.

F

Farr, J. M. (1999). *America's top jobs for college graduates*. Indianapolis, In: JIST Works.

Frank, S. (1996). *The everything study book*. Holbrook, MA: Adams Media.

Fulghum, R. (1997). Pay attention. In R. Carlson & B. Shield (Eds.), *Handbook for the soul*. Boston: Little, Brown.

G

Gardner, H. (1989). *Frames of mind*. New York: Basic Books.

Gewertz, K. (2000). *Harvard University Gazette*. http://www.news.harvard.edu/gazette/2000/06.08/ellison.html

Giles, D. E., Jr., & Eyler, J. (1998). A service learning research agenda for the next five years. *New Directions for Teaching and Learning, 73*, 65–72.

Goldberg, H. (1980). *The new male*. New York: Signet.

Goleman, D., Kaufmann, P., and Ray, M. (1992). *The creative spirit*. New York: Plume.

Gordon, T. (1970). *Parent effectiveness training*. New York: McGraw-Hill.

Gottman, J., & Silver, N. (1999). *The seven principles for making marriages work*. New York: Crown.

Grandin, T. (1995). *Thinking in pictures*. New York: Doubleday.

Griffith-Joyner, F., & Hanc, J. (1999). *Running for dummies*. Foster City, CA: IDG Books.

H

Haines, M. E., Norris, M. P., & Kashy, D. A. (1996). The effects of depressed mood on academic performance in college students. *Journal of College Student Development, 37*, 519–526.

Halonen, J. S., & Gray, C. (2000). *The critical thinking companion for introductory psychology*. New York: Worth.

Halpern, D. F. (1997). *Critical thinking across the curriculum*. Mahwah, NJ: Erlbaum.

Hamburg, D. A. (1997) Meeting the essential requirements for healthy adolescent development in a transforming world. In R. Takanishi & D. Hamburg (Eds.), *Preparing adolescents for the twenty-first century*. New York: Cambridge University Press.

Hansen, R. S., & Hansen, K. (1997). *Write your way to a higher GPA*. Berkeley, CA: Ten Speed Press.

Harbin, C. E. (1995). *Your transfer planner*. Belmont, CA: Wadsworth.

Hurtado, S., Dey, E. L., & Trevino, J. G. (1994). *Exclusion or self-segregation? Interaction across racial/ethnic groups on college campuses*. Paper presented at the meeting of the American Educational Research Association, New York.

I

Ishikawa, K. (1986). *What is total quality control? The Japanese way*. Englewood Cliffs, NJ: Prentice-Hall.

J

Jendrick, M. P. (1992). Students' reactions to academic dishonesty. *Journal of College Student Development, 33*, 260–273.

Johnson, M. K., Beebe, T., Mortimer, J. T., & Snyder, M. (1998). Volunteerism in adolescence: A process perspective. *Journal of Research in Adolescence, 8*, 309–332.

Johnston, L. D., O'Malley, P. M. & Bachman, J. G. (1996). *National survey results on drug use from the Monitoring the Future study, 1975–1994: Vol. 2*. Rockville, MD: National Institute on Drug Abuse.

Jonassen, D. H., & Grabowski, B. L. (1993). *Handbook of individual differences, learning, and instruction*. Mahwah, NJ: Erlbaum.

K

Kagan, J. (1965). Reflection-impulsivity and reading development in primary grade children. *Child Development, 36*, 609–628.

Kaplan, R. M., & Saccuzzo, D. P. (1993). *Psychological testing: Principles, applications, and issues* (3rd ed.). Pacific Grove, CA: Brooks/Cole.

Keith-Spiegel, P. (1992, October). *Ethics in shades of pale gray*. Paper presented at the Mid-America Conference for Teachers of Psychology, Evansville, IN.

Keller, P. A., & Heyman, S. R. (1987). *Innovations in clinical practice*. Sarasota, FL: Professional Resource Exchange.

Kelly, J. (2000). Sexually transmitted diseases. In A. Kazdin (Ed.), *Encyclopedia of psychology*. Washington, DC, and New York: American Psychological Association and Oxford University Press.

King, A. (2000). Exercise and physical activity. In A. Kazdin (Ed.), *Encyclopedia of psychology*. Washington, DC, and New York: American Psychological Association and Oxford University Press.

Kolb, D. A. (1984). *Experiential learning: Experience as the source of learning and development*. Englewood Cliffs, NJ: Prentice-Hall.

Koss, M., & Boeschen, L. (1998). Rape. In H. S. Friedman (Ed.), *Encyclopedia of mental health: Vol. 3* San Diego, CA: Academic Press.

Kurose, J. F., & Ross, K. W. (2001). *Computer networking.* Boston: Addison-Wesley.

L

Lakein, A. (1973). *How to get control of your time and your life.* New York: Signet.

Langer, E. (1989). *Mindfulness.* Reading, MA: Addison-Wesley.

Langer, E. (1997). *The power of mindful learning.* Reading, MA: Addison-Wesley.

Lazarus, R. S. (1993). Coping theory and research: Past, present, and future. *Psychosomatic Medicine, 55,* 234–247.

Lazarus, R. S. (1998). *Fifty years of the research and theory of R. S. Lazarus.* Mahwah, NJ: Erlbaum.

Lerner, H. G. (1989). *The dance of intimacy.* New York: HarperCollins.

Levinger, E. E. (1949). *Albert Einstein.* New York: Julian Messner.

Lin, J. G., & Yi, J. K. (1997). Asian international students' adjustments. *College Student Journal, 31,* 473–479.

Loftus, E. F. (1980). *Memory.* Reading, MA: Addison-Wesley.

Lorayne, H., & Lucas, J. (1996). *The memory book.* New York: Ballantine.

M

Maas, J. (1998). *Power sleep: The program that prepares your mind for peak performance.* New York: Villard.

Maris, R. W. (1998). Suicide. In H. S. Friedman (Ed.), *Encyclopedia of mental health: Vol. 3.* San Diego, CA: Academic Press.

Matlin, M. (1998). *Cognitive psychology* (3rd ed.). New York: Harcourt Brace.

McDonald, R. L. (1994). *How to pinch a penny till it screams.* Garden City, NY: Avery.

McNally, D. (1990). *Even eagles need a push.* New York: Dell.

McNett, J., Harvey, C., Athanassiou, N. & Allard, J. (2000, July 17). *Bloom's taxonomy as a teaching tool: An experiment.* Paper presented at Improving University Teaching Conference, Frankfurt, Germany.

Michael, R. T., Gagnon, J. H., Laumann, E. O., & Kolata, G. (1994). *Sex in America.* Boston: Little, Brown.

Miller, G. A. (1956). The magical number seven, plus or minus two: Some limits on our capacity for information-processing. *Psychological Review, 48,* 337–442.

Miller, J. B. (1986). *Toward a new psychology of women* (2nd ed.). Boston: Beacon Press.

Murphy, M. C. (1996). Stressors on the college campus: A comparison of 1985 and 1993. *Journal of College Student Development, 37,* 20–28.

Mussell, M. P., & Mitchell, J. E. (1998). Anorexia nervosa and bulimia nervosa. In H. S. Friedman (Ed.), *Encyclopedia of mental health: Vol. 1.* San Diego, CA: Academic Press.

N

Nichols, R. B. (1961, March). Do we know how to listen? Practical helps in a modern age. *Speech Teacher, 10,* 22.

Nolen-Hoeksema, S. (2001). *Abnormal psychology* (2nd ed.). New York: McGraw Hill.

O

Occupational outlook handbook. (2000–2001). Washington, DC: U.S. Department of Labor.

P

Paludi, M. A. (1998). *The psychology of women.* Upper Saddle River, NJ: Prentice-Hall.

Pennebaker, J. (1990). *Opening up.* New York: Avon.

Perkins, D. N. (1984, September). Creativity by design. *Educational Leadership,* pp. 18–25.

Perlman, D., & Peplau, L. A. (1998). Loneliness. In H. S. Friedman (Ed.), *Encyclopedia of psychology: Vol. 2.* San Diego, CA: Academic Press.

Peterson, C., & Stunkard, A. J. (1986). *Personal control and health promotion.* Unpublished manuscript, Department of Psychology, University of Michigan, Ann Arbor.

Pomerleau, O. (2000). Smoking. In A. Kazdin (Ed.), *Encyclopedia of psychology.* Washington, DC, and New York: American Psychological Association and Oxford University Press.

Poole, B. J. (1998). *Education for an information age* (2nd ed.). Burr Ridge, IL: McGraw Hill.

R

Rodin, J., & Langer, E. J. (1977). Long-term effects of a control-relevant intervention with the institutionalized aged. *Journal of Personality and Social Psychology, 35,* 397–402.

Ruggerio, V. R. (1996). *Becoming a critical thinker* (2nd ed.). Boston: Houghton-Mifflin.

S

Sax, L. J., Astin, A. W., Korn, W. S., & Mahoney, K. M. (1995). *The American college freshman: National norms for fall, 1995.* Los Angeles: Higher Education Research Institute, UCLA.

Sax, L. J., Astin, A. W., Korn, W. S., & Mahoney, K. M. (1999). *The American freshman: National norms for fall 1999.* Los Angeles: Higher Education Research Institute, UCLA.

Sears, D. O., Peplau, L. A., & Taylor, S. E. (2000). *Social psychology* (10th ed.). Upper Saddle River, NJ: Prentice-Hall.

Seligman, M. E. P. (1991). *Learned optimism.* New York: Pocket Books.

Sher, K. J., Wood, P. K., & Gotham, H. J. (1996). The course of psychological distress in college: A prospective high-risk study. *Journal of College Student Development, 37,* 42–51.

Skinner, K. (1997). *The MSE Oracle System*. Dallas, TX: Southern Methodist University.

Stark, R. (1994). *Sociology* (5th ed.). Belmont, CA: Wadsworth.

Sternberg, R. J. (1988). *The triangle of love*. New York: Basic Books.

Stukas, A. A., Clary, E. G., & Snyder, M. (1999). Service learning: Who benefits and why. *Social Policy Report: Vol. 13, no. 4*. Chicago: Society for Research in Child Development.

T

Tan, Amy. (1996, June 28). [Interview]. Posted at www.achievement.org/autodoc/page/tanoint-1

Tavris, C. (1992). *The mismeasure of woman*. New York: Touchstone.

Taylor, S. E. (1999). *Health psychology* (4th ed.). New York: McGraw Hill.

Tiene, D., & Ingram, A. (2001). *Exploring current issues in educational technology*. New York: McGraw Hill.

Treagust, D. F., Duit, R., & Fraser, B. J. (1996). *Improving teaching and learning in science and mathematics*. New York: Teachers College Press.

U

University of Illinois Counseling Center. (1984). *Overcoming procrastination*. Urbana-Champaign, IL: Department of Student Affairs.

V

van Praag, H., Kempermann, G., & Gage, F. H. (1999). Running increases cell proliferation and neurogenesis in the adult mouse dentate gyrus. *Nature Neuroscience, 3*, 266–270.

Vickery, D. M., & Fries, J. F. (2000). *Take care of yourself* (7th ed.). Reading, MA: Addison-Wesley.

Von Oech, Roger. (1990). *A whack on the side of the head: How you can be more creative*. New York: Warner, 1990.

W

Walters, A. (1994). Using visual media to reduce homophobia: A classroom demonstration. *Journal of Sex Education and Therapy, 20*, 92–100.

Wechsler, H., Davenport, A., Sowdall, G., Moetykens, B., & Castillo, S. (1994). Health and behavioral consequences of binge drinking in college. *Journal of the American Medical Association, 272*, 1672–1677.

Wechsler, H., Lee, J. E., Kuo, M., & Lee, H. (2000). College binge drinking in the 1990s—a continuing health problem: Results from the Harvard University School of Health 1999 College Alcohol Study. *Journal of American College Health, 48*, 1999–1210.

Weinstein, N. D. (1984). Reducing unrealistic optimism about illness susceptibility. *Health Psychology, 3*, 431–457.

Whimbey, A., & Lochhead, J. (1991). *Problem solving and comprehension*. Mahwah, NJ: Erlbaum.

Winston, S. (1995). *Stephanie Winston's best organizing tips*. New York: Simon & Schuster.

Y

Yate, M. (2000). *Knock 'em dead*. Boston: Adams Media.

Yates, M. (1995, March). *Community service and political-moral discussions among black urban adolescents*. Paper presented at the meeting of the Society for Research in Child Development, Indianapolis, IN.

Z

Zeidner, M. (1995). Adaptive coping with test situations: A review of the literature. *Educational Psychologist, 30*, 123–133.

Credits

These pages constitute an extension of the copyright page. We have made every effort to trace the ownership of all copyrighted material and to secure permission from copyright holders. In the event of any question arising as to the use of any material, we will be pleased to make the necessary corrections in future printings. Thanks are due to the following authors, publishers, and agents for permission to use the material indicated.

Photo Credits

p. 1 David Young-Wolff/Stone. **p. 2** Theo Westenberger/ The Gamma Liaison Network. **p. 4** © Barbara Stitzer/ PhotoEdit. **p. 8** © Bettmann/CORBIS. **p. 20** © Michael Newman/PhotoEdit/PictureQuest. **p. 27** © Jeff Greenberg/PhotoEdit. **p. 28** Barbra Witt. **p. 44** Robert Ginn/PhotoEdit. **p. 53** © Susan Vanetten/Stock, Boston. **p. 54** © Bettmann/CORBIS. **p. 59** Michael Matisse/ PhotoDisc. **p. 60** Palm is a trademark of Palm, Inc. **p. 71** (top) Gary A. Conner/PhotoEdit. (bottom) Barbara Stitzer/PhotoEdit. **p. 77** © Tom Levy/Photo 20-20/ PictureQuest. **p. 78** Mark Richards/Contact Press Images. **p. 81** D. Young-Wolff/PhotoEdit. **p. 89** Jon Riley/Stone Images. **p. 92** (top) Babriel Covian/The Image Bank. (bottom) Index Stock Photography. **p. 94** Courtesy of Bob Grauer. **p. 101** © Frank Siteman/Stock, Boston. **p. 102** © C. J. Gunther. **p. 114** Francis Hogan/Electronic Publishing Services Inc., NYC. **p. 118** Flip Chalfant/The Image Bank. **p. 133** © Tom & DeeAnn McCarthy/The Stock Market. **p. 134** © Reuters Newmedia, Inc./CORBIS. **p. 136** Barbara Stitzer/PhotoEdit. **p. 151** (left) © Ed Kashi/CORBIS. (center) Cliff Lipson/Courtesy of CBS. (right) © Reuters Newmedia, Inc./CORBIS. **p. 161** © Gary Conner/ PhotoEdit. **p. 162** © Bettmann/CORBIS. **p. 166** © Bonnie Kamin/PhotoEdit/PictureQuest. **p. 189** © Tom Levy/Photo 20-20/PictureQuest. **p. 190** © Rosalie Winard. **p. 194** Gary A. Conner/PhotoEdit. **p. 207** (all) Courtesy of National Inventors Hall of Fame. **p. 217** © Gary Conner/ PhotoEdit. **p. 218** © Reuters/CORBIS. **p. 228** Mryleen Ferguson/PhotoEdit. **p. 243** Don Smetzer/Stone. **p. 244** © Reuters/CORBIS. **p. 256** Rob Gage/FPG International. **p. 258** Losh/FPG International. **p. 261** Jonathan Novrok/PhotoEdit. **p. 269** © Tom Stewart/The Stock Market. **p. 270** © Reuters Newmedia, Inc./CORBIS. **p. 281** Paula A. Scully/The Gamma Liaison Network. **p. 282** Bachmann/PhotoEdit. **p. 297** Cindy Charles/PhotoEdit. **p. 298** Erica Lansner/Black Star.

Cartoon Credits

p. 6 © The New Yorker Collection 1992, Mike Twohy, from cartoonbank.com. All Rights Reserved. **p. 15** DILBERT reprinted by permission of United Feature Syndicate, Inc. **p. 16** © 1973 News America Syndicate, Mell Lazarus. **p. 19** (top) © The New Yorker Collection 1992, Michael Maslin, from cartoonbank.com. All Rights Reserved. (bottom) © 2000. Reprinted courtesy of Bunny Hoest and Parade Magazine. **p. 30** © 2000 by Sidney Harris. **p. 34** © The New Yorker Collection 1997, Mike Twohy, from cartoonbank.com. All Rights Reserved. **p. 41** © The New Yorker Collection 1999, Danny Shanahan, from cartoonbank.com. All Rights Reserved. **p. 55** © 2000 Charles Barsotti, from cartoonbank.com. All Rights Reserved. **p. 58** © The New Yorker Collection 1990, Robert Weber, from cartoonbank.com. All Rights Reserved. **p. 82** © The New Yorker Collection 1974, J. B. Handelsman, from cartoonbank.com. All Rights Reserved. **p. 84** 1982 Universal Press Syndicate. ZIGGY © 1982, 1995 ZIGGY AND FRIENDS, INC. Dist. by Universal Press Syndicate. Reprinted with permission. All rights reserved. **p. 93** Reprinted by permission. www.cartoon-stock.com. **p. 95** Reprinted with permission of Carole Cable. **p. 105** Reprinted by permission of Vivian Scott Hixson. **p. 119** © Gahan Wilson. **p. 142** © 2000 by Sidney Harris. **p. 149** © 2000 by Sidney Harris. **p. 150** © The New Yorker Collection 1986, Bud Handelsman, from cartoonbank.com. All Rights Reserved. **p. 163** © The New Yorker Collection 1991, Mike Twohy, from cartoonbank.com. All Rights Reserved. **p. 169** © Harald Carl Bakken. **p. 174** ©1987 FarWorks, Inc. **p. 176** PEANUTS reprinted by permission of United Feature Syndicate, Inc. **p. 180** © The New Yorker Collection 1990, Danny Shanahan, from cartoonbank.com. All Rights Reserved. **p. 193** Reprinted with permission of the artist, Carol Cable. **p. 200** © 2000 by Sidney Harris. **p. 202** © 1990 by Universal Press Syndicate. Used with permission. **p. 206** © The New Yorker Collection 1990, Eric Teitelbaum, from cartoonbank.com. All Rights Reserved. **p. 226** PEANUTS reprinted by permission of United Feature Syndicate, Inc. **p. 233** The Far Side, © FarWorks, Inc. All Rights Reserved. **p. 236** Reprinted with permission of United Media. **p. 246** PEANUTS reprinted by permission of United Features Syndicate, Inc. **p. 259** © Joel Pett. All Rights Reserved. **p. 275** © 1982 FarWorks, Inc. All rights reserved. **p. 278** The Far Side, © FarWorks, Inc. All Rights Reserved. **p. 285** (top) © 2000 by Sidney Harris.

Text Credits

Index

Note: Italicized letters *b*, *f*, and *t* following page numbers indicate boxes, figures, and tables, respectively.